The Transgender Compendium

Medical, Psychological, Social, and
Legal Aspects of Gender Diversity

The Transgender Compendium

Medical, Psychological, Social, and Legal Aspects of Gender Diversity

By
Diane Saunders

With contributions from
Joanna Clark and Jude Patton

Published by
TransGender Publishing

an imprint of
Castle Carrington Publishing Group
Victoria, BC
Canada

2022

The Transgender Compendium

Medical, Psychological, Social, and Legal Aspects of Gender Diversity

Copyright © Diane Saunders 2022

All rights reserved. No part of this publication may be reprinted, reproduced, stored in a retrieval system or transmitted in any form or by any means, electronic, mechanical, photocopying and recording or otherwise, now known or hereafter invented without the express prior written permission of the author, except for brief passages quoted by a reviewer in a newspaper or magazine. To perform any of the above is an infringement of copyright law.

We are not lawyers. The content provided herein is intended for educational purposes and does not take the place of legal advice from your attorney. Every effort has been made to ensure that the content provided is accurate at publishing time. However, this is not an exhaustive treatment of the subject matter. No liability is assumed for losses or damages that might result from the information provided. You are responsible for your own choices, actions, and results. You should consult your attorney for specific questions and/or advice.

First published in paperback in 2022

Cover Art: Yalila Rivero

ISBN: 978-1-990096-59-4 (Hardcover)
ISBN: 978-1-990096-56-3 (Paperback)
ISBN: 978-1-990096-57-0 (Kindle e-book)
ISBN: 978-1-990096-58-7 (Smashwords e-book)

Published in Canada by
TransGender Publishing
www.transgenderpublishing.ca

an imprint of
Castle Carrington Publishing Group
www.castlecarringtonpublishing.ca
Victoria BC
Canada

Contents

DISCLOSURE STATEMENT xxvii
AUTHOR'S COMMENTS xxix
PREFACE xxxiii
    Why I Chose to Write This Book xxxiii
    ACLU Transsexual Rights Committee xxxiii
    Audience xxxiv
    A Few Additional Words xxxiv
FOREWORD xxxvi
INTRODUCTION 1
BASIS OF DISCRIMINATION 5
BACKGROUND 9
METHODOLOGY 12
EARLY RESEARCH 15
    Terminology 15
    Disclosure 15
    Early Research 16
    Etiology 17
    Endocrinology of Transsexualism 17
    The Birth of WPATH 19
    Conversion or Reparative Therapy 20
CURRENT RESEARCH 26
    Stigmatization 26
    Neurological Aspects 27
    Genetic Component 28
    The Genetics of Sex and Gender 28
    Transgender Athletics 30
    Discrimination Against Transgender Athletes 31
DIAGNOSTIC CRITERIA 34
SOCIOLOGICAL ISSUES 37
    Conversion or Reparative Therapy 37
    Bias, Prejudice, and the Basis of Discrimination 39
    Sex and Gender Stereotyping in Sports 40
CLINICAL CARE PROGRAMS 43

- ALABAMA 43
- ARIZONA 43
- ARKANSAS 44
- CALIFORNIA 44
- COLORADO 46
- CONNECTICUT 47
- FLORIDA 47
- ILLINOIS 48
- IOWA 48
- MAINE 49
- MARYLAND 49
- MASSACHUSETTS 50
- MICHIGAN 51
- MINNESOTA 52
- MISSOURI 52
- NEBRASKA 53
- NEW YORK 53
- NORTH CAROLINA 54
- OHIO 54
- OKLAHOMA 56
- OREGON 56
- PENNSYLVANIA 57
- RHODE ISLAND 58
- SOUTH CAROLINA 59
- TENNESSEE 59
- VERMONT 59
- WASHINGTON 60
- WASHINGTON, D.C. 60
- WISCONSIN 61

LEGAL ASPECTS 62
- FEDERAL/NATIONAL 62
  - *Constitutional Provisions* 62
- Laws Enacted by Congress 64
  - *Title VII of the Civil Rights Act of 1964, as Amended, Discrimination in Employment* 64

Equal Employment Opportunity Commission (EEOC) 69

Title VI of the Civil Rights Action of 1964 69

The Affordable Care Act 70

Title IX of the Education Amendments of 1972 70

Fair Housing Act of 1968 74

Discrimination in Occupational Licensing 75

Marriage 76

Military Service 76

Passports 78

Discrimination by Federal Law Enforcement Agencies 78

Changing Your Gender with the Social Security Administration 79

Veterans Administration (VA) 79

Federal Religious Freedom Restoration Act (RFRA) of 1993 79

STATE LAWS 83

Birth Certificates and Driver's Licenses 83

State Religious Exemption Laws in General 84

Sports 86

Public Accommodations 93

Final Note on State laws 94

Alabama 97

Alabama Non-Discrimination Laws 97

Birth Certificates 97

Driver's Licenses 97

Public Accommodations 97

Sports and Sporting Events 97

Law Enforcement, Jails, and Prisons 98

Health Care and Health Care Benefits 98

Marriage and Parental Rights 98

LGBTQ Youth Laws 98

Religious Exemption Laws 98

Alabama Overall Tally 99

Alaska 100

Alaska Non-Discrimination Laws 100

Birth Certificates 100

- *Driver's Licenses* 101
- *Public Accommodations* 101
- *LGBTQ Youth Laws* 101
- *Law Enforcement, Jails, and Prisons* 102
- *Health Care and Health Care Benefits* 102
- *Marriage and Parental Rights* 102
- *Religious Exemption Laws* 102
- *Alaska Overall Tally* 102

Arizona 103
- *Arizona Non-Discrimination Laws* 103
- *Birth Certificates* 107
- *Driver's Licenses* 108
- *Public Accommodation* 108
- *LGBTQ Youth Laws* 109
- *Law Enforcement, Jails, and Prisons* 110
- *Health Care and Health Care Benefits* 111
- *Marriage and Parental Rights* 111
- *Religious Exemption Laws* 111
- *Arizona Overall Tally* 111

Arkansas 112
- *Arkansas Anti-Discrimination Laws* 112
- *Birth Certificates* 112
- *Driver's Licenses* 112
- *Public Accommodation* 112
- *Sports* 113
- *Law Enforcement, Jails, and Prisons* 113
- *Health Care and Health Care Benefits* 113
- *Marriage* 114
- *LGBTQ Youth Laws* 114
- *Religious Exemption Laws* 115
- *Arkansas Overall Tally* 115

California 116
- *California Anti-Discrimination Laws* 116
- *Birth Certificates* 116

- *Driver's Licenses* 116
- *Public Accommodation Laws* 116
- *Sports* 116
- *LGBTQ Youth Laws and Policies* 117
- *Law Enforcement, Jails, and Prisons* 117
- *Health Care and Health Care Benefits* 117
- *Marriage* 117
- *Religion* 117
- *California Overall Tally* 117

Colorado 118
- *Colorado Non-Discrimination Laws* 118
- *Birth Certificates* 118
- *Driver's Licenses* 118
- *Public Accommodation Laws* 118
- *Sports* 118
- *Law Enforcement, Jails, and Prisons* 118
- *Health Care and Health Care Benefits* 118
- *Marriage* 119
- *Youth Laws and Policies* 119
- *Religious Exemption Laws* 119
- *Colorado Overall Tally* 119

Connecticut 120
- *Connecticut Non-Discrimination Laws* 120
- *Birth Certificates* 120
- *Driver's Licenses* 120
- *Public Accommodation Laws* 120
- *Sports* 121
- *Law Enforcement, Jails, and Prisons* 121
- *Health Care and Health Care Benefits* 121
- *Marriage* 121
- *LGBTQ Youth Laws and Policies* 121
- *Religious Exemption Laws* 121
- *Connecticut Overall Tally* 121

Delaware 122

Delaware Non-Discrimination Laws 122
Birth Certificates 122
Driver's Licenses 122
Public Accommodations 122
Sports 123
Law Enforcement, Jails, and Prisons 123
Health Care and Health Care Benefits 123
Marriage 123
LGBTQ Youth Laws and Policies 123
Religious Exemption Laws 123
Delaware Overall Tally 124

District of Columbia 125
District of Columbia Non-Discrimination Laws 125
Birth Certificates 125
Driver's Licenses 125
Public Accommodations 125
Sports 126
Law Enforcement, Jails, and Prisons 126
Health Care and Health Care Benefits 126
Marriage 126
LGBTQ Youth Laws and Policies 126
Religious Exemption Laws 126
District of Columbia Overall Tally 126

Florida 127
Florida Non-Discrimination Laws 127
Birth Certificates 127
Driver's Licenses 127
Public Accommodations 127
Sports 127
Law Enforcement, Jails, and Prisons 128
Health Care and Health Care Benefits 128
Religious Exemption Laws 128
Marriage 128
LGBTQ Youth Laws and Policies 128

- *Religious Exemption Laws* 128
- *Florida Overall Tally* 129

Georgia 130
- *Georgia Non-Discrimination Laws* 130
- *Birth Certificates* 130
- *Driver's Licenses* 130
- *Public Accommodations* 130
- *Sports* 130
- *Law Enforcement, Jails, and Prisons* 131
- *Health Care and Health Care Benefits* 131
- *Marriage* 131
- *LGBTQ Youth Laws and Policies* 131
- *Religious Exemption Laws* 131
- *Georgia Overall Tally* 132

Hawai'i 133
- *Hawai'i Non-Discrimination Laws* 133
- *Birth Certificates* 133
- *Driver's Licenses* 133
- *Public Accommodations* 133
- *Sports* 133
- *Law Enforcement, Jails, and Prisons* 134
- *Health Care and Health Care Benefits* 134
- *Marriage* 134
- *LGBTQ Youth Laws and Policies* 134
- *Religious Exemption Laws and Policies* 134
- *Hawai'i Overall Tally* 134

Idaho 135
- *Idaho Non-Discrimination Laws* 135
- *Birth Certificates* 135
- *Driver's Licenses* 136
- *Public Accommodations* 136
- *Sports* 136
- *Law Enforcement, Jails, and Prisons* 136
- *Health Care and Health Care Benefits* 136

Marriage 136

LGBTQ Youth Laws and Policies 136

Religious Exemption Laws 136

Idaho Overall Tally 137

Illinois 138

Illinois Non-Discrimination Laws 138

Birth Certificates 138

Driver's Licenses 138

Public Accommodations 138

Sports 139

Law Enforcement, Jails, and Prisons 139

Health Care and Health Care Benefits 139

Marriage 139

LGBTQ Youth Laws and Policies 139

Religious Exemption Laws 139

Illinois Overall Tally 140

Indiana 141

Indiana Non-Discrimination Laws 141

Birth Certificates 141

Driver's Licenses 141

Public Accommodations 141

Sports 141

Law Enforcement. Jails, and Prisons 141

Health Care and Health Care Benefits 141

Marriage 141

LGBTQ Youth Laws and Policies 142

Religious Exemption Laws 142

Indiana Overall Tally 142

Iowa 143

Iowa Non-Discrimination Laws 143

Birth Certificates 143

Driver's Licenses 143

Public Accommodations 143

Sports 144

Contents

- *Law Enforcement, Jails, and Prisons* *144*
- *Health Care and Health Care Benefits* *144*
- *Marriage* *144*
- *LGBTQ Youth Laws and Policies* *144*
- *Religious Exemption Laws* *144*
- *Iowa Overall Tally* *144*

Kansas 145
- *Kansas Non-Discrimination Laws* *145*
- *Birth Certificates* *145*
- *Driver's Licenses* *146*
- *Public Accommodations* *147*
- *Sports* *147*
- *Law Enforcement, Jails, and Prisons* *147*
- *Health Care and Health Care Benefits* *147*
- *Marriage* *148*
- *LGBTQ Youth Laws and Policies* *148*
- *Religious Exemption Laws* *148*
- *Kansas Overall Tally* *148*

Kentucky 149
- *Kentucky Non-Discrimination Laws* *149*
- *Birth Certificates* *149*
- *Driver's Licenses* *149*
- *Public Accommodations* *149*
- *Sports* *149*
- *Law Enforcement, Jails, and Prisons* *150*
- *Health Care and Health Care Benefits* *150*
- *Marriage* *150*
- *LGBTQ Youth Laws and Policies* *150*
- *Religious Exemption Laws* *150*
- *Kentucky Overall Tally* *150*

Louisiana 151
- *Louisiana Non-Discrimination Laws* *151*
- *Birth Certificates* *151*
- *Driver's Licenses* *151*

- Public Accommodations 151
- Sports 152
- Law Enforcement, Jails, and Prisons 152
- Health Care and Health Care Benefits 152
- Marriage 152
- LGBTQ Youth Laws and Policies 152
- Religious Exemption Laws 152
- Louisiana Overall Score 152

Maine 153
- Maine Non-Discrimination Laws 153
- Birth Certificates 153
- Driver's Licenses 153
- Public Accommodations 153
- Sports 153
- Law Enforcement, Jails, and Prisons 154
- Health Care and Health Care Benefits 154
- Marriage 154
- LGBTQ Youth Laws and Policies 154
- Religious Exemption Laws 154
- Maine Overall Tally 154

Maryland 155
- Maryland Non-Discrimination Laws 155
- Birth Certificates 155
- Driver's Licenses 155
- Public Accommodations 155
- Sports 155
- Law Enforcement, Jails, and Prisons 155
- Health Care and Health Care Benefits 156
- Marriage 156
- LGBTQ Youth Laws and Policies 156
- Religious Exemption Laws 156
- Maryland Overall Tally 156

Massachusetts 157
- Massachusetts Non-Discrimination Laws 157

Birth Certificates	*157*
Driver's Licenses	*157*
Public Accommodations	*157*
Sports	*157*
Law Enforcement, Jails, and Prisons	*157*
Health Care and Health Care Benefits	*157*
Marriage	*157*
LGBTQ Youth Laws and Policies	*157*
Religious Exemption Laws	*158*
Massachusetts Overall Tally	*158*
Michigan	159
Michigan Non-Discrimination Laws	*159*
Birth Certificates	*159*
Driver's Licenses	*159*
Public Accommodations	*159*
Sports	*160*
Law Enforcement, Jails, and Prisons	*161*
Health Care and Health Care Benefits	*161*
Marriage	*161*
LGBTQ Youth Laws and Policies	*161*
Religious Exemption Laws	*161*
Michigan Overall Tally	*162*
Minnesota	163
Minnesota Non-Discrimination Laws	*163*
Birth Certificates	*163*
Driver's Licenses	*163*
Public Accommodations	*164*
Sports	*164*
Law Enforcement, Jails, and Prisons	*165*
Health Care and Health Care Benefits	*165*
Marriage	*165*
LGBTQ Youth Laws and Policies	*165*
Religious Exemption Laws	*165*
Minnesota Overall Tally	*165*

Mississippi 166
Mississippi Non-Discrimination Laws 166
Birth Certificates... 166
Driver's Licenses... 166
Public Accommodations... 166
Sports 166
Law Enforcement, Jails, and Prisons 166
Health Care and Health Care Benefits 166
Marriage... 166
LGBTQ Youth Laws and Policies 166
Religious Exemption Laws 166
Mississippi Overall Tally... 167

Missouri 168
Missouri Non-Discrimination Laws 168
Birth Certificates... 169
Driver's Licenses... 169
Public Accommodations... 169
Sports 170
Law Enforcement, Jails, and Prisons 170
Health Care and Health Care Benefits 170
Marriage... 170
LGBTQ Youth Laws and Policies 170
Religious Exemption Laws 170
Missouri Overall Tally... 171

Montana 172
Montana Non-Discrimination Laws.. 172
Birth Certificates... 172
Driver's Licenses... 172
Public Accommodations... 173
Sports 173
Law Enforcement, Jails, and Prisons 173
Health Care and Health Care Benefits 173
Marriage... 173
LGBTQ Youth Laws and Policies 173

Religious Exemption Laws 174

Montana Overall Tally 174

Nebraska 175

Nebraska Non-Discrimination Laws 175

Birth Certificates 175

Driver's Licenses 175

Public Accommodations 176

Sports 176

Law Enforcement, Jails, and Prisons 176

Health Care and Health Care Benefits 176

Marriage 176

LGBTQ Youth Laws and Policies 176

Religious Exemption Laws 176

Nebraska Overall Tally 177

Nevada 178

Nevada Non-Discrimination Laws 178

Birth Certificates 178

Driver's Licenses 179

Public Accommodations 179

Sports 179

Health Care and Health Care Benefits 179

Marriage 180

LGBTQ Youth Laws and Policies 180

Religious Exemption Laws 180

Nevada Overall Tally 180

New Hampshire 181

New Hampshire Non-Discrimination Laws 181

Birth Certificates 181

Driver's Licenses 181

Public Accommodations 182

Sports 182

Law Enforcement, Jails, and Prisons 182

Health Care and Health Care Benefits 182

Marriage 183

LGBTQ Youth Laws and Policies 183

Religious Exemption Laws 183

New Hampshire Overall Tally 183

New Jersey 184

New Jersey Non-Discrimination Laws 184

Birth Certificates 184

Driver's Licenses 184

Public Accommodations 184

Sports 185

Law Enforcement, Jails, and Prisons 185

Health Care and Health Care Benefits 185

Marriage 185

LGBTQ Youth Laws and Policies 185

Religious Exemption Laws 185

New Jersey Overall Tally 186

New Mexico 187

New Mexico Non-Discrimination Laws 187

Birth Certificates 187

Driver's Licenses 187

Public Accommodations 187

Sports 188

Law Enforcement, Jails, and Prisons 189

Health Care and Health Care Benefits 189

Marriage 189

LGBTQ Youth Laws and Policies 189

Religious Exemption Laws 189

New Mexico Overall Tally 190

New York 191

New York Non-Discrimination Laws 191

Birth Certificates 191

Driver's Licenses 191

Public Accommodations 192

Sports 193

Law Enforcement, Jails, and Prisons 193

Health Care and Health Care Benefits 193

Marriage 193

LGBTQ Youth Laws and Policies 193

Religious Exemption Laws 193

New York Overall Tally 194

North Carolina 195

North Carolina Non-Discrimination Laws 195

Birth Certificates 195

Driver's Licenses 195

Public Accommodations 195

Sports 196

Law Enforcement, Jails, and Prisons 196

Health Care and Health Care Benefits 196

Marriage 196

LGBTQ Youth Laws and Policies 196

Religious Exemption Laws 196

North Carolina Overall Tally 196

North Dakota 197

North Dakota Non-Discrimination Laws 197

Birth Certificates 198

Driver's Licenses 199

Public Accommodations 199

Sports 199

Law Enforcement, Jails, and Prisons 199

Health Care and Health Care Benefits 199

Marriage 200

LGBTQ Youth Laws and Policies 200

Religious Exemption Laws 200

North Dakota Overall Tally 200

Ohio 201

Ohio Non-Discrimination Laws 201

Birth Certificates 201

Driver's Licenses 203

Public Accommodations 203

- Sports 203
- Law Enforcement, Jails, and Prisons 204
- Health Care and Health Care Benefits 204
- Marriage 204
- LGBTQ Youth Laws and Policies 204
- Religious Exemption Laws 204
- Ohio Overall Tally 204

Oklahoma 205
- Oklahoma Non-Discrimination Laws 205
- Birth Certificates 205
- Driver's Licenses 206
- Public Accommodations 206
- Sports 206
- Law Enforcement, Jails, and Prisons 207
- Health Care and Health Care Benefits 207
- Marriage 207
- LGBTQ Youth Laws and Policies 207
- Religious Exemption Laws 207
- Oklahoma Overall Tally 208

Oregon 209
- Oregon Non-Discrimination Laws 209
- Birth Certificates 209
- Driver's Licenses 210
- Public Accommodations 210
- Sports 211
- Law Enforcement, Jails, and Prisons 211
- Health Care and Health Care Benefits 211
- Marriage 211
- LGBTQ Youth Laws and Policies 211
- Religious Exemption Laws 211
- Oregon Overall Tally 212

Pennsylvania 213
- Pennsylvania Non-Discrimination Laws 213
- Birth Certificates 213

- *Driver's Licenses* 213
- *Public Accommodations* 213
- *Sports* 213
- *Law Enforcement, Jails, and Prisons* 214
- *Health Care and Health Care Benefits* 214
- *Marriage* 214
- *LGBTQ Youth Laws and Policies* 214
- *Religious Exemption Laws* 214
- *Pennsylvania Overall Tally* 214

Rhode Island 215
- *Rhode Island Non-Discrimination Laws* 215
- *Birth Certificates* 215
- *Driver's Licenses* 215
- *Public Accommodations* 215
- *Sports* 216
- *Law Enforcement, Jails, and Prisons* 216
- *Health Care and Health Care Benefits* 216
- *Marriage* 216
- *LGBTQ Youth Laws and Policies* 216
- *Religious Exemption Laws* 216
- *Rhode Island Overall Tally* 216

South Carolina 217
- *South Carolina Non-Discrimination Laws* 217
- *Birth Certificates* 217
- *Driver's Licenses* 218
- *Public Accommodations* 218
- *Sports* 218
- *Law Enforcement, Jails, and Prisons* 218
- *Health Care and Health Care Benefits* 219
- *Marriage* 219
- *LGBTQ Youth Laws and Policies* 219
- *Religious Exemption Laws* 219
- *South Carolina Overall Tally* 219

South Dakota 220

South Dakota Non-Discrimination Laws 220
Birth Certificates 220
Driver's Licenses 220
Public Accommodations 221
Sports 221
Law Enforcement, Jails, and Prisons 221
Health Care and Health Care Benefits 221
Marriage 221
LGBTQ Youth Laws and Policies 221
Religious Exemption Laws 221
South Dakota Overall Tally 222

Tennessee 223
Tennessee Non-Discrimination Laws 223
Birth Certificates 223
Driver's Licenses 223
Public Accommodations 223
Sports 224
Health Care and Health Care Benefits 224
Marriage 224
LGBTQ Youth Laws and Policies 224
Religious Exemption Laws 224
Tennessee Overall Tally 224

Texas 225
Texas Non-Discrimination Laws 225
Birth Certificates 225
Driver's Licenses 225
Public Accommodations 225
Sports 225
Law Enforcement, Jails, and Prisons 226
Health Care and Health Care Benefits 226
Marriage 226
LGBTQ Youth Laws and Policies 226
Religious Exemption Laws 226
Texas Overall Tally 227

Utah 228
Utah Non-Discrimination Laws 228
Birth Certificates 228
Driver's Licenses 228
Public Accommodations 228
Sports 229
Law Enforcement, Jails, and Prisons 229
Health and Health Care Benefits 229
Marriage 229
LGBTQ Youth Laws and Policies 229
Religious Exemption Laws 229
Utah Overall Tally 230

Vermont 231
Vermont Non-Discrimination Laws 231
Birth Certificates 231
Driver's Licenses 231
Public Accommodations 231
Sports 232
Law Enforcement, Jails, and Prisons 232
Health and Health Care Benefits 232
Marriage 232
LGBTQ Youth Laws and Policies 232
Religious Exemption Laws 232
Vermont Overall Tally 232

Virginia 233
Virginia Non-Discrimination Laws 233
Birth Certificates 233
Driver's Licenses 233
Public Accommodations 234
Sports 234
Law Enforcement, Jails, and Prisons 235
Health and Health Care Benefits 235
Marriage 235
LGBTQ Youth Laws and Policies 235

Religious Exemption Laws *235*

Virginia Overall Tally *236*

Washington 237

Washington Non-Discrimination Laws *237*

Birth Certificates *237*

Driver's Licenses *237*

Public Accommodations *238*

Sports *238*

Law Enforcement, Jails, and Prisons *240*

Health and Health Care Benefits *240*

Marriage *240*

LGBTQ Youth Laws and Policies *240*

Religious Exemption Laws *240*

Washington Overall Tally *241*

West Virginia 242

West Virginia Non-Discrimination Laws *242*

Birth Certificates *242*

Driver's Licenses *242*

Public Accommodations *242*

Sports *242*

Law Enforcement, Jails, and Prisons *244*

Health and Health Care Benefits *244*

Marriage *244*

LGBTQ Youth Laws and Policies *244*

Religious Exemption Laws *244*

West Virginia Overall Tally *245*

Wisconsin 246

Wisconsin Non-Discrimination Laws *246*

Birth Certificates *246*

Driver's Licenses *246*

Public Accommodations *247*

Sports *247*

Law Enforcement, Jails, and Prisons *247*

Health and Health Care Benefits *247*

Marriage	*247*
LGBTQ Youth Laws and Policies	*247*
Religious Exemption Laws	*247*
Wisconsin Overall Tally	*248*
Wyoming	249
Wyoming Non-Discrimination Laws	*249*
Birth Certificates	*249*
Driver's Licenses	*250*
Public Accommodations	*250*
Sports	*250*
Law Enforcement, Jails, and Prisons	*251*
Health and Health Care Benefits	*251*
Marriage	*251*
LGBTQ Youth Laws and Policies	*251*
Religious Exemption Laws	*251*
Wyoming Overall Tally	*251*
United States Territories and Possessions	252
American Samoa	*252*
Commonwealth of the Northern Mariana Islands	*252*
Guam	*252*
Puerto Rico	*252*
United States Virgin Islands	*253*
SUMMARY	254
ACKNOWLEGEMENTS	256
ABOUT THE AUTHOR	257
DEFINITIONS	258
REFERENCES	264
Periodicals	264
Books	268
Clinical Practice Guidelines	268
Organization Policy Statements	269
Reports	269
Constitutional Provisions	270
Laws of the United States	270

Code of Federal Regulations 270
U.S. Departmental Policies 270
Legal Cases 270
    Federal Courts 270
    United States Circuit Courts of Appeals 271
    United States District Courts 271
    Law Review Articles 272
    State Courts 272
    Additional Cases Not Cited 272
NOTES 273

DISCLOSURE STATEMENT

Throughout this book, the author cites sources from websites where information was obtained but cannot guarantee that the Universal Resource Locators (URLs) for those websites will always remain the same. Companies and government agencies routinely update or make significant revisions to their websites, resulting in changed content and website addresses. The URLs contained in this book were current as of the date of publication. The author takes no responsibility for changes that occur after publication.

AUTHOR'S COMMENTS

The opinions expressed here are those of the author. They are not attributable to anyone else, and the author takes full responsibility. My comments and opinions, offered here, are based on scientific evidence, which the author believes to be correct, given the current political climate surrounding the ongoing attack on the civil rights of the trans community.

Frequently, the more we learn, the more questions are raised. Like much of the scientific knowledge in other areas of human experience, the science dealing with sex and gender-related issues grows as concepts are verified or disproved when peer-reviewed. For example, when Galileo discovered that the earth orbits the sun, the Vatican refused to accept that the earth was not the center of the universe until 359 years later. Similarly, in 1687, Sir Isaac Newton published his book *Principia*, which set out the laws of motion and universal gravitation. Gravity is a universal physical constant, which exists regardless of the presence of humans. I mention these two examples because, even to this day, some people still believe that the answers to many questions are best left to something other than science.

Our understanding of gender identity disorders is subject to change as the scientific research that explains it changes. Like many areas of human knowledge, as further research is undertaken, the body of knowledge we possess grows and evolves. This is the nature of scientific discovery. The quest for new knowledge and understanding explains why humans continue to strive to discover testable (objective) truths.

This book describes what I believe to be objective truths regarding gender identity disorders based on a wide range of research in medical, psychological, and sociological disciplines, which has been undertaken, peer-reviewed, and replicated to demonstrate that sex and gender represent two distinct, but related, aspects of human nature. Working with the people who present symptoms characteristic of gender identity disorders, researchers from various disciplines have reached the same or similar conclusions. Psychological research tells us that gender roles are dictated by sociological and cultural distinctions, rather than biological ones. Thus, gender roles are socially and culturally constructed to define accepted and expected behaviors, usually based on one's sex as assigned at birth. But not everyone agrees with or is able to comply with those expectations. Some individuals prefer to be viewed as being different from, or outside of, the gender roles as determined by the sex they were assigned at birth. Accordingly, old concepts about a person's place in society based on sex have changed over time. The heteronormative nuclear family, characteristic of the first half of the 20th Century, is no longer accepted by many.

Much of the early research on gender identity and gender identity disorders began in the 1960s. A number of researchers came to the same conclusion—that not all humans are born cisgender and/or heterosexual. The literature references the possibility of a genetic component that may result in individuals identifying later in childhood as homosexual or trans. Much scientific evidence demonstrates that being trans, for example, is, indeed, a legitimate human condition about which we have empirical and clinical evidence. Still, some people refuse to accept this eventuality—focusing instead on disinformation, obfuscation, innuendo, and proceeding by way of false preconceptions and/or denial, or, more recently, by redirecting the narrative toward something else (often religious conviction), which they believe supports their view.

This form of "willful ignorance"[1] is demonstrated by many White Christian Republicans, who, for example, do not accept (or respect) this evidence, as demonstrated on January 6, 2021, when

Republican members of Congress and the Senate, who continue to support Donald J. Trump, actively sought to overturn the results of the 2020 Presidential election based on false claims that the election was "stolen" and there was widespread election fraud.

Following on this, the current narrative in some circles is that male-to-female transgender people possess an "unfair advantage" in sports, for example. These allegations are based on a false presumption that trans athletes enjoy some innate physical advantage conferred by testosterone, which non-trans, cisgender female athletes do not possess. The literature tells us otherwise. There is no unfair advantage: rather, the focus on testosterone levels in transfeminine athletes is misplaced. It amounts to subterfuge, primarily when the goal of excluding trans athletes has no connection to the actual intent. I believe the true objective is to force a religiously based set of values on society, even though others may not accept this perspective. Numerous authors have written about how White Christian values mixed with White supremacy have influenced political discourse in this country. We have witnessed that influence in numerous events that have occurred in the last ten years, where southern White Christian values of exclusion have become the driving force behind attempts to restrict the civil rights of people who challenge the *status quo* by not conforming to a preconceived social order. White Christian doctrine defines a clear delineation of male and female heterosexuality—a delineation they claim to be God's creation and does not allow for any differences or deviation. Texts in the Old Testament of the Christian Bible are used to discriminate against anyone who expresses a sexual orientation or "preference" that is different. The Bible, they claim, interprets this as an "abomination." This is a narrative that completely ignores and rejects scientific evidence to the contrary.

Despite an established understanding of gender identity disorders through the rigorous use of the scientific method, a political agenda has emerged that attempts to refute science in favor of an alternative, non-scientific viewpoint that permits the twisting of facts to suit their agenda. The alternate reality of the four years of the Trump Administration comes to mind. If one wishes to dispute facts, it is necessary to provide verifiable alternatives that demonstrate that previously established information no longer fits the outcomes of new inquiry. This new research must be peer-reviewed to confirm that the methodology used, and the conclusions drawn, are valid and replicable. Simply calling previous research into question without any evidence to the contrary is not rigorous. This is the situation when certain people in power try to make claims based on their belief in "alternative facts," particularly when the "alternative facts" have never been produced or reviewed by others. An example of this is when people claim that "biological males"—a term used by the ultra-conservative religious right to describe male-to-female transgender people—cannot participate in school sports because they were assigned male at birth. They completely discount and ignore the existence of gender identity disorders in this belief.

It is my opinion that many Republicans, who support or identify with Donald J. Trump, want to push back the clock on human rights to a time when such rights did not exist. They mock the rule of law when well-reasoned court decisions do not go in their favor. They try to subvert the rule of law by engaging in tactics that sow rebellion instead of accepting the result. Further, they have undertaken certain behaviors approved by their followers—primarily evangelical Christians—in order to secure their re-election. For many years, the Southern Baptist community has been highly influential in Republican politics (for example, consider the Southern Baptist Convention policy statement from June 2014—see below for details[2]). New legislation is being introduced and passed by state legislatures across the country to "dial back" civil rights for the trans community. The U.S. Supreme Court, in a well-written opinion by Justice Neil Gorsuch, ruled that trans people cannot be discriminated against in employment.

But rather than accept that ruling as being in line with what the Court has previously said about the provisions in the Constitution that deal with the rights of the governed, some, who have other non-inclusive views, choose to enact harmful, restrictive laws in the state legislatures to subvert the rule of law as interpreted by the nation's highest court.

For example, when one reads the text of the Bills in state legislatures proposing to ban participation in interscholastic and intercollegiate sports, it is easy to see this as a coordinated effort on the part of ultra-conservative Republicans nationwide to put restrictions in place that purportedly solve a problem that does not exist. Less than one percent of the United States population identifies as trans. In some states that have enacted such laws, there have been no trans athletes desiring to participate in school sports programs. Nevertheless, these laws have been enacted to protect cisgender female students from the *potential* that boys "pretending to be girls" (i.e., transgirls) might, at some point in the future, wish to compete against students assigned female at birth. This legislative position confirms ultra-conservative Republican views on this issue. The laws define transfeminine athletes as boys and completely ignore the findings of the professional medical and psychological communities regarding these students in terms of their gender identity. Further, they completely ignore and dispute the research showing that students assigned male at birth, who have completed transition-related medical care, do not demonstrate an unfair advantage against their cisgender counterparts. Their objections are based on out-of-date misinformation about trans athletes' supposedly high testosterone levels allowing them to dominate in girls' sports.

Described in an article in *Scientific American* (March 16, 2021, "Trans Girls Belong on Girls' Sports Teams"), a lawsuit was filed in Connecticut challenging a policy that had previously allowed transfeminine athletes to compete in girls' sports, claiming that cisgender girls could not win, despite one of the cisgender plaintiffs in the lawsuit having beaten a trans athlete in a statewide championship. The article states that studies with trans athletes do not show any clear or consistent link between testosterone and athletic performance. So, why are ultra-conservative Republicans pushing this narrative so forcefully? I suspect they are not all that interested in whether a trans athlete competes or not: but rather, they are pushing these restrictive laws to declare to their base of supporters, "See what I have done to further the White Christian conservative cause?" To date, none of the laws that have been proposed or enacted demonstrate a basis in scientific evidence. Instead, they are based on religious belief that scorns anything that differs from what they claim God has ordained. Resolutions of the Southern Baptist Convention of June 1, 2014, underscore this intent.

> WHEREAS, God's design was the creation of two distinct and complementary sexes, male and female (Genesis 1:27; Matthew 19:4; Mark 10:6) which designate the fundamental distinction that God has embedded in the very biology of the human race; and
>
> WHEREAS, Distinctions in masculine and feminine roles as ordained by God are part of the created order and should find expression in every human heart (Genesis 2:18, 21–24; 1 Corinthians 11:7–9; Ephesians 5:22–33; 1 Timothy 2:12–14); and
>
> WHEREAS, Many LGBT activists have sought to normalize the transgender experience and to define gender according to one's self-perception apart from biological anatomy; and

> WHEREAS, The separation of one's gender identity from the physical reality of biological birth sex poses the harmful effect of engendering an understanding of sexuality and personhood that is fluid; now, therefore, be it
>
> **RESOLVED, That we oppose efforts to alter one's bodily identity (e.g., cross-sex hormone therapy, gender reassignment surgery) to refashion it to conform with one's perceived gender identity; and be it further;**
>
> **RESOLVED, That we continue to oppose steadfastly all efforts by any governing official or body to validate transgender identity as morally praiseworthy (Isaiah 5:20); and be it further;**
>
> **RESOLVED, That we oppose all cultural efforts to validate claims to transgender identity.**[3] (emphasis added)

In their disregard for the research that has been performed in the last 60 years and the World Professional Association for Transgender Health (WPATH) Standards of Care (SOC) that professional associations have promulgated since 1979, Conservative Christian Republicans espouse a narrative that completely denies the scientific evidence.

Furthermore, in their disregard for the position statements issued by dozens of medical, psychological, psychiatric, and other professional organizations in the field of gender and sexuality, supporting the availability of care for the trans community and for the inclusion of trans athletes in school sports, Conservative Christian Republicans ignore all that and push a narrative that supports discrimination and non-inclusion of the trans community.

It seems as though Conservative Christian Republicans have decided *en masse* that the scientific evidence about gender diversity is in dispute. They appear to have forgotten that similar scientific undertakings provided their cellphones, the computers they use to promulgate their narrative on gender diversity (or lack thereof), the cars they drive, and the many other modern conveniences that make their lives better. Beyond this, it was scientific research that provided the health care they take for granted and that they would deny to the adolescent and youth trans community when it is related to their transition.

I don't think many of us want to return to the day when "The Church" imprisoned people because they said the sun was at the center of our solar system, rather than the earth. Further, I don't think ultra-conservative Christian Republicans speak for the majority of people. Society must protect the civil rights of minorities, who the majority has systematically mistreated for over 200 years. When that fails to happen, we all suffer. The Fourteenth Amendment to the U.S. Constitution provides for equal protection under the law for all, not just a privileged few.

PREFACE

Why I Chose to Write This Book

I initially agreed to write this book because earlier editions, titled *Legal Aspects of Transsexualism*, had become outdated. Originally ghost written by Harriet Slavitz and published by the Erickson Educational Foundation in 1971,[4] *Legal Aspects of Transsexualism* (sometimes with the subtitle *A Handbook for Transsexuals*) was rewritten and updated by Joanna Clark (Sister Mary Elizabeth) and republished in 1980 by JANUS Information Facility[5], in 1988 by J2CP Information Services, and again, in 1990 by The International Foundation for Gender Education (IFGE). But then, I didn't do anything with it for a couple of years. The events that inspired me to start writing finally began to happen in the last year of the Trump administration and continue to the present. Specifically, I have been deeply concerned with the efforts by Republicans across the nation to introduce legislation that adversely affects the rights of one specific segment of the LGBTQ population, the trans community. Legislative proposals banning student-athletes who are trans from participating in interscholastic and intercollegiate sports are becoming law. Other legislation prohibiting transition-related health care for trans youth and adolescents is also being passed, potentially causing life-threatening harm to young people.

I have a health care background, having worked as a respiratory therapist in acute care and critical care medicine for twenty-one years in hospitals in Wisconsin and Minnesota, and as a member of a Disaster Medical Assistance Team (DMAT). In 2006 through 2008, I helped with the effort to build a cache of portable ventilators for stockpiling by the Minnesota Department of Health.

My previous work with the ACLU Foundation of Southern California, along with my medical background, has been beneficial to me in terms of my education and training. I have a deep appreciation for science, technology, and other fields, such as astrophysics, spaceflight, and particle physics.

I regularly keep up on advancements in virology, because viruses often impact the respiratory and cardiovascular systems.

Realizing the knowledge and research skills that I possessed could help address the issues being raised by the laws being passed by Republican-led legislatures, I decided, in February 2021, that I had to take action to help the community by producing this work for their benefit. When reasonable people know of something that can alleviate pain and suffering, and they do nothing, they bring down the human spirit in an inhumane way. To me, they are unworthy of my respect.

ACLU Transsexual Rights Committee

The author, along with Joanna Clark, and Jude Patton, who have both contributed to this volume, were members of the ACLU Foundation of Southern California Transsexual Rights Committee between 1980 and 1985, along with Joy Shaffer, Carol Katz, and Candice Brown. At that time, the committee was responsible for advocating for the rights of the transsexual community. The committee members assisted in bringing to the attention of the legal community those cases where trans individuals were being discriminated against in employment, housing, education, and other areas. Our major accomplishment was working on a civil lawsuit that was filed on behalf of a transgender woman who was incarcerated in the prison system. The author supported two attorneys in that office, the Lesbian and Gay Rights attorney and the Death Penalty attorney. The author typed legal briefs for cases pending in the federal court system in California and was responsible for filing court documents. The ACLU Foundation of Southern California also employed the author in the capacity of legal assistant. The author gained much of her knowledge of transsexual rights during this employment and volunteerism with the ACLU.

Figure 1: ACLU Transsexual Rights Committee, San Jose, California, June 1982
Joanna Clark (Chairperson), Jude Patton, Candice Brown, Joy Shaffer, Diane Saunders

The committee was dissolved when the above individuals left the ACLU for various reasons. Most of us have returned to individual and collective advocacy positions to help address current issues.

Audience

The primary audience for this book is two-fold.

First, is the professional community and the need for up-to-date information (as of the publication date) on research and case law in the United States. The research, diagnostic criteria, and case law sections will be of particular interest to clinicians and lawyers.

A second segment that will find the book helpful includes members of the LGBTQ community and their allies, who are looking for resources to point them in the direction of finding help and advice. Accordingly, the sections on clinic locations and the laws and regulations of the various states will be of particular interest to those individuals. I am writing this for you just as much as I am writing it for professionals.

A Few Additional Words

I also want to add a few words for those who might say, "I am not transsexual or transgender. So, why should I read this book?" This book is intended as a resource for transsexual, transgender, non-binary, Two -Spirit, and other gender diverse individuals as well as professionals, clinicians, and allies who work with, are related to, or have an interest in the trans community. Moreover, although this book could cover a wide range of different subject areas related to being trans, had I tried to cover them all, it would be twice the length it already is. Since I cannot cover every aspect of sex and gender in one volume, those are subjects best left for another day. Still, much of the information presented here is applicable and of interest, more broadly, to the LGBTQ+ community.

In preparing to write this book, I searched for scholarly works, including articles in medical, psychological, and sociological journals and their subspecialties. My review of the research includes articles from media, books, and internet sources. In 2018 and 2019, I also used the resources of the Kathryn A. Martin Library at the University of Minnesota Duluth campus. I provide a more detailed explanation of my methodology in that section of the book. My writing also involved many consultations with my contributors and my publisher over the many issues that present themselves whenever one undertakes a project that encompasses the size and complexity of a book of this type.

Every person experiences differences in the ways in which the issues surrounding gender, sex, and identity impact our lives. Thus, even though the book's primary focus is various aspects of the trans community experience intended to help individuals understand many of the issues they will encounter as trans people, there is plentiful and valuable information contained in this book for the entire LGBTQ+ community. Even if you are not trans, you may have friends, family members, colleagues, or clients who are. The knowledge gained by reading this book will help you to understand their experiences and their responses to those experiences. Furthermore, this book contains resources that can help you find levels of support that are appropriate. I discuss this further in the Introduction.

I hope you will find this revision of *The Legal Aspects of Transsexualism* helpful.

~Diane Saunders

FOREWORD

Legal Aspects of Transsexualism, a small booklet originally published under the auspices of the Erickson Educational Foundation (EEF) in 1971, was not the first publication, nor was EEF the first organization, involved in addressing legal concerns affecting transgender, non-binary, and gender non-conforming citizens of the US. Most early laws dealt with crossdressing, masquerade, sodomy, homosexuality, pornography, and "public indecency."

Adopted as part of a broader anti-decency campaign, in 1863, San Francisco's Board of Supervisors passed a law that criminalized appearing in public "in a dress not belonging to his or her sex." This became a template for other laws policing multiple "gender transgressions," resulting in more than 100 known arrests before the end of the 19th century. More than 40 other U.S. cities passed similar laws during this time.

For a timeline of anti-cross-dressing laws in the United States, read the article, "Arresting Dress: A timeline of anti-cross-dressing laws in the United States," in *Nation*, May 31, 2015. For further reading, see the book, *Arresting Dress: Cross-dressing, Law, and Fascination in Nineteenth-Century San Francisco* by Clare Sears, published in 2014 by Duke University Press. Also, see Wikipedia's pages on the subjects of crossdressing and sodomy laws for additional information. Prior to 1962, sodomy was a felony offense in every state, punishable by imprisonment (up to a lifetime sentence in Idaho) and/or by hard labor. Most of the sodomy offenses were applied to gay men. Sodomy laws were finally struck down in the U.S. Supreme Court decision, *Lawrence vs Texas*, in 2003.

By the 1950s and early 1960s, several homophile organizations began campaigns to publicly support gay liberation, including One, Inc. in Los Angeles. Dorr Legg, President of One, Inc. (founded in 1952) was one of my mentors in the early 1970s, along with Virginia Prince, who fought for the civil rights of cross dressers.

While not defined as "legal organizations," early examples of "trans liberation organizations" included: Queens Liberation Front (QLF) in New York City founded in 1969; the Transvestite-Transsexual Organization (TAO) in Los Angeles and in Coconut Grove, Florida; the Cockettes in San Francisco; Street Transvestites Action Revolutionaries (STAR) in New York City; Fems Against Sexism and Transvestites and Transsexuals (TATS) in New York City; and Radical Queens in Milwaukee, Wisconsin, all founded in 1970. Later, Transsexual Menace was a well-known and outspoken group. Some of these early trans groups and some LGBT groups were involved in "riots" with police. In May 1959, drag queens clashed with police at Cooper's Donuts in Los Angeles. In August 1966, LGBT riots occurred at Compton's Cafeteria in San Francisco. In June 1969, the infamous Stonewall Inn riots occurred over several consecutive days in Manhattan's West Village.

Diane Saunders, author of this updated version of the *Legal Aspects of Transsexualism*, invited Joanna Clark and me to contribute some of the historical background information for this updated volume. In the text of this book, Diane has described her own history of becoming involved with the ACLU Transsexual Rights Committee and her commitment to rewriting the *Legal Aspects of Transsexualism*.

I am certainly not a legal scholar, but I *am* a long-time activist and advocate for transgender rights, having "transitioned" myself in 1970. I also consider myself to be somewhat of an amateur historian. I have a large private library and a large collection of trans-related materials, all planned for donation to the Transgender Library Archives at the University of Victoria in Victoria BC, upon my demise.

The ACLU Transsexual Rights Committee was founded by Joanna Clark in 1980. Chief Counsel at the time for the Los Angeles Chapter of the ACLU was Susan D. McGreivy (a cisgender woman), who worked with Diane who was her legal aid/secretary. The other (all trans-identified) committee members were: Joy Shaffer, Kay (Candice) Brown, Carol Katz, and Jude Patton. Diane lobbied many times for Susan to support trans rights, but Susan was primarily focused on other law projects at the time. At least one historian has described the ACLU Transsexual Rights Committee as being "the first serious legal organization addressing transgender rights."

I want to give a personal "shout-out" to Vern Bullough RN, Ph.D. for his advocacy in the early 1960s and beyond, to involve the Los Angeles Chapter of the ACLU in legal interventions related to the LGBTQ+ community, which likely aided the creation and support later on by the ACLU for the Transsexual Rights Committee. Both Vern and his wife, Bonnie Bullough RN, Ph.D., were highly valued as mentors to me when I began my own career as a sex therapist and sex educator in 1980. (See the Bulloughs' many books published about the history of sex.)

Since the inception of the ACLU Transsexual Rights Committee in 1980, I have remained in personal contact with Joanna Clark over the past 41 years. After leaving the ACLU Transsexual Rights Committee in 1985, Diane dropped out of her political/legal involvement in trans issues, pursuing other private interests and career activities. However, she became very concerned about the plight of trans youth when Trump was elected as U.S. President and began making radical changes in laws which offered some protection to trans people. This was the impetus driving her to write *The Transgender Compendium*.

Early in 2021, when Diane contacted Joanna about writing this book, I joined her and Joanna in this project. Since then, we have spent one to two mornings each week via Zoom meetings online, in conversation/planning the book together, along with one morning each week in a Zoom meeting with the editor/publisher, Margot Wilson. I have also maintained limited contact with Kay (Candice) Brown and with Carol Katz since 1985. I lost contact with Joy Shaffer sometime in the late 1990s. Joy had established her Seahorse Medical Clinic in San Jose, California in 1995, serving mostly trans clientele. Joy also participated in early brain research MRI studies, hoping to locate a possible etiology of trans identity. Joy wrote the introduction to the book, *Transgender Care: Recommended Guidelines, Practical Information, and Personal Accounts*, by Gianna Israel and Donald Tarver, published in 1997 by Temple University Press. Eventually, Joy moved to New Zealand and began working in a rural medical clinic.

Carol Katz has been living in one of the Dakotas for at least the past 30 years, having dropped out of most of her earlier public work in the Los Angeles area, as an openly lesbian trans activist, but remaining as an advocate, working behind the scenes for trans rights. Carol and Diane both are avid ham radio operators, working as volunteers with local, state, and federal disaster relief teams in their respective geographic areas. Carol worked in mostly security positions until her retirement a few years ago. Diane has mostly worked as a respiratory therapist in hospital settings before her retirement. Additionally, she has worked in organizing disaster relief programs, having had specialized training in this field.

In 1975, Joanna Clark waged a legal battle with the U.S. Army after she was discharged from the Army subsequent to being "outed" as a trans woman. She had previously successfully served in the U.S. Navy as a male while on active duty. On active duty, she served in naval air operations and as a diver. She is the first known 20th Century trans person to have "served both as a man and as a woman" in U.S. military service. In 1977, Joanna successfully lobbied for a California state law that allows replacement birth certificates. She later wrote two revised editions of *Legal Aspects of Transsexualism*.

In 1983, Joanna left the ACLU Transsexual Rights Committee and Diane took over as the Chair of the committee.

I have a copy of an article written by Diane Saunders to *Phoenix*, a publication of Gateway Gender Alliance in Sunnyvale, California, dated May 3, 1983 in which Diane announces that she is now the Chair of the Transsexual Rights Committee, lauding Joanna's previous work as Chair, and seeking donations. Most of the funding for the ACLU Transsexual Rights Committee's work was provided by Committee members, who also volunteered all of their time.

I also have a copy of a letter from Lou Sullivan (considered by many as an "FTM hero"), dated June 19, 1987, addressed to "Diane Saunders, ACLU Transsexual Rights Committee," describing himself as "a member of the ACLU through the Transsexual Rights Committee for several years" and seeking legal advice for how to change his name on his Wisconsin birth certificate. Joanna Clark sent back a hand-written note to Lou, advising him that the Committee was disbanded "two years ago" due to lack of financial support and Diane's move to Wisconsin. Joanna was attempting to reply to correspondence addressed to the Committee through J2CP (an organization founded by Joanna and myself to serve the trans community). J2CP had also taken over the work Paul Walker had been doing for the Erickson Educational Foundation, after it disbanded, and for the work done previously by Renaissance Gender Identity Services, an organization established by me in the later 1970s. The work of J2CP was eventually turned over in the early 1990s to Dallas Denny. Joanna Clark became an Episcopal Sister, Sister Mary Elizabeth, taking her vows at St. Clements by the Sea Episcopal Church in San Clemente, California in 1988. In 1990, Joanna founded AIDS Education Global Information System (AEGiS), the largest AIDS and HIV information online service in the world. Today, Joanna works from home as a conservation and climate change advocate, spending hours daily, penning letters to various politicians, advocating to save our environment.

Kay Brown (Candice H. Brown Elliott) has gone on to write and publish about transgender science, history, and politics. Kay has worked for improved legal and social treatment of transsexuals (her preferred term) all of her life. She has a dual degree in physics and psychology, with a minor in biology. Her successful career as a scientist speaks for itself. She has been granted over 100 U.S. patents. She is also the proud mother of two (now grown) foster/adopted daughters and enjoys her family life, living in northern California. See Kay's two self-published books: *On the Science of Changing Sex: A Layman's Guide to Transsexuality and Transgenderism;* and *Rainbow's End: A Parent's Guide to Understanding Transsexual Teens and Children.* She has also written science fiction novels under the pen name, "Seaby Brown." Candice is a commercial pilot and flight instructor at a local airport.

Below, Diane describes the establishment and evolution of The Harry Benjamin International Gender Dysphoria Association (HBIGDA), starting in 1979. I was elected to serve as a Board member, as a "consumer advocate," at that first meeting. HBIGDA's name was later changed to The World Professional Association for Transgender Health (WPATH). Richard Green was the President of their organization between 1997 through 1999. During his Presidency, he gave a speech at their world conference in the United Kingdom in 1999 that Diane cites.

> In closing, I address a remarkable evolution in this field—the dual role now played by persons with a history of gender identity disorder, or gender dysphoria, or transsexualism, as both professional and consumer. This previously marginalized population is increasingly taking its position as respected professional colleagues. As President of this association, I am pleased that our Executive Board contains both transsexual and non-transsexual persons. As Chair of the Program Committee, I am

pleased that our program has included both transsexual and non-transsexual professionals. It would make Harry Benjamin proud.

In 1999, both I, a trans man, and Sheila Kirk M.D., a trans woman, were elected to serve on the WPATH Executive Board. Since that time, trans men, Jamison Green Ph.D., J.D. and Stephen Whittle Ph.D., J.D. have served as President. Importantly, mainstream professional, medical, and legal organizations all over the world have written positive "Position Papers" supporting the health care needs and civil rights of trans people. Just recently, WPATH released to the public, for public comment, its latest revisions to their Guidelines for Care, Version SOC8. The first Guidelines for Care were written by Paul Walker and introduced at the initial HBIGDA meeting in 1979.

We are all still awaiting the passage of the Equality Act, which was introduced by Congress in 2019. This piece of legislation would explicitly and strongly extend civil rights protections to cover all LGBTQ+ people in the United States. The Equality Act prohibits discrimination based on an individual's sexual orientation or gender identity in employment, housing, credit, education, jury service, federally funded programs, health care, and businesses that serve the public. Hopefully, during the Biden administration, this important legislation will be passed.

With the above historical comments serving to introduce the invaluable legal information contained within this volume, I wish to congratulate Diane Saunders on the creation of this Compendium.

Jude Patton LMHC, LMFT, PA
December 19, 2021

INTRODUCTION

Descriptions from classical mythology[6] and history[7], the Renaissance[8], and nineteenth-century history,[9] plus anthropology[10,11] point to the longstanding and widespread pervasiveness of the trans phenomenon.[12,13] These descriptions were largely hidden away in historical or scientific documents, unavailable and of little interest to the public.

However, this situation changed in late-1952 when sex reassignment surgery[14] burst publicly upon the world. On December 1, 1952, the *New York Daily News* carried the banner headline, "Ex-GI Becomes Blonde Beauty."[15] For the next few months, transsexualism became a household topic as story after story about Christine Jorgensen's journey of personal life enhancement emerged. Eventually, interest in the subject dwindled, and one-time front-page stories were lost within the inner pages of the tabloids.

Few articles appeared during the period 1954 to 1976. Those that did seldom rated front-page coverage. During the summer of 1976, however, the world of professional tennis was disrupted by the controversy surrounding a player (Renee Richards) who had undergone sex reassignment and, subsequently, desired to play professional tennis as a woman.[16] The controversy once again sparked the nation's curiosity concerning trans people. During the following months, numerous magazine articles, newspaper reports, and television programs dealt with the scientific phenomenon of a "female mind trapped in a male body." Or vice versa.[17] An article by Betty Liddick, featuring text and photos of Jude Patton and Canary Conn appeared on the front page of the *Los Angeles Times*, moving over wire services on October 11, 1976.

Interest in trans people would have dwindled once again had it not been for a seemingly endless series of newsworthy stories involving trans individuals, such as "Transsexual Wars With The Army"[18] and "Sex Changed Teacher Seeks Job Back." [19] Further, the courts were suddenly alive with trans litigation, the common denominator in each case being a persistent pattern of severe discrimination.

In the early nineteen-fifties, systematic medical treatment of gender dysphoria was instituted by Harry Benjamin, M.D., a prominent New York endocrinologist.[20] The first gender clinics opened during the 1965 to 1967 period at Johns Hopkins Medical Institutions, the University of Minnesota, the University of California at Los Angeles (UCLA), and others. The Harry Benjamin International Gender Dysphoria Association (HBIGDA) was formed in 1979.[21] The first professional organization focused specifically on trans issues and devoted to the development of standards of care for trans individuals, HBIGDA was the precursor to the World Professional Association for Transgender Health (WPATH) and USPATH. It set the standard of care that is the benchmark of the field to this day.

The professionals involved in providing care for trans individuals realized early on that differential diagnosis would be complex and controversial. Consequently, international symposiums were established to resolve many of the issues surrounding the treatment of gender dysphoria.[22] International symposiums have taken place in London (1969)[23], Denmark (1971)[24], Yugoslavia (1973)[25]—now the Republic of Macedonia—Stanford (1975), Norfolk (1977), San Diego (1979), Tahoe (1981), Bordeaux, France (1983), Minneapolis (1985), and Amsterdam (1987). The first USPATH Conference occurred in November 2021.[26]

By 1976, gender dysphoria was no longer seriously questioned as an accepted medical entity. Today, gender dysphoria syndrome[27] and gender identity disorders are described thoroughly in the literature, which suggests that:

(1) the causes are still unknown[28], but there is believed to be a genetic component;[29,30]

(2) presurgical trans people, as a group, are among the most miserable of people,[31] often exhibiting extreme unhappiness, which frequently brings them to the verge of suicide[32] or self-mutilation;[33] and

(3) a satisfactory outcome to sex reassignment surgery, in terms of improved social and emotional adjustment, is at least ten times more likely than an unsatisfactory outcome in appropriately selected patients.[34,35]

The literature describes being trans as a disturbance of gender identity, where individuals experience a sense of incongruence between their innate sense of their gender and their anatomic sex.[36] Other disorders are described but frequently confused with being trans, including homosexuality and transvestism.[37]

They are, however, distinct entities. Homosexuals, who are sexually attracted to members of the same sex, and transvestites, who occasionally dress in clothes of the opposite sex, experience conflicts that are only superficially similar to those experienced by trans people. Unlike trans individuals, they do not necessarily desire to alter their anatomy.[38] The trans person, *by contrast*, may feel trapped in a body of the wrong sex and seeks release, either through skilled surgical intervention or through whatever means—including suicide—available to effectively escape.[39]

The literature shows a consistent trend towards rejection by family and friends, as well as harassment and discrimination.[40] The literature also shows that some in the legal and medical professions have refused to render services, either because they question the validity of such a diagnosis or perhaps due to fear of potential peer and community sanctions.[41]

Discrimination in employment, public accommodations, and the retail industry, as a consequence of stated religious beliefs of people who perceive only the heterosexual model as acceptable, has become rampant in our society. The interpretation of what is written in religious texts is often situated in one's own biases and prejudices, which are routinely handed down from one generation to the next.

In the last ten years, the public view of the LGBTQ+ community has become more favorable. Like homosexuality, being trans is now becoming more widely accepted. Still, in some segments of society, to be trans is still considered "abnormal."[42,43] In the political realm, transsexualism is often not represented well, especially from conservative voices. Some have characterized being trans as a kind of "freak show,"[44] despite gender dysphoria having been identified as a genuine issue for which the medical, psychiatric, psychological, sociological, and legal communities have fashioned remedies.

A lot has changed in today's medical community, medical centers of excellence, and university health programs. University-based health care systems, and others, provide services related to presurgical and hormone therapies, psychological and psychiatric screening, and other services.

It is clear from the literature[45,46,47,48] that transgender and gender nonconforming (TGNC) adolescents are significantly affected by mental health disparities and have difficulty accessing and receiving health care[49,50,51] compared with cisgender youth. Previous research in this field is limited by reliance on small, nonrepresentative, and adult samples.

> TGNC adolescents reported poorer health, fewer health checkups, and more nursing visits than their cisgender peers. TGNC adolescents whose gender expression strongly matched their birth-assigned sex had better health and fewer long-term mental health problems compared with other gender presentations.[52]

The case for trans adolescents and youth has recently become a great deal more complex. This is due to the enactment of laws meant to ban trans athletes from participating in school sports in many so-called "Red" states or states where conservative Republicans control the legislatures. Laws have been enacted to ban outright the provision of medical care to trans adolescents and youth. More on this later in the book.

My intentions in writing this revision are that it will provide a resource for anyone who works with individuals who are experiencing gender discomfort. In addition, I want this book to be a resource for individuals dealing with gender-related issues but who do not know where to turn for help. The list of gender clinics in the U.S. will interest anyone looking for help for themselves, a loved one, or a friend.

The topics addressed in the sections that follow include:

1. a brief background on the trans phenomenon and trans-related issues. Other people have written more in-depth historical volumes on trans history, so I will leave it to the reader to explore that area as they desire.
2. a review of the medical, psychiatric, psychological, and sociological research undertaken between the early nineteen-sixties to approximately nineteen-ninety. This was the early period of research conducted on gender dysphoria as the issue first presented itself in the United States.
3. a review of the more recent period of research, from nineteen-ninety to the present shows that our understanding of gender dysphoria and persons who identify as transgender or gender nonconforming (TGNC) has exploded, mainly when various media outlets began covering the subject. This was a period of new organizations coming into the fray to undertake research and advocate for the rights of this population.
4. organizations in medicine, psychiatry, psychology, sociology, and associated disciplines have produced diagnostic criteria, standards of care, and clinical practice guidelines for professionals to use in evaluating, assessing, treating, and providing follow-up care or services to people with gender-related symptoms.
5. along with the fields of study and practice mentioned above, there are other sociological issues involved that are separate from the medical, psychiatric, and psychological phenomenology.
6. when persons present in doctors' offices with symptoms of gender dysphoria or gender-nonconforming feelings, family physicians, and others, need to know where to refer patients for more definitive care, particularly if they are unsure how to treat such patients. Accordingly, I have listed those transgender specialty clinics of which I am aware at the time of publication. This list is by no means all-inclusive. Nevertheless, the list includes the names and contact information for those larger organizations that may be able to point readers in the right direction.

This revision provides readers with up-to-date medical, psychological, and psychiatric research, the availability of clinics specializing in the care and treatment of gender-related disorders, and an overview of the Federal and State legal landscape as it now exists.

Finally, I have included some personal comments that reflect my deep concern about the laws being passed in Republican-led states, which severely restrict or eliminate the civil rights now enjoyed by the trans community.

BASIS OF DISCRIMINATION

The literature shows that discrimination can be based on conscious bias,[53] implicit bias,[54] marginalization,[55] stigmatization,[56] and even explicit or implicit stereotyping[57] where the individual seeks to exclude those viewed as undesirable or objectionable for a variety of reasons, including those of a political nature. In this section, I describe and discuss how these concepts fit together to form the basis of discrimination against individuals in the trans community.

Discrimination is not simply a choice based on preferences, but often, is an overt choice to exclude others with the intent of gaining an advantage, economically, socially, politically, or by artificial construct. The history of this country is replete with instances where people who are different because of their race, nationality, country of origin, sex, religious beliefs, color of their skin, shape of their eyes, or other characteristics have been shunned, hung, shot, burned at the stake, and made to feel as though they are not considered human, simply because of those differences. We have killed indigenous people for no other reason than that we considered them to be "savages." We took the land of others simply because we could. To this day, there are members of this society who believe that they are superior to others (e.g., White supremacy), as we have recently seen during riots in Charlotte, North Carolina, Charlottesville, Virginia, and other cities. All of these are examples of how and why we discriminate.

The Merriam-Webster Dictionary Online defines marginalization[58] as "to relegate to an unimportant or powerless position within a society or group." Trans persons have been in a position of powerlessness for decades, as demonstrated in numerous studies.[59,60]

Stigmatization is defined as describing someone or something as worthy of disapproval or hatred simply because of a characteristic or trait that the stigmatized person possesses. When people are stereotyped, marginalized, and stigmatized—as the trans community has been—it results in members of that group or class of people having a low sense of self and/or low self-esteem. When coupled with a lack of educational opportunity, this often results in that group living in poverty. Furthermore, poverty, itself, becomes another reason why the trans community suffers from chronic and often severe discrimination.[61] The harm done to members of the trans community is real and has been well-documented in the legal cases brought before the courts in the last 40 years or so.

Stereotyping is defined as unfairly believing that all people with similar characteristics should be treated differently than those who do not share that characteristic. In social psychology, a stereotype is defined as a fixed, over-generalized belief about a particular group or class of people. In 1968, Jane Elliott, a schoolteacher in Riceville, Iowa, performed an exercise with her third-grade class to highlight the effects of discrimination. She separated her class into those students with blue eyes and those with brown eyes. The exercise was described in detail by a story on the Public Broadcasting System (PBS) program "Frontline," on January 1, 2003:[62]

> On the first day, the blue-eyed children were told they were smarter, more sociable, neater, and better than those with brown eyes. Throughout the day, Elliott praised them and allowed them privileges, such as taking a longer recess and being first in the lunch line. In contrast, the brown-eyed children had to wear collars around their necks and their behavior and performance were criticized and ridiculed by Elliott. On the second day, the roles were reversed, and the blue-eyed children were made to feel inferior while the brown eyes were designated the dominant group.

What happened over the course of this unique two-day exercise astonished both students and teacher. On both days, children designated as inferior took on the look and behavior of genuinely inferior students, performing poorly on tests and other work. In contrast, the "superior" students—students who had been sweet and tolerant before the exercise—became mean-spirited and seemed to like discriminating against the "inferior" group. The exercise highlights that people often discriminate against others on the basis of their physical differences. Blue eyes, brown eyes, right-handed, left-handed, and other traits or characteristics can be, and have been, the basis for discrimination. Much like racial discrimination, a person is rejected or excluded simply because of a trait or characteristic that sets them apart from others.

Similar to discrimination on the basis of eye color is discrimination on the basis of sex. Discrimination on the basis of sex began with men viewing women as property, rather than as humans deserving equal treatment either by them or by society. In the 1700s, women were considered to be coverture, an inherited practice from the English common law where a woman's property rights were not her own, but her father's and, later, her husband's. Moreover, a married woman had no right to refuse her husband's sexual advances. To this day, some men still feel this way and objectify women as nothing more than vessels for sex and/or procreation. Even after many years of advocacy, women's rights still have a long way to go in some settings. The ultimate discrimination against women is men telling women they do not merit having control over their own bodies in the health care decisions they make, when men take such control for granted.

Likewise, discrimination because of sex is equally problematic for homosexual or transgender individuals. Today, the Civil Rights Act prohibits any individual in the U.S. from being excluded from participation in, denied the benefits of, or be subjected to discrimination because of race, color, national origin, sex, age, or disability. Perhaps, Justice Neil Gorsuch said it best when he wrote the majority U.S. Supreme Court opinion in *Bostock v. Clayton County, GA*, 590 U.S. ____ 2020:

> An individual's homosexuality or transgender status is **not relevant** to employment decisions. That's because it is impossible to discriminate against a person for being homosexual or transgender without discriminating against that individual based on sex (emphasis added).

When we treat people differently solely on the basis of a single attribute or even in connection with other reasons, we act in contravention of the law. It really doesn't matter whether the discrimination has a rational basis or can withstand strict scrutiny (or not). Nevertheless, it appears that sex discrimination is particularly pervasive in our society, despite there being no legitimate, socially mandated, or legal reason for it. Such discrimination only serves to exclude those some may deem objectionable for one reason or another. Discriminating against anyone because of some perceived difference has no legitimate purpose.

Still, humans often display a built-in, implicit bias toward seeing the world from our own perspective. A heterosexual person sees the world from a heteronormative perspective, while a homosexual person may see the world differently. Further, a trans person may see the world from yet another perspective. As most people take sex and gender for granted, rarely giving it a second thought, it may never occur to them that the person standing next to them might not be what they appear to be and may not share the same perspective on the world. In addition, most people view sex and gender as being the same—they consider their sex as inherently male or female and their gender to be the same, i.e., either male or female.

However, sex and gender are ***not*** the same.[63] Why would we consider sex and gender any differently than the rest of human diversity? Human beings display an infinite diversity. Just look around, and you will see this to be true. We are not alike, although we do share some common characteristics. Still, people continue to look at the world around them through the looking glass of their own biases and prejudices and often choose to see only what they want to see. Sex is at the center of how we perceive ourselves and others[64], and, in many ways, it is the first label we attach to another human being.

As we grow up early in life, we learn from our parents, siblings, friends, and others with whom we interact. The values, biases, and prejudices of those with whom we interact help to shape us. Values and beliefs are passed from one generation to the next and unless we reject the values, biases, and prejudices that form the basis of misunderstanding or hatred, they become part of who we are. Sometimes, we form opinions not based in fact but on preconception, preconceptions that come from books, articles, other people, or stories that misinterpret or misstate the facts for reasons that are antiquated, suspect, or lost to memory. Thus, the narrative becomes one based on misinformation, supposition, or the furtherance of a political agenda. An example of this is the current narrative put forth by conservative Republicans in Congress and state legislatures that trans athletes have an unfair advantage when competing against cisgender athletes in interscholastic and intercollegiate sports.

In the section of this book titled "The Research: Endocrinology of Transsexualism" about research into the effects of testosterone in trans athletes, it is pointed out that once a trans person has been on hormone therapy for at least one to two years, testosterone levels drop to "levels within the normal female range because of estrogen effects on sex hormone binding globulin, only 32.1% reached normal free testosterone levels."[65] For male-to-female trans persons who have obtained sex reassignment surgery, testosterone levels drop even further because the adrenal gland atrophies along with the prostate, and the lack of testes means other masculinizing hormones, such as certain gonadotropins, as well as testosterone, are reduced even further. Muscle mass can also decline over time. Based on the above and other research reviewed in this book, it is clear the narrative espoused by these legislators is not based in fact.

The trans community has suffered from economic, social, and legal marginalization for over 60 years.[66] Trans people have been systematically denied employment, housing, medical care, social and legal services, and other benefits simply because of who they are. For years, the trans community has been treated as a group of misfits who choose to live their lives apart from accepted norms. Only recently has the trans community been increasingly accepted since court decisions have begun to recognize trans people as having the same civil rights as others in our society.

Yet, discrimination persists because some people are not prepared to examine and/or give up their beliefs that anything other than a White Christian heteronormative representation of society has value. This is in sharp contrast to other segments of society, which have begun to accept LGBTQ+ people more generally. According to the Williams Institute at the UCLA School of Law, support for gay men and lesbians has doubled in the last 30 years. Similarly, public support for trans people has increased by forty percent between 2005 and 2011.[67]

The conservative movement to deny medical and other treatments required for adolescents and youth who have been diagnosed with a gender identity disorder is flawed, because professional Standards of Care[68,69] have been established that provide for safe and effective assessment, diagnosis, and treatment with reversible modalities. Studies show that when these patients receive appropriate transition-related care, they are less likely to harbor thoughts of self-mutilation or suicide.[70] When patients present with symptoms of a gender identity disorder, such as discomfort with or abhorrence for their genitals, constant, unrelenting statements that they feel they were born in the wrong body, and a desire to alter their anatomy to match their innate sense of self as being of one gender or another, such statements cannot be downplayed or ignored. They are the statements of a person who presents with symptoms of gender dysphoria. The literature clearly shows these patients benefit from appropriate therapy, including psychiatric and psychological counseling, diagnosis, hormone therapy, and follow-up care. Other transition-related care can include assisting the individual in living in the gender role with which they identify and strengthening social support mechanisms. Legal advice can be obtained for changing names and birth records. A supportive parent can provide these supports to their trans child.

When medical care for gender dysphoric adolescents and older trans persons is denied, the literature clearly shows that they are at significantly increased risk of suicide or self-mutilation.[71] It is unfathomable that certain segments of society would not only advocate for laws that deny medical care to this population but advocate against care on the basis of inaccurate information and misplaced belief. It is inhumane to deny medical care to anyone who needs it.

BACKGROUND

The following is taken from the "Introduction" in "Transgender History in the United States: A Special Unabridged Version of a book chapter from *Trans Bodies, Trans Selves*"[72]

> Can there be said to be a "transgender history," when "transgender" is a contemporary term and when individuals in past centuries who would perhaps appear to be transgender from our vantage point might not have conceptualized their lives in such a way? And what about individuals today who have the ability to describe themselves as transgender, but choose not to for a variety of reasons, including the perception that it is a White, middle-class Western term and the belief that it implies transitioning from one gender to another? Should they be left out of "transgender history" because they do not specifically identify as transgender?
>
> These questions complicate any attempt to write a history of individuals who would have been perceived as gender nonconforming in their eras and cultures. While it would be inappropriate to limit this chapter to people who lived at a time and place when the concept of "transgender" was available and used by them, it would also be inappropriate to assume that people who are "transgender," as we currently understand the term, existed throughout history. For this reason, we cannot claim that gender non-conforming individuals were "transgender" or "transsexual" if these categories were not yet named or yet to be embraced. However, where possible, we can seek to distinguish between individuals whose actions would seem to indicate that they would be what we would call "transgender," "transsexual," or a "crossdresser" today and those who might have presented as a gender different from the one assigned to them at birth for reasons other than a sense of gender difference (such as to escape narrow gender roles or pursue same-sex sexual relationships). While all these can admittedly be fine lines, the distinctions are worth trying to make clear when presenting any specific "transgender history."[73]

Minority groups all experience some of the same social consequences of being in the minority in society. History is replete with discussions about what it is like to be shunned by a majority population simply because one is a member of a minority. Women, Blacks, Asians, Hispanics, anyone who has not conformed to a White, Anglo-Saxon, Christian, heteronormative view of the world, regardless of any other attribute, has experienced,

> significant forms of discrimination and prejudice, including religious condemnation. Because most people have great difficulty recognizing the humanity of another person if they cannot recognize that person's gender, encounters with gender changing or gender-challenging people can sometimes feel for others like an encounter with a monstrous and frightening unhumanness [sic].[74]

Throughout history, anyone who looks, acts, or espouses feelings contrary to these culturally constructed norms have been subject to the inhumanness of being treated as though they are not deserving of dignity and respect, simply because of their differences.

Members of the lesbian, gay, bisexual, transgender and queer+ (LGBTQ+) community, have been stoned, burned, hung, shot, disparaged, dragged, drowned, arrested and imprisoned, and made to feel subhuman by those who think they are superior, and, therefore, the rightful inheritors of the earth. Many of these behaviors are based on White Christian[75] mythology and perpetrated by its followers.[76] In some countries, being homosexual is a crime for which one can be executed.[77] For example, in England, the Witchcraft Act of 1542,[78] under which more than 300 women were burned at the stake, demonstrates the degree to which some are prepared to go in order to prosecute their fellow humans who hold different beliefs. A more recent example is the "ethnic cleansing" of Bosnian Muslims by Slobodan Milosevic in the Yugoslav war in the nineteen-nineties where more than two hundred thousand people lost their lives simply for belonging to the "wrong" group. Other examples of ethnic or religious "cleansing" can be found in current, ongoing disputes involving different cultures or religions. Almost every war ever fought had its origins in disputes over religious beliefs.

Our history is littered with stories about transgendered or even gay people killed simply because of who or what they were. One of the most famous cases involved Matthew Shepard, who was a gay student at the University of Wyoming. Two men, Aaron McKinney and Russell Henderson, abducted Matt on October 7, 1998, and drove him to a remote area east of Laramie, Wyoming. He was tied to a split-rail fence where the two men severely assaulted him with the butt of a pistol. He was beaten and left to die in the cold of the night. Almost eighteen hours later, he was found by a bicyclist who initially mistook him for a scarecrow.

Matt died on October 12, 1998, at 12:53 a.m. at Poudre Valley Hospital in Fort Collins, Colorado with his family by his side. His memorial service was attended by friends and family from around the world and garnered immense media attention that brought Matt's story to the forefront of the fight against bigotry and hate.[79]

On November 20, 2021, National Transgender Day of Remembrance[80] saw the highest number of trans persons killed in the United States thus far at 47 people. That number was 44 in 2020, 25 in 2019, and 22 in 2018.[81]

Even today, people who call themselves "Christians," who consider members of the LGBTQ+ community to be "abnormal," vile, and evil creatures to be banned from society, can be found in almost any community. By their words and actions, they exact an incredible mental and emotional toll on transgender persons, often in the name of religion.[82] Some have even called for the execution of members of the LGBTQ+ community.[83]

Similarly, discrimination against those of another race has deep roots in American history. We engaged in a civil war over issues of race and slavery.[84] Yet, we have not come to terms with race issues that have roots dating back hundreds of years. Events of the last few years continue to bear this out. People who gain power often use that power to enslave other people or to control the wealth of the society through oppressive measures. Charismatic "stable geniuses" have amassed herds of supporters who would follow them off a cliff if asked to do so.

Treating someone differently solely because of the traits, characteristics, color of one's skin or eyes, the shape of one's face, or any other distinguishing feature by individuals who, for whatever reason, believe that religious writings support their beliefs has become a way of life in this country.

Today, some people rationalize this disparate treatment of others as "deeply-held religious belief." Later in the book, I discuss the rise of "Religious Exemption Laws" that have been passed by state legislatures solely because Christian groups did not like it when, in 1997, the United States Supreme Court overturned the Federal Religious Freedom Restoration Act of 1993. History shows that adherents of Christianity have long followed vaguely worded religious writings, especially from the Old Testament, as support for their beliefs. They base their beliefs about homosexuality and other sex or gender-related conditions solely on what they say is "in The Bible."[85]

The practice of so-called "conversion therapy" or "reparative therapy," which will be discussed later in this book, is practiced by people of the Christian faith who falsely believe they can "cure" homosexual or trans people.[86] The practice has been widely condemned, and cities across the U.S. are instituting bans on the practice. Some states have already banned or are considering banning the practice.[87] Former Minnesota Republican Congresswoman, Michelle Bachman, and her husband, Marcus, operated a Lake Elmo, Minnesota "pray away the gay" clinic.[88] Like so many others, who see political advantage in discriminating on the basis of sexual orientation, the Bachman's also use their religious beliefs to argue against certain medical practices in women's clinics that they believe are immoral.

The Southern Poverty Law Center has named eighteen religious-based organizations, such as the Family Research Council, the Liberty Counsel, Alliance Defending Freedom, Abiding Truth Ministries, American Family Association, Americans for Truth About Homosexuality, and others as organizations that "pump out demonizing propaganda aimed at homosexuals and other sexual minorities."[89] Several of the groups also participate in filing lawsuits that relentlessly challenge laws, regulations, or government policies that favor transgender rights.

The transgender community has long suffered from severe discrimination, as outlined in this brief background review. A lot of work remains to be done to counter those belief mechanisms that foster hatred and discrimination.

METHODOLOGY

In writing this book, I relied on a large number of external resources, along with other resources that I already possess, which are part of a sizable library of texts and other resources gathered over several years. That library is continually expanding.

In the research sections of the book, I relied heavily on Google Scholar[90] and the search functions of the Library of Congress,[91] National Library of Medicine,[92] National Institutes of Health,[93] National Archives,[94] National Academies[95] and publishing companies where much of the literature from various disciplines can be found. Google Scholar was also used for researching court cases, as I do not have access to Westlaw, Lexis-Nexus, or any other commercial case reporting company websites. Most, if not all, of these companies require a subscription, and the subscriptions can be very costly.

I also used online media outlets to find stories that pointed me to further research by data-mining the articles for freely available information on topics included in the book. Newsprint stories and stories from online news providers infrequently supply the complete details about the court cases or stories on which they report. Often what is missing are links or complete citations to sources discussed in the articles. Other information is often omitted for brevity. I found this inconsistency in citing sources to be widespread throughout the news media. As a result, I used the internet to search for and locate additional information and sources and to locate and provide full citations in this book. I verified the sources and/or the stories by contacting either the author or publisher of the story. Where needed, I bought copies of research articles and books on the subject, which I read and then cite in the book.

I visited websites of organizations whose work in LGBTQ advocacy or in providing professional services and guidance, and developing policies impact the LGBTQ community most directly. The list of organizations is a long one and is not provided here. Nevertheless, citations are available in the endnotes and references list.

Where available, I downloaded copies of policies, regulations, laws, published scholarly research, professional organizational policy statements relating to the LGBTQ community, and Court documents in cases with relevance to the book. I also used Pacer, a federal government website, to retrieve documents filed with the Federal District and Appellate Courts. I also used the Circuit Courts of Appeals and the United States Supreme Court websites to research Appellate Court and Supreme Court cases and download documents from those cases. State court decisions and cases were researched using state court websites. Where websites or pertinent information were not available, I used the websites of organizations involved in state and federal court cases to locate information about cases. Some of these organizations provide downloadable copies of court briefs on their websites.

To further aid in my research, I used the websites of well-known legal advocacy groups and legal firms who make information freely available on court cases in which they represent an individual or a group of individuals, such as the ACLU, Lambda Legal, Southern Poverty Law Center, National Center for Lesbian Rights, National Center for Transgender Equality, and others. These cases are included in the appropriate areas of the book.

In researching federal and state laws and regulations, I used resources such as the Federal Register, the electronic Code of Federal Regulations (eCFR) Court websites, agency websites at the federal and state level, the U.S. Congress' websites, and the various states' legislatures to locate and cite active Bills, laws, and regulations. Where legislative reports were available, I downloaded them for future use. In researching laws or active Bills on legislatures' websites, I often found them difficult to navigate, which required additional research to locate useful information. For a time, I also used the county law library located in the Saint Louis County, Minnesota Courthouse, as well as the law library located in the U.S. Courthouse in Duluth, Minnesota.

Clinic locations were researched online. They are accurate to the best of my knowledge at the time of publication. If a listing is inaccurate, please email me through the publisher.

The section on state laws and policies was researched by me and verified through other sources, including state websites. I visited state agency websites when main state websites did not provide the information for which I was looking or if they referred me to the agency or county website.

During this process, I found many instances where I had to email or call state agencies, sometimes numerous times, to get the information I was requesting. Many state agency websites do not list email addresses for staff or provide a general contact email where a visitor can ask questions or seek clarification. Many state agencies were slow to respond to inquiries, and some never responded at all, requiring me to use other methods, typically Freedom of Information Act (FOIA) requests, to get the information. One agent of the State of Utah told me, "We don't give out our policies."

Under many state FOIA laws, agencies must disclose the information requested unless it has been classified as "private," or "confidential." In those cases, the agency must state why the information cannot be disclosed and provide the statutory authority that supports non-disclosure.

I visited state high school sports associations or organizations and other sports-related websites, such as the NCAA and others. Included in the search were the websites for the International Olympic Committee and World Athletics (formerly known as the International Association of Athletics Federations (IAAF)).

Permission for extensive use of tables and the data contained therein was obtained from "The Movement Advancement Project."[96]. This organization provided their full support and permission to use their data in this book. I am incredibly grateful to them for such a high level of support.

I also made extensive use of the websites of the World Professional Association for Transgender Health (WPATH),[97] the American Medical Association,[98] the American Psychiatric Association,[99] the American Psychological Association,[100] the American Association of Family Physicians,[101] the American Academy of Pediatrics,[102] the American College of Surgeons,[103] the Academy of Emergency Physicians,[104] the National Association of Social Workers,[105] the American Civil Liberties Union,[106] the National Center for Transgender Equality,[107] the National Center for Lesbian Rights[108], the Endocrine Society[109] and others, where I was able to download and cite both scholarly and legal research, and Federal Court cases involving discrimination against the transgender community nationwide.

Further, when the websites of organizations and government agencies I visited did not make information relevant to the book readily available, I emailed them, if email addresses were available on the website, to get the information I was seeking. In the case where the website did not provide an email address to request information, and no email addresses were provided for staff members from whom clarification could be sought, I searched for a phone number, either on the website or through an online search, where I could call the agency to get the information I was seeking. This process was ongoing throughout the writing of the manuscript.

A note on state agencies

Many states that I contacted, either by email, by phone, or through the website, responded to my inquiries in a timely manner. Others, however, did not provide a timely response, if I received a response at all. Where this occurred, it is noted in the appropriate section of the manuscript.

The timeframe during which the most recent research was received and during which the manuscript was written was approximately March through September 2021. Earlier research occurred during 2018 and up until the end of 2019, but the section on the laws and policies of the states was researched and written between May and September 2021. This section is, by far, the most extensive in the book.

EARLY RESEARCH

Terminology

Since this book was first published and throughout its several revisions, the terminology has changed significantly. Indeed, the language used by and within the trans community changes on a yearly if not weekly basis. A number of websites provide regularly updated definitions for terminologies currently in use. Readers interested in the nuances of trans language are encouraged to consult (in no particular order): The National Center for Transgender Equality (NCTE),[110] the Human Rights Campaign (HRC),[111] Egale Canada Human Rights Trust,[112] PFLAG,[113] the GLAAD Media Reference Guide,[114] the QMUNITY Queer Terminology Guide[115] or LGBTA Wiki.[116] See also the Definitions section below for explanations for how words are used specifically by the author in this volume.

The terms "transgender" or "trans" have come into widespread use to cover a broad range of gender-related issues and presentations. But, in my opinion, these terms do not accurately describe the ways in which sex reassignment surgery provides an ultimate solution to some individuals. Let me explain.

The term "transgender," taken at face value, applies to someone who is uncomfortable in the gender role expected of them based on their sex as assigned at birth. These individuals alter their gender presentation to conform to how they perceive their authentic selves, but they may not express an overt desire to change their sex (i.e., their bodies).[117] In many cases, a transgender individual may not necessarily express a desire to engage in chemotherapy and/or sex reassignment surgery, sometimes referred to as "gender-confirming surgery."

Before the establishment of the Harry Benjamin International Gender Dysphoria Association (HBIGDA) in 1979 and the publication of the first edition of the HBIGDA "Standards of Care" that same year, the term "transgender" was not widely used in the literature, if at all,[118] although, Williams[119] suggests that either Christine Jorgensen or Virginia Prince may have been early proponents of the term.

By contrast, the term "transsexual," when taken at face value, describes someone who not only believes that they are trapped in the wrong body (whether it be male or female) but hates their genitals to the point of wishing to have them removed. These are the individuals who seek out sex reassignment surgery in order to alter their bodies to conform to their innate sense of their gender. I believe that this perspective separates "transsexuals" as a separate subset of individuals who would include themselves under the more global category of "transgender."

Disclosure

I should disclose here that I do not believe the term "transgender" accurately describes who I am. I did not seek approval to change my gender. I like my gender. But as far back as I can remember, I felt as though I was trapped in the wrong body. Yes, I was assigned male at birth, at least in terms of my mother's physician looking at my genitals, waving his magic wand, and pronouncing me male at birth. My perceptions of myself from about age nine onward were that I was a female trapped in a male body. My gender was fixed (as female), and it has never changed. So, in actuality, I did not seek to change my gender: I sought to change my sex (i.e., my physical body) to match the image in my brain, which is (and always has been) female. So, for me (and for many others like me), the term "transgender" is not correct. The term "post-operative transsexual" *is*. Accordingly, I do not perceive myself as transgender and that perspective likely emerges in my writing. I use the pronouns her/hers/she.

I understand that "transgender" is an umbrella term used to describe gender-distressed or gender dysphoric individuals who may not seek sex reassignment surgery. Thus, in my opinion, the term "transsexual" more accurately reflects a group of individuals who are more correctly classified as a subclassification under the umbrella of "transgender."

Now, having declared my personal perspective on this issue, I use the terms "transsexual" and "transsexualism" throughout this portion of the literature review, where appropriate, as these were the terms most commonly in use during the time period under consideration. Throughout other sections of the book, I use the terms "trans" and "transgender" in a generic sense (in compliance with how these terms are widely used today). I've chosen to do this as I believe the information contained in this volume is valuable for, and of interest to, all gender diverse individuals (and their allies) and has broad application throughout the trans community.

Finally, it bares noting that much of the discussion that follows in this chapter refers to male-to-female transsexual persons. This is the result of a preponderance of known male-to-female transsexual cases available to researchers during this time period and the resulting research bias.

Early Research

Early studies have shown that psychological and psychiatric treatment and/or other forms of therapy to rid a person of these persistent feelings of gender dysphoria have not been successful. Furthermore, during this early period, clinicians found that attempting to change a transsexual's mind to conform to their body is equally unsuccessful. In these circumstances, many individuals find themselves feeling that there is no hope for their future. As a result, the suicide rate for trans people is extremely high.[120,121]

Much of the early literature[122] and even some more recent historical writings[123] describe the problem of transsexualism as a disturbance of gender identity, where individuals experience a sense of incongruence between their psychological sex and their anatomic sex.[124] Other disturbances described, but frequently confused with transsexualism, include homosexuality and transvestism.[125] These are, however, distinct from it. No other situation comes close to the level of incongruence presented by the person who feels themselves to be trapped in the body of the wrong sex. This salient feature of transsexualism sets us apart from either homosexuality and transvestism, although same sex attraction and/or cross dressing may also be aspects of the trans experience. Still, the importance of separating gender presentation from sexual preference cannot be understated.

Homosexual individuals are attracted to members of the same sex, while cross dressers occasionally dress in clothes of the opposite sex. Unlike the transsexual, they usually do not desire to alter their anatomy.[126] The transsexual, in sharp contrast, feels trapped in the body of the wrong sex and seeks release, either through skilled surgical intervention or through whatever means available—including suicide—to effectively escape.[127] I realize to say this again is repetitive, but this point needs emphasizing. It is that important.

Other research refines the history of transsexualism further.[128] Researchers, such as John Money, Ph.D., Richard Green, M.D., J.D., Harry Benjamin, M.D., Robert J. Stoller, M.D., Charles.L. Ihlenfeld, M.D., Jan Walinder, M.D., Walter Bockting, Ph.D., and Ira Pauly, M.D., and others, working together or separately, have authored many research papers on transsexualism.[129]

Past literature indicates a consistent trend toward rejection by both family and friends, harassment and discrimination[130] in varying degrees by most of society, and often, a refusal by many in the legal[131] and medical professions[132] to render services, either because of questioning the validity of such a diagnosis, or perhaps for fear of potential peer and community sanctions.[133] More recent literature suggests specific segments of the public are becoming more receptive to transgender issues. Today, parents of trans adolescents and youth are supporting their children who are going through one of the most difficult experiences they will ever encounter.

Etiology

Previously, the literature showed that the causes of transsexualism were disputed among professionals. Most of the controversy focuses on whether the etiology of transsexualism is psychogenic or organic.[134]

Money and Ehrhart have suggested that a fetal metabolic or hormonal component may predispose a person toward gender confusion.[135] Block and Tessler discussed an endocrine theory that assumes that chromosomal sex and endocrine sex do not always correspond. Seyer and associates demonstrated that the response of female transsexuals to diethylstilbestrol (DES) and luteinizing-releasing hormone (LRH) was intermediate between the female and male patterns, suggestive of a biological component being present.[136,137] Other researchers have discussed in more detail the endocrinological factor in transsexuals.[138]

In another study, Foreman et al. have argued that:

> The results of our study of transgender women support the hypothesis that gender dysphoria has a polygenic basis, involving interactions among multiple genes and polymorphisms that may alter the sexual differentiation of the brain in utero, contributing to the development of gender dysphoria in transgender women."[139]

Ettner probed deeper into the etiology of transsexualism, explaining that:

> Human behavior is exceedingly complex and largely unfathomable; just as the precursors of genius intelligence or other prodigies remain obscured, the etiology of transgenderism remains unknown. The goal of treatment, however, *is* known and is indisputable: to assist gender-variant patients who request medical interventions by providing state-of-the-art treatment.[140]

Even with the studies that have been performed, the etiology of transsexualism is still being debated. Several other challenges include not all transsexuals wanting to participate in research. Secondly, designing a study that avoids contaminants or other confounding variables is challenging. Studies have considered brain structure and function, endocrine factors before and during fetal gestation, psychosocial factors, and the like. Most recently, studies in the genetic makeup of trans people and those experiencing gender distress have pointed to a possible genetic link, but further research is needed before we can point to one primary factor that causes gender dysphoria.

Endocrinology of Transsexualism

The hormone testosterone is synthesized from cholesterol or acetyl coenzyme A in the testes. It is the principal male hormone (androgen) and has a number of effects on the body. It controls the development, growth, and maintenance of the male sex organs.[141] Similarly, the hormone β-estradiol exerts a major effect in the female. It is synthesized from cholesterol or acetyl coenzyme A in the ovaries.[142] Further examination of the action of these hormones is covered elsewhere in the book.[143]

The Endocrine Society published its Clinical Practice Guidelines, which updated prior guidelines for the treatment of persons with gender dysphoria.[144] The guidelines established specific protocols for the assessment, diagnosis, and treatment of gender dysphoria with endocrinologic interventions. The interventions include, in specific situations, the administration of hormone blockers, followed by hormone treatment to either feminize or masculinize the body.

In a study from the *Journal of Clinical Endocrinology and Metabolism*, the authors found, in part, that:

> The number of neurons in the BSTc of male-to-female transsexuals was similar to that of the females ($P = 0.83$). In contrast, the neuron number of a female-to-male transsexual was found to be in the male range. Hormone treatment or sex hormone level variations in adulthood did not seem to have influenced BSTc neuron numbers. The present findings of somatostatin neuronal sex differences in the BSTc and its sex reversal in the transsexual brain clearly support the paradigm that in transsexuals, sexual differentiation of the brain and genitals may go in opposite directions and point to a neurobiological basis of gender identity disorder.[145]

Countless theories have been proffered over the years concerning the etiology of transsexualism, with research failing to support one idea alone. The result has been that many professionals accepted the concept that best corresponded with their background, education, and clinical experience.[146]

Adding to the controversy was a lack of standardized criteria to determine the presentation of true transsexualism, the diagnostic process being one of inference and ruling out of other disorders. Definitive diagnostic tools, such as standardized physical or psychological tests, did not exist.[147] That has changed with the development of diagnostic criteria accepted by medical, psychological, psychiatric, and sociological professionals. Also, professional organizations in numerous disciplines accept and adhere to the Clinical Practice Guidelines for assessing and treating gender dysphoria.

In the only study of its kind, to date, regarding transsexual athletes competing in sports, Louis Gooren and Mathijs Bunck found that:

1. Testosterone exposure has profound effects on muscle mass and strength, justifying the practice that men and women compete in sports in separate categories.
2. The response to testosterone exposure in men is idiosyncratic; similar plasma levels of testosterone do not produce similar effects on muscle mass and strength.
3. The effects of cross-sex hormones in the dosages commonly used have reached their maximum effects after 1 year of administration.
4. In spite of a large difference in testosterone exposure between men and women, there is a large overlap of muscle area between them.
5. Androgen deprivation of men induces a loss of muscle area, further increasing this overlap with women.
6. Therefore, depending on the levels of arbitrariness one wants to accept, it is justifiable that reassigned M–F compete with other women.[148]

In her study about race times of transgender women versus cisgender women in sports, Joanna Harper found:

> Transgender women who have undertaken testosterone suppression change from normal male testosterone levels to normal female levels, in fact, after surgery their testosterone levels are below the mean for 46, XX women (Gooren and Bunck, pp. 425–

429). Largely as a result of their vastly reduced testosterone levels, transgender women lose strength, speed, and virtually every other component of athletic ability."[149]

Studies have also been performed on the assessment and treatment of pediatric patients with gender dysphoria.[150, 151]

The Birth of WPATH

The Harry Benjamin International Gender Dysphoria Association Standards of Care, Sixth Version (2001) was discussed in the *Journal of Psychology and Human Sexuality*.[152]

Since this book was first published, experienced practitioners have found ways to differentiate primary from secondary transsexualism and predict outcomes accurately. Extensive patient histories, psychometric testing, and psychiatric evaluations are part of the program during intake, mid-transition (following the administration of hormone therapy and full time living in the gender-role of reassignment), and just before surgery is used to monitor patient progress and adjustment to/suitability for sex reassignment surgery. Coupled with this evaluative process is the real-life test, extending from one to two years, supplemented by private group therapy to solve non-gender-related emotional problems, etc., and develop realistic patient expectations *before* surgery.[153]

Today, the World Professional Association for Transgender Health (WPATH) has on its website the 2011, 7th Edition of the Standards of Care (SOC).[154]

> to provide clinical guidelines for the health care of transsexual, transgender, and gender non-conforming persons to maximize health and well-being by revealing gender dysphoria.[155]

Chapter I of the Standards of Care specifies that the SOC are "flexible clinical guidelines" Intended to:

> Be flexible in order to meet the diverse health care needs of transsexual, transgender, and gender-nonconforming people. While flexible, they offer standards for promoting optimal health care and guiding the treatment of people experiencing gender dysphoria—broadly defined as discomfort or distress that is caused by a discrepancy between a person's gender identity and that person's sex assigned at birth (and the associated gender role/or primary and secondary sex characteristics)[156]

In Chapter VI of the Standards of Care, WPATH notes that a quick and dramatic progression in children and adolescents is involved with greater flexibility and variability in outcomes, especially in prepubertal children.[157] The section provides specific guidelines for the "assessment and treatment of gender dysphoric children and adolescents."[158] The assessment and treatment guidelines for adults are covered at length on pages 23-33.

Despite the controversy surrounding transsexualism, the literature on the subject has not reflected recurrent themes.

> First, each individual's gender identity is well established early in childhood.[159,160,161]

> Second, transsexualism usually manifests before puberty, and once the pattern is found, it is *highly* resistant, if not *impossible,* to change.[162]

> Third, *true* transsexuals do not respond to psychotherapy, rejecting this mode of treatment because they see their problem as physical and the solution as surgical, not

psychiatric.[163] Consequently, therapy aimed at other than sex reassignment has consistently failed,[164] rendering self-castration or suicide a real risk.[165]

Fourth, transsexuals suffer from a distinct gender disorder of unknown etiology that is capable of amelioration, if not cure,[166] uniquely through sex reassignment.[167]

Fifth, as might be expected, surgical complications are more frequent when individual surgeons or surgical teams are making their initial attempts at vaginal construction. As the experience of each group develops, the complications may be vastly reduced or eliminated.[168]

Sixth, sex reassignment, while often treated as cosmetic in the literature, has consistently been deemed non-cosmetic and, in most cases, as medically necessary by the courts.[169]

Conversion or Reparative Therapy

In reference to the second point above, a number of religiously-based individuals and groups claim to have the answer to "curing" gay, bisexual, cross dressing, or transsexual people by what is known as "reparative or conversion therapy." They have found their beliefs discredited, and a growing number of states and communities in the United States have outlawed these approaches through legislation.

So-called "conversion therapy," sometimes known as "reparative therapy," is a range of dangerous and discredited practices that falsely claim to change a person's sexual orientation or gender identity or expression. Such practices have been rejected by every mainstream medical and mental health organization for decades, but due to continuing discrimination and societal bias against LGBTQ people, some practitioners continue to conduct conversion therapy. Minors are especially vulnerable, and conversion therapy can lead to depression, anxiety, drug use, homelessness, and suicide.[170,171,172,173]

Despite favorable non-cosmetic and medically necessary judicial decisions, the American judicial system has failed to keep pace with medical and scientific advances, particularly in regard to gender dysphoria syndrome and transsexualism. This failure is aptly demonstrated by a diversity of decisions, rendering the transsexual person vulnerable to discrimination in various socioeconomic contexts, especially in the area of civil rights and health care. This vulnerability was clearly described in an article by Tim Alger.

There [are few] provisions for transsexuals under the law. They're kind of left out there, hanging in space. Each time they go into court, depending on the empathy of the judge, it is unknown how they will be treated.[174]

There can be little doubt about the complexity of the sociolegal problems surrounding transsexualism. The limited size of this field makes research difficult. Furthermore, the professional may find that once a body of information has been accumulated, it may fail to answer the question that motivated the research. On the other hand, few fields of endeavor offer more of a challenge.

In his August 1999 address to the Sixteenth Harry Benjamin International Gender Dysphoria Association Symposium, Richard Green, M.D., J.D., made the following remarks. I quote his comments here, at some length, in their entirety, and with permission, as they provide a comprehensive, historical, state-of-the-art overview of the perspectives of the medical community at that point in time.

I co-edited the textbook *Transsexualism and Sex Reassignment,* with John Money, in 1969. The Johns Hopkins Press published it.

In retrospect, it was a groundbreaking work. It was the first interdisciplinary professional text published only three years after Harry Benjamin's pioneering *The Transsexual Phenomenon*. In it, transsexualism was promoted as "consistent with the tradition of scientific inquiry and medicine, 'examining' deviations from the norm in the hope of better understanding normal processes." To justify serious professional attention, transsexualism was packaged in time-honored wrapping.

Many changes have evolved in these 30 years.

In 1969, the subject of transsexualism was exotic and esoteric. In the 1960s and 1970s, my professional papers on transsexualism needed to define the term at the outset. Now children know it. They have seen lots of transsexuals on television talk shows.

Does transsexualism still pose the most controversial subject in medicine as it did then? Although it is still contentious, other topics such as abortion and euthanasia also exercise emotions. But they do not challenge psychodynamic theories of psychosexual development or anxieties about the genitalia in the same measure as transsexualism.

Transsexualism was characterized in *Transsexualism and Sex Reassignment* as the most atypical pattern of psychosexual development, with all three components of gender identity being atypical. The transsexual was atypical on basic identity as male or female, for behaviors as masculine or feminine, and for sexual orientation as homosexual or heterosexual. Today the relation between components one and two versus three is being refined. We have considerable experience with lesbian women male transsexuals and limited experience with gay men female transsexuals. But it remains true as in 1969 that "the variables on which transsexualism, transvestism, and homosexuality overlap and on which they are separate are not entirely clear."

The prevalence of transsexualism appears higher than previously thought, perhaps double. Probably this is not a true increase. Rather it is an expression of patient optimism that coming forward for help will be respected by the healing professionals.

In the intervening 30 years, surgeons have harnessed the transsexual's request as technological challenge. Vaginoplasty is excellent. As we have seen at this meeting, phalloplasty is evolving. But the surgical quip of the 1960s remains: "It's easier to build a hole than a pole."

There has been something of a "help-hurt" role reversal in these thirty years between physician and patient. In 1969, with rare exceptions, such as Harry Benjamin, physicians were the worst enemies of transsexual patients. As I documented in my research during that period, most doctors, even psychiatrists, would rather let transsexual patients die than treat them with sex reassignment. By contrast, today some patients have become their own worst enemies in the face of physicians attempting to help.

One reason there are relatively few professionals who commit their time to trying to help gender dysphoric persons is that many find the experience very frustrating, far more so than with other types of patients. They conclude that it is just not worth the effort.

It is difficult to identify another psychiatric or medical condition where the patient makes the diagnosis and prescribes the treatment. Anything short of fulfilling those judgements is objected to, perhaps vigorously. The administration overseeing the Gender Identity Clinic at Charing Cross Hospital is besieged by patient complaints. This is mostly because the clinic professionals have not acquiesced quickly enough to the patient's demands for sex reassignment. The expense of handling these complaints has made the Gender Identity Clinic unpopular with administration and has at times threatened its existence. Unhappily, not only are such patients self-defeating but they make it difficult for the great majority of patients who are in genuine collaboration with professionals.

Mysteries of the origins of transsexualism remain. It remains true as in 1969 that "no one now, be he psychoanalyst or neuro-endocrinologist or expert in any other science, can claim to have the complete explanation of transsexualism… Much (still) remains to be discovered about how masculinity and femininity develop." And the "eventual availability of measures of circulating gonadal hormones during prenatal development" to help explain the neuroendocrine origins of gender identity remains that—a potential.

There was a flurry of excitement fifteen years ago over the possibility that the HY antigen on the male Y chromosome was absent in male-to-female transsexuals. However, our research at Stony Brook put this provocative theory to rest. More recently there has been some excitement over demonstration of a possible variant in congenital adrenal hyperplasia responsible for transsexualism. There has been substantial excitement generated over the finding of a size difference in the brain's bed nucleus in male-to-female transsexuals.

Of what relevance is it if biological or genetic bases of transsexualism can be demonstrated? Why should it matter? The same issue is raised in the discussion of the origins of homosexuality. On the one hand, the person with a variant in sexual orientation in gender identity may be seen as more "legitimate" if the variation is biologically based, not due to psychological trauma during formative years, or worse yet, sin. But from the perspective of John Stuart Mill, the original civil libertarian should be irrelevant whatever the basis of same-sex attraction or wish to be the other sex, providing this is not harmful to another.

An additional concern is that reliance on a "biological" basis of atypical sexual orientation or gender identity may leave such individuals wanting for understanding and legal protection if such a basis is not found. In American law, there is a class of individuals protected against discrimination when the source of their difference from the majority is innate. The classic example is race, a feature over which few have a say. But acceptance and protection should not be tethered to such an origin.

Research on patients' post-sex reassignment has been reassuring. Very early follow-up data in the late 1960s "support(ed) the contention that in the majority of persons in whom cross-gender identity is extensive and of longstanding duration—conflict can be significantly lessened by sex reassignment." This remains true.

The methodologically flawed Johns Hopkins study of 1979 questioning benefits of sex reassignment surgery served as an excuse for discontinuing that hospital's pioneering program. But it made only a dent in the worldwide professional recognition of the legitimacy of sex change. The methodologically sound study from London's Charing Cross of 1990 clearly demonstrated the benefits.

Some professionals remain opposed to hormonal or surgical reassignment, retreating into psychodynamic formulations of pathology. They falsely equate providing psychological insight with a change of gender identity, reminisce about a poorly adjusted postoperative patient they once saw, and indict the sex reassignment follow-up literature as methodologically flawed. But when pressed to recount their success rate in modifying gender identity or cite others psychiatrically treated successes, they retreat to their armchairs. There they reign.

Thirty years after *Transsexualism and Sex Reassignment*, it remains a truism that "the law must share with medicine responsibility for some of the transsexual's plight… The problem remains… whether what has been granted medically will be acknowledged legally".

Cross-gender living before surgery, the "real-life test," was coined by John Money, has proved to be a critical *rite de passage*. But the real-life test can be obstructed by employment discrimination. In the US, the *Ulane* case, where I was an unsuccessful expert witness, was the death knell for protecting transsexuals under federal sex discrimination law. Eastern Airlines (now defunct) prevented a previously male pilot with an impeccable record from flying as a woman. However, in the United Kingdom, a lawsuit against employment discrimination reached a more successful outcome in the European Court of Human Rights, the latter court only a dream option of 1969.

The 30-year debate continues "whether it should be the rightful concern of the law to deny one the right to dress as one wishes, conduct one's life in a preferred gender role, privately conduct one's sexual relationship as preferred by oneself and one's partner, and even to marry in the preferred sexual role." Not only does U.S. employment law neglect the transsexual, but the Veteran's Administration also refuses to treat them, and half the states still criminalize same-sex genital contact. In the U.K., post-operative transsexuals cannot marry.

The United Kingdom has been fighting a rearguard action against most of Europe's refusal to grant post-sex reassigned transsexuals a revised birth certificate. Andorra and Albania join the UK, with Ireland, in its march out of step. The U.S. is not that far behind, where many states still refuse to issue a changed birth certificate.

The UK position on birth certificate change is that the sex designation at birth is a historical event that cannot be undone. This concern should not preclude the issuance of a new certificate with retention of the original on file. Considering that the incidence of transsexualism is 1 in 30,000 females and 1 in 10,000 males, it would not appear that the actuarial foundation of the UK would crumble with this rate of "error."

Allocating resources for transsexual treatment is the new discrimination. Government funding agencies and insurance companies marginalize transsexuals. They are an easy target: a small constituency. But in July 1999, in the United Kingdom, the Court of Appeal ruled that a National Health Service authority couldn't deny treatment in blanket fashion for transsexual patients. In my position as Head of our Gender Identity Clinic, I authored an 18-page affidavit supporting the transsexual patients in that landmark case.

Risks of medical negligence suits for facilitating sex reassignment have been substantially reduced, in these 30 years, when standards adopted by the professional community are followed. The "Harry Benjamin Guidelines" are in effect, at least for the adult. But with adolescents, similar concerns for medical negligence confront us as previously existed for adults. What is (will be) the standard for accepted practice? Should the physical changes of puberty that handicap later cross-gender passing be interrupted? Will research reveal that benefits to most teenagers outweigh the risks that some will regret the intervention?

Newer ethical concerns in these 30 years have evolved from whether clinicians *should* grant a request for sex reassignment, to the question, are clinicians *necessary*? Should sex change be available on demand? That was hardly the issue in 1969, as the nearly insurmountable hurdle then was professionally endorsed reassignment. If gender patients can procure surgeons who do not require psychiatric or psychological referral, research should address outcome for those who are professionally referred versus self-referred. Then an ethical issue could be, if success is less (or failure more significant) among the self-referred, should otherwise competent adults nevertheless have that autonomy of self-determination?

The ramifications of surgery on demand for gender dysphoric persons or persons discontent with some aspect of their anatomy, be it sexual or otherwise, engage legal and ethical issues. Should there be a limit to a person's autonomy over the body? This question is involved in debates over pregnancy termination. It is engaged in issues of drug use during pregnancy. It is involved in the refusal of religious groups to sanction life-saving medical treatment.

It is not just in gender identity disorder that requests for surgery that radically alter the body are controversial. Some men and women demand amputation of limbs to meet their ideal body image. Should surgeons reflexively grant such requests? Should surgeons require psychiatric screening? If screening were deemed appropriate, what criteria would be used to accept or reject an individual's request?

Intermediary between these limb amputation requests and what is considered the "conventional" requests for sex-change procedures are demands of persons who might be termed the emergent "third gender." These include requests of females who want bilateral mastectomy but no other surgery and no virilizing hormone treatment, or males who want castration or penectomy, or both, but no feminizing hormone treatment.

A practical dilemma for the clinician engaged with such persons, whether it is for amputation of a limb or amputation of a sex-typed body part, is that the *rite de passage* to determine whether the patient has a realistic anticipation of life after surgery is not possible. There is no "Real Life Test" for the would-be limb amputee or the would-be third gender sex-part amputee.

The civil libertarian, John Stuart Mill, argued forcefully that adults should be able to do with their bodies as they wish providing that it did not bring harm to another. Thus, if the third gender, the transsexual, or the would-be limb amputee can continue to shoulder social responsibilities post-surgery, then the surgical requests are not society's business.

But, accepting that philosophical base, a subsequent question asks who will share the financial burden of meeting such requests? Should that be borne by the society? If so, the argument can be that society is affected adversely by needing to meet the expense. However, if the individual is willing to pay for the intervention, then it becomes the individual's responsibility without spreading financial adversity.

Another current political movement argues for removing gender identity disorder or transsexualism, or whatever it may be called next, from the list of disorders of the American Psychiatric Association and the World Health Organization. But an argument put to insurance companies or a National Health Service for payment is that those persons for whom funding is requested have a medical disorder requiring a specific treatment. Absent that, the procedures are viewed as purely "elective" or "cosmetic", which traditionally have not been gleefully funded by third party payers.

Children of transsexuals continue to engage courts of law and the anxieties of transsexual parents and their former spouses. I am saddened at the number of cases in which I have testified as an expert witness where children and transsexual parent have been denied the opportunity to continue their parent-child relationship. From the many cases that I have seen, a transsexual parent does not have a deleterious effect on the children. There is no objective basis for the non-transsexual spouse's acrimonious denial of continuing a relationship between the co-parent and child. Yet transsexuals are not popular parties in courts of law. In the United Kingdom implacable opposition by one parent to continuing contact with the other parent often trumps. Emotional blackmail rules the day. Dig in your heels and win the fray.

In closing, I address a remarkable evolution of this field—the dual role now played by persons with a history of gender identity disorder, or gender dysphoria or transsexualism, as both professional and consumer. This previously marginalized population is increasingly taking its position as respected professional colleague. As President of this Association, I am pleased that our Executive Board contains both transsexual and non-transsexual persons. As Chair of the Program Committee, I am pleased that our program has included both transsexual and non-transsexual professionals.

This would have made Harry Benjamin very proud.[175]

Lawyers, legislators, and judges need to better understand the human condition as it relates to gender dysphoria or gender identity disorder (GID), particularly transsexualism. Only through this group of professionals can the advancement of equal rights and equal protection under the law be reached.

Every member of society, regardless of race, national origin, religious belief, sex, sexual orientation, or gender identity, should be entitled to live under, and to be judged by, laws that are free of prejudice and the weaknesses of government enacted by men or women acting without regulation.

CURRENT RESEARCH

Research shows that there is "an association between gender-affirming or sex reassignment surgery and improved mental health outcomes. These results contribute new evidence to support the provision of gender-affirming surgical care for TGD people"—TGD stands for Transgender and Gender Diverse.[176] Likewise, it has been shown that there is "a marked reduction in psychopathology [that] occurs during the process of sex reassignment therapy, especially after the initiation of hormone therapy."[177]

As previously reported, transsexual individuals experience a wide range of issues related to how society perceives them, including stigmatization. "Transgender individuals belong to one of the most stigmatized groups in society."[178] Social stigmatization has been well documented, as can be seen in the article available on *Wikipedia, "Social Stigma."*[179,180]

Stigmatization

According to Hughto, Reisner, and Pachankis,[181] Stigma "is the social process of labeling, stereotyping, and rejecting human difference as a form of social control." Stigmatization is the basis for discrimination against others we deem unacceptable due to a variety of characteristics, e.g., the color of one's skin, one's country of origin, the shape and color of one's eyes, sex (male or female), sexual orientation, gender identity, religious beliefs (this one is a double-edged sword because religion can be the basis used for discriminating against others), socioeconomic status, mental health status, or any other physical or behavioral characteristic or trait an individual deems unacceptable. Groups historically stigmatized face an even more significant burden to overcome because discrimination becomes institutionalized.

> Institutional stigma, is more systemic, involving policies of government and private organizations that intentionally or unintentionally limit opportunities for people with mental illness. Examples include lower funding for mental illness research or fewer mental health services relative to other health care.[182]

Stigmatization coupled with marginalization—marginalized populations are groups of people and "communities" that experience discrimination and exclusion (social, political, and economic) because of unequal power relationships across economic, political, social, and cultural dimensions—are conditions that the transgender community has experienced for many decades.

> Despite the strong advocacy of notable individuals who are transgender and allies, including Laverne Cox, Chaz Bono, Dr. Jamison Green, Janet Mock, and Jazz Jennings, the transgender community continues to face widespread injustice in various segments of their lives: discrimination, bullying, as well as harassment at school, work, within health care, criminal justice, and many other public and private settings (Grant, et. al., 2011; Lombardi, Wilchins, Priesing, and Malouf, 2002; Nadal, Skolnik, and Wong, 2012; Reisner, et. Al., 2015; Stotzer, 2009).[183]

Transgender individuals can develop effective strategies to cope with this stigmatization and discrimination.

But as one individual described,

> I think that there is a high level of survival instinct in trans culture in general. As transgender people, we have to be resilient. We have to be strong. Because when we

say, "I am going ahead with and making this transition," well, we know we could lose everything—our family, our children, our friends, our employment, our places of worship, our standing in the community. And even in some cases, we could lose our lives.[184,185]

In more than fifty percent of cases, transgender individuals experience discrimination in the workplace.[186] Transgender individuals experience discrimination in virtually every facet of life. The legal issues transgender individuals face will be covered in depth later in this work.

Su and Irwin, et al.[187] indicate that "emerging evidence suggests within the LGBT population the odds of depression symptoms are even higher among transgender individuals compared with nontransgender [sic] individuals."

Society often looks at transgender individuals with emotional revulsion directed at individuals who do not conform to society's assumptions of gender. People look at others, and when they see someone who appears to be female, assume that the person's gender is in tune with their physical appearance. When gender does not conform with physical appearance, people instinctually respond with disbelief, disgust, and sometimes physical violence directed at the transgender person.

Sometimes, without saying a word, people will turn their heads to look at the transgender person as they continue to walk by; at other times, they will stop and yell obscenities at the person; and still may physically confront the transgender person with outrage. If the voice of the transgender person is low in pitch, they may address the person as "sir" or some other male-identified honorific rather than "miss" or "ma'am." It is often intentional misgendering that causes the most harm. Especially when a transgender person is in the early stages of their transition, intentional, even hateful comments can cause long-lasting emotional distress because the trans person is looking for affirmation, not disparaging remarks.

People will often say they look at someone who is transgender as a "freak" or another derogatory term. These responses are outgrowths of stigmatism and learned social constructs where anyone who looks or acts differently from the antagonist is reviled and even hated.

How one perceives self, body image, and quality of life are essential factors in determining successful outcomes of interventions. In one study,[188] the authors found scores of body image and quality of life were significantly higher in the group which completed sex reassignment surgery. The effects of hormone therapy on quality of life and mental health were found to improve the psychological health of transgender individuals. Two studies[189] assessed psychological functioning, anxiety, depression, and quality of life.

While the lesbian, bisexual, and gay populations have shown an increased acceptance by the public, transgender individuals continue to lag behind these groups by a significant percentage. In "Friendship, attitudes, and behavioral intentions of cisgender heterosexuals toward transgender individuals,"[190] the authors demonstrate that although "friendship experiences with transgender individuals do impact cisgender heterosexuals' reported attitudes and intentions concerning transgender individuals, the exact nature of this interaction remains unclear."[191]

Neurological Aspects

In terms of a transsexual's neurological brain structure and functioning, it has been found that "signs of *feminization* or *masculinization* are observable in transsexual individuals, which, during hormonal treatment partly seem to further adjust to characteristics of the desired sex."[192]

Magnetic Resonance Imaging (MRI) studies have found some differences in brain structural makeup, and some have found few if any differences.[193, 194, 195, 196]

Genetic Component

Concerning the oft-heard descriptions of transsexuality having a possible genetic component, Fernandez, R., et al., stated, in "The Genetics of Transsexualism,"

> No karyotype aberration has been linked to transsexualism (FtM or MtF), and prevalence of aneuploidy (3%) appears to be slightly higher than in the general population (0.53%). Concerning the molecular study, FtMs differed significantly from control females with respect to the median repeat length polymorphism Erβ (P=0.002) but not to the length of the other two studied polymorphisms. The repeat numbers in Erβ were significantly higher in FtMs than in the female control group. The likelihood of developing transsexualism was higher (odds ratio: 2.001 [1.15-3.46]) in the subjects with the genotype homozygous for long alleles.
>
> No significant difference in allele or genotype distribution of any gene examined as found between MtFs and control males. Moreover, molecular findings presented no evidence of an association between the sex hormone-related genes (Erβ, AR, and CYP19A1) and MtF transsexualism. *Id.* at pp. 122.[197]

Further, in a separate study, Garcia-Falgueras and Swaab found that INAH3 volume and neuron number in transsexual MtF individuals were in the female range. FtM individuals were in the male range. Their conclusion was:

> Differences in adult testosterone levels can only partly explain the observed differences in the INAH3 subdivision of transsexual people while estrogen levels do not seem to have an influence. In male-to-female [MtF] subjects the number of neurons in the INAH3 does not seem to be related to sexual orientation, nor to the onset time of transsexuality, but rather to atypical early female-biased gender. The differences observed between the INAH3 structure, its innervation in relation to sexual orientation and gender identity and its putative connection to the BSTc suggest that these two nuclei, together with the SDN-POA (= intermediate nucleus, = INAH1 and 2) and the SCN (Swaab, et. al., 1985) are part of a complex network involved in various aspects of sexual behaviour. For the INAH4 subdivision of the uncinate nucleus, the only difference found among the groups was in relation to its shape, which was similar in all genetically male groups studied.[198,199]

See also, the section above under the heading "Endocrinology of Transsexualism" about the study article by Gooren and Bunck.[200]

The Genetics of Sex and Gender

People typically have 46 chromosomes in each cell, two of which are designated as the sex chromosomes. Females have two X chromosomes (46, XX), and males have one X and one Y chromosome (46, XY). But what about XXX, XO, or XYY, XXY, or YO?

Being a man or a woman is a matter of gender identity, not a simple matter of chromosomal algebra. Certainly, the genes on our chromosomes contribute to our development, but they don't simply dictate our gender identities as boys or girls, men or women.

The X and Y chromosomes are called "sex chromosomes" because they contribute to how a person's sex develops. Most males have XY chromosomes, and most females have XX chromosomes.

But there are girls and women who have XY chromosomes. This can happen, for example, when a girl has androgen insensitivity syndrome (AIS).[201] And there are boys and men who have XX chromosomes. This can happen, for example, when an SRY gene on the Y chromosome ends up on an X chromosome, causing that X chromosome to function more like a Y.

There are genes on chromosomes other than the X or Y that also contribute to sex development. Because of all this, the term "sex chromosomes" is really something of a misnomer. Just looking at whether a person has XX or XY (or some other variation) won't tell you conclusively about that person's sex development, and it certainly won't tell you about that person's gender identity.

It is worth remembering that most of us know whether we are men or women even though we have no idea what our "sex chromosomes" are. We just assume that because we see ourselves as male or female that our chromosomes are in alignment. Gender identity is about who you know yourself to be, not about how your sex chromosomes look on a microscope slide. Doctors look at the "sex chromosomes" of people with Disorders of Sex Differentiation (DSD)[202] as part of coming up with a diagnosis, but they don't treat the "sex chromosomes" alone as a simple answer to anything. Our "sex chromosomes" are just part of the picture of who we are.

An allele is a variant form of a gene. Some genes have a variety of different forms, which are located at the same position, or genetic locus, on a chromosome. Humans are called diploid organisms because they have two alleles at each genetic locus, with one allele inherited from each parent. Each pair of alleles represents the genotype of a specific gene. Genotypes are described as homozygous if there are two identical alleles at a particular locus and as heterozygous if the two alleles differ. Alleles contribute to the organism's phenotype, which is the outward appearance of the organism.

Some alleles are dominant or recessive. When an organism is heterozygous at a specific locus and carries one dominant and one recessive allele, the organism will express the dominant phenotype. Alleles can also refer to minor DNA sequence variations between alleles that do not necessarily influence the gene's phenotype.[203]

Concerning brain development, another group of researchers found that areas of the brain's white matter are different in transsexuals than in cisgender females and males.[204,205]

See "Changing your sex changes your brain: influences of testosterone and estrogen on adult human brain structure" for a discussion on hormone treatment in male-to-female and female-to-male transsexuals.[206,207] For a detailed discussion of the effects and expected timeline for feminizing hormones on male-to-female (MtF) trans persons, and for the effects and expected timeline of masculinizing hormones on female-to-male (FtM) trans persons see the WPATH Standards of Care.[208]

It is becoming more evident that the treatment of transsexualism involves the treatment of youth and adolescents. Many studies have been published that show how advances in the care of this patient population impact this area of medical, psychological, and psychiatric care.

In their article on "Advances in the care of transgender Children and Adolescents," the authors describe that:

> Children and adolescents with gender dysphoria are presenting for medical attention at increasing rates. Standards of Care have been developed which outline appropriate mental health support and hormonal interventions for transgender youth... terminology

related to gender identity reviews the history of medical interventions for transgender persons, outlines what is known about gender identity development, and reviews mental health disparities faced by this patient population.[209]

Richard Green studied whether there was co-occurrence of gender dysphoria in ten sibling or parent-child pairs and found:

> The prevalence of male transsexualism is estimated at 1 in 10,000 and female transsexualism at 1 in 30,000 (Kesteran et al., 1996). Thus, for a set of male twins or two brothers in a two-sibling family, the odds for both being transsexual are 1/100,000,000 [1 in 100 million], assuming random selection, or 1/10,000 when one sibling is already identified as transsexual. It is somewhat lower in larger families with more siblings, but higher in male-female sibling pairs. The rarity of both transsexualism and transvestism makes the chance occurrence in father and child very improbable. The cases here are called from a patient pool of about 1,500.[210]

In another paper by Dr. Green, the subject of what is meant by the term "sex" is explored in-depth. Dr. Green explains that a person's sex can be determined by a multitude of factors that include the outward physical appearance of female or male genitalia, gonads (ovaries/testes), the individual's chromosomes, hormone levels of testosterone, progesterone, and estrogen, and one's perception of self as male or female or gender identity.[211] All people have a sense of their gender identity, and for most of the population, gender identity and physical appearance as male or female are congruent. It is unfathomable that gender identity cannot be seen as an indistinguishable part of one's "sex." As more than one researcher has pointed out, a person's sex is not ultimately determinable only by a cursory look at the external genitalia at birth. It is part of the complex makeup of who we are as humans, and despite the efforts of some to claim otherwise, science dictates fact, not ancient traditions, myths, and religious teachings.

Transgender Athletics

Concerning the possible differences between transgender and non-transgender athletes, articles and studies too numerous to mention conclude that there is no significant difference. For example:

> The inclusion of trans people in sport challenges a number of long-standing traditions and beliefs. For instance, the segregation of female and male athletes as well as perceptions related to gendered athletic ability leave little space for trans athletes. As Morgan Dickens, a former college athlete, stated, "The clear delineation between male and female in the sporting world doesn't leave room for someone like me" (quoted in Griffin and Carroll, 2010a, pp.49). We believe an important first step in creating more welcoming climates for trans athletes is to recognize and counter common falsehoods and misinformation about them.[212]

Another article describes the slowness of acceptance at College and University campuses nationwide. The literature has frequently addressed the unknown size of the LGBTQ community,[213] and estimates ranging from 10-15% are typical.

> Colleges have been slow to recognize, much less provide support to, transgender people. Although many lesbian, gay, and bisexual student organizations and almost all existing campus LGB administrative offices have added a "T" to their names in the last decade, this move toward greater inclusiveness has been more symbolic than substantive. Most LGB student leaders and center directors still have little understanding

of the experiences of trans people and continue to engage in trans-exclusive practices. Other administrators and faculty typically are even less educated about transgender issues, and only become cognizant of the needs of transgender students when a crisis arises, such as a conflict over a transitioning woman using the women's restroom.[214]

So, institutions of higher learning, places where knowledge and science are the rules of the day, seem unable to grasp gender identity and sex concepts and have promulgated rules and regulations that discriminate against transgender students. This has most recently come to light in two areas. First, transgender students' use of campus bathrooms that most closely align with their gender identities has been curtailed and resulted in lawsuits by transgender students to enforce their rights under Title IX of the Education Amendments of 1972. Second, transgender students' ability to play in intercollegiate sports has also been the subject of lawsuits to enforce their rights under Title IX. Similar actions have been happening in interscholastic sports, lawsuits have been filed and won, and some states have been attempting to restrict access to sports by enacting laws explicitly aimed at the transgender student population.

Discrimination Against Transgender Athletes

In recent years (2020-2021), we have seen a significant rise in the number of laws proposed by legislatures in many states and Bills signed into law that prohibit or severely limit transgender athletes from competing in school sports. These attempts to severely restrict transgender athletes' ability to compete significantly and adversely impact this population. The evidence proponents of such legislation are using to justify the laws is entirely based on misinformation, outright falsehoods, and the belief, based on religious teachings, that "biological sex" means if you were assigned male or female at birth, your gender is the same and should not be "changed." They also argue that "males" who are transgender females have an unfair advantage because of their testosterone levels. But this amounts to nothing more than people in politics meddling in medical science.

It's common for people to confuse sex, gender, and gender identity. But they're actually all different things. In an article on the Planned Parenthood website, sex, gender, and gender identity are discussed in detail.

- Sex is a label—male or female—that you're assigned by a doctor at birth based on the genitals with which you're born (and possibly the chromosomes you have). It goes on your birth certificate. The doctor looks at your genitals, and presto, you're a male or a female.

- Gender is much more complex: It's a social and legal status, and set of expectations from society, about behaviors, characteristics, and thoughts. Each culture has standards about the way that people should behave based on their gender, generally male or female. But instead of being about body parts, it's more about how you're expected to act, because of your sex.

- Gender identity is how you feel inside and how you express your gender through clothing, behavior, and personal appearance. It's a feeling that begins very early in life. It's a personal internal sense of self belonging to one gender (male or female) or no gender (non-binary) or all genders (gender-fluid). [215]

As discussed above, the notion that testosterone could be at work here has already been disproven. Male individuals who have undergone hormone therapy, experience a reduction in the adrenal gland, the prostate, testicles, and an increase in breast tissue growth. Males who have undergone castration (surgical removal of the testes) as the first step toward final genital surgery have significantly reduced testosterone levels because the testes produce the bulk of testosterone in males. When added, treatment with an estrogen and the lack of the testes, blood testosterone levels are dramatically reduced. The adrenal cortex produces, among other hormones, Adrenal androgens, male sex hormones mainly consisting of dehydroepiandrosterone (DHEA) and testosterone. All have weak effects but play a role in the early development of the male sex organs in childhood and female body hair during puberty.

The studies cited above clearly show that the claims of the unfair advantage of male-to-female (MtF) transsexuals being litigated by people wanting to restrict transgender athletes' participation in school sports are unfounded. They seem inexorably committed to asserting the position that male-to-female trans individuals are males, period, even if they have been treated with hormone therapy to feminize the body's characteristics. It seems as though they deny the science of the last 50 years in favor of their preconceptions of what is male or female. This amounts to nothing more than Orwellian thinking.

Finally, in 2016 at least one study showed "no direct or consistent research suggesting transgender female individuals (or male individuals) have an athletic advantage at any stage of their transition (e.g., cross-sex hormones, gender-confirming surgery) and, therefore, competitive sport policies that place restrictions on transgender people need to be considered and potentially revised."[216]

Another study, this one in the *Asian Journal of Andrology*, states:

> Eventually, it is illusionary to arrive at 100% fairness in competition based on serum testosterone levels. First of all, there are the well-known methodological difficulties of measuring serum testosterone levels reliably. Second, serum testosterone levels provide an indicator of the strength of the androgen signal but have limited predictive value of the biological effects of testosterone which are codetermined by properties of the androgen receptor. This is exemplified in people with abnormalities of the androgen receptor who have high circulating serum androgen levels, but androgen action is impaired due to genetically determined abnormalities of the molecular properties of the androgen receptor (androgen insensitivity syndrome)."[217] See also, "Beyond Fairness: The Biology of Inclusion for Transgender and Intersex Athletes.[218] [internal footnotes omitted.]

One final note. Some not in the multidisciplinary fields that deal with transgender individuals have claimed that it is unknown whether transition-related health care results in long-term benefits for the person who has undergone transition-related care. This notion has already been dispelled. Transgender wellbeing is beneficial for those who have received such care. An article entitled, "What does the Scholarly research say about the effect of gender transition on transgender well-being," published by Cornell University Public Policy Research Portal,[219] lists eight findings that show that transition-related care to transgender persons "is effective in treating gender dysphoria and can significantly improve the well-being of transgender individuals."[220]

From the author's own experience, I can tell you going through the transition from male to female, including hormone therapy for at least two years, participating in psychological counseling for at least a year to both verify that I met the diagnostic criteria for gender dysphoria and that any preexisting mental health issues I may have had were addressed, obtaining sex reassignment surgery, and living the life I have lived since having had the surgery, the treatment saved my life. The average person cannot possibly know and sometimes may not even understand the extent of the emotional and physical toll being a pre-op transsexual takes on a person. My experience prior to surgery was different than the vast majority simply because suicide was never an option for me. Obtaining the surgery, for me, was like putting the period at the end of the sentence. All the pain and suffering I experienced before my transition is gone. If that, in and of itself, is not a benefit, I don't know what is. It has allowed me to participate in life more fully.

The people who are proposing and enacting the bans on transgender athletes in sports and the bans on transition-related health care for youth and adolescents are calling FtM transgender youth and adolescents who have been diagnosed with gender dysphoria "males" and are only looking at what these individuals were stated to be at the time of their birth by the doctor. It is what they are calling, for example, a "biological male." Almost all of us are pronounced male or female at birth by nothing more than a cursory look at our genitals. Got a penis, bingo, you're a male; got a vagina, bingo, you're a female.

However, as science has shown us, there is much more to sex and gender than meets the eye.

DIAGNOSTIC CRITERIA

In 1980, "Gender Identity Disorder" was introduced into the Diagnostic and Statistical Manual (DSM), 3rd Edition, published by the American Psychiatric Association. The current DSM-5 Diagnostic Criteria for Gender Dysphoria (2013) provides the following definitions:

> The term "transgender" refers to a person whose sex assigned at birth (i.e., the sex assigned by a physician at birth, usually based on external genitalia) does not match their gender identity (i.e., one's psychological sense of their gender). Some people who are transgender will experience "gender dysphoria," which refers to psychological distress that results from an incongruence between one's sex assigned at birth and one's gender identity. Though gender dysphoria often begins in childhood, some people may not experience it until after puberty or much later.
>
> People who are transgender may pursue multiple domains of gender affirmation, including social affirmation (e.g., changing one's name and pronouns), legal affirmation (e.g., changing gender markers on one's government-issued documents), medical affirmation (e.g., pubertal suppression or gender-affirming hormones), or surgical affirmation (e.g., vaginoplasty, facial feminization surgery, breast augmentation, masculine chest reconstruction, etc.). Of note, not all people who are transgender will desire all domains of gender affirmation, as these are highly personal and individual decisions.
>
> It is important to note that gender identity is different from gender expression. Whereas gender identity refers to one's psychological sense of one gender, gender expression refers to how one presents in the world in a gendered way. For example, in much of the U.S., wearing a dress is considered a "feminine" gender expression, and wearing a tuxedo is considered a "masculine" gender expression. Such expectations are culturally defined and vary across time and culture. One's gender expression does not necessarily align with one's gender identity. Diverse gender expressions, much like diverse gender identities, are not indications of a mental disorder.
>
> Gender identity is also different from sexual orientation. Sexual orientation refers to the types of people towards which one is sexually attracted. People who are transgender have the same diversity of sexual orientations as people who are cisgender (people whose sex assigned at birth matches their gender identity).[221]

The DSM-5 provides one overarching diagnosis of gender dysphoria with separate specific criteria for children, adolescents, and adults.

The DSM-5 defines gender dysphoria in adolescents and adults as a marked incongruence between one's experienced/expressed gender and their assigned gender, lasting for at least 6 months, and manifested by at least two of the following:

- A marked incongruence between one's experienced/expressed gender and primary and/or secondary sex characteristics (or in young adolescents, the anticipated secondary sex characteristics)
- A strong desire to be rid of one's primary and/or secondary sex characteristics because of a marked incongruence with one's experienced/expressed gender

(or in young adolescents, a desire to prevent the development of the anticipated secondary sex characteristics)

- A strong desire for the primary and/or secondary sex characteristics of the other gender
- A strong desire to be of the other gender (or some alternative gender different from one's assigned gender)
- A strong desire to be treated as the other gender (or some alternative gender different from one's assigned gender)
- A firm conviction that one has the typical feelings and reactions of the other gender (or some alternative gender different from one's assigned gender).

In order to meet criteria for the diagnosis, the condition must also be associated with clinically significant distress or impairment in social, occupational, or other important areas of functioning.

The DSM-5 defines gender dysphoria in children as a marked incongruence between one's experienced/expressed gender and assigned gender, lasting at least 6 months, as manifested by at least six of the following (one of which must be the first criterion):

- A strong desire to be of the other gender or an insistence that one is the other gender (or some alternative gender different from one's assigned gender),
- In boys (assigned gender), a strong preference for cross-dressing or simulating female attire; or in girls (assigned gender), a strong preference for wearing only typical masculine clothing and a solid resistance to the wearing of typical feminine clothing,
- A strong preference for cross-gender roles in make-believe play or fantasy play,
- A strong preference for the toys, games or activities stereotypically used or engaged in by the other gender,
- A strong preference for playmates of the other gender,
- In boys (assigned gender), a strong rejection of typically masculine toys, games, and activities and a strong avoidance of rough-and-tumble play; or in girls (assigned gender), a strong rejection of typically feminine toys, games, and activities,
- A strong dislike of one's sexual anatomy,
- A strong desire for the physical sex characteristics that match one's experienced gender.

As with the diagnostic criteria for adolescents and adults, the condition in children must also be associated with clinically significant distress or impairment in social, occupational, or other important areas of functioning."[222,223] Zucker discusses the changes in the DSM diagnostic criteria between Edition 4 and the most recent Edition 5.[224]

In 2012, the American Psychiatric Association (APA) published a report concerning the treatment of Gender Identity Disorder (GID). The report contains recommendations for several groups and subgroups. For adults, the report concluded that:

With subjective improvement as the primary outcome measure, the existing evidence base combined with clinical consensus is sufficient for developing recommendations in the form of an APA Practice Guideline.[225]

Then, in 2015, the American Psychological Association issued guidelines to assist psychologists in providing care to people with gender dysphoria-like symptoms.[226]

Together, the Clinical Practice Guidelines of the Endocrine Society, the American Psychiatric Association and American Psychological Association's practice guidelines, the World Professional Association for Transgender Health, Standards of Care (WPATH SOC), and treatment recommendations from other organizations, these widely accepted practice guidelines demonstrate the efficacy of treating gender dysphoric patients of all ages.

The benefits of treatment are clear. Clinically appropriate treatment of gender dysphoria, according to well-established practice guidelines, saves lives. To do anything else amounts to malpractice.

SOCIOLOGICAL ISSUES

Besides the medical, psychological, and psychiatric issues faced by individuals who are transgender, there are many sociological, socioeconomic, and other issues.

In "The Report of the 2015 U.S. Transgender Survey" (hereinafter "USTS Report, Executive Summary"),[227] the authors confirm:

> Disturbing patterns of mistreatment and discrimination, and startling disparities between transgender people in the survey and the U.S. population when it comes to the most basic elements of life, such as finding a job, having a place to live, accessing medical care, and enjoying the support of family and community. Survey respondents also experienced harassment and violence at alarmingly high rates. Several themes emerge from the thousands of data points presented in the full survey report.[228]

Societal reactions to individuals who are transgender, as discussed above, vary widely. One stress factor transgender individuals experience is statements made by others, including misgendering. One trans individual reported that being misgendered is "like a gut punch, visceral feeling of alienation and being misunderstood."[229]

Another said,

> I especially hate it when people refer to me by birth name online. It makes me panic and want to hit them because why would you use my birth name when I keep telling you to use my preferred name, the fuck?[230]

These and other factors have a significant impact on a person's transition where successfully passing in the gender and sex of reassignment is a requirement of the WPATH guidelines.

The WPATH Standards of Care outline the requirements for assessment and referral, which include: assessing the individual's gender dysphoria; providing information regarding options for gender identity and expression, and possible medical interventions; assessing, diagnosing, and discussing treatment options for coexisting mental health concerns; assessment of eligibility, preparation for, and referral for hormone therapy; assessment of eligibility, preparation for, and referral for surgery.[231]

Conversion or Reparative Therapy

Extensive clinical evidence shows that transgender, homosexual, and/or bisexual people cannot be changed to heterosexual through psychological or psychiatric therapeutic modalities (see also the section on conversion therapy above). Yet, despite this evidence, some people continue to believe, based on various factors including religious belief, that members of the LGBTQ+ community can be "converted" using techniques, such as "prayer and group support and pressure," as well as aversion therapy.[232] Aversion therapy includes applying an electric shock to the hands or genitals and/or nausea-inducing drugs, administered while the individual is watching homoerotic images, in what is called "masturbatory reconditioning." These techniques have been widely condemned by professional mental health and medical communities nationwide. Nevertheless, some American Christian organizations and individuals continue to provide these conversion sessions even though the practices are banned in a growing number of states.[233]

According to the APA, "no credible evidence exists that any mental health intervention can reliably and safely change sexual orientation; nor, from a mental health perspective does sexual orientation need to be changed."[234] Additionally, The Trevor Project[235] provides additional commentary regarding these practices:

> These harmful practices are based on the false claim that being gay or transgender is a mental illness that should be cured. In fact, the American Psychiatric Association determined that homosexuality was not a mental illness, but a normal variant of human nature, in 1973. Unfortunately, young lesbian, gay, bisexual, transgender, and questioning (LGBTQ) people may be coerced and subject to these harmful practices, resulting in a range of negative outcomes including depression, anxiety, substance abuse, and suicidality.

Conversion therapy comes in many forms and is sometimes known by other names, including (but not limited to):

- gender critical therapy
- reparative therapy
- ex-gay ministries
- sexual orientation change efforts (SOCE)
- gender identity change efforts.

Conversion therapy may be performed by licensed professionals, unlicensed ministries, and/or life coaches. It may be undertaken one-on-one or in groups, in practitioners' offices and/or at retreats or conferences. It may be done for money or for free. Faith-based conversion therapy can be found across various religious traditions. Faith communities have also played a significant and growing role in protecting LGBTQ youth from conversion therapy.

While some conversion therapists continue to use physical methods, including painful aversive conditioning, the most common techniques in the United States today include "talk therapies" where licensed or unlicensed practitioners attempt to "treat" a person's sexual orientation or gender identity. They may falsely claim that a person's sexual orientation or gender identity results from abuse and/or childhood trauma or is otherwise due to their environment and upbringing. Modern science has thoroughly rejected conversion practices. Thus, practitioners are not certified mental health professionals and have no accredited training. This also means there is no ethical standard of care for any therapy claiming to effectively change a person's sexual orientation or gender identity.

Especially for faith-based providers, conversion therapy often involves teachings pulled from religious texts, prayer, spiritual discipline, and/or practices modeled on twelve-step programs, targeting "sexual brokenness," "unwanted same-sex attractions," or "gender confusion."

Notably, conversion therapy does not include counseling that helps people find social supports to explore their gender identity. Laws against conversion therapy also do not prevent people from providing treatment for sexual assault, harassment, and abuse."[236]

The list of organizations that condemn the practice of "reparative" or "conversion therapy" is a long one and includes:

> The American Psychological Association,
> The American Psychiatric Association,
> The American Medical Association,
> American Academy of Child and Adolescent Psychiatry,
> American Academy of Pediatrics,

American Academy of Physician Assistants,
American Association for Marriage and Family Therapy,
American Association of School Administrators,
American Association of Sexuality Educators, Counselors, and Therapist,
American College of Physicians,
American Counseling Association,
American Federation of Teachers,
American Osteopathic Association,
American Psychoanalytic Association,
American School Counselor Association,
American School Health Association,
Interfaith Alliance Foundation,
National Association of School Psychologists,
National Association of Secondary School Principals,
National Association of Social Workers,
National Education Association,
School Social Work Association on America,
United Nations High Commissioner of Human Rights,
World Health Organization,
Religious leaders in 35 countries sign petition on Declaring LBGTQ principles,[237]
And many more.

Bias, Prejudice, and the Basis of Discrimination

Finally, why do people discriminate against others, taking into consideration only our differences rather than our commonalities? Implicit bias (implicit social cognition)[238] provides one explanation. Implicit bias is defined as "an *unconscious* association, belief, or attitude toward any social group."[239] People may act on prejudice and stereotypes, sometimes without intending to do so. Similarly, people may harbor implicit gender biases,[240] even though they may outwardly express a more accommodating attitude, for example, that men and women, should be treated equally.

By contrast, according to the Georgetown University's National Center for Cultural Competence (NCCC):

> In the case of explicit or conscious [bias], the person is very clear about their feelings and attitudes, and related behaviors are conducted with intent. This type of bias is processed neurologically at a conscious level as declarative, semantic memory, and in words. Conscious bias in its extreme is characterized by overt negative behavior that can be expressed through physical and verbal harassment or through more subtle means such as exclusion.[241]

Thus, explicit bias, defined as "outward, clear, conscious thoughts, beliefs, and actions expressed in words and/or overt negative behavior," is directed verbally or physically against specific persons or groups viewed as undesirable based on prejudice.[242]

Prejudice—defined as "a conscious, preconceived judgment or opinion about an individual or group of individuals and/or an irrational attitude of hostility directed against an individual, a group, a race, or any other characteristic, or their supposed characteristics," very often forms the basis of discrimination in the United States. Whether overt or covert, the result is the same. People are discriminated against because of any characteristic considered to be objectionable by the discriminating person. Groups of people who have been historically discriminated against include: people of color, people whose place of national origin is different than the person discriminating against them, women, the disabled, certain religious groups, and, in the case of this book, the lesbian, gay, bisexual, transgender, and queer (LGBTQ) community and the individuals who make up that community.

Stereotyping is:

> Something conforming to a fixed or general pattern especially, a standardized mental picture that is held in common individually by members of a group and that represents an oversimplified opinion, prejudiced attitude, or uncritical judgment.[243]

For many, religious belief comprises an important part of their lives. Belief in a higher power or a spiritual deity can, for many people, provide a sense of balance. But problems arise when people attempt to inflict their religious beliefs on others, especially those who are not receptive. When fundamental American Christian belief (often based on the Old Testament) provides a prejudicial basis for discrimination and when individuals who subscribe to these perspectives mix religious ideology with political rhetoric, claims of First Amendment rights are used to excuse, justify, and substantiate prejudicial behaviors. Accordingly, religion becomes the basis for discrimination. If one doesn't subscribe to the same belief system as others, one may be subject to discrimination and ostracism. When certain perspectives (especially those based on particular religious beliefs) become entrenched, institutionalized discrimination emerges.

For a long time, members of the LGBTQ community have been stereotyped or stigmatized by those who consider the LGBTQ community to be undesirable and not entitled to experience equality under the law. Many LGBTQ people have experienced discrimination in various forms. Only recently are we beginning to see our rights under the law being validated in the courts.

Sex and Gender Stereotyping in Sports

Traditionally, sports have been separated into men's and women's divisions at the interscholastic, intercollegiate, and professional levels. Men's sports dominate the media and society generally. The attention, glamor, funding, and media coverage favor men's sports over women's sports in every aspect. Sports organizations, stadium builders and owners, and the media spend billions of dollars on sports every year. Of course, it doesn't include the billions of dollars spent on marketing and advertising of sporting events. In this category alone, beer advertising far surpasses all other advertising. As this is being written, the 2021 Summer Olympics are in progress in Tokyo, Japan, with the first transgender athletes competing from Canada, New Zealand, and the United States.[244] Television networks cover the games live, dedicating millions of dollars to secure well-known sports broadcasters on location to provide the public with a second-by-second accounting of the events. Fifty-six sports are represented at the games.

As of 23 October 2012, the International Olympic Committee (IOC), along with the International Association of Athletics Federations (IAAF) (now World Athletics), has sanctioned the following policy:

> The IAAF Medical/Anti-Doping Commission has adopted the IOC Medical Commission's statement on sports participation for athletes who have undergone sex reassignment.
>
> 1. Before Puberty

Individuals undergoing sex reassignment of male to female before puberty should be regarded as girls and women. Similarly, this also applies to female to male reassignment, and they should be regarded as boys or men.

2. After Puberty

Individuals undergoing sex reassignment from male to female, or the reverse, after puberty are eligible to participate in their reassigned gender under the following conditions:

    a. Surgical anatomic changes have been completed, including external genitalia changes and gonadectomy.

    b. Legal recognition of their assigned sex has been conferred by the appropriate official authorities.

    c. Hormonal therapy appropriate for the assigned sex has been administered in a verifiable manner and for sufficient length of time to minimize gender-related advantages in sport competitions.

Further guidelines:

    a. Eligibility should begin no sooner than two years after gonadectomy.

    b. A confidential case-by-case evaluation will occur.

    c. In the event that the gender of a competing athlete is questioned, the medical delegate (or equivalent) of the relevant sporting body shall have the authority to take all appropriate measures for the determination of the gender of a competitor.[245]

Despite international sports organizations attempting to develop science-based eligibility standards, in the United States, sex stereotyping and discrimination against transgender athletes continues to this day. In their article entitled, "Sport and Transgender People: A Systematic Review of the Literature Relating to Sport Participation and Competitive Sport Policies,"[246] Jones et al. document that transgender athletes generally have a negative experience when participating in competitive sports. The article reports no direct or consistent research demonstrating that transgender female athletes have an athletic advantage in sport. As a result, they conclude that:

> The majority of competitive sport policies are discriminatory against [the transgender] population.[247]

Yet, certain members of society continue to stereotype transgender athletes purely on the basis of sex and gender. Their objections appear to be based on an unsupported belief that to allow transgender athletes to participate at all is unfair in some generalized way. Even if they accept that transgender athletes have a right to participate, they want to put arbitrary restrictions in place with little to no support for such restrictions.

For example, in 2019, the IAAF (World Athletics)[248] issued new eligibility criteria for female athletes with Differences of Sex Development (DSD).

> Most females (including elite female athletes) have low levels of testosterone circulating naturally in their bodies (0.12 to 1.79 nmol/L in blood); while after puberty the normal male range is much higher (7.7 to 29.4 nmol/L). Absent a DSD or a tumor, no female

would have serum levels of testosterone of 5 nmol/L and above, but individuals with DSDs can have very high levels of natural testosterone, extending into and even beyond the normal male range...

If a female athlete wishing to participate in a Restricted Event at an International Competition has a DSD that results in levels of circulating testosterone greater than 5 nmol/L, and her androgen receptors function properly, such that those elevated levels of circulating testosterone have a material androgenizing effect... she must reduce those levels down below 5 nmol/L for six months (e.g., by use of hormonal contraceptives) before competing in such events, and must maintain them below that level until she no longer wishes to participate in Restricted Events at International Competitions.[249]

This despite a 2014 study by Bermon et al. of serum androgen concentrations in elite female athletes, which found that for most:

The DHEAS [dehydroepiandrosterone sulphate, a precursor of testosterone] concentration observed is very similar to the one reported in age-matched healthy sedentary women (mean 4.72 μmol/L)... However, in our study [n=839], 19 female athletes [2.3%] showed a DHEAS concentration greater than 10 μmol/L, whereas 82 subjects [9.8%] showed DHEAS concentrations greater than 7.8 μmol/L,[250]

Further, Bermon et al. observed that DHEAS concentrations differed depending on which athletic event the women were involved in, such as throwing, sprinting, and to a lesser degree jumping, where women demonstrated higher levels of androgenic hormones than, for example, long-distance runners.[251] Thus, it appears that the 5 nmol/L threshold set by World Athletics is not supported by scientific research.

The bottom line is that transgender athletes who have completed sex reassignment surgery *and* a hormone therapy regime aimed specifically at reducing testosterone and other androgen levels to correspond to cisgender female levels, and who have done so at least one to two years prior to competing can, and should, be allowed to compete as females in female sports.

Jones et al. concluded that:

There is limited research from which to draw any conclusion about whether transgender people have an athletic advantage in competitive sport or not.[252]

Without research that definitively responds to this question, policies prohibiting transgender individuals from participating in school sports are, at the very least, misplaced.

CLINICAL CARE PROGRAMS FOR TRANSGENDER AND GENDER-EXPANSIVE YOUTH

Following is a listing of the Clinical Care Programs in the United States that provide clinical services for transgender and gender-expansive youth and adolescents. If a state is not listed, no programs are available in that state. Data were obtained from the Human Rights Campaign website.[253]

Note: If you have a clinic or a clinical program that is not listed here, or if the entry is inaccurate or out of date, please contact the author through the publisher to have your program included in any future book revision.

Also, if you provide non-clinical services to the transgender community, please provide that information to the author through the publisher. Non-clinical services include housing assistance, employment assistance, or other social services of a non-clinical nature.

ALABAMA

Facility Name: **Pediatric Endocrinology**
Healthcare Facility: University of Alabama Birmingham
Address: 1601 Fourth Avenue South, Room M30, Birmingham, AL 35233
Website: None

Description: UAB Pediatrics offers gender health care at our clinic under the department of Pediatrics, the Division of Pediatric Endocrinology. We offer all patients access to a dedicated pediatric Endocrinologist, a General Pediatrician, and a licensed psychologist. We also have an administrator that is supportive of patients and families and a nurse that is well versed in care of Gender non-conforming children and adolescents. There is also a social worker available to help navigate the challenges for healthcare and access to medications. Our Chaplain office at the Children's Hospital of Alabama is supportive of our effort and are willing to help families that need spiritual and religious support.

Contact Name: Hussein Abdullatif, M.D.

Contact Email: hlatif@uab.edu
Contact Phone: 205-638-9107

ARIZONA

Facility Name: **El Rio Medical Home for Transgender and Gender Non-Conforming Youth**
Healthcare Facility: El Rio Community Health Center
Address: 101 West Irvington, Tucson, AZ 85714
Website: https://www.elrio.org/transgender-medicine/

Description: El Rio Community Health Center's Medical Home for Transgender and Gender Non-Conforming Youth serves patients from first identification of gender dysphoria until age 21 (current youth ages in our program are 4-20). The medical team provides primary care, including puberty blockers, hormones, and referrals for surgical consultation. Our behavioral health team of psychiatry, social work, and counselors supports families with acute behavioral and mental health needs. We have built a strong network with local mental health specialists for ongoing counseling and assessments. We also refer to community organizations, subspecialty medical providers as needed, and education for other primary care providers in the region.

Contact Name: Andrew Cronyn, M.D., FAAP
Contact Email: AndrewC@elrio.org
Contact Phone: (520) 670-3909

ARKANSAS

Facility Name: **Gender Spectrum Clinic**
Healthcare Facility: Arkansas Children's Hospital
Address: 16101 Cantrell Dr. S. 114, Little Rock, AR 72223
Website: https://tinyurl.com/39ee8bxx

Description: The Gender Spectrum Clinic provides healthcare services to youth with gender dysphoria, using a gender affirmative model of care and individualized treatment plans developed for each patient. The Gender Spectrum interdisciplinary team collaborates with patients, parents/guardians, mental health therapy providers, and schools to ensure the best possible health care outcomes.

We recognize the unique barriers that youth experiencing gender dysphoria face in pursuing health care and want to ensure that our patients and families feel valued and respected under the care of our clinic. Our ultimate goal is to provide high-quality, evidence-based, and gender-affirming care in a comfortable and safe environment.

Conditions and Treatments

- Gender dysphoria
- Hormone therapy (cross-sex hormone therapy)
- Feminizing therapy
- Masculinizing therapy
- Menstruation suppression
- Puberty suppression therapy

Contact Name: Kirsten Sowell, Gender Spectrum Clinic Social Worker

Contact Email: Sowellkl@archildrens.org
Contact Phone: (501) 364-2935

CALIFORNIA

Facility Name: **The Center for Transyouth Health and Development**
Healthcare Facility: Children's Hospital Los Angeles
Address: 5000 Sunset Blvd. 4th Floor, Los Angeles, CA 90027
Website: https://tinyurl.com/2md43chb

Description: The Center's Medical services include a thorough evaluation of transgender patients, including gaining an understanding of the youth's experience of gender non-conformity and an assessment of medical readiness for hormones. Physicians determine, in collaboration with the youth, mental health therapists, ancillary support staff, and families, the best treatment plan for each individual. Ongoing monitoring of efficacy, safety, and side effects are essential for youth, especially in the first year of treatment.

Facility Name: **Gender Management Clinic**
Healthcare Facility: Rady Children's Hospital
Address: 3020 Children's Way, San Diego, CA 92123
Website: https://tinyurl.com/3ury2nv8

Description: The Gender Management Clinic provides care for children and adolescents under age 21 years with gender dysphoria and related issues. The team comprises two pediatric endocrinologists who provide gonadotropin-releasing hormones (puberty blockers) and hormonal therapy. Mental health services include individual outpatient assessments, therapy (through the Department of Psychiatry), and referrals to local therapists and support groups.

Contact Name: Maja Marinkovic, M.D. (or Claudia Juarez, secretary), Assistant Professor, Department of Pediatric Endocrinology
Contact Email: mmarinkovic@rchsd.org
Contact Phone: 858-966-4032

Facility Name: **Dimensions Clinic**
Healthcare Facility: Castro-Mission Health Center
Address: 3850 17th St., San Francisco, CA 94114
Website: http://www.dimensionsclinic.org

Description: Dimensions Clinic serves lesbian, gay, bisexual, transgender, queer, and intersex young people and their partners and allies ages 12 to 25 years (with more than 80% of their served population identifying as transgender and/or gender-nonconforming). Dimensions Clinic has a team that provides primary medical care (MDs, NPs, RNs, and health workers) under internal medicine and family medicine, as well as care in psychology and psychiatry. Dimensions Clinic offers access to hormones and puberty blockers and can make surgery referrals. Mental health services include individual and group therapy services and assessments.

Facility Name: **Child and Adolescent Gender Center Clinic**
Healthcare Facility: UCSF Benioff Children's Hospital
Address: 1825 Fourth St., San Francisco, CA 94158
Website: https://tinyurl.com/ytzf66j4

Description: The Child and Adolescent Gender Center (CAGC) serves transgender and gender-nonconforming children and adolescents (ages 2 to 24 years) and their families. The team provides care in psychology, endocrinology, adolescent medicine, and pediatrics and additionally includes a social worker, attorney, and educational advocate. The team can provide puberty blockers and hormones. Mental health services include screenings, family support, referrals for assessments, individual and group therapy, and psychiatric care through their CAGC mental health consortium.

Contact Name: Stephen Rosenthal, M.D., Medical Director, and Joel Baum, MS, Director of education and training at Gender Spectrum and Director of Advocacy at CAGC, Dr. Rosenthal
Contact Email: rosenthals@peds.ucsf.edu
Contact Phone: 415-476-2266

Facility Name: **Teen Health Van—Mobile Clinic Program for Adolescents**

Healthcare Facility: Lucile Packard Children's Hospital Stanford
Address: 725 Welch Road, Palo Alto, CA 94304
Website: http://www.stanfordchildrens.org/en/service/teen-van

Description: The Teen Health Van — Mobile Clinic Program for Adolescents provides care for uninsured, underinsured, and homeless youth ages 10 to 25 years. The team provides adolescent medicine and psychiatry care as needed and includes a social worker, nurse practitioner, and registered dietitian. The team can provide hormones. Mental health services include individual therapy and referrals for assessments and group therapy through community partners.

Contact Name: Seth Ammerman, M.D., Medical Director, Teen Health Van
Contact Email: seth.ammerman@stanford.edu
Contact Phone: 650-736-9557

COLORADO

Facility Name: **LGBT Center of Excellence**
Healthcare Facility: Denver Health and Hospital Authority
Address: 777 Bannock St, Denver, CO 80204
Website: https://tinyurl.com/jtrs55xx

Description: Denver Health LGBT Center of Excellence is committed to caring for LGBTQIA patients of any age. Young people have access to open, affirming providers that will help patients start on cross-sex hormones, provide young people and their families access to LGBT meet-up groups in the "child zone", provide mental health services, and more. We have identified LGBT champions at all 17 school-based clinics and all 9 of our community health clinics. Denver health also provides gender-affirming surgeries. (Bottom surgeries coming in late 2017) Call our Patient navigator today to learn more about how and where you can get the care you need.

Contact Name: Paige Jackson
Contact Email: Paige.Jackson@dhha.org
Contact Phone: 303-602-6736

Facility Name: **TRUE Center for Gender Diversity**

Healthcare Facility: Children's Hospital Colorado
Address: 860 N Potomac Circle, Aurora CO 80011
Website: https://tinyurl.com/4tra8y9t

Description: Our multidisciplinary team supports and cares for every aspect of the gender-diverse experience of children, adolescents, and young adults in the Rocky Mountain Region. Our care team includes experts in adolescent medicine, endocrinology, nursing, psychology, and social work. We specialize in helping our patients achieve the gender expression that's right for them. We understand the medicines and medical concerns that gender transitions involve, but we also understand the emotional challenges of gender diversity. In short, we speak your language. We see not just patients but people: We understand, empathize, and treat each patient as unique. That means we work together with you and your family to meet your needs and goals. Your unique care plan considers factors like your: Gender expression, Age, Stage of puberty, Goals, Plans for future treatments or procedures, Health and Support system.

Contact Name: TRUE Center
Contact Email: TRUE@childrenscolorado.org
Contact Phone: 720-777-8783

CONNECTICUT

Facility Name: **Yale Gender Program**
Healthcare Facility: Yale School of Medicine
Address: 1 Long Wharf Drive Floor 2, New Haven, CT 06511 United States
Website: https://www.yalemedicine.org/departments/pediatric-gender-program/

Description: We are a safe, supportive resource and treatment center for gender-variant children, adolescents, and young adults who are exploring their gender identity. Our team, which includes doctors and mental health professionals, provides comprehensive, interdisciplinary, family-centered care for children, teens, and young adults questioning their assigned gender and/or seeking gender-affirming consultation and treatment. We are committed to providing care in compassionate and respectful ways. Our multidisciplinary team includes pediatric endocrinologists, a psychologist, psychiatrists, a medical ethicist, and a lawyer. We all work closely together, in addition to consulting with and referring to our wide array of specialists within Yale Medicine and Yale-New Haven Health. For example, we consult with fertility experts, gynecology, plastic surgeons, and ear, nose, and throat specialists.

Contact Name: Christy Olezeski, Ph.D.
Contact Email: christy.olezeski@yale.edu
Contact Phone: (203) 737-7169

Facility Name: **Gender Identity Program**

Healthcare Facility: Connecticut Children's Medical Center
Address: 282 Washington Street, Hartford, CT 06106
Website: https://tinyurl.com/7tuvsfs5

Description: The Gender Identity Program at Connecticut Children's Medical Center serves patients with gender dysphoria from the start of puberty until age 21 years. The team provides care in psychology, psychiatry, endocrinology, and urology and includes a plastic surgeon. The team can provide puberty blockers, hormones, and breast surgery. Mental health services include individual therapy, assessments, family therapy specific to medical transition, general group therapy for LGBTQ youth facilitated by the team's psychologist, and referrals to support groups for children and adolescents with gender dysphoria, their parents, and their siblings.

Contact Name: Priya Phulwani, M.D., Pediatric Endocrinologist, Connecticut Children's Medical Center
Contact Email: Pphulwa@connecticutchildrens.org
Contact Phone: 860-545-9370

FLORIDA
Facility Name: **UF Health Youth Gender Program**
Healthcare Facility: UF Health Shands Children's Hospital
Address: 2000 SW Archer Rd, Gainesville, FL 32608

Website: https://tinyurl.com/347vmb6z

Description: The UF Health Youth Gender Program provides medical care and psychologic support for transgender and gender non-conforming youth with gender dysphoria. We provide counseling for youth and their families, readiness assessment for pubertal suppression and cross-sex hormonal therapy, and gender-affirming therapies, including pubertal blockers, cross-sex hormones, and referrals for gender-affirming surgery when appropriate.

Contact Name: Kristin Dayton, M.D.
Contact Email: kristinjohnson23@peds.ufl.edu
Contact Phone: 352-265-7337

ILLINOIS
Facility Name: **Department of Pediatrics, Divisions of Adolescent Medicine and Endocrinology and Diabetes**
Healthcare Facility: Washington University School of Medicine
Address: St. Louis Children's Hospital, 1 Childrens Place, St. Louis, MO 63110
Website: None available

Description: The Washington University School of Medicine Department of Pediatrics, Divisions of Adolescent Medicine and Endocrinology and Diabetes, serves children and adolescents with gender dysphoria up to age 18 years in psychology, ages 13 to 21 years in adolescent medicine, and from early puberty to age 21 years in endocrinology. The team offers care in psychology, endocrinology, and adolescent medicine and includes a social worker. The endocrinologist can provide puberty blockers and hormones. Mental health services include individual therapy, assessments, and referrals to parent and peer support groups.

Contact Name: Abby Hollander, M.D., pediatric endocrinologist
Contact Email: hollander@kids.wustl.edu
Contact Phone: 314-454-6051

IOWA
Facility Name: **Lesbian, Gay, Bisexual, Transgender, Queer, and Questioning Clinic**
Healthcare Facility: University of Iowa
Address: 105 East 9th Street, Coralville, Iowa 52241
Website: http://www.uihealthcare.org/lgbt

Description: The team at the University of Iowa Lesbian, Gay, Bisexual, Transgender, Queer, and Questioning Clinic serves LGBTQ people of all ages. The team offers psychology, psychiatry, pediatric endocrinology, general medicine, and obstetrics and includes a pharmacist on site. The team provides primary care for LGBTQ populations, including hormone therapy, wellness exams, acute care, chronic disease management, STI testing and treatment, and referrals for puberty blockers and surgery (breast augmentation, male chest reconstruction, hysterectomy and oophorectomy, and orchiectomy). Mental health services include individual therapy, family and couple therapy, and assessments.

Contact Name: Katie Imborek, M.D., Co-Director
Contact Email: katherine-imborek@uiowa.edu
Contact Phone: 319-384-7444 (option 1)

MAINE

Facility Name: **Gender Clinic**
Healthcare Facility: The Barbara Bush Children's Hospital at Maine Medical Center
Address: 22 Bramhall Street, Portland, ME 04102
Website: None available

Description: The Gender Clinic at Barbara Bush Children's Hospital at Maine Medical Center serves trans* and gender-nonconforming children, teens, and young adults in northern New England. The team provides care in the areas of psychiatry, endocrinology, and pediatric gynecology. The endocrine team can provide puberty blockers, hormones, and surgical counseling. Mental health services include individual and/or family therapy, assessments, psychiatric medication management, and connection with support groups.

Contact Name: Heather Shanholtz, RN (Coordinator for the Gender Clinic)
Contact Email: shanhh@mmc.org
Contact Phone: 207-662-5795

MARYLAND

Facility Name: **Pediatric Endocrinology**
Healthcare Facility: University of Maryland Medical Center
Address: 22 S. Greene Street, Baltimore, M.D. 21201
Website: https://umm.edu/programs/childrens/services/endocrinology

Description: Pediatric Endocrinology at University of Maryland Medical Center serves children, adolescents, and adults with gender variance through age 21 years. The team offers care in pediatric and adult endocrinology, with adolescent medicine care available at their Adolescent and Young Adult Clinic. A multi-disciplinary program is being developed. The team can provide puberty blockers, hormones, and referrals for surgery. The team can make referrals for services in therapy and psychiatry.

Contact Name: Elyse Pine-Twaddell, M.D., Clinical Assistant Professor of Pediatrics, Division of Pediatric Endocrinology
Contact Email: epine@peds.umaryland.edu
Contact Phone: 410-328-3410

Facility Name: **Gender JOY (Journeys of Youth)**
Healthcare Facility: Chase Brexton Health Care
Address: 1111 N Charles Street, Baltimore, M.D. 21201
Website: http://www.chasebrexton.org/our-services/trans-care

Description: Chase Brexton Health Care provides trans-specific health care across the lifespan, including specialized, high-quality care for transgender and gender-diverse children, adolescents, and young adults. Gender JOY services include routine pediatric medical care, puberty blockers, cross-sex hormone therapy, gynecological care, counseling regarding fertility preservation, behavioral health support including individual, group, and family therapy, case management, pharmacy services, and an on-site laboratory. Additionally, the LGBT Health Resource Center of Chase Brexton Health Care can connect patients and their families to services, programs, and resources to support the full spectrum of optimal health.

Contact Name: The LGBT Health Resource Center of Chase Brexton
Contact Email: lgbt@chasebrexton.org
Contact Phone: 410-837-2050

Facility Name: **Center for Adolescent and Young Adult Health**
Healthcare Facility: Johns Hopkins Children's Center
Address: 1800 Orleans St., Baltimore, Maryland 21287
Website: None available

Description: The Center for Adolescent and Young Adult Health offers a provision of services for adolescents aged 12 to 24 years under adolescent medicine, including hormones and hormone blockers. The center also offers support services, on-site psychology services, and access to endocrinology consultants.

Contact Name: Renata Arrington-Sanders, M.D., MPH, ScM, Assistant Professor
Contact Email: rarring3@jhmi.edu
Contact Phone: 410-502-8166

MASSACHUSETTS

Facility Name: **The Adolescent Center**
Healthcare Facility: Boston Medical Center
Address: Boston Medical Center Department of Pediatrics, Adolescent Center, 5th Floor, 850 Harrison Avenue, Boston, MA 02118
Website: http://www.bmc.org/pediatrics-adolescentcenter.htm

Description: The Adolescent Center at Boston Medical Center serves transgender and gender-nonconforming youth aged 22 years, primarily from inner-city Boston and many from immigrant communities in the Boston area. The team provides care in adolescent medicine and can provide puberty blockers and hormones. The team offers consultation in endocrinology when needed. Mental health services include individual therapy conducted by an on-site social worker and referrals in psychiatry and psychology.

Contact Name: Mandy Coles, M.D., MPH
Contact Email: mandy.coles@bmc.org
Contact Phone: 617-414-4086

Facility Name: **Transgender Health Program**
Healthcare Facility: Fenway Health
Address: 1340 Boylston St, Boston, MA 02215
Website: http://www.fenwayhealth.org/transhealth

Description: Fenway Health's Transgender Health Program is a leader in high-quality, informed health care. In conjunction with Fenway's Family Medicine department, we serve transgender patients of all ages. Services include: Medical care, including hormone therapy and referrals to outside providers for gender-affirming medical procedures; Behavioral Healthcare, including support groups for the parents of transgender and gender non-conforming individuals; Information and counseling on reproductive health issues; Our Peer Listening Line for LGBT young people (800-399-PEER) offers a supportive ear and linkage to care and services for transgender youth. Other services, like HIV testing and counseling, dental, optometry, and pharmacy, are also available to transgender young people. Transgender patients of all ages are seen at all three Fenway Health clinical locations.

Contact Name: Ruben Hopwood
Contact Email: transhealth@fenwayhealth.org
Contact Phone: 857-313-6589

Facility Name: **The Adolescent Center**
Healthcare Facility: Boston Medical Center
Address: Boston Medical Center Department of Pediatrics, Adolescent Center, 5th Floor, 850 Harrison Avenue, Boston, MA 02118
Website: http://www.bmc.org/pediatrics-adolescentcenter.htm

Description: The Adolescent Center at Boston Medical Center serves transgender and gender-nonconforming youth up to age 22 years, primarily from inner-city Boston and many from immigrant communities in the Boston area. The team provides care in adolescent medicine and can provide puberty blockers and hormones. The team offers consultation in endocrinology when needed. Mental health services include individual therapy conducted by an on-site social worker and referrals in psychiatry and psychology.

Contact Name: Mandy Coles, M.D., MPH
Contact Email: mandy.coles@bmc.org
Contact Phone: 617-414-4086

Facility Name: **Transgender Clinic (Northampton Office) and Gender Specialty Clinic (Springfield Office)**
Healthcare Facility: Baystate Health
Address: 140 High Street, Springfield MA, 01105 and 325B King Street, Northampton, MA 01060.
Website: https://tinyurl.com/bvamd9fk

Description: The Transgender Clinic (Northampton Office) and Gender Specialty Clinic (Springfield Office) serve trans* and gender-nonconforming people ages 18 years and older; the program includes a provider who sees patients 18 years and younger through the provider's pediatric endocrinology office. The team offers care in pediatric endocrinology and can make referrals for care in psychology and psychiatry. The team can provide hormones, puberty blockers, top surgery, breast augmentation surgery, orchiectomy on a case-by-case referral basis, and management of psychotropic medications on a case-by-case basis. Providers at these clinics can make basic mental health assessments for hormones and can refer out for individual therapy, group therapy, crisis management, and additional assessments.

Contact Name: J. Aleah Nesteby, Nurse Practitioner, Adult Internal Medicine
Contact Email: J.Aleah.Nesteby@baystatehealth.org
Contact Phone: 413-794-1316 (for questions). 413-794-2511 (to set up a new patient visit).

MICHIGAN
Facility Name: **Child and Adolescent Gender Clinic**
Healthcare Facility: Mott Children's Hospital - University of Michigan
Address: 1500 E. Medical Center Drive, Ann Arbor, MI 48109

Website: http://www.mottchildren.org/conditions-treatments/gender-management

Description: The Child and Adolescent Gender Clinic at the University of Michigan offers comprehensive gender-affirming care for youth and adolescents, including gender assessment, hormone blockers, and cross-sex hormones. The team consists of pediatrics endocrinology, adolescent medicine, child and adolescent psychiatry, social work, and nursing. It is housed within the Division of Pediatric Endocrinology at Mott Children's Hospital.

Contact Name: Dr. Daniel Shumer
Contact Email: dshumer@med.umich.edu
Contact Phone: 734-764-5175

MINNESOTA

Facility Name: **Program in Human Sexuality**
Healthcare Facility: Center for Sexual Health, University of Minnesota Medical School
Address: 1300 South 2nd Street, Suite 180, Minneapolis, MN 5545
Website: https://tinyurl.com/ey4t3syh

Description: The Center for Sexual Health specializes in treating children and adolescents with gender issues and a range of medical conditions. The Center provides psychological assessments, has coordination of care with psychiatric services, and provides medical exams that are needed to provide puberty-delaying medication as well as hormones. Individual, group, and family therapy are also offered. The clinic collaborates with a pediatric endocrinologist when puberty blockers are indicated and offers hormone therapy. Referrals are given for surgery also when appropriate.

Contact Name: Ethan Turcotte, Communications Officer
Contact Email: phs@umn.edu
Contact Phone: 612-625-1500

MISSOURI

Facility Name: **Department of Pediatrics, Divisions of Adolescent Medicine and Endocrinology and Diabetes**
Healthcare Facility: Washington University School of Medicine
Address: St. Louis Children's Hospital, 1 Childrens Place, St. Louis, MO 63110
Website: None available

Description: The Washington University School of Medicine Department of Pediatrics, Divisions of Adolescent Medicine and Endocrinology and Diabetes, serves children and adolescents with gender dysphoria up to age 18 years in psychology, ages 13 to 21 years in adolescent medicine, and from early puberty to age 21 years in endocrinology. The team offers care in psychology, endocrinology, and adolescent medicine and includes a social worker. The endocrinologist can provide puberty blockers and hormones. Mental health services include individual therapy, assessments, and referrals to parent and peer support groups.

Contact Name: Abby Hollander, M.D., pediatric endocrinologist
Contact Email: hollander@kids.wustl.edu
Contact Phone: 314-454-6051

NEBRASKA

Facility Name: **College of Medicine Department of Obstetrics and Gynecology**
Healthcare Facility: University of Nebraska Medical Center
Address: 4400 Emile Street, Omaha, NE 68198
Website: http://www.unmc.edu/obgyn/amoura_njean.htm

Description: Dr. Jean Amoura at the University of Nebraska Medical Center sees trans* and gender-nonconforming children and adults of all ages. Dr. Amoura (in General Obstetrics and Gynecology) works with an adolescent specialist and a therapist in private practice to provide primary care to patients and prescribe puberty blockers and hormones for patients seeking these medical interventions. The team can make referrals for care in psychiatry and therapy.

Contact Name: Jean Amoura, M.D., MSc, Associate Professor, OB/GYN
Contact Email: jamoura@unmc.edu
Contact Phone: 402-?559-4500

NEW YORK

Facility Name: **Health Outreach to Teens (HOTT)**
Healthcare Facility: Callen-Lorde Community Health Center
Address: 356 W 18th St New York, NY 10011
Website: http://callen-lorde.org/

Description: The Callen-Lorde Community Health Center serves lesbian, gay, bisexual, transgender, queer, and questioning youth and youth who are HIV+ ages 13 and up. Callen Lorde's team offers care in psychiatry, social work, adolescent medicine, and gynecology. The team can provide hormones and referrals for puberty blockers and surgery. Mental health services include individual and group therapy and assessments.

Contact Name: Manel Silva, M.D., MPH, Clinical Director
Contact Email: msilva@callen-lorde.org
Contact Phone: 212-271-7200

Facility Name: **Gender and Sexuality Service**
Healthcare Facility: NYU Langone Medical Center
Address: NYU Child Study Center, One Park Avenue, 7th Floor, New York, NY 10016
Website: https://tinyurl.com/3bb3vkjf

Description: The New York University Gender and Sexuality Service provides care for trans* and gender-nonconforming people from birth through adulthood across multiple clinical sites. The team offers care in psychology and psychiatry and refers out of their private clinic for endocrinology and adolescent medicine. The team also offers family therapy and services in social work. The team can provide mental health evaluations for puberty suppression, cross-sex hormones, and surgery and makes referrals outside their clinic for all three. Mental health services include individual therapy, assessments, family therapy, and inpatient treatment.

Contact Name: Aron Janssen, M.D. Clinical Director, Gender and Sexuality Service; Assistant Professor of Child and Adolescent Psychiatry
Contact Email: aron.janssen@nyumc.org
Contact Phone: 646-754-4885

Facility Name: **Susquehanna Family Practice**
Healthcare Facility: A.O. Fox Hospital, Bassett Healthcare Network
Address: 1 FoxCare Drive, Suite 103, Oneonta, NY 13820
Website: https://tinyurl.com/3hvc4yrs

Description: Practitioners at Susquehanna Family Practice provide primary care for gender-nonconforming children/teens and adult patients. The team can prescribe puberty blockers and cross-sex hormones and offers mental health services, including therapy in the office. The team can also make referrals to Fox Hospital, the same hospital at which the Susquehanna Family Practice is housed.

Contact Name: Carolyn Wolf-Gould, M.D.
Contact Email: cawolf-gould@aofmh.org
Contact Phone: 607-431-5757

Facility Name: **Gender Health Services at Golisano Children's Hospital**
Healthcare Facility: University of Rochester Medical Center
Address: 601 Elmwood Avenue, Rochester, New York 14642
Website: https://tinyurl.com/3vsfmxdf

Description: We offer appointments to youth and young adults from puberty through age 25 and their families/care providers. Our team provides transition support, including puberty blockers and hormone therapies; our team includes mental health providers, surgeons, speech-language pathologists, and gynecologists. Mental health services through our behavioral health partners includes individual therapy, hormone assessments, group therapy, and referral to family and patient support groups.

Contact Name: Katherine Blumoff Greenberg M.D.
Contact Email: katherine_greenberg@urmc.rochester.edu
Contact Phone: (585) 275-2964

NORTH CAROLINA
Facility Name: **Duke Child and Adolescent Gender Care**
Healthcare Facility: Duke Children's Hospital
Address: 2301 Erwin Rd, Durham, NC 27710
Website: https://www.dukehealth.org/locations/duke-child-and-adolescent-gender-care

Description: Our clinic is staffed by pediatric endocrinology, pediatric urology, clinical social workers, and counselors in psychology/psychiatry and spiritual care. We partner with doctors, surgeons, and counselors in neonatology, genetics, family and community medicine, adolescent medicine, voice care services, fertility, and nutrition. Our mission is to provide holistic and compassionate care for youth and their families.

Contact Name: Deanna Adkins, M.D.
Contact Email: Deanna.adkins@duke.edu
Contact Phone: 919-684-8225

OHIO
Facility Name: **Center for Gender Affirming Medicine**

Healthcare Facility: Akron Children's Hospital
Address: 215 W Bowery St., Akron, Oh 44308
Website: https://www.akronchildrens.org/departments/Adolescent-Medicine.html

Description: The Akron Children's Hospital Center for Gender-Affirming Medicine provides care for LGBTQ+ youth aged 7 through 23. Our multidisciplinary team includes adolescent medicine, social work, endocrinology, and behavioral health. We provide puberty blockers, gender-affirming hormones, mental health care coordination, and supportive care for patients and their families.

Contact Name: Crystal Cole, M.D.
Contact Email: ccole@akronchildrens.org
Contact Phone: (330) 543-8538

Facility Name: **The MetroHealth Pride Clinic**
Healthcare Facility: MetroHealth
Address: 4242 Lorain Avenue, Cleveland, OH 44113
Website: http://www.metrohealth.org/prideclinic

Description: The MetroHealth Pride Clinic is the first in the region devoted to serving the health needs of the lesbian, gay, bisexual, and transgender (LGBT) community. The clinic provides transgender health services, including hormonal medical care and behavioral health services for LGBT and questioning youth.

Contact Name: Henry Ng, M.D., MPH, FAAP, FAC, Clinical Director
Contact Email: hng@metrohealth.org
Contact Phone: 216-957-4905 (to schedule an appointment)

Facility Name: **Transgender Health Clinic**
Healthcare Facility: Cincinnati Children's Hospital Medical Center
Address: 3333 Burnet Avenue, Cincinnati, Ohio 45229-302
Website: https://tinyurl.com/sz5dj2v7

Description: The Transgender Clinic at Cincinnati Children's Hospital Medical Center serves trans* and gender-nonconforming adolescents and young adults aged 5 to 22 years. The team provides care in endocrinology, adolescent medicine, pediatric gynecology, nutrition, referrals for voice communication (speech pathology), legal services, and psychology and psychiatry care; the team also offers social work services and nursing education and primary care. The team can provide puberty blockers and gender-affirming hormones. Mental health services include assessments in the clinic, individual therapy, and referrals to support groups.

Contact Name: Dr. Lee Ann Conard, RPh, DO, MPH, Assistant Professor of Adolescent Medicine, Director of the Transgender Clinic
Contact Email: leeann.conard@cchmc.org
Contact Phone: 513-636-2153

Facility Name: **THRIVE Program**
Healthcare Facility: Nationwide Children's Hospital
Address: 700 Children's Drive, Columbus, Ohio 43205

Website: http://www.nationwidechildrens.org/THRIVE

Description: THRIVE provides care for individuals (of any age) with disorders of sexual development and complex urological conditions, as well as gender concerns for individuals up to 22 years old. The team provides care in urology, endocrinology including hormone suppressants and hormone therapy, genetics, psychiatry, psychology, and social work, with services for adolescent medicine underway. Mental health services include assessments, psychiatry, medication management services, individual therapy, and systems support.

Contact Name: Bethanie Combs, MSW, LISW–Program Coordinator
Contact Email: Bethanie.combs@nationwidechildrens.org
Contact Phone: 614-72215765

OKLAHOMA

Facility Name: **The OU Children's Physicians Adolescent Medicine Clinic**
Healthcare Facility: University of Oklahoma Children's Hospital
Address: 1200 Children's Ave. Suite 12200, Oklahoma City, OK 73104
Website: https://tinyurl.com/yvfkam4c

Description: The OU Children's Physicians Adolescent Medicine Clinic offers the Roy G. Biv Program to support and care for LGBTQ youth, including those seeking gender-affirming treatment up to age 25 years. The interdisciplinary team serves the mental health, nutritional and medical needs for all LGBTQ youth, including those moving toward gender affirmation. Gender-affirming treatment includes pausing puberty, managing gender-affirming hormones, and helping patients find surgeons who perform fertility preservation and gender-affirming surgeries. Mental health services include assessment, individual and family therapy as needed. Support groups for transgender teens ages 13-18 and their parents are also hosted at OU Children's by the team.

Contact Name: Shauna M. Lawlis, M.D., Assistant Professor of Pediatrics
Contact Email: shauna-lawlis@ouhsc.edu
Contact Phone: 405-271-6208

OREGON

Facility Name: **The Doernbecher Gender Clinic**
Healthcare Facility: Oregon Health and Science University
Address: 3181 SW Sam Jackson Park Rd., Portland, OR 97239 United States
Website: http://www.ohsu.edu/transhealth

Description: The Doernbecher Gender Clinic at OHSU is designed to provide a safe and inclusive environment for delivering education and medical care options to transgender and gender-diverse youth and their families. It functions under the umbrella of the OHSU Transgender Health Program (THP), serving transgender and gender non-conforming communities of all ages. The clinic provides pediatric, adolescent, and young adult patients and offers puberty blockers and hormone therapy. As a service of the THP, the clinic also works collaboratively with the full complement of gender-affirming services by referring to social work, psychology, psychiatry, family medicine, plastic surgery, urology, gynecology, reproductive endocrinology, and dermatology. Patient/family education, care navigation, and care coordination are also available through the THP.

Contact Name: Amy Penkin, LCSW Program Supervisor

Contact Email: transhealth@ohsu.edu
Contact Phone: 503-494-7970

Facility Name: **T- Clinic Providing Excellence in Multidisciplinary Care to Transgender and Gender Expansive Youth**
Healthcare Facility: Randall Children's Clinic
Address: 501 N Graham St, Portland, OR 97227
Website: https://tinyurl.com/26dtc6et

Description: The Randall Children's Hospital T Clinic offers medical and mental health care for transgender and gender-expansive youth. We have 2 Pediatric Endocrinologists, Dr. Karin Selva, and Dr. Maya Hunter, who provide medical and hormonal treatment. Our mental health services include a gender-affirming evaluation by Dr. Laura Edwards Leeper, as well as. ongoing therapy and psychiatric medical management if needed by Valerie Tobin PPNP. Our Nurse, Connie, is an expert in care coordination, education, and injection education for our patients and families. The T clinic works with several area support networks to facilitate wrap-around care in schools, homes, and community. We all work as a team together to help our patients and families along their gender journey in an individualized approach.

Contact Name: Connie Earnest-Ritchey, RN
Contact Email: cearnest@lhs.org
Contact Phone: 503-413-1619

PENNSYLVANIA
Facility Name: **Gender and Sexuality Development Clinic**
Healthcare Facility: The Children's Hospital of Philadelphia
Address: 34th St and Civic Center Blvd, Philadelphia, PA 19104
Website: http://www.chop.edu/service/adolescent-medicine/home.html

Description: The Children's Hospital of Philadelphia (CHOP) Gender and Sexuality Development Clinic serves gender-variant, gender nonconforming, and/or transgender children and youth through age 21. CHOP's team provides care in psychology, endocrinology, and adolescent medicine and has connections with and access to psychiatrists in the CHOP and University of Pennsylvania Health Systems. CHOP offers access to hormones and puberty blockers and provides assessments and short-term in-house individual therapy and referrals to longer-term therapy, and provides parent support and psychoeducation. The multidisciplinary team also offers consultation and training about gender-variant children and adolescents to local pediatric health care providers and other youth-serving professionals.

Contact Name: Linda A. Hawkins, Ph.D., LPC, Co-Director and Nadia Dowshen, M.D., Medical Director
Contact Email: hawkins@email.chop.edu
Contact Phone: 215-280-7128

Facility Name: **Pediatric and Adolescent Comprehensive Transgender Services "PACTS"**
Healthcare Facility: Mazzoni Center
Address: 809 Locust Street, Philadelphia, PA 19107
Website: http://www.mazzonicenter.org/PACTS

Description: Mazzoni Center's PACTS program is Philadelphia's only community-based and multi-disciplinary program of its kind. Mazzoni Center staff are experts in providing transgender-specific care and have years of experience working with transgender-identified individuals and their loved ones. The PACTS team consists of affirming and competent medical providers, licensed social workers, therapists, attorneys, and RNs. Collaboration between our care team and the patient and family seeking care involves assessing knowledge, educating the patient and family on treatment options, and offering ongoing support around issues surrounding the social, legal, and medical transition process. Mazzoni is a non-profit agency committed to ensuring that families have access to quality care. We accept most health insurance plans and offer a sliding scale, making often unattainable care possible for many.

Contact Name: L. Elaine Dutton, LSW Trans* Clinical Services Coordinator
Contact Email: edutton@mazzonicenter.org
Contact Phone: 215-563-0658

Facility Name: **Gender and Sexual Development Program**
Healthcare Facility: Children's Hospital of Pittsburgh of UPMC
Address: 3420 Fifth Ave. Pittsburgh, PA 15213
Website: Adolescent Medicine: http://www.chp.edu/CHP/am
        Endocrinology: http://www.chp.edu/CHP/endocrinology

Description: The Gender and Sexual Development Program of Children's Hospital of Pittsburgh of UPMC serves gay, lesbian, bisexual, transgender, questioning, intersexed, and ally (GLBTQIA) and gender-fluid children and youth up to age 26 years, as well as anyone with questions about or who needs support regarding gender and sexual development. The interdisciplinary team includes specialists in endocrinology, behavioral health, and adolescent medicine who provide individualized care, including diagnostics, puberty blockers/hormone treatment, psychiatric evaluation, and transition to adult care. The team offers education related to gender, sexual development, and the social aspects of transition. Social work support, counseling, and care coordination through a network of community partners are also available.

Contact Name: Joanne Goodall, CRNP (Family Practice), Center for Adolescent and Young Adult Health
Contact Phone: 412-692-6677 (Ask specifically for "gender care" visit to ensure adequate time and resources can be coordinated).

RHODE ISLAND
Facility Name: **Health Care for Gender and Sexually Diverse Individuals**
Healthcare Facility
Hasbro Children's Hospital (Pediatric Division of Rhode Island Hospital)
Address: 593 Eddy Street, Providence, RI 02903
Website: http://www.hasbrochildrenshospital.org

Description: Warren Alpert School of Medicine at Brown University and Hasbro Children's and Rhode Island Hospitals offer specialty and primary care health services to all gender diverse and gender-nonconforming individuals from early childhood through maturity. The program operates out of adolescent medicine and medicine-pediatrics clinics in the Providence, RI area and serves patients in New England and the east coast. The team, using a consent-based model of care, provides gender-affirming hormones, puberty blockers, referrals for surgery, and general medical follow-up. The team can also work with the patient's local primary care doctor to coordinate care. The team offers other sex-positive health services, including sexually transmitted infection (STI) testing, family planning, and other sexuality concerns.

Contact Name: Michelle Forcier, M.D., MPH, Associate Professor Pediatrics
Contact Email: mforcier@lifespan.org
Contact Phone: 401-444-5980 Adolescent young adult medicine at (Jessica)

SOUTH CAROLINA

Facility Name: **Division of Pediatric Endocrinology and Diabetes**
Healthcare Facility: MUSC Children's Hospital
Address: 169 Ashley Avenue, Charleston, SC 29425
Website: http://www.musckids.org/pediatrics/divisions/endocrinology

Description: The Division of Pediatric Endocrinology and Diabetes provides services to pediatric patients (ages 0 to 17 years) with gender dysphoria. The team includes in-house care in endocrinology and has a dedicated social worker; the team can refer to community partners in psychology and psychiatry. The team can provide puberty blockers and hormones and can make referrals to surgeons. Mental health services include referrals to community partners for assessments and individual therapy.

Contact Name: Deborah Bowlby, M.D.; Division Chief
Contact Email: bowlbyd@musc.edu
Contact Phone: 843-792-6807

TENNESSEE

Facility Name: **Vanderbilt Program for LGBTI Health**
Healthcare Facility: Vanderbilt University Medical Center
Address: 1301 Medical Center Drive, Nashville, TN 37232
Website: http://www.vanderbilthealth.com

Description: The Program for LGBTI Health at Vanderbilt University Medical Center serves patients with gender dysphoria of all ages. The team provides care in psychology, psychiatry, endocrinology, urology, and plastic surgery. The team can provide puberty blockers, hormones, and breast surgery. Mental health services include individual therapy, assessments, therapy specific to medical transition, and referrals to support groups for children and adolescents with gender dysphoria, their parents, and their siblings.

Contact Name: Jesse M. Ehrenfeld, M.D. MPH - Director, Vanderbilt Program for LGBTI Health
Contact Email: lgbti.health@vanderbilt.edu
Contact Phone: 615-936-3879

VERMONT

Facility Name: **Transgender Youth Program**
Healthcare Facility: UVM Medical Center
Address: Main Campus, 111 Colchester Avenue, Burlington, Vermont 05401
Website: https://tinyurl.com/fbvrwkc3

Description: The Transgender Youth Program at the UVM Children's Hospital strives to provide gender-variant and transgender children and their families with comprehensive education and resources about available options. Ages of patients for whom we provide services: up to 18 years old.

Contact Name: Dr. Gibson
Contact Email: Erica.Gibson@uvmhealth.org
Contact Phone: (802) 847-3811

WASHINGTON

Facility Name: **Seattle Children's Gender Clinic**
Healthcare Facility: Seattle Children's Hospital
Address: 4800 Sand Point Way NE, Seattle, WA 98105
Website: http://www.seattlechildrens.org/clinics-programs/gender-clinic/

Description: Seattle Children's Gender Clinic is a multidisciplinary clinic that provides care for transgender and gender-nonconforming youth up to age 21. Our team members include adolescent medicine specialists, endocrinologists, psychologists, and mental health therapists, social workers, nurses, and medical assistants. Services available include mental health support, readiness assessment, puberty blockers, cross-sex hormones, and management of other related issues, including menstrual suppression and acne. We base our treatments on the most current research and tailor treatment to each patient and family based on the patient's age, stage of puberty, desired future treatments, support systems, and any health problems.

Contact Name: Lara Hayden, MSW LICSW, Program Manager and Care Navigator
Contact Email: lara.hayden@seattlechildrens.org
Contact Phone: 206-987-8319

Facility Name: **Pediatric Gender Health Program**
Healthcare Facility: Mary Bridge Children's
Address: 311 S L St, Tacoma, WA 98407
Website: https://tinyurl.com/ysj55db2

Description: The Mary Bridge Children's Gender Health Clinic will provide gender-affirming care for people up to age 18. Our services are for children and adolescents who identify as transgender, gender non-conforming, non-binary, gender-neutral, and all other honored gender-diverse identities.

Our priority is to ensure a safe space for your child or adolescent to receive gender-affirming care tailored to their needs and those of your family. With our family-centered care philosophy, you can count on us to work with you to provide the highest quality, sensitive, and specialized healthcare.

Our multidisciplinary team of M.D.s, Ph.Ds, and LICWs provides mental health services through our social worker and psychology as well as pubertal blockers and hormones.

Contact Name: Barbara Thompson, M.D.
Contact Email: brthompson@multicare.org
Contact Phone: (253) 792-6630

WASHINGTON, D.C.

Facility Name: **Gender and Sexuality Development Programs**

Healthcare Facility: Children's National Medical Center
Address: 111 Michigan Avenue, NW Washington, DC 20010
Website: https://tinyurl.com/3ev6z42y

Description: The Gender and Sexuality Psychosocial Programs team provides care for transgender and gender-nonconforming children and adolescents up to age 21 years. The team offers care in psychology, psychiatry, pediatric gynecology, endocrinology, pediatric urology, and genetics and includes disorders of sexual development multidisciplinary team. The team can provide puberty blockers, hormone therapy, and hysterectomies and can make referrals for surgery. Mental health services include group therapy, assessments, and parent support groups.

Contact Name: Martine Solages, M.D., Psychiatrist
Contact Email: gender@childrensnational.org
Contact Phone: 202-476-5158

WISCONSIN

Facility Name: **Pediatric Adolescent Transgender Health Clinic**
Healthcare Facility: American Family Children's Hospital, UW Health
Address: 1675 Highland Ave. Madison, WI 53792
Website: http://www.uwhealthkids.org/path

Description: The Pediatric Adolescent Transgender Health Clinic sees adolescents across the gender spectrum (toddlers through young adults, primarily ten years and older). The team provides care in adolescent medicine, endocrinology, reproductive endocrinology, and psychology. This clinic can provide hormones and puberty blockers and can make referrals for surgery. Mental health services include assessments and referrals for individual therapy and local support groups.

Contact Name: Jennifer Rehm, M.D., and Betsy Bazur-Leidy, Nurse Coordinator
Contact Email: jrehm@wisc.edu
Contact Phone: 608-263-9059

Facility Name: **Gender Health Clinic**
Healthcare Facility: Children's Hospital of Wisconsin
Address: 9000 West Wisconsin Avenue, Milwaukee, WI 53226
Website: http://www.chw.org

Description: The Gender Health Clinic at Children's Hospital of Wisconsin is a multidisciplinary clinic focused on children and youth seeking assistance with gender identity development and transition concerns. Our medical providers prescribe puberty-suppressing hormone therapy and gender-affirming hormone therapy when appropriate. Our psychologist provides consultation to clinic patients and families designed to help support them and collaborate with other mental health providers. She may meet with patients outside of the clinic to provide a more comprehensive psychological evaluation of gender concerns. We have a clinic nurse and social worker who support patients with their treatment plans and goals.

Contact Name: Loretta L Bush, APNP
Contact Email: lbush@mcw.edu
Contact Phone: 414-266-6750

LEGAL ASPECTS

This section discusses the legal landscape for trans persons under federal government legislation, followed by separate sections for each state. Provisions that protect the rights of other members of the LGBTQ+ community are beyond the scope of this work, although aspects of sexual orientation are discussed in situations where sexual orientation is lumped together with gender identity. There are many different legal issues discussed, some of which include:

- Health Care Benefits,
- Employment Discrimination,
- Public Accommodations,
- Public Transportation,
- Discrimination in Housing,
- Educational Institutions,
- Change of Name and Birth Certificate Issues,
- Driver's Licenses/I.D. Cards,
- Sports and Sporting Events,
- Law Enforcement, Jails, and Prisons,
- And others.

Federal or national issues also include:

- Federal Employment Discrimination,
- Military Service (including the National Guard),
- Passports,
- Transportation Security Administration,
- Discrimination by Federal Law Enforcement Agencies,
- Federal benefits from the Social Security Administration, Department of Health and Human Services, Veteran's Administration,
- Issuance of government contracts,
- Memberships in federally chartered organizations.

FEDERAL/NATIONAL

Constitutional Provisions

There are many laws and constitutional provisions that protect the LGBTQ+ community from discrimination. First is the United States Constitution. Specifically, the Fourteenth Amendment to the U.S. Constitution states:

Section 1.

All persons born or naturalized in the United States, and subject to the jurisdiction thereof, are citizens of the United States and of the state wherein they reside. No state shall make or enforce any law which shall abridge the privileges or immunities of citizens of the United States; nor shall any state deprive any person of life, liberty, or property, without due process of law; nor deny to any person within its jurisdiction the equal protection of the laws.

Overview

A civil right is an enforceable right or privilege, which if interfered with by another gives rise to an action for injury.

Discrimination occurs when the civil rights of an individual are denied or interfered with because of the individual's membership in a particular group or class. Various jurisdictions have enacted statutes to prevent discrimination based on a person's race, sex, religion, age, previous condition of servitude, physical limitation, national origin, and in some instances sexual orientation and gender identity.

Civil Rights and Civil Liberties

People often confuse civil rights and civil liberties. Civil rights refer to legal provisions that stem from notions of equality. Civil rights are not in the Bill of Rights; they deal with legal protections. For example, the right to vote is a civil right. A civil liberty, on the other hand, refers to personal freedoms protected by the Bill of Rights. For example, the First Amendment's right to free speech is a civil liberty.[254]

In the Executive Summary of their landmark study, "Injustice at Every Turn: A Report of the National Transgender Discrimination Survey," Grant et al. studied the ways in which transgender persons are discriminated against.

This study brings to light what is both patently obvious and far too often dismissed from the human rights agenda. Transgender and gender non-conforming people face injustice at every turn: in childhood homes, in school systems that promise to shelter and educate, in harsh and exclusionary workplaces, at the grocery store, the hotel front desk, in doctors' offices and emergency rooms, before judges and at the hands of landlords, police officers, health care workers, and other service providers.[255]

Key findings from the study include:

1. Discrimination was pervasive throughout the entire sample, yet **the combination of anti-transgender bias and persistent, structural racism was especially devastating**. People of color in general fare worse than White participants across the board, with African American transgender respondents faring worse than all others in many areas examined.

2. Respondents **lived in extreme poverty**. Our sample was nearly four times more likely to have a household income of less than $10,000/year compared to the general population.

3. A staggering **41% of respondents reported attempting suicide** compared to 1.6% of the general population, with rates rising for those who lost a job due to bias (55%), were harassed/bullied in school (51%), had low household income, or were the victim of physical assault (61%) or sexual assault (64%). [emphasis in original]

And in the educational setting, the study found that:

1. Those who expressed a transgender identity or gender non-conformity while in grades K-12 reported **alarming rates of harassment (78%), physical assault (35%) and sexual violence (12%)**; harassment was so severe that it led to **almost one-sixth (15%) to leave a school** in K-12 settings or in higher education.

2. Respondents who have been **harassed and abused by teachers** in K-12 settings showed dramatically worse health and other outcomes than those who did not experience such abuse. Peer harassment and abuse also had highly damaging effects. [emphasis in original]

Grant et al. found similar results in employment discrimination and economic insecurity, housing discrimination and homelessness, discrimination in public accommodations, barriers to receiving updated documents, abuse by police and in prison, and discrimination in health care and poor health outcomes.[256]

Laws Enacted by Congress

Title VII of the Civil Rights Act of 1964, as Amended, Discrimination in Employment

Title VII of the Civil Rights Act of 1964, as amended (Pub. L. 88-352) (42 U.S.C. §2000e), prohibits discrimination in employment because of one's race, color, religion, sex, or national origin.[257]

For many years, Federal District Courts held that Title VII did not protect trans people (or homosexual people) whose employers fired them. Courts defined the word "sex" very narrowly, claiming that the term "sex" specifically meant one's "biological sex" as assigned at birth. But since the Supreme Court's ruling in *Obergefell v. Hodges*, 576 U.S. 644 (2015),[258] Federal Courts began to recognize that "sex" encompasses more than just one's anatomy. And in this case, which involved same-sex marriage, the Court ruled that the Fourteenth Amendment *does* protect same-sex couples' right to marry just as it protects the rights of cisgender couples.

What follows is an exceptionally long quote from the Obergefell decision. The intent of including it here is to demonstrate the Court's progression in recent cases involving discrimination resulting from or based on "sex." This decision was crucial because it sets the stage for decisions rendered in succeeding years.

The Supreme Court, in *Obergefell*, with Justice Kennedy writing for the majority, said:

> (a) Before turning to the governing principles and precedents, it is appropriate to note the history of the subject now before the Court.[259]
>
>> (1) The history of marriage as a union between two persons of the opposite sex marks the beginning of these cases. To the respondents, it would demean a timeless institution if marriage were extended to same-sex couples. But the petitioners, far from seeking to devalue marriage, seek it for themselves because of their respect—and need—for its privileges and responsibilities, as illustrated by the petitioners' own experiences.[260]
>>
>> (2) The history of marriage is one of both continuity and change. Changes, such as the decline of arranged marriages and the abandonment of the law of coverture, have worked deep transformations in the structure of marriage, affecting aspects of marriage once viewed as essential. These new insights have strengthened, not weakened, the institution. Changed understandings of marriage are characteristic of a Nation where new dimensions of freedom become apparent to new generations.
>>
>> This dynamic can be seen in the Nation's experience with gay and lesbian rights. Well into the 20th century, many States condemned same-sex intimacy as

immoral, and homosexuality was treated as an illness. Later in the century, cultural and political developments allowed same-sex couples to lead more open and public lives. Extensive public and private dialogue followed, along with shifts in public attitudes. Questions about the legal treatment of gays and lesbians soon reached the courts, where they could be discussed in the formal discourse of the law. In 2003, this Court overruled its 1986 decision in *Bowers* v. *Hardwick*, 478 U.S. 186, which upheld a Georgia law that criminalized certain homosexual acts, concluding laws making same-sex intimacy a crime "demea[n] the lives of homosexual persons." *Lawrence* v. *Texas*, 539 U. S. 558, 575 (2003). In 2012, the federal Defense of Marriage Act was also struck down. *United States* v. *Windsor*, 570 U.S. ___744 (2012). Numerous same-sex marriage cases reaching the federal courts and state supreme courts have added to the dialogue.[261]

(b) The Fourteenth Amendment requires a State to license a marriage between two people of the same sex.[262]

(1) The fundamental liberties protected by the Fourteenth Amendment's Due Process Clause extend to certain personal choices central to individual dignity and autonomy, including intimate choices defining personal identity and beliefs. See, *e.g., Eisenstadt* v. *Baird*, 405 U.S. 438, 453 (1972); *Griswold* v. *Connecticut*, 381 U.S. 479, 484–486 (1965). Courts must exercise reasoned judgment in identifying interests of the person so fundamental that the State must accord them its respect. History and tradition guide and discipline the inquiry but do not set its outer boundaries. When new insight reveals discord between the Constitution's central protections and a received legal stricture, a claim to liberty must be addressed.

Applying these tenets, the Court has long held the right to marry is protected by the Constitution. For example, *Loving* v. *Virginia*, 388 U.S. 1, 12 (1967), invalidated bans on interracial unions, and *Turner* v. *Safley*, 482 U.S. 78, 95 (1987), held that prisoners could not be denied the right to marry. To be sure, these cases presumed a relationship involving opposite-sex partners, as did *Baker* v. *Nelson*, 409 U.S. 810 (1972), a one-line summary decision issued in 1972, holding that the exclusion of same-sex couples from marriage did not present a substantial federal question. But other, more instructive precedents have expressed broader principles. See, *e.g., Lawrence, supra,* at 574. In assessing whether the force and rationale of its cases apply to same-sex couples, the Court must respect the basic reasons why the right to marry has been long protected. See, *e.g., Eisenstadt, supra,* at 453–454. This analysis compels the conclusion that same-sex couples may exercise the right to marry.[263]

(2) Four principles and traditions demonstrate that the reasons marriage is fundamental under the Constitution apply with equal force to same-sex couples. The first premise of this Court's relevant precedents is that the right to personal choice regarding marriage is inherent in the concept of individual autonomy. This abiding connection between marriage and liberty is why *Loving* invalidated

interracial marriage bans under the Due Process Clause. See 388 U.S., at 12. Decisions about marriage are among the most intimate that an individual can make. See *Lawrence, supra*, at 574. This is true for all persons, whatever their sexual orientation.

A second principle in this Court's jurisprudence is that the right to marry is fundamental because it supports a two-person union unlike any other in its importance to the committed individuals. The intimate association protected by this right was central to *Griswold* v. *Connecticut*, which held the Constitution protects the right of married couples to use contraception, 381 U.S., at 485, and was acknowledged in *Turner, supra,* at 95. Same-sex couples have the same right as opposite-sex couples to enjoy intimate association, a right extending beyond mere freedom from laws making same-sex intimacy a criminal offense. See *Lawrence, supra*, at 567.

A third basis for protecting the right to marry is that it safeguards children and families and thus draws meaning from related rights of childrearing, procreation, and education. See, *e.g., Pierce* v. *Society of Sisters*, 268 U.S. 510 (1925). Without the recognition, stability, and predictability marriage offers, children suffer the stigma of knowing their families are somehow lesser. They also suffer the significant material costs of being raised by unmarried parents, relegated to a more difficult and uncertain family life. The marriage laws at issue thus harm and humiliate the children of same-sex couples. See *Windsor, supra,* at ___. This does not mean that the right to marry is less meaningful for those who do not or cannot have children. Precedent protects the right of a married couple not to procreate, so the right to marry cannot be conditioned on the capacity or commitment to procreate.

Finally, this Court's cases and the Nation's traditions make clear that marriage is a keystone of the Nation's social order. See *Maynard* v. *Hill*, 125 U.S. 190, 211 (1888). States have contributed to the fundamental character of marriage by placing it at the center of many facets of the legal and social order. There is no difference between same- and opposite-sex couples with respect to this principle, yet same-sex couples are denied the constellation of benefits that the States have linked to marriage and are consigned to an instability many opposite-sex couples would find intolerable. It is demeaning to lock same-sex couples out of a central institution of the Nation's society, for they too may aspire to the transcendent purposes of marriage.

The limitation of marriage to opposite-sex couples may long have seemed natural and just, but its inconsistency with the central meaning of the fundamental right to marry is now manifest.[264]

(3) The right of same-sex couples to marry is also derived from the Fourteenth Amendment's guarantee of equal protection. The Due Process Clause and the Equal Protection Clause are connected in a profound way. Rights implicit in liberty and rights secured by equal protection may rest on different precepts and are not always co-extensive, yet each may be instructive as to the meaning and reach of the other. This dynamic is reflected in *Loving,* where the Court invoked

both the Equal Protection Clause and the Due Process Clause; and in *Zablocki v. Redhail*, 434 U.S. 374 (1978), where the Court invalidated a law barring fathers delinquent on child-support payments from marrying. Indeed, recognizing that new insights and societal understandings can reveal unjustified inequality within fundamental institutions that once passed unnoticed and unchallenged, this Court has invoked equal protection principles to invalidate laws imposing sex-based inequality on marriage, see, *e.g., Kirchberg* v. *Feenstra*, 450 U.S. 455, 460–461 (1981), and confirmed the relation between liberty and equality, see, *e.g., M. L. B.* v. *S. L. J.*, 519 U. S. 102, 120–121 (1996).

The Court has acknowledged the interlocking nature of these constitutional safeguards in the context of the legal treatment of gays and lesbians. See *Lawrence*, 539 U.S., at 575. This dynamic also applies to same-sex marriage. The challenged laws burden the liberty of same-sex couples, and they abridge central precepts of equality. The marriage laws at issue are in essence unequal: Same-sex couples are denied benefits afforded opposite-sex couples and are barred from exercising a fundamental right. Especially against a long history of disapproval of their relationships, this denial works a grave and continuing harm, serving to disrespect and subordinate gays and lesbians.[265]

(4) The right to marry is a fundamental right inherent in the liberty of the person, and under the Due Process and Equal Protection Clauses of the Fourteenth Amendment couples of the same sex may not be deprived of that right and that liberty. Same-sex couples may exercise the fundamental right to marry. *Baker* v. *Nelson* is overruled. The State laws challenged by the petitioners in these cases are held invalid to the extent they exclude same-sex couples from civil marriage on the same terms and conditions as opposite-sex couples.[266]

(5) There may be an initial inclination to await further legislation, litigation, and debate, but referenda, legislative debates, and grassroots campaigns; studies and other writings; and extensive litigation in state and Federal courts have led to an enhanced understanding of the issue. While the Constitution contemplates that democracy is the appropriate process for change, individuals who are harmed need not await legislative action before asserting a fundamental right. *Bowers,* in effect, upheld state action that denied gays and lesbians a fundamental right. Though it was eventually repudiated, men and women suffered pain and humiliation in the interim, and the effects of these injuries no doubt lingered long after *Bowers* was overruled. A ruling against same-sex couples would have the same effect and would be unjustified under the Fourteenth Amendment. The petitioners' stories show the urgency of the issue they present to the Court, which has a duty to address these claims and answer these questions. Respondents' argument that allowing same-sex couples to wed will harm marriage as an institution rests on a counterintuitive view of opposite-sex couples' decisions about marriage and parenthood. Finally, the First Amendment ensures that religions, those who adhere to religious doctrines, and others have protection as they seek to teach the principles that are so fulfilling and so central to their lives and faiths.[267]

So, with this foundation, laid by the *Obergefell* decision, the Supreme Court was poised to rule on Title VII protections against discrimination in employment on the basis of sex.

Amendments to Title VII of the Civil Rights Act of 1964 prohibit discrimination because of one's sex and include that prohibition of discrimination because an applicant or an employee is gay, or trans. In his opinion, in *Bostock v. Clayton County GA*, 590 U.S. ____ (2020), 140 S. Ct. 1731, 1753 (2020), Justice Neil Gorsuch stated unequivocally:[268]

> An employer who fires an individual merely for being gay or transgender violates Title VII.[269]
>
> (a) Title VII makes it "unlawful… for an employer to fail or refuse to hire or to discharge any individual, or otherwise to discriminate against any individual because of such individual's race, color, religion, sex, or national origin." 42 U.S.C.. §2000e–2(a)(1). The straightforward application of Title VII's terms interpreted in accord with their ordinary public meaning at the time of their enactment resolves these cases.[270]
>
> > (1) The parties concede that the term "sex" in 1964 referred to the biological distinctions between male and female. And "the ordinary meaning of 'because of' is 'by reason of' or 'on account of,'" *University of Tex. Southwestern Medical Center* v. *Nassar,* 570 U.S. 338, 350 [2013]. That term incorporates the but-for causation standard, *id.,* at 346, 360, which, for Title VII, means that a defendant cannot avoid liability just by citing some *other* factor that contributed to its challenged employment action. The term "discriminate" meant "[t]o make a difference in treatment or favor (of one as compared with others)." Webster's New International Dictionary 745. In so-called "disparate treatment" cases, this Court has held that the difference in treatment based on sex must be intentional. See, *e.g.,* *Watson* v. *Fort Worth Bank and Trust*, 487 U. S. 977, 986 [1988]. And the statute's repeated use of the term "individual" means that the focus is on "[a] particular being as distinguished from a class." Webster's New International Dictionary, at 1267.[271]
> >
> > (2) These terms generate the following rule: An employer violates Title VII when it intentionally fires an individual employee based in part on sex. It makes no difference if other factors besides the plaintiff's sex contributed to the decision or that the employer treated women as a group the same when compared to men as a group. A statutory violation occurs if an employer intentionally relies in part on an individual employee's sex when deciding to discharge the employee. Because discrimination on the basis of homosexuality or transgender status requires an employer to intentionally treat individual employees differently because of their sex, an employer who intentionally penalizes an employee for being homosexual or transgender also violates Title VII. There is no escaping the role intent plays: Just as sex is necessarily a but-for cause when an employer discriminates against homosexual or transgender employees, an employer who discriminates on these grounds inescapably intends to rely on sex in its decisionmaking.[272]

In *Price Waterhouse v. Hopkins,* 490 U.S. 228 (1989), wherein the Court, in section II(C), discussed how sex stereotyping applies to gender in general and transgender specifically, the Court said this about gender stereotyping:[273]

> An employer who objects to aggressiveness in women but whose positions require this trait places women in an intolerable and impermissible catch 22: out of a job if they behave aggressively and out of a job if they do not. Title VII lifts women out of this bind.
>
> Remarks at work that are based on sex stereotypes do not inevitably prove that gender played a part in a particular employment decision. The plaintiff must show that the employer actually relied on her gender in making its decision. In making this showing, stereotyped remarks can certainly be *evidence* that gender played a part. In any event, the stereotyping in this case did not simply consist of stray remarks. On the contrary, Hopkins proved that Price Waterhouse invited partners to submit comments; that some of the comments stemmed from sex stereotypes; that an important part of the Policy Board's decision on Hopkins was an assessment of the submitted comments; and that Price Waterhouse in no way disclaimed reliance on the sex-linked evaluations. This is not, as Price Waterhouse suggests, "discrimination in the air"; rather, it is, as Hopkins puts it, "discrimination brought to ground and visited upon" an employee.

Equal Employment Opportunity Commission (EEOC)

The Equal Employment Opportunity Commission (EEOC) is the Federal agency responsible for implementing and enforcing regulations for Title VII of the Civil Rights Act.[274]

The laws enforced by EEOC make it unlawful for Federal agencies to discriminate against employees and job applicants based on race, color, religion, sex, national origin, disability, or age. A person who files a complaint or participates in an investigation of an EEOC complaint or opposes an employment practice made illegal under any of the laws that EEOC enforces is protected from retaliation. As a result, employers cannot refuse to hire or treat the trans person any differently than other employees "but for" one's sex, which includes homosexual and transgender people.

> Under the laws enforced by EEOC, it is illegal to discriminate against someone (applicant or employee) because of that person's race, color, religion, sex (including gender identity, sexual orientation, and pregnancy), national origin, age (40 or older), disability or genetic information. It is also illegal to retaliate against a person because he or she complained about discrimination, filed a charge of discrimination, or participated in an employment discrimination investigation or lawsuit.
>
> The law forbids discrimination in every aspect of employment.[275]

The EEOC has a formal complaint process for filing a charge of discrimination in employment. One can file the complaint oneself or through an attorney. Filing a complaint through an attorney is recommended because the complaint process sets the stage for everything that happens after that.

Title VI of the Civil Rights Action of 1964

Title VI of the Civil Rights Act of 1964 protects people from discrimination based on race, color, and national origin in programs and activities receiving federal financial assistance. The Federal Transit Administration (FTA) works to ensure nondiscriminatory transportation to support and enhance all Americans' social and economic quality of life. The FTA Office of Civil Rights monitors FTA recipients' Title VI programs and ensures compliance with Title VI requirements.[276]

While Title VI does not explicitly prohibit discrimination based on sex, the FTA Office of Civil Rights maintains that discrimination because of sex in Federal Transit Programs is illegal. Other federal statutes also prohibit discrimination based on sex.

The Affordable Care Act (ACA)

Section 1557 of the Patient Protection and Affordable Care Act (42 U.S.C. §18116) ("ACA") and its implementing regulations provide that an individual shall not be excluded from participation in, be denied the benefits of, or be subjected to discrimination on the grounds prohibited under Title VI of the Civil Rights Act of 1964, 42 U.S.C. §2000d et seq. (race, color, national origin), Title IX of the Education Amendments of 1972, 20 U.S.C.. §1681 et seq. (sex), the Age Discrimination Act of 1975, 42 U.S.C. §6101 et seq. (age), or Section 504 of the Rehabilitation Act of 1973, 29 U.S.C. §794 (disability), under any health program or activity, any part of which is receiving federal financial assistance; any program or activity administered by the Department under Title I of the Act; or any program or activity administered by any entity established under such Title. The Office for Civil Rights (OCR) at the U.S. Department of Health and Human Services has enforcement authority with respect to health programs and activities that receive federal financial assistance from the Department of Health and Human Services (HHS) or are administered by HHS or any entity established under Title I of the Affordable Care Act. OCR is responsible for enforcing regulations issued under Section 1557 of the Affordable Care Act, protecting the civil rights of individuals who access or seek to access covered health programs or activities. Section 1557 prohibits discrimination on the basis of race, color, national origin, sex (including sexual orientation and gender identity), age, or disability in covered health programs or activities.[277]

Under the ACA, a medical provider, clinic, hospital, or other medical facility cannot discriminate on the basis of sex in the provision of medical services. This includes long-term health care facilities, such as nursing homes, assisted living facilities, and rehabilitation centers.

Title IX of the Education Amendments of 1972, as amended (20 U.S.C. §1681, et. seq.)

Title IX, Section 1681(a), prohibits discrimination "on the basis of sex, be excluded from participation in, be denied the benefits of, or be subjected to discrimination under any education program or activity receiving Federal financial assistance."[278]

Title IX cases differ from Title VII cases only insofar as Title IX relates to the educational setting versus the employment setting covered by Title VII. Both prohibit discrimination based on or because of sex.

In one of the first court cases involving Title IX, the U.S. Court of Appeals for the Eighth Circuit, in *Torbin H. Brenden, et al., v. Independent School District*,[279] the Court held:

> That where high schools attended by plaintiffs, two female students, provided teams for males in noncontact sports of tennis and cross-country skiing and running but did not provide such teams for females and where plaintiffs were qualified to compete with boys in such sports, application of rule prohibiting females from participating in the boys' interscholastic athletic program as to plaintiffs was arbitrary and unreasonable and in violation of equal protection clause of Fourteenth Amendment.[280]

Title IX cases have primarily involved trans students' use of bathrooms in secondary and post-secondary schools and institutions of higher learning. In *Dodds v. U.S. Department of Education*, 845 F. 3d 217, 6th Circuit (2016), the Appellate Court wrote:

We are not convinced that Highland has made its required showing of a likelihood of success on appeal. Under settled law in this Circuit, gender nonconformity, as defined in *Smith v. City of Salem,* is an individual's "fail[ure] to act and/or identify with his or her gender... Sex stereotyping based on a person's gender non-conforming behavior is impermissible discrimination." 378 F.3d 566, 575 (**6th Cir. 2004**); *see also Glenn v. Brumby,* 663 F.3d 1312, 1316 (**11th Cir. 2011)** ("A person is defined as transgender precisely because of the perception that his or her behavior transgresses gender stereotypes."); *G.G. ex rel. Grimm v. Gloucester County. School Bd.,* 822 F.3d 709, 729 (**4th Cir. 2016**) (Davis, J., concurring) ("[T]he weight of authority establishes that discrimination based on transgender status is already prohibited by the language of federal civil rights statutes, as interpreted by the Supreme Court.").[281]

See also *Smith v. City of Salem,* cited Id., 378 F.3d 566, **6th Circuit**, (2004) at pp. 571-574; *GG v. Gloucester County School Board,* 822 F.3d 709 (2016), **4th Circuit**; *Doe v. Boyertown, supra.,* 897 F.3d 518 (2018), **3rd Circuit**; *Evancho v. Pine-Richland School District,* et al., 237 F.Supp.3d 267 (2017) (USDC Western Dist. PA); *Johnston v. University of Pittsburgh,* 97 F.Supp.3d 657 (2015) (USDC Western Dist. PA) holding no Title IX violation; *Vandiver Elizabeth GLENN, f.k.a. Glenn Morrison, Plaintiff-Appellee, v. Sewell R. BRUMBY, Defendant-Appellant,* 663 F.3d 1312 (2011) **11th Circuit**; *Oncale v. Sundowner Offshore Services, Inc.,* 523 U.S. 75 (1998); *Michelle Nichols v. Azteca Restaurant Enterprises, Inc,* 256 F.3d 864 (2001) **9th Circuit**; *Finkle v. Howard County MD,* 12 F.Supp.3d 780 (USDC Dist. MD 2014); and *Joaquín CARCAÑO, et al., Plaintiffs, v. Patrick McCrory,* 203 F.Supp.3d 615 (USDC MD North Carolina 2016), which all involved cases (Title VII and Title IX) where plaintiffs had alleged sex stereotyping (homosexual, transgender) as the basis for discrimination because of sex. [emphasis here and in the quote above highlights the Circuits which have ruled that sex encompasses sexual orientation and gender identity]

On July 14, 2018, in *Parents for Privacy, et al. v. Dallas School District,* the U.S. District Court for the District of Oregon, Portland Division, 326 F.Supp.3d 1075 (USDC D.Or 2018) dismissed the case in which parents and students complained that Title IX of the Education Amendments of 1972 did not protect transgender students from using the school's bathrooms. The Parents appealed the case to the U.S. Court of Appeals for the Ninth Circuit on November 29, 2018. The ACLU of Oregon moved to intervene on behalf of Basic Rights Oregon. On February 12, 2020, the Court of Appeals ruled that the School District's policy of allowing transgender students to use the bathrooms that most closely match their gender identity does not violate Title IX, __ F.3d __ (2020). The parents then filed a Petition for a Writ of Certiorari in the U.S. Supreme Court to the United States Court of Appeals for the Ninth Circuit on November 13, 2017. On December 7, 2020, the Court denied the Petitioner's Petition for a Writ of Certiorari.

Transgender individuals have also been discriminated against in student sports activities. In *Hecox, et al., v. Little, et al.,* U.S. District Court, Case No. 1:20-cv-00184-DCN (Dist. Idaho 2020), the Court ruled that "the Court finds Plaintiffs are likely to succeed in establishing the Act is unconstitutional as currently written, it must issue a preliminary injunction at this time pending trial on the merits."[282] See also other cases from the 3rd, 4th, 6th, 7th, and 9th Circuits.[283]

A recent (2016-2020) trend, in which people who claim to have "deeply held religious beliefs," attempts to challenge anti-discrimination laws that prohibit discrimination against the LGBTQ+ community. The reasoning behind this claim is that their First Amendment rights to freedom of expression and freedom of speech are being violated because anti-discrimination laws prevent them and their children from bullying or confronting those who express different sexual orientations or gender identities.

In *Reynolds, et al. v. Talberg, et al.*, Case No. 1:18-cv-69 (USDC W.D. Mich. S. Dist. October 30, 2020):

> Citing their Christian faith, Plaintiffs contend the Challenged Policies force their children to disregard their sincerely held religious beliefs and to "affirm… alternative sexual lifestyles" or else face punishment (see Compl. ¶¶ 1, 37, ECF No.1). The crux of Plaintiffs' claim is that the Challenged Policies "promote and force the approval of alternate sexual lifestyles and behavior [in a manner] that infringes upon Plaintiffs' personal identity, autonomy, and their sincerely held religious beliefs and convictions and constitutional right to oppose such policies and freely speak out on such issues in accordance with their sincerely held religious beliefs.[284]

The parents, in this case, complained that their children were being forced to accept or affirm the so-called "alternative lifestyles" of other children who expressed a sexual orientation or gender identity different from that of their children. The School District had revised policies to indicate that the "guidance and counseling services of the district shall be available to any student and shall not discriminate against any student on the basis of sex, race, age, color, national origin, religion, sexual orientation, gender identity, gender expression, or disability."[285]

The Court held that the Plaintiffs lacked standing to sue, that the Court lacked jurisdiction over the case, and that the Plaintiffs had failed to state a claim upon which relief could be granted. See also *Morrison II v. Board of Education of Boyd County, Kentucky*, 419 F.Supp.2d 937 (USDC E.D. Kentucky (2006)), wherein a different District Court came to essentially the same conclusion, that parents have a right to educate and bring up their children in the manner they choose but cannot dictate to schools how the schools teach their children. Schools also have a right to establish anti-discrimination policies so long as they are directed toward ensuring the safety of children while they are at school. That safety includes educating children that bullying and harassment of other children will not be tolerated at school. The courts have also said that free exercise of one's "deeply held" religious beliefs does not include disrupting the educational process to express disapproval of other students' sexual orientation or gender identity.

So, it seems that several U.S. Court of Appeals Circuits (3rd Circuit, 4th Circuit, 6th Circuit, 7th Circuit, and 9th Circuit) have addressed Title IX cases involving transgender students and have ruled that Title IX's provisions that prohibit discrimination because of "sex," include prohibiting discrimination because of transgender status. One case, Parents for Privacy (cited above), is pending before the Supreme Court as of May 2021. The Hecox case (cited above), is currently pending before the 9th Circuit Court of Appeals. If those cases are decided before the publication of this book occurs, they will be included here. In *Gavin Grimm v. Gloucester County School Board*, 822 F.3d 709 (USCA 4th 2016), the U.S. Court of Appeals for the Fourth Circuit ruled that Title IX of the Education Amendments of 1972 prohibited discrimination based on sex in Grimm's use of the boy's restrooms at school. On June 28, 2021, the U.S. Supreme Court denied the Appellee's Petition for a Writ of Certiorari to the Fourth Circuit Court of Appeals. The denial of Certiorari means the decision of the Court of Appeals stands.

Additionally, Title IX regulations (Title 45 CFR §86.31) explicitly prohibit discrimination because of sex.

The Title IX regulation states that "except for provided elsewhere in this part, no person shall, on the basis of **sex**, be excluded from participation in, be denied the benefits of, or be subjected to discrimination under any academic, extracurricular, research, occupational training, or other education program or activity operated by a recipient which receives... Federal financial assistance...

(b) *Specific prohibitions.* Except as provided in this subpart, in providing any aid, benefit, or service to a student, a recipient shall not, on the basis of sex:

> (1) Treat one person differently from another in determining whether such person satisfies any requirement or condition for the provision of such aid, benefit, or service;
>
> (2) Provide different aid, benefits, or services or provide aid, benefits, or services in a different manner;
>
> (3) Deny any person any such aid, benefit, or service;
>
> (4) Subject any person to separate or different rules of behavior, sanctions, or other treatment;
>
> (5) Discriminate against any person in the application of any rules of appearance;
>
> (6) Apply any rule concerning the domicile or residence of a student or applicant, including eligibility for in-state fees and tuition;
>
> (7) Aid or perpetuate discrimination against any person by providing significant assistance to any agency, organization, or person which discriminates on the basis of sex in providing any aid, benefit or service to students or employees;
>
> (8) Otherwise limit any person in the enjoyment of any right, privilege, advantage, or opportunity. 45 C.F.R. § 86.31[286] [emphasis added]

Finally, on June 22, 2021, the U.S. Department of Education, through its Office of Civil Rights, issued its updated interpretation of Title IX of the Education Amendments of 1972, referencing the Supreme Court's decision in *Bostock*, by saying:

> Title IX Prohibits Discrimination Based on Sexual Orientation and Gender Identity. Consistent with the Supreme Court's ruling and analysis in *Bostock,* the Department interprets Title IX's prohibition on discrimination "on the basis of sex" to encompass discrimination on the basis of sexual orientation and gender identity. As was the case for the Court's Title VII analysis in *Bostock,* this interpretation flows from the statute's "plain terms."[287]
>
> Addressing discrimination based on sexual orientation and gender identity thus fits squarely within OCR's responsibility to enforce Title IX's prohibition on sex discrimination."[288]

See also the "Dear Educator" letter the Department of Education sent to schools dated June 23, 2021.[289]

As discussed earlier, state legislatures pushed by conservative Republicans have been enacting laws prohibiting transgender students' participation in interscholastic and intercollegiate sports. These laws now seem more in jeopardy than before the OCR interpretation was issued.

Fair Housing Act of 1968

The Fair Housing Act is administered by the United States Department of Housing and Urban Development (HUD). The Fair Housing Act prohibits housing discrimination based on race, color, national origin, religion, sex, familial status, and disability. A person who identifies as LGBTQ who has experienced (or is about to experience) discrimination under any of these bases may file a complaint with HUD. HUD is committed to investigating the Fair Housing Act violations against all individuals regardless of their sexual orientation or gender identity.

Examples:

The owner asks a transgender woman of her apartment building not to dress in women's clothing in the property's common areas. This may violate the Fair Housing Act's prohibition against sex discrimination, including discrimination based on non-conformity with gender stereotypes.

A gay man is evicted because his landlord believes he will infect other tenants with HIV/AIDS. This may violate the Fair Housing Act's prohibition against disability discrimination, which includes discrimination against people who have or are perceived to have HIV/AIDS.

About HUD's Equal Access Rules

On February 3, 2012, HUD issued the first of three rules to ensure fair and equal access to housing for all Americans, regardless of their sexual orientation, gender identity, nonconformance with gender stereotypes, or marital status. The first rule, "Equal Access to Housing in HUD Programs Regardless of Sexual Orientation or Gender Identity," required that a determination of eligibility for housing that is assisted by HUD or subject to a mortgage insured by the Federal Housing Administration shall be made following the eligibility requirements provided for such program by HUD. Such housing shall be made available without reference to actual or perceived sexual orientation, gender identity, or marital status. The rule also included a definition for sexual orientation and gender identity and expanded the definition of family in most of HUD's programs.

Building on that rule, on September 21, 2016, HUD issued a final rule, "Equal Access in Accordance with an Individual's Gender Identity in Community Planning and Development Programs Rule" (Gender Identity Rule). The Gender Identity Rule ensures that all individuals have equal access to many of the Department's core shelter programs following their gender identity. Following what had previously been a practice encouraged by HUD, providers that operate single-sex projects using funds awarded through the Office of Community Planning and Development (CPD) are required by the rule to provide all individuals, including transgender individuals and other individuals who do not identify with the sex they were assigned at birth, with access to programs, benefits, services, and accommodations following their gender identity without being subjected to intrusive questioning or being asked to provide documentation. HUD's rule will require a recipient, sub-recipient, or provider to establish, amend, or maintain program admissions, occupancy, and operating policies and procedures (including policies and procedures to protect individuals' privacy and security) so that equal access is provided to individuals based on their gender identity. This requirement includes tenant selection and admission preferences. The rule also updates the definition of sexual orientation and gender identity.

Lastly, on November 17, 2016, HUD issued a third final rule, "Equal Access to Housing in HUD's Native American and Native Hawaiian Programs—Regardless of Sexual Orientation or Gender

Identity." This rule applied the same equal access provisions from the first rule to HUD's Native American and Native Hawaiian programs. Therefore, those programs are also required to decide of eligibility for housing that is assisted by HUD or subject to a mortgage insured by HUD, per the eligibility requirements provided for such program by HUD, and such housing shall be made available without regard to actual or perceived sexual orientation, gender identity, or marital status.

How to File a Housing Discrimination Complaint

If you believe you have experienced (or are about to experience) housing discrimination, you should contact HUD's Office of Fair Housing and Equal Opportunity for help.[290] You may also download the Apple App, Android App, or file a housing discrimination complaint online. HUD will thoroughly review your allegation to determine if the claims you raise are jurisdictional under the Fair Housing Act and the Equal Access Rule.

Additionally, in a situation where you have experienced (or are about to experience) housing discrimination in a HUD-funded program or when seeking a HUD-insured mortgage, you should contact your local HUD office for assistance with alleged violations of HUD program regulations.

Cyndi Lauper's True Colors Fund and the Forty to None Project

Since 2013, HUD and the True Colors Fund have partnered to end homelessness among lesbian, gay, bisexual, transgender, and questioning youth, creating a world where young people can be their true selves. Together, HUD and the True Colors Fund launched an initiative to help Houston and Cincinnati prevent homelessness for LGBTQ youth. A recent report describes lessons learned from the planning phase in those two communities and offers recommendations for other communities looking to champion similar efforts.

> HOW TO GET INVOLVED:
>
> Read the report and learn how your community can implement similar planning efforts to those in Houston and Cincinnati, and
>
> Look to the Cincinnati and Houston plans as examples of community-wide strategies for preventing LGBTQ youth homelessness.

For information and resources about this community change process and the initiative's outcomes, visit HUD's Youth Homelessness resource page.

Visit the True Colors website to learn more about how you can help.[291] In addition, interested people can also participate in an ongoing Forty to None conversation.[292,293]

Discrimination in Occupational Licensing

The law generally considers it to be illegal for professional or occupational licensing boards to discriminate against an applicant on account of one's sex, as well as other classifications.

> It is undoubtedly the right of every citizen of the United States to follow any lawful calling, business, or profession he may choose, subject only to such restrictions as are imposed upon all persons of like age, sex, and condition. This right may in many respects be considered as a distinguishing feature of our republican institutions. Here all vocations are open to everyone on like conditions. All may be pursued as sources of livelihood, some requiring years of study and great learning for their successful prosecution. The interest, or, as it is sometimes termed, the estate acquired in them, that is, the right to

continue their prosecution, is often of great value to the possessors, and cannot be arbitrarily taken from them, any more than their real or personal property can be thus taken.[294]

Additionally, an individual, who feels they have been discriminated against because of any statute, ordinance, regulation, custom, or usage, of any State or Territory or the District of Columbia, or because of their race, religion, color, sex, or country of origin, may be able to file a lawsuit under Title 42 United States Code Section 1983 to protect those rights. While licensing boards may undertake background checks to prevent licenses from being granted to those with criminal records specifically relating to the license sought or to those with mental health issues that may keep them from performing the functions of the license, licensing boards cannot refuse to issue an occupational license on impermissible grounds.

Marriage

Marriage is a state issue, and the states have passed marriage license laws. Historically, many laws prevented the LGBTQ+ community from obtaining a license because states interpreted "sex" to mean sex as assigned at birth.

The now-famous case of a Rowan County Clerk, Kim Davis, who refused to issue a marriage license to members of the LGBTQ community after the U.S. Supreme Court's decision in *Obergefell v. Hodges*, 576 U.S. 644, 135 S. Ct. 2584 (2015), held that state bans on same-sex marriage and on recognizing same-sex marriages duly performed in other jurisdictions are unconstitutional under the Due Process and Equal Protection Clauses of the Fourteenth Amendment to the United States Constitution highlight the ongoing discrimination members of the LGBTQ community experience every day. Davis claimed that to do so (i.e., issue marriage licenses) violated her religious objections to same-sex marriage. Two couples for whom she refused to issue licenses sued her in federal court, and the Sixth Circuit affirmed the District Court's decision, which ordered her to issue marriage licenses.[295,296] The U.S. Supreme Court, in *Davis v. Ermold*, 592 US____ (2020), denied Petitioner Davis's petition for a Writ of Certiorari.

State laws that provide for the issuance of marriage licenses will be covered in the section for each state. It should be noted, however, that the *Obergefell* decision means states can no longer deny marriage licenses to same-sex couples.

Military Service

Service in the military has historically been restricted to those assigned as male at birth, and not until 1948 were women allowed to serve in non-combat roles. But the military has had a longstanding practice of banning service in the military by homosexual men and women. In 1993, President Bill Clinton signed the "Don't Ask, Don't Tell" policy, which lasted until 2011, when President Barack Obama repealed it. Women began serving in combat roles in 2015 after the ban was lifted.

From the creation of the military to 1960, there was no official policy banning transgender individuals from military service. A ban existed from 1960 to 2016 that categorically prohibited service in the U.S. military by transgender individuals. From June 2016 to January 2018, transgender persons were allowed to serve under certain conditions. In 2016, under the Secretary of Defense, Ash Carter, the Obama Administration requested that the Rand Corporation study service in the military by transgender persons and issue recommendations. The Rand Report concluded that provided they received appropriate treatment while serving, there was no evidence to support the claim that transgender persons could not serve. The Rand Report stated:

> The available research we reviewed found no significant effect of openly serving transgender military members on cohesion, operational effectiveness or readiness."[297]

Despite the findings of the Rand Report, in 2017, the Trump Administration, at the direction of the President, undertook another effort to find that transgender individuals were not fit for military service. In their report, the Department of Defense found that:

> Transgender persons who have not transitioned to another gender and do not have a history or current diagnosis of gender dysphoria—i.e., they identify as a gender other than their biological sex but do not currently experience distress or impairment of functioning in meeting the standards associated with their biological sex—are eligible for service, provided that they, like all other persons. satisfy all mental and physical health standards and are capable of adhering to the standards associated with their biological sex. This is consistent with the Carter policy, under which a transgender person's gender identity is recognized only if the person has a diagnosis or history of gender dysphoria.[298]

The Trump policy completely excluded transgender individuals from serving in the U.S. military, including those currently serving at the time of Trump's order on April 12, 2019.

On January 25, 2021, the Biden Administration quickly rescinded the Trump policy. In President Biden's Executive Order, he stated:

> It is my judgment that the Secretary of Defense's 2016 conclusions remain valid, as further demonstrated by the fact that, in 2018, the then-serving Chief of Staff of the Army, Chief of Naval Operations, Commandant of the Marine Corps, and Chief of Staff of the Air Force all testified publicly to the Congress that they were not aware of any issues of unit cohesion, disciplinary problems, or issues of morale resulting from open transgender service. A group of former United States Surgeons General, who collectively served under Democratic and Republican Presidents, echoed this point, stating in 2018 that "transgender troops are as medically fit as their non-transgender peers and that there is no medically valid reason—including a diagnosis of gender dysphoria—to exclude them from military service or to limit their access to medically necessary care."

> Therefore, it shall be the policy of the United States to ensure that all transgender individuals who wish to serve in the United States military and can meet the appropriate standards shall be able to do so openly and free from discrimination.[299]

The Department of Defense has instituted a policy that prohibits discrimination in the armed forces based on a recruit or currently serving member being or suffering from gender dysphoria.

1.2. POLICY.

> a. DoD and the Military Departments will institute policies to provide Service members a process by which they may transition gender while serving. These policies are based on the conclusion that open service by transgender persons who are subject to the same high standards and procedures as other Service members with regard to medical fitness for duty, physical fitness, uniform and grooming standards, deployability, and retention is consistent with military service and readiness.

b. All Service members must be treated with dignity and respect. No person, solely on the basis of his or her gender identity, will be:

> (1) Involuntarily separated or discharged from the Military Services;
>
> (2) Denied reenlistment or continuation of service in the Military Services; or
>
> (3) Subjected to adverse action or mistreatment.[300]

The Department of Defense also updated DoD Instruction 6130.03 Volume 1, "Medical Standards for Military Service, Appointment, Enlistment, or Induction," dated April 30, 2021.[301]

Passports

The United States Department of State, Bureau of Consular Affairs, issues passports for travel abroad by U.S. citizens. Transgender individuals can obtain a passport by providing the appropriate documentation and a properly filled-out Form DS-11. The guidelines and fees are listed on the website of the State Department.[302,303]

A transgender applicant should read through the information on the State Department website very carefully. Once you have your passport, you can travel abroad and travel within the United States, its territories, and possessions.

Discrimination by Federal Law Enforcement Agencies

Federal law enforcement agencies are prohibited from discriminating because of sex pursuant to 42 U.S.C. §1983. Yet, in a report by *The Williams Institute*, of the University of California at Los Angeles (UCLA) Law School, in March 2015, the Executive Summary stated:

> Discrimination and harassment by law enforcement based on sexual orientation and gender identity is an ongoing and pervasive problem in LGBT communities. Such discrimination impedes effective policing in these communities by breaking down trust, inhibiting communication and preventing officers from effectively protecting and serving the communities they police. While a patchwork of state, local and federal laws provides some protection against certain forms of discrimination, there is no nationwide federal statute that comprehensively and consistently prohibits discrimination based on actual or perceived sexual orientation and gender identity.[304]

Besides the discrimination felt by the LGBTQ community in policing, law enforcement agencies have discriminated against their employees who are members of the LGBTQ community. The Center for American Progress website claims:

> There are approximately 1 million gay or transgender individuals in America today working in state, local, or municipal government. They are firefighters, teachers, police officers, nurses, librarians, child-care providers, sanitation workers, and more. These public servants care for our children, protect our communities, clean our streets, and keep America functioning.
>
> Unfortunately, far too many gay and transgender public-sector employees arrive at work each day fearing that they may lose their job due to discrimination. Moreover, these workers often have little or no legal recourse when discrimination occurs. Research and data reveal that gay and transgender employees experience rates of discrimination on the job comparable to other protected groups, but they lack the same legal protections afforded to those groups.[305]

However, now with the U.S. Supreme Court's decision in *Bostock,* employment opportunities for the LGBTQ community in public safety employment should open up.

Changing Your Gender with the Social Security Administration

The Social Security Administration (SSA) has a procedure requiring the applicant to file certain documents and an Application for a Social Security Card. The procedure is outlined on the SSA website.[306]

Veterans Administration (VA)

Patient Care Services at the VA has a website that provides information to veterans who are members of the LGBTQ community.[307]

According to VHA Directive 1341(2), issued May 23, 2018:

> [The] Veterans Health Administration (VHA) directive revises VHA policy for the respectful delivery of health care to transgender and intersex Veterans who are enrolled in the Department of Veterans Affairs (VA) health care system or are otherwise eligible for VA care.[308]

Transgender individuals cannot be discriminated against in issuing federal contracts pursuant to Title VI of the Civil Rights Act of 1964.

Federal Religious Freedom Restoration Act (RFRA) of 1993

Title 42 U.S. Code, Section 2000bb-1 states, in part:

> (a) In general
>
> > Government shall not substantially burden a person's exercise of religion even if the burden results from a rule of general applicability, except as provided in subsection (b).
>
> (b) Exception
>
> > Government may substantially burden a person's exercise of religion only if it demonstrates that application of the burden to the person:
> >
> > > (1) is in furtherance of a compelling governmental interest; and
> > >
> > > (2) is the least restrictive means of furthering that compelling governmental interest.[309]

Religious groups and persons around the country have used the RFRA as a model for enacting similar state religious freedom laws. Their stated beliefs are that their religious freedom is being attacked: therefore, other measures must be taken to protect it. These laws are used by people to claim that their religious beliefs prevent them from doing certain things and allow them to discriminate based on sex in various contexts. The argument is that because the Christian Bible says men are men and women are women, they will not recognize male-to-female or female-to-male transgender individuals as female or male, respectively, and to do so flies in the face of their religious beliefs. They claim that "biological sex" means you are either male or female as designated at birth. Accordingly, they use male and female pronouns inappropriately to refer to those who have changed or are in the process of transitioning from one sex to the other because they have been diagnosed with gender dysphoria syndrome.

One problem persists: whether the First Amendment's free exercise and establishment clauses are to be construed as overstepping those of the Equal Protection Clause contained in the Fourteenth Amendment. The Fourteenth Amendment to the U.S. Constitution's equal protection clause states that the states cannot make laws that treat people differently. The text of the equal protection clause is unmistakable in its meaning:

> Nor shall any State... deny to any person within its jurisdiction the **equal protection** of the laws.[310] [Emphasis in original]

Just because the First Amendment came before all the others does not mean it is more important than the others. The law says we are to be treated equally. There are those in this country who, for whatever reason, do not want to treat all people the same: instead, they want to treat those who may be different from them unequally. Look at racism. The world has a long history of treating people of color differently solely because they are different.

> The roots of racism stem from differing religions, the mission to Christianize, and the global acceptability of owning those of a different faith. It was acceptable for Christians to have non-Christian slaves, Muslims to have non-Muslim slaves, or African peoples to own others from enemy tribes. However, in the late Middle Ages, slave owners began to pivot toward making a profit when the Portuguese began their exploration and triggered Western exploitation of African goods, services, and bodies. Original justifications were because African peoples were not vastly Christian, but after Christianization, slavers needed a new reason to justify their highly profitable industry.[311]

See, for example, the three-volume set on the Civil War by author Shelby Foote. Many televised programs have examined why the Civil War took place, and, as we see today, we still find it inexorably challenging to break ourselves free from what I am calling the "American Apartheid" era. Christians have believed that people of color were subhuman in order to justify the oppression and killing of Black people since this country was founded. Until American Christianity comes to terms with its role in racism, how can we ever expect it to treat the LGBTQ community differently than they do now? This is not an indictment of all of Christianity. However, it is an indictment of those Christians who use their religious beliefs as an excuse to discriminate against those they view as different and, therefore, unacceptable.

The King James Bible says, "Thou shall Love thy neighbor as thyself."[312] Also that all humans were made in "God's image." If God made us the way we are, then why don't Christians accept us "the way we are"? If God made people gay, why don't Christians accept gay people? I certainly did not wake up one day and decide that I wanted to be a woman. This is where the disconnect between science and religion occurs. Science explains why gay people are gay and why transgender people are transgender. Religious mythology, however, supports a different perspective. For example: why did the apple fall from the tree? Science says it is because of gravity. Religion says God made the apple fall. In science, we can replicate that experiment and judge the results. Thank you, Isaac Newton. This issue is considered in greater depth in the section below on state laws and their application to the LGBTQ community.

Finally, the Federal RFRA was struck down by the U.S. Supreme Court in *City of Boerne v. Flores, Archbishop of San Antonio, et al.*, 521 U.S. 507 (1997) (cited post at En. 219) as being an unconstitutional overreach by Congress. Some of the language of the *Boerne* decision[313] is now being used in state RFRA-style laws. The Court in *Boerne*, 521 U.S. at 532, states unequivocally:

> RFRA is not so confined. Sweeping coverage ensures its intrusion at every level of government, displacing laws and prohibiting official actions of almost every description and regardless of subject matter. RFRA's restrictions apply to every agency and official of the Federal, State, and local Governments. 42 U.S.C. § 2000bb–2(1). RFRA applies to all federal and state law, statutory or otherwise, whether adopted before or after its enactment. § 2000bb–3(a). RFRA has no termination date or termination mechanism. Any law is subject to challenge at any time by any individual who alleges a substantial burden on his or her free exercise of religion.[314]

The High Court even went so far as to say the Act was so broad in its scope that it literally would impact every aspect of modern life and law.

> The stringent test RFRA demands of state laws reflects a lack of proportionality or congruence between the means adopted and the legitimate end to be achieved. If an objector can show a substantial burden on his free exercise, the State must demonstrate a compelling governmental interest and show that the law is the least restrictive means of furthering its interest. Claims that a law substantially burdens someone's exercise of religion will often be difficult to contest. See *Smith*, 494 U. S., at 887 ("What principle of law or logic can be brought to bear to contradict a believer's assertion that a particular act is 'central' to his personal faith?"); *id.,* at 907 ("The distinction between questions of centrality and questions of sincerity and burden is admittedly fine…") (O'Connor, J., concurring in judgment). Requiring a State to demonstrate a compelling interest and show that it has adopted the least restrictive means of achieving that interest is the most demanding test known to constitutional law. If "'compelling interest' really means what it says… many laws will not meet the test… [The test] would open the prospect of constitutionally required religious exemptions from civic obligations of almost every conceivable kind." *Id.,* at 888. Laws valid under *Smith* would fall under RFRA without regard to whether they had the object of stifling or punishing free exercise. We make these observations not to reargue the position of the majority in *Smith* but to illustrate the substantive alteration of its holding attempted by RFRA. Even assuming RFRA would be interpreted in effect to mandate some lesser test, say, one equivalent to intermediate scrutiny, the statute nevertheless would require searching judicial scrutiny of state law with the attendant likelihood of invalidation. This is a considerable congressional intrusion into the States' traditional prerogatives and general authority to regulate for the health and welfare of their citizens.

> The substantial costs RFRA exacts, both in practical terms of imposing a heavy litigation burden on the States and in terms of curtailing their traditional general regulatory power, far exceed any pattern or practice of unconstitutional conduct under the Free Exercise Clause as interpreted in *Smith*. Simply put, RFRA is not designed to identify and counteract state laws likely to be unconstitutional because of their treatment of religion. In most cases, the state laws to which RFRA applies are not ones which will have been motivated by religious bigotry. If a state law disproportionately burdened a particular class of religious observers, this circumstance might be evidence of an impermissible legislative motive. Cf. *Washington* v. *Davis,* 426 U. S. 229, 241 (1976). RFRA's substantial-burden test, however, is not even a discriminatory-effects or disparate-impact test. It is a reality of the modern regulatory state that numerous state laws, such

as the zoning regulations at issue here, impose a substantial burden on a large class of individuals. When the exercise of religion has been burdened in an incidental way by a law of general application, it does not follow that the persons affected have been burdened any more than other citizens, let alone burdened because of their religious beliefs. In addition, the Act imposes in every case a least restrictive means requirement—a requirement that was not used in the pre-*Smith* jurisprudence RFRA purported to codify—which also indicates that the legislation is broader than is appropriate if the goal is to prevent and remedy constitutional violations.[315]

Legal Aspects | **83**

STATE LAWS

State laws encompass many of the same issues found at the federal level. However, specific issues, such as changing your name on a birth certificate, driver's license, state I.D. card, or other legal documents, engaging in sports activities, professional occupations requiring a state-issued license, and public accommodations, to name a few, are state-level issues that are addressed in the following pages.

One of the most pervasive new trends in the states—specifically states where the majority political party is the Republican Party—are religious exemption laws. These laws allow owners or employees of businesses that provide goods and services to the public to refuse to serve specific individuals or groups by stating that to do so would violate their "deeply held" religious beliefs. This scenario plays out chiefly when the business is patronized by someone who is a member of the LGBTQ community. Some commentators have suggested that the religious exemption laws appear to be a run-around of the U.S. Supreme Court's decision in the *Obergefell* case. This subject will be covered in-depth in the section on Public Accommodations.

In government services, such as the issuance of marriage licenses (see the discussion on the *Obergefell* decision above), state government and local government agencies in some states have enacted regulations that make obtaining amended or corrected documents difficult at best. Other states refuse outright to amend or correct legal documents, claiming to do so violates state laws.

Birth Certificates and Driver's Licenses

For each of the states, the laws and regulations that govern how, or if, a person who is transgender can get their name and designation of sex changed on documents to reflect the person's stated gender identity may be different.

In the case of birth certificates, in most instances, a transgender person *first* needs to get a court order changing their name. Most of the other steps require this document, so it is a good first step to get out of the way.

If you have already had surgery, another good first step is to get documentation of that from your primary care physician or surgeon, even before you go to court to get your name changed. Several copies of a letter stating you have had sex reassignment surgery may be required, and it is advisable that you keep several copies for yourself. If you haven't had surgery yet, or even if you don't plan on seeking surgery, you will still need proof from your doctor(s) that you are being treated for a gender issue.

Once you have the documentation from your surgeon, you can file a change of name petition in court. If possible, also include in the petition that you want the judge to instruct the state agency that handles birth records—called "Vital Records" or "Vital Statistics"—to change the designation of sex on your birth certificate to reflect your stated gender identity. The same is true for driver's license offices. States differ on what they require for documentation, the forms to be filled out, and the fees they may charge. Make sure you visit the state agency's website to be fully informed beforehand.

Once you have the new birth certificate, you can pursue a change of name and designation of sex on your driver's license.

This whole process could take several months depending on how long it takes to get through each step. State agencies can be very slow in responding to your requests. Also, if you are required to make an appointment to visit a government office during the COVID-19 pandemic, make sure you wear a mask. With the Delta variant gaining ground in many states, you may be required to wear a mask when visiting any government offices. Even if you are fully vaccinated, it can help to keep you safe.

Finally, if you find this to be overwhelming, many states have legal aid offices where you may be able to get assistance with changing your legal documents. At the least, they usually can walk you through the process with the courts. Many have self-help brochures or pamphlets that provide valuable information.

If you are unsure how to find legal help in your state, you can go to the State Side Legal website, which lists legal aid organizations by state.[316]

One last note on identity documents.

KEEP COPIES OF THE DOCUMENTS YOU SUBMIT TO GOVERNMENT AGENCIES OR COURTS AND KEEP COPIES OF THE DOCUMENTS THEY SEND BACK TO YOU. THIS INCLUDES ANY STATE AGENCY AND STATE OR COUNTY COURTS. Doing this is vitally important if your requests are denied. Any lawyer who later may represent you will want to have copies of all these documents for their records.

I highly recommend The Movement Advancement Project (MAP) website,[317] which provides the most up-to-date information on the laws, regulations, and state agency rules that the reader will need to follow. Some of their data tables are presented below.

State Religious Exemption Laws in General

Religious exemption laws are laws that exempt persons who claim to hold certain religious beliefs that prohibit them from undertaking a particular action, or from performing that action, because their religion requires them to abstain. People who run businesses, for example, have claimed that to serve a member of the LGBTQ community violates their religious beliefs. Some of these laws date back to the era of the Jim Crow laws in the south, where food counters refused to serve people of color. Separate facilities for public restrooms, water fountains, and the like existed for people of color. They represented a codified system of racial apartheid in the south for approximately seventy-five years, beginning in the 1890s. The policy was one of segregation and separation from the White establishment. The owners of such establishments often justified segregation on the false, often religious, pretext that people of color were inferior to Whites.

Religious exemption laws attempt to put the religious beliefs of some people and their free exercise rights under the First Amendment *before* the rights of other people as guaranteed by the Constitution. The Hobby Lobby case was an outgrowth of this concept. In *Burwell, Secretary of Health and Human Services et al., v. Hobby Lobby Stores, Inc., et al.* 573 U.S. 682 (2014), the U.S. Supreme Court held that the religious views of the company's owner permissibly allowed him to refuse to provide birth control coverage to female employees of the company.

Yet, in the case of *Employment Division, Department of Human Resources of Oregon, et al., v. Alfred L. Smith, et al.*, 494 U.S. 872, 110 S.Ct. 1595, 108 L.Ed.2d 876 (1990), which involved an employee's claimed religious use of a scheduled drug (Peyote) under the Controlled Substances Act of 1987, 21 U.S.C. §§ 811-812, the Court ruled:

> "Laws," we said, "are made for the government of actions, and while they cannot interfere with mere religious belief and opinions, they may with practices... Can a man excuse his practices to the contrary because of his religious belief? To permit this would

be to make the professed doctrines of religious belief superior to the law of the land, and in effect to permit every citizen to become a law unto himself."[318]

Then, in 1997, the Supreme Court ruled in *City of Boerne v. Flores, Archbishop of San Antonio, et al.*, 521 U.S. 507 (1997),[319] that the RFRA exceeded Congress' authority under Section 5 of the Fourteenth Amendment, Section 5:

> The Congress shall have power to enforce, by appropriate legislation, the provisions of this article.[320]

The Court reversed the decision of the Fifth Circuit Court of Appeals, which had found RFRA to be constitutional. The Supreme Court said:

> Congress enacted RFRA in direct response to the Court's decision in *Employment Div., Dept. of Human Resources of Ore. et al. v. Smith*, 494 U. S. 872 (1990).[321]

The Court went on to explain why RFRA was so intrusive into everyday lives:

> Requiring a State to demonstrate a compelling interest and show that it has adopted the least restrictive means of achieving that interest is the most demanding test known to constitutional law. If "compelling interest" really means what it says... many laws will not meet the test.... [The test] would open the prospect of constitutionally required religious exemptions from civic obligations of almost every conceivable kind.[322]

> Laws valid under Smith would fall under RFRA without regard to whether they had the object of stifling or punishing free exercise. We make these observations not to reargue the position of the majority in Smith but to illustrate the substantive alteration of its holding attempted by RFRA. Even assuming RFRA would be interpreted in effect to mandate some lesser test, say, one equivalent to intermediate scrutiny, the statute nevertheless would require searching judicial scrutiny of state law with the attendant likelihood of invalidation. This is a considerable congressional intrusion into the States' traditional prerogatives and general authority to regulate for the health and welfare of their citizens.[323]

Compare this with an article in the Columbia Law Review,[324] which came to the conclusion that RFRA's application to state law (RFRASTA) and RFRA's application to federal law (RFRAF) were both unconstitutional, but for differing reasons.

Today, an increasing number of state religious exemption laws are coming into force that allow individuals claiming religious belief to be excluded from obeying laws prohibiting discrimination because of sex, among other laws. For example, one such law, the Alabama Religious Freedom Amendment to the state Constitution, says in part:

> The purpose of the Alabama Religious Freedom Amendment is to guarantee that the freedom of religion is not burdened by state and local law; and to provide a claim or defense to persons whose religious freedom is burdened by government.[325]

"Not burdened by state and local law" seems to mean that those who subscribe to certain religious beliefs are not required to abide by anti-discrimination laws, essentially putting religious belief above the laws enacted by states or local governments. A person who is a law unto themself was never envisioned by our forefathers when they wrote the Constitution.

As of the date of publication, other states that have enacted religious exemption provisions include Virginia, South Carolina, Michigan, Illinois, Tennessee, Mississippi, Arkansas, Texas, Oklahoma, Kansas, and North and South Dakota.

Deeply conservative Christians seem to be saying that their religious beliefs constitute a superior power to human law. They consistently put that superior power, and their belief in it, before human-made laws. They appear to be arguing against the separation of church and state even though the Constitution explicitly forbids it. The Establishment Clause of the First Amendment to the United States Constitution says that, "Congress shall make no law respecting an establishment of religion." That is the essence of the *separation of church and state.*

The religious right went to great extremes to ensure that former President Trump appointed people to the nation's highest Court who they felt held similar beliefs to their own, expecting that this would ensure that the Court ruled in their favor when it came to issues of religion. The current Roberts court has to date, not fulfilled the dreams of these conservatives. So, rather than accept the Court's rulings on cases involving LGBTQ rights, they are attempting an end-run around the Supreme Court by enacting these state laws.

Nevertheless, this approach, may soon be tested by the actions that states are taking to exclude the LGBTQ community—in particular, the transgender population—from participating fully in society. It appears that they did not like what the Supreme Court said about RFRA and decided to take matters into their own hands. By enacting RFRA-style laws at the state level, they are able to accomplish what they could not at the federal level.

In a report released by the Human Rights Campaign in 2015,[326] 14 of the top 20 companies in the Fortune 1000 listing had a Corporate Equality Index of 100 percent. Those companies included Chevron, Apple, General Motors, General Electric, Ford Motor Co., AT&T, Federal National Mortgage Association (Fannie Mae), CVS Caremark, McKesson, Hewlett-Packard, UnitedHealth Group, JP Morgan Chase, Cardinal Health, and IBM. Many of them issued statements saying they opposed the passage of Bills like the federal RFRA because it could be used to discriminate against the LGBTQ community, many of whom are employed by the companies listed above.

In the last ten years alone, American businesses have recognized that a sizable portion of their workforce belongs to the LGBTQ community. Many of them are highly talented individuals. These RFRA-like Bills impact their businesses when LGBTQ employees turn down employment offers in or refuse transfers to the states where such laws exist.

Sports

According to the ACLU, more than 18 states have introduced or passed legislation in 2020 to ban transgender athletes from participating in school sports. Further, as of February 2021, at least 24 states have introduced such legislation. One state, where the U.S. District Court for the District of Idaho initially struck down such a law, continues seeking to re-enact it. Accordingly, the case (*Hecox et al., v. Little, et al.*) is now before the U.S. Court of Appeals for the Ninth Circuit on an appeal by the Governor and other parties. Similarly, another state law, unartfully titled "The Arkansas Save Adolescents From Experimentation (SAFE) Act," was voted into law by overriding the Governor's veto. Similar laws are being considered or have already been introduced in Tennessee, Mississippi, Montana, South Dakota, Florida, and Utah. Lawsuits in other Court of Appeals Circuits either have ruled or will soon be ruling whether Title IX prohibits discrimination in school sports based on sex.

These issues are brought into the limelight through media coverage when state legislation, motivated by specious political concerns, has been enacted, and when Governors sign into law prohibitions against transgender participation in interscholastic K-12 and intercollegiate sporting events because the sponsors of such laws and their supporters believe that only "biological" males and females should be allowed to compete. The argument central to all these laws seems to be the definition of "sex" as "biological," that is, as assigned at birth based on a cursory examination of the infant's genitals. Accordingly, advocates of the terms "biological male" or "biological female" presume that sex is biologically based. Nevertheless, this perspective does not allow for individuals whose gender identity is different from the "sex" they were assigned at birth or that of "preferred" cisgender participants. In my opinion, "biological sex" is a misnomer.

All these laws are supported by Christian organizations that wrongfully claim that transgender females have an unfair advantage over their cisgender female counterparts. Some state laws also specifically exclude transgender males from competing in male sports activities. The American Academy of Pediatrics News and Journals website reports, in part:

> AAP chapters have argued that the bills discriminate against transgender youths. Pediatricians testifying against the legislation said it is based on myths and misinformation about transgender children and adolescents and a misunderstanding about medical and surgical aspects of gender-affirmative care. They are presenting science, explaining policies of national and international medical and athletic organizations and describing harms the bills would cause.[327]

The introduction of these Bills is related to a politically conservative agenda to curtail many of the civil rights won by the LGBTQ community in recent years. Some have described it as a litmus test to identify the most conservative person worthy of being the party standard-bearer. Conservative pastors in churches all over the country have long wanted to see a community they view with disdain lose rights they portray as "special" or unnecessary. I believe the opposite is true. The LGBTQ community has had to fight tooth and nail for decades to achieve even a modicum of equal protection under the law for the exact reasons religious groups want to see us lose them. The Constitution guarantees us equality. Equality is not a "special right."

Such legislation is not based on science but on the false belief that Title IX of the Education Amendments of 1972 does not cover discrimination because of gender identity or transgender status. Accordingly, transgender persons need not be accorded the same rights as everyone else. Some of the Bills are modeled after text suggested by a conservative legal organization. In an article in the New York Times, Jeremy Peters wrote,

> South Dakota is just one of a growing number of states where Republicans are diving into a culture war clash that seems to have come out of nowhere. A coordinated and poll-tested campaign has been brought about by social conservative organizations like the American Principles Project and Concerned Women for America. They say they are determined to move forward with what may be one of their last footholds in the fight against expanding L.G.B.T.Q. Rights.[328]

The text of these laws seems to be essentially the same from state to state. The text quoted at some length here ("Save Women's Sports Act") is an example from the State of Arizona Senate, 55th Legislature, 1st Regular Session of 2021 introduced by Senator Wendy Rogers.

Be it enacted by the Legislature of the State of Arizona: Section 1. Title 15, chapter 1, article 1, Arizona Revised 3 Statutes, is amended by adding section 15-120.01, to read: 4 15-120.01.

<u>Designation of athletic teams; educational 5 institutions; cause of action; definition</u>

A. AN INTERSCHOLASTIC OR INTRAMURAL ATHLETIC TEAM OR SPORT THAT IS SPONSORED BY AN EDUCATIONAL INSTITUTION IN THIS STATE MUST BE EXPRESSLY DESIGNATED AS ONE OF THE FOLLOWING BASED ON BIOLOGICAL SEX:

1. MALES, MEN OR BOYS.

2. FEMALES, WOMEN OR GIRLS.

3. COED OR MIXED SEX.

B. ATHLETIC TEAMS OR SPORTS DESIGNATED FOR FEMALES, WOMEN OR GIRLS MAY NOT BE OPEN TO STUDENTS OF THE MALE SEX.

C. IF DISPUTED, A STUDENT MAY ESTABLISH THE STUDENT'S SEX BY PRESENTING A SIGNED PHYSICIAN'S STATEMENT THAT INDICATES THE STUDENT'S SEX BASED ON AN ANALYSIS OF THE STUDENT'S GENETIC MAKEUP.

D. A GOVERNMENTAL ENTITY, A LICENSING OR ACCREDITING ORGANIZATION OR AN ATHLETIC ASSOCIATION OR ORGANIZATION MAY NOT ENTERTAIN A COMPLAINT, OPEN AN INVESTIGATION OR TAKE ANY OTHER ADVERSE ACTION AGAINST AN EDUCATIONAL INSTITUTION FOR MAINTAINING SEPARATE INTERSCHOLASTIC OR INTRAMURAL ATHLETIC TEAMS OR SPORTS FOR STUDENTS OF THE FEMALE SEX.

E. ANY STUDENT WHO IS DEPRIVED OF AN ATHLETIC OPPORTUNITY OR SUFFERS DIRECT OR INDIRECT HARM AS A RESULT OF A VIOLATION OF THIS SECTION HAS A PRIVATE CAUSE OF ACTION FOR INJUNCTIVE RELIEF, DAMAGES AND ANY OTHER RELIEF AVAILABLE UNDER LAW AGAINST THE EDUCATIONAL INSTITUTION.

F. ANY STUDENT WHO IS SUBJECT TO RETALIATION OR OTHER ADVERSE ACTION BY AN EDUCATIONAL INSTITUTION OR ATHLETIC ASSOCIATION OR ORGANIZATION AS A RESULT OF REPORTING A VIOLATION OF THIS SECTION TO AN EMPLOYEE OR REPRESENTATIVE OF THE EDUCATIONAL INSTITUTION OR ATHLETIC ASSOCIATION OR ORGANIZATION OR TO ANY STATE OR FEDERAL AGENCY WITH OVERSIGHT OF EDUCATIONAL INSTITUTIONS IN THIS STATE HAS A PRIVATE CAUSE OF ACTION FOR INJUNCTIVE RELIEF, DAMAGES AND ANY OTHER RELIEF AVAILABLE UNDER LAW AGAINST THE EDUCATIONAL INSTITUTION OR ATHLETIC ASSOCIATION OR ORGANIZATION.

G. ANY ELIGIBLE INSTITUTION THAT SUFFERS ANY DIRECT OR INDIRECT HARM AS A RESULT OF A VIOLATION OF THIS SECTION HAS A PRIVATE

CAUSE OF ACTION FOR INJUNCTIVE RELIEF, DAMAGES AND ANY OTHER RELIEF AVAILABLE UNDER LAW AGAINST THE GOVERNMENTAL ENTITY, LICENSING OR ACCREDITING ORGANIZATION OR ATHLETIC ASSOCIATION OR ORGANIZATION.

H. A CIVIL ACTION UNDER THIS SECTION MUST BE INITIATED WITHIN TWO YEARS AFTER THE HARM OCCURS. A PERSON THAT PREVAILS ON A CLAIM BROUGHT UNDER THIS SECTION IS ENTITLED TO MONETARY DAMAGES, INCLUDING FOR ANY PSYCHOLOGICAL, EMOTIONAL AND PHYSICAL HARM SUFFERED, ANY REASONABLE ATTORNEY FEES AND COSTS AND ANY OTHER APPROPRIATE RELIEF.

I. FOR THE PURPOSES OF THIS SECTION, "EDUCATIONAL INSTITUTION" MEANS ANY OF THE FOLLOWING:

1. A PUBLIC SCHOOL, WHETHER OR NOT THE PUBLIC SCHOOL IS A MEMBER OF AN INTERSCHOLASTIC ATHLETIC ASSOCIATION OR ORGANIZATION.

2. A PRIVATE SCHOOL THAT IS A MEMBER OF AN INTERSCHOLASTIC ATHLETIC ASSOCIATION OR ORGANIZATION.

3. A UNIVERSITY UNDER THE JURISDICTION OF THE [Fill in state name] BOARD OF REGENTS, WHETHER OR NOT THE UNIVERSITY IS A MEMBER OF ANY ASSOCIATION LISTED IN PARAGRAPH 5 OF THIS SUBSECTION.

4. A COMMUNITY COLLEGE AS DEFINED IN SECTION 15-1401, WHETHER OR NOT THE COMMUNITY COLLEGE IS A MEMBER OF ANY ASSOCIATION LISTED IN PARAGRAPH 5 OF THIS SUBSECTION.

5. ANY OTHER INSTITUTION OF HIGHER EDUCATION THAT IS A MEMBER OF ANY OF THE FOLLOWING:

(a) A NATIONAL COLLEGIATE ATHLETIC ASSOCIATION.

(b) A NATIONAL ASSOCIATION OF INTERCOLLEGIATE ATHLETICS.

(c) A NATIONAL JUNIOR COLLEGE ATHLETIC ASSOCIATION.

Sec. 2. Legislative findings and purpose

The legislature finds that:

1. There are "'[i]nherent differences' between men and women," and that these differences "remain cause for celebration, but not for denigration of the members of either sex or for artificial constraints on an individual's opportunity." *United States v. Virginia*, 518 U.S. 515, 24 533 (1996).

2. These "inherent differences" range from chromosomal and hormonal differences to physiological differences.

3. Men generally have "denser, stronger bones, tendons, and ligaments" and "larger hearts, greater lung volume per body mass, a higher red blood cell count, and higher hemoglobin." Neel Burton, The Battle of the Sexes, PSYCHOL. TODAY, July 2, 2012.[329]

4. Men also have higher natural levels of testosterone, which affects traits such as hemoglobin levels, body fat content, the storage and use of carbohydrates and the development of Type 2 muscle fibers, all of which result in men being able to generate higher speed and power during physical activity. Doriane Lambelet Coleman, Sex in Sport, 80 LAW and CONTEMP. PROBS. 63, 74 (2017) (quoting Gina Kolata, Men, Women and Speed. 2 Words: Got Testosterone? N.Y. TIMES, Aug. 21, 2008).

5. The biological differences between females and males, especially as they relate to natural levels of testosterone, "explain the male and female secondary sex characteristics which develop during puberty and have lifelong effects, including those most important for success in sport: categorically different strength, speed, and endurance." Doriane Lambelet Coleman and Wickliffe Shreve, Comparing Athletic Performances: The Best Elite Women to Boys and Men, DUKE LAW CTR. FOR SPORTS LAW AND POLICY.[330]

6. While classifications based on sex are generally disfavored, the United States Supreme Court has recognized that "[s]ex classifications may be used to compensate women for particular economic disabilities [they have] suffered… to promote equal employment opportunity… [and] to advance full development of the talent and capacities of our Nation's people." *United States v. Virginia*, 518 U.S. 515, 533 (1996) (internal citations and quotation marks omitted).

7. One place where sex classifications allow for the "full development of the talent and capacities of our Nation's people" is in the context of sports and athletics.

8. Courts have recognized that the inherent, physiological differences between males and females result in different athletic capabilities. *See, e.g., Kleczek v. R.I. Interscholastic League, Inc.*, 612 A.2d 734, 738 (R.I. 1992) ("Because of innate physiological differences, boys and girls are not similarly situated as they enter athletic competition."); *Petrie v. Ill. High Sch. Ass'n*, 394 N.E.2d 855, 861 (Ill. App. Ct. 1979) (noting that "high school boys [generally possess physiological advantages over] their girl counterparts" and that those advantages give them an unfair lead over girls in some sports like "high school track").

9. A recent study of female and male Olympic performances since 1983 found that, although athletes from both sexes improved over the time span, the "gender gap" between female and male performances remained stable. "These suggest that women's performances at the high level will never match those of men." Valerie Thibault, et al., Women and Men in Sport Performance: The Gender Gap has not Evolved since 1983, 9 J. SPORTS SCI. and MED. 214, 219 (2010).

10. As Duke Law professor and all-American track athlete Doriane Coleman, tennis champion Martina Navratilova and Olympic track gold medalist Sanya Richards-Ross recently wrote: "The evidence is unequivocal that starting in puberty, in every sport except sailing, shooting and riding, there will always be significant numbers of boys and men who would beat the best girls and women in head-to-head competition. Claims to the contrary are simply a denial of science." Doriane Coleman, Martina Navratilova, et al., Pass the Equality Act,

But Don't Abandon Title IX, WASH. POST, Apr. 29, 2019, https://wapo.st/2VKlNN1.

11. The benefits that natural testosterone provides to male athletes are not diminished through the use of puberty blockers and cross-sex hormones. A recent study on the impact of such treatments found that even "after 12 months of hormonal therapy," a man who identifies as a woman and is taking cross-sex hormones "had an absolute advantage" over female athletes and "will still likely have performance benefits" over women. Tommy Lundberg, et al., Muscle strength, size and composition following 12 months of gender-affirming treatment in transgender individuals: retained advantage for the transwomen, Karolinksa Institutet, (Sept. 26, 2019).

12. Having separate sex-specific teams furthers efforts to promote sex equality. Sex-specific teams accomplish this by providing opportunities for female athletes to demonstrate their skill, strength and athletic abilities while also providing them with opportunities to obtain recognition and accolades, college scholarships and the numerous other long-term benefits that flow from success in athletic endeavors.

Sec. 3. Severability

If a provision of this act or its application to any person or circumstance is held invalid, the invalidity does not affect other provisions or applications of the act that can be given effect without the invalid provision or application, and to this end the provisions of this act are severable. [Spacing, line numbering, and page numbers omitted for clarity and ease of reading. Caps in original] [331]

Since early 2020, members of the Republican Party have sought to change the laws in so-called "red states" to reflect the far-right conservative view that the term "sex" means sex assigned at birth. The Republican effort runs against decisions by federal courts in several of the 11 U.S. Courts of Appeal Circuits that discrimination because of "sex" violates Title IX of the Education Amendments of 1972. In the latest case on employment discrimination, the Court determined that Title VII of the Civil Rights Act of 1964, covers discrimination because of sex, and that sexual orientation and transgender status are part of sex. The U.S. Supreme Court's decision in *Bostock*, 590 U.S. ____ (2020), did not specifically address discrimination in school sports, but it did say that to discriminate based on sex, including sexual orientation and transgender status, violates federal law; in this case Title VII of the Civil Rights Act of 1964.

Since many federal anti-discrimination laws ban discrimination based on sex (as in the *Bostock* case), logically, if discriminating because of sex in one context violates the law, this should also be true in other contexts. Further, the U.S. Supreme Court has already ruled that discrimination based on sex includes discrimination based on transgender status. Thus, state laws designed to exclude transgender persons from participation in school sports and/or the provision of health care *are* discriminating based on sex. The Court has said,

In the language of law, this means that Title VII's "because of" test incorporates the "simple" and "traditional" standard of "but-for" causation.[332]

In an article written for the Annual Labor and Employment Law Conference (2019), the "but-for" causation standard is described like this:

The employer community, bolstered by court decisions, has however, won the messaging war (so far) by framing but-for cause as a "heightened," "elevated" or "more demanding" standard. The question is compared to what? If the comparison is the but-for standard to the motivating factor standard, then obviously but-for is a higher standard because it always resolves the case. But-for means proof that a factor... had a "determinative influence" on the adverse decision.[333]

If this concept applies to Title VII, why would it not apply to Title IX or to The Affordable Care Act's Section 1557 prohibitions (discussed below) on discrimination—again—based on sex?

In *Bostock*, Justice Gorsuch also wrote that the "determinative influence" only has to be one cause. If there are several reasons for discharging an employee in the case of employment discrimination, if sex was a determinative influence on the decision, that employer has discriminated based on sex regardless of whether other factors were considered in the decision to terminate the employee. Sex doesn't even have to be a significant influence, it has only to have been a motivating factor.

When one looks at the totality of decisions from the federal courts over the last six years, it appears that many federal courts at the District Court and Appeals Court levels now understand that there is more to sex than meets the eye.

This situation highlights a battle that is being waged in the Republican party over conservative views, which appear to base its understanding of human characteristics on fundamental Christian belief. These views are contrary to what science tells us, which is that sex is a complex phenomenological issue that cannot be understood by simply defining male as having a penis and female as having a vagina. This perspective appears to take the Christian point of view as valid and must, therefore, be valid for science and the law as well. The dichotomy is striking and amounts to a war over the alleged supremacy of religion over human law, whether religious belief or human law should adjudicate human behavior. Since this country is founded on principles embodied in our Constitution, it seems the argument is already settled. We all must live by the laws our representatives in government enact, not by the tenets of any particular religion. Our forefathers fled 17th Century England because of King James's taxation of the poor and religious persecution. That fear of religion intimately tied to government is why we are pledged to the separation of church and state.

Since we live in an ordered society, we are obliged to obey the laws written by those we elect to government office, whether that office is a city or municipal government, country or parish government, state government, or federal government. Imagine what it would be like to live in a society where no human laws existed. Life would be quite different because we would be left to various interpretations of the law based on whichever religious text we read. Almost certainly, these interpretations would conflict. Case in point: Afghanistan or Somalia, where tribes of different religious sects do not co-mingle. For example, Shiite and Sunni Muslims are constantly at war with each other. Without human rule of law, who would interpret the conflicts? When someone commits a crime—stealing, for example—some religions dictate to cut off the hand that did the crime. Such a simplistic approach simply does not work in an ordered society. Human laws are essential to government. The Preamble to the Constitution *does not* say, "We, the people under God."

Rather, the Preamble says:

> **We the People of the United States**, in Order to form a more perfect Union, establish Justice, insure domestic Tranquility, provide for the common defense, promote the

general Welfare, and secure the Blessings of Liberty to ourselves and our Posterity, do ordain and establish this Constitution for the United States of America. [emphasis added]

As discussed above, federal courts have ruled that prohibiting transgender individuals from competing in sports activities sponsored by school districts violates Title IX. However, no policy statement about discrimination in public schools based on sex has been found on the American Federation of High School Associations website. But on April 12, 2021, the National Collegiate Athletic Association (NCAA) issued the following statement regarding transgender athletes in NCAA-sponsored sports:

> The NCAA Board of Governors firmly and unequivocally supports the opportunity for transgender student-athletes to compete in college sports. This commitment is grounded in our values of inclusion and fair competition.
>
> The NCAA has a long-standing policy that provides a more inclusive path for transgender participation in college sports. Our approach—which requires testosterone suppression treatment for transgender women to compete in women's sports—embraces the evolving science on this issue and is anchored in participation policies of both the International Olympic Committee and the U.S. Olympic and Paralympic Committee. Inclusion and fairness can coexist for all student-athletes, including transgender athletes, at all levels of sports. Our clear expectation as the Association's top governing body is that all student-athletes will be treated with dignity and respect. We are committed to ensuring that NCAA championships are open for all who earn the right to compete in them.
>
> When determining where championships are held, NCAA policy directs that only locations where hosts can commit to providing an environment that is safe, healthy, and free of discrimination should be selected. We will continue to closely monitor these situations to determine whether NCAA championships can be conducted in ways that are welcoming and respectful of all participants.[334]

Public Accommodations

Public accommodations are businesses that provide goods and services to the public. It includes restaurants, theaters, hotels, hospitals, libraries, gas stations, and other retail stores. It also includes bakeries, flower shops, and services, such as wedding planners and financial services, to name only a few. Public accommodation statutes are a cornerstone of civil rights law. They were one of the primary mechanisms used to end Jim Crow segregation and discrimination in everyday commerce.

Like racial discrimination, discrimination against the trans community has roots in religion, specifically southern Baptist Christianity, where Whites have historically found justification for their bigotry. I remember traveling through Georgia in the 1960s and seeing signs that barred people of color from using restrooms for Whites, sitting at lunch counters (again meant only for Whites), and other public accommodations. Rosa Parks, a Black woman from Alabama, who I once met at an ACLU Foundation of Southern California gathering, refused to give up her seat in the Black section of the bus to accommodate a White man because the white section was fully occupied.

Public accommodations laws typically provide two kinds of protection:

(1) they prohibit a business from discriminating in its provision of service based on protected characteristics, such as race, gender, religion, sexual orientation, or disability; and

(2) they prohibit third parties from discriminatorily interfering with someone seeking to patronize a business.[335]

While there are no federal laws prohibiting discrimination in public accommodations based on sex, 44 states and the District of Columbia prohibit discrimination in public accommodations based on sex.

If a state has a public accommodations law or Human Rights Law, it will be listed in each state's section below.

Final Note on State laws

The state sections include data extracted from many sources, including my own research. Where state websites provide information relative to each state's subjects covered in the state section, links to state agency websites are provided. Still, the vast amount of data reported here (used with permission) comes from the Movement Advancement Project (MAP). The author thanks MAP for regularly updating these data and making them available on their website in both printable and pdf formats.[336]

The Movement Advancement Project methodology consists of tracking LGBTQ-related laws and policies in all 50 states, Washington D.C., and the five populated U.S. territories. MAP assigns a score or point value and creates a total "Overall Tally" for each state. The totals are divided into simple categories (negative, low, fair, medium, and high) to provide an overall LGBTQ policy climate across the U.S. Harmful or discriminatory policies earn negative points, while LGBTQ-inclusive or protective laws earn positive points. Fractions of points are awarded when states have enacted a portion of a law, or in cases where local laws provide protections that do not extend to the entire state. The MAP tally system is:

dynamic and updated in real time—meaning that as new laws pass, whether anti-LGBTQ or pro-LGBTQ, we will update the maps and include the new laws in the tally.[337]

Policies are evaluated and scored for their relevance to Sexual Orientation and Gender Identity.

Sexual Orientation is defined by MAP as:

a person's pattern of emotional, romantic, or sexual attraction, or lack thereof, to other people. Laws that explicitly mention sexual orientation primarily protect or harm lesbian, gay, bisexual, queer, and other non-heterosexual people. That said, transgender people who are also lesbian, gay, bisexual, or queer can be affected by laws that explicitly mention sexual orientation.[338]

Gender Identity is defined by MAP as:

a person's deeply-felt inner sense of their own gender, including being male, female, or something else or in-between. For transgender people, their gender identity typically does not match the sex they were thought to be at birth. "Gender expression" refers to a person's characteristics and behaviors such as appearance, dress, mannerisms and speech patterns that can be described as masculine, feminine, or something else. Gender identity and expression are each independent of sexual orientation, and transgender people may identify as heterosexual, lesbian, gay, bisexual, queer, or another orientation. Laws that explicitly mention "gender identity" or "gender identity and expression" primarily protect or harm transgender people. These laws also can apply to people who are not transgender, but whose sense of self or gender expression does not adhere to gender stereotypes.[339]

Thus, the MAP Overall Tally for each state (possible total of 42.5 points) is calculated based on the Sexual Orientation Tally (20.5 total possible points) and the Gender Identity Tally (22 total possible points). The tallies illustrate how LGBQ-related, versus transgender-related, policies are progressing differentially both within individual states and across the country more generally.

Total scores can result from consistent scores between the Sexual Orientation and Gender Identity tallies or from divergent scores in the two categories. The table below demonstrates the cut-offs set by MAP for each categorization. MAP notes that:

> Tallies look only at existing laws. They do not look at the social climate, nor do they take into account implementation of each state's laws. The tally also does not reflect the efforts of advocates and/or opportunities for future change. States with low tallies might shift rapidly with an influx of resources, and states with higher tallies might continue to expand equality for LGBTQ people in ways that can provide models for other states.[340]

CATEGORY	SEXUAL ORIENTATION TALLY	GENDER IDENTITY TALLY	TOTAL TALLY
HIGH (75-100% OF POINTS POSSIBLE)	15.5 to 20.5	16.5 to 22	32 to 42.5
MEDIUM (50-74.9% OF POINTS POSSIBLE)	10.25 to 15.25	11 to 16.25	21.25 to 31.75
FAIR (25-49.9% OF POINTS POSSIBLE)	5.25 to 10	5.5 to 10.75	10.75 to 21
LOW (0-24.9% OF POINTS POSSIBLE)	0 to 5	0 to 5.25	0 to 10.5
NEGATIVE POINTS	<0	<0	<0
TOTAL POINTS POSSIBLE	20.5	22	42.5

Equality Maps Snapshot: LGBTQ Equality by State.
Source: Movement Advancement Project. [341]

The Overall Tally tables (presented below) allow states to be ranked on the basis of their overall score. A summary table of state Overall Tallies is presented in the summary section at the end of this section of the book.

Topics discussed in the sections for each state include:

- State Non-Discrimination Laws,
- Birth Certificates,
- Driver's Licenses,
- Public Accommodations,
- Sports,
- Law Enforcement, Jails, and Prisons,
- Health Care and Health Care Benefits,

- Marriage,
- LGBTQ Youth Laws and Policies, and
- Religious Exemption Laws.

In the sections for each individual state that follow, if there is little or no information presented on any specific topic, it is because the state agency either does not have the information posted on their website or they did not respond to my email and/or telephone requests for that information. In such cases, I have indicated that, as of the date of publication, no information was available.

In those instances where a response was received, it often required additional digging by me to verify the information. Sometimes, email responses provided links to the information, which I then pursued and included. My experience, however, is that not everyone in state government believes in transparency. In searching through state statutes to find state laws on specific topics, the results were hit and miss. State agency regulations for many states were, at best, difficult to find and when I did find them, they did not always address the issue directly. It appears that under the current climate of highly restrictive legislation being introduced and passed, some people are evasive when asked questions specifically about transgender issues. A few issues where information may have been difficult to find were the areas of Law Enforcement, Jails and Prisons, Health Care and Health Care Benefits, and LGBTQ Youth Laws and Policies. When no information is available, I refer the reader to the Movement Advancement Project website. The issue of same-sex marriage after the *Obergefell* decision means states now have to issue marriage licenses even though their marriage laws may not yet have been updated.

Suffice it to say that I found that states, where the state government and state legislatures are controlled by members of the Republican party, were often openly hostile to the transgender community. Although not every state's government or legislature was, or is, openly hostile, there are those that make life very difficult for those who are transgender. It can be particularly perplexing when these same individuals make statements such as they are just looking out for the safety and wellbeing of their constituencies, when, in fact, they are doing the exact opposite. The hypocrisy is sometimes overwhelming.

Finally, I want to stress that the rights of the trans community are being challenged at every turn by conservative Republicans at the state level. Laws will continue to be introduced in state legislatures that will affect the lives of those in the trans community. It is up to all of us to keep abreast of the changing legal landscape.

Alabama

Alabama Non-Discrimination Laws

Alabama does not have a specific anti-discrimination law. The state primarily relies on federal anti-discrimination law regarding employment and housing discrimination, and other areas. The state has a separate statute covering age discrimination, the Alabama Age Discrimination in Employment Act (AADEA). As a whole, Alabama ranks as one of the worst states in the country for protecting the civil rights of transgender individuals. In terms of social progress on issues involving minority populations, including the transgender population, the state seems not to have come out of the reconstruction era. In a state where the population is 69.1% White, 26.8% Black, and an average per capita income, in 2019, of $28,650, minorities here are the poorest of any state in the country.[342]

Birth Certificates

Alabama Code Title 22, Health, Mental Health, and Environmental Control § 22-9A-19(d),[343] provides:

> (d) Upon receipt of a certified copy of an order of a court of competent jurisdiction indicating that the sex of an individual born in this state has been changed by surgical procedure and that the name of the individual has been changed, the certificate of birth of the individual shall be amended as prescribed by rules to reflect the changes.

The Rules of the Alabama State Board of Health, Alabama Department of Public Health, Chapter 420-7-1.-16 states, "Amendment or Correction of Birth Certificates," does not specifically cover changes to birth certificates for transgender persons.

To get a court ordered name change you will need to fill out and file a name change form[344] with the local Alabama Probate Court.

Driver's Licenses

The Alabama Law Enforcement Agency (ALEA) issued Policy Order 63 in 2012, which states that transgender persons wishing to get an Alabama Driver's License must complete sex reassignment surgery and provide a proof of surgery letter on the surgeon's letterhead that confirms that the person has undergone surgery to change their genitals. The case of *Corbitt, et al. v. Taylor*, CIVIL ACTION NO. 2:18cv91-MHT (WO) (M.D. Ala. Jan. 15, 2021) went before the U.S. District Court for the Middle District of Alabama, Northern Division. The District Court ruled that Policy Order 63 was unconstitutional because it classified drivers' licenses based on sex and enjoined policy enforcement.[345] The State has appealed the District Court's decision to the U.S. Court of Appeals for the 11th Circuit. If there is a ruling from the 11th Circuit before the publication of this book, it will be included here.

Public Accommodations

Alabama's public accommodation law only protects people with disabilities. See Alabama Code §§21-4-1 to 21-4-7.[346]

Sports and Sporting Events

The Associated Press (AP) announced on Friday, April 23, 2021, that:

> Republican Gov. Kay Ivey on Friday signed legislation restricting transgender students from participating in K-12 sports, making Alabama the latest conservative state to ban transgender girls from playing on female sports teams.[347]

The AP also reported that

> Supporters of the Bill, HB 391, say transgender girls are born bigger and faster and have an unfair advantage in competition. Opponents argue the Bills are rooted in discrimination and fear and violate the federal law barring sex discrimination in education.
>
> "HB 391 is nothing more than a politically motivated Bill designed to discriminate against an already vulnerable population. By signing this legislation, Gov. Ivey is forcefully excluding transgender children. Let's be clear here: transgender children are children. They deserve the same opportunity to learn valuable skills of teamwork, sportsmanship, and healthy competition with their peers," Human Rights Campaign President Alphonso David said in a statement.[348]

Law Enforcement, Jails, and Prisons

The 2015 U.S. Transgender Survey reports that:

> Respondents experienced high levels of mistreatment and harassment by police. In the past year, of respondents who interacted with police or other law enforcement officers who thought or knew they were transgender, 57% experienced some form of mistreatment. The mistreatment included being verbally harassed repeatedly, referred to as the wrong gender, physically assaulted, or sexually assaulted, including being forced by officers to engage in sexual activity to avoid arrest, 53% of respondents said they would feel uncomfortable asking the police for help if they needed it.[349]

No Alabama state law prohibits discrimination by law enforcement based on sex in their interactions with the transgender community.

Health Care and Health Care Benefits

Alabama currently has no anti-discrimination law that prohibits discrimination because of sex in providing private health care to anyone, including the transgender community. This also applies to the health insurance industry in Alabama. There is also no law banning best-practice medical care for transgender youth and adolescents. Further, no law bans insurance providers from excluding coverage for transgender-specific care. Furthermore, no Medicaid law in the state provides coverage for transgender health care. No law exists that provides benefits for state employees who are transgender.

Marriage and Parental Rights

For information on this topic, see the state data on the MAP website.[350] Please also review the section above under federal laws on marriage.

LGBTQ Youth Laws

For information on this topic, please see the state data on the MAP website.

Religious Exemption Laws

The Alabama Religious Freedom Amendment to the state Constitution says in part:

> The purpose of the Alabama Religious Freedom Amendment is to guarantee that the freedom of religion is not burdened by state and local law; and to provide a claim or defense to persons whose religious freedom is burdened by government.[351]

Alabama Overall Tally

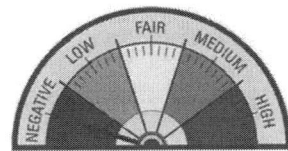

Grand Totals	Sexual Orientation Policy Tally	Gender Identity Policy Tally	Overall Tally
Totals	-0.5/20.5	-3.5/22	-4/42.5
Ratings	NEGATIVE	NEGATIVE	NEGATIVE

Alaska

Alaska Non-Discrimination Laws

Alaska fairs reasonably well in terms of its laws that prohibit discrimination in a variety of contexts. The Alaska Human Rights Law, Alaska Statutes, Title 18, Chapter 80, Article 4, §18.80.200, et. seq., states, in part:

> The opportunity to obtain employment, credit and financing, public accommodations, housing accommodations, and other property without discrimination because of sex, physical or mental disability, marital status, changes in marital status, pregnancy, parenthood, race, religion, color, or national origin is a civil right.[352]

Sections on discrimination in employment, housing, public accommodations, financing, and financial services are all covered in this law.

Birth Certificates

The Alaska Department of Vital Records will amend the gender marker on a birth certificate upon receiving a letter from a medical or mental health provider attesting to appropriate clinical treatment for gender transition.

To apply for an amended birth certificate, the applicant should submit:

1. A Birth Certificate Request Form
2. Photocopy of the ID of the registrant or the parent or guardian
3. To update the name, a certified copy of the Decree of Name Change
4. To update the gender marker, a letter from a medical or mental health provider OR a certified copy of a court-ordered change of sex
5. Fee ($60 for the amendment fee and one certified copy)

Submit the application to this address:

Alaska Vital Records Office
Attn: Corrections
PO Box 110675
Juneau, AK 99811-0675

Notes :

- Unfortunately, please note that the amended birth certificate will list the amended information in fine print below the child and parent's names.

- If you use a gender change letter, the letter must be signed by a physician, social worker, psychologist, professional counselor, physician assistant, or advanced nurse practitioner. See the Department of Vital Records gender change policy for additional information.

- If you are applying for a legal name change in Alaska, you can request the court to include a sex change in the same proceeding. A court-ordered name and sex change is sufficient evidence to update the name and gender on a birth certificate.[353]

To change your name in Alaska, you can visit the website of the Alaska Court System Self-Help Center[354] for more information and to download the forms packet.

Driver's Licenses

To update name and gender on an Alaska ID, the applicant must first change their name with the Social Security Administration and then submit (1) court order for a name change, (2) an application for a new ID, and (3) a Certification for Change of Sex signed by a licensed provider certifying that the applicant has undergone the appropriate clinical treatment. Instead of a signature by a licensed provider, an applicant may present an updated birth certificate, U.S. Passport, or court order for gender change. The applicant must update the name on their license within 30 days of receiving a legal name change.[355]

Public Accommodations

Alaska's statutes also prohibit discrimination in public accommodations:

(a) It is unlawful for the owner, lessee, manager, agent, or employee of public accommodation,

(1) to refuse, withhold from, or deny to a person any of its services, goods, facilities, advantages, or privileges because of sex, physical or mental disability, marital status, changes in marital status, pregnancy, parenthood, race, religion, color, or national origin;

(2) to publish, circulate, issue, display, post, or mail a written or printed communication, notice, or advertisement that states or implies

(A) that any of the services, goods, facilities, advantages, or privileges of the public accommodation will be refused, withheld from, or denied to a person of a certain race, religion, sex, physical or mental disability, marital status, color, or national origin or because of pregnancy, parenthood, or a change in marital status, or

(B) that the patronage of a person belonging to a particular race, creed, sex, marital status, color, or national origin or who, because of pregnancy, parenthood, physical or mental disability, or a change in marital status, is unwelcome, not desired, or solicited.

(b) Notwithstanding (a) of this section, a physical fitness facility may limit public accommodation to only males or only females to protect the privacy interests of its users. Public accommodation may be limited under this subsection only to those rooms in the facility that are primarily used for weight loss, aerobic, and other exercises, or for resistance weight training. Public accommodation may not be limited under this subsection to rooms in the facility primarily used for other purposes, including conference rooms, dining rooms, and premises licensed under AS 04.11. This subsection does not apply to swimming pools or golf courses.[356]

LGBTQ Youth Laws

On May 12, 2021, Alaska Senate Majority Leader Shelley Hughes introduced SB140 to exclude transgender athletes from participating in school sports. Like many other Bills being introduced around the country, SB140 defines "sex" as one's "biological" sex. The legislation does not define "biological" sex.

Law Enforcement, Jails, and Prisons

For information on this topic, please see the state data on the MAP website.

Health Care and Health Care Benefits

For information on this topic, please see the state data on the MAP website.

Marriage and Parental Rights

For information on this topic, please see the state data on the MAP website. Please also review the section above under federal laws on marriage.

Religious Exemption Laws

For information on this topic, please see the state data on the MAP website.

Alaska Overall Tally

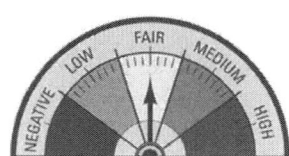

Grand Totals	Sexual Orientation Policy Tally	Gender Identity Policy Tally	Overall Tally
Totals	8.75/20.5	9/22	17.75/42.5
Ratings	FAIR	FAIR	FAIR

Arizona

Arizona Non-Discrimination Laws

Generally speaking, Arizona law prohibits discrimination because of race, color, religion, *sex*, age, or national origin or on the basis of disability in a variety of contexts. The following is Arizona Revised Statute 41-1463:

41-1463. Discrimination; unlawful practices; definition

- A. Nothing contained in this article shall be interpreted to require that the less qualified be preferred over the better qualified simply because of race, color, religion, *sex*, age or national origin or on the basis of disability. [emphasis added]

- B. It is an unlawful employment practice for an employer:
  1. To fail or refuse to hire or to discharge any individual or otherwise to discriminate against any individual with respect to the individual's compensation, terms, conditions or privileges of employment because of the individual's race, color, religion, *sex*, age or national origin or on the basis of disability. [emphasis added]
  2. To limit, segregate or classify employees or applicants for employment in any way which would deprive or tend to deprive any individual of employment opportunities or otherwise adversely affect the individual's status as an employee, because of the individual's race, color, religion, *sex*, age or national origin or on the basis of disability. [Emphasis added]
  3. To fail or refuse to hire, to discharge, or to otherwise discriminate against any individual based on the results of a genetic test received by the employer, notwithstanding subsection I, paragraph 2 of this section.

- C. It is an unlawful employment practice for an employment agency to fail or refuse to refer for employment or otherwise to discriminate against any individual because of the individual's race, color, religion, *sex,* age or national origin or on the basis of disability or to classify or refer for employment any individual on the basis of the individual's race, color, religion, sex, age or national origin or on the basis of disab[ility]. [Emphasis added]

- D. It is an unlawful employment practice for a labor organization:
  1. To exclude or to expel from its membership or otherwise to discriminate against any individual because of the individual's race, color, religion, *sex*, age or national origin or on the basis of disability. [emphasis added]
  2. To limit, segregate or classify its membership or applicants for membership or to classify or fail or refuse to refer for employment any individual in any way which would deprive or tend to deprive the individual of employment opportunities or would limit those employment opportunities or otherwise adversely affect the individual's status as an employee or as an applicant for employment because of the individual's race, color, religion, *sex*, age or national origin or on the basis of disability. [emphasis added]

3. To cause or attempt to cause an employer to discriminate against an individual in violation of this section.

E. It is an unlawful employment practice for any employer, labor organization or joint labor-management committee controlling apprenticeship or other training or retraining programs, including on-the-job training programs, to discriminate against any individual because of the individual's race, color, religion, **sex**, age or national origin or on the basis of disability in admission to or employment in any program established to provide apprenticeship or other training and, if the individual is an otherwise qualified individual, to fail or refuse to reasonably accommodate the individual's disability. [emphasis added]

F. With respect to a qualified individual, it is an unlawful employment practice for a covered entity to:

1. Participate in any contractual or other arrangement or relationship that has the effect of subjecting a qualified individual who applies with or who is employed by the covered entity to unlawful employment discrimination on the basis of disability.

2. Use standards, criteria or methods of administration that have the effect of discriminating on the basis of disability or that perpetuate the discrimination of others who are subject to common administrative control.

3. Exclude or otherwise deny equal jobs or benefits to an individual qualified for the job or benefits because of the known disability of an individual with whom the individual qualified for the job or benefits is known to have a relationship or association.

4. Not make reasonable accommodations to the known physical or mental limitations of an otherwise qualified individual who is an applicant or employee unless the covered entity can demonstrate that the accommodation would impose an undue hardship on the operation of the business of the covered entity or the individual only meets the definition of disability as prescribed in § 41-1461, paragraph 4, subdivision (c).

5. Deny employment opportunities to a job applicant or employee who is an otherwise qualified individual if the denial is based on the need of the covered entity to make reasonable accommodation to the physical or mental impairment of the applicant or employee.

6. Use qualification standards, employment tests or other selection criteria, including those based on an individual's uncorrected vision, that screen out or tend to screen out an individual with a disability or a class of individuals with disabilities, unless the standard, test or other selection criteria, as used by the covered entity, is shown to be job related for the position in question and is consistent with business necessity.

7. Fail to select and administer tests relating to employment in the most effective manner to ensure that, when the test is administered to a job applicant or employee who has a disability that impairs sensory, manual or speaking

skills, the test results accurately reflect the skills or aptitude or whatever other factor of the applicant or employee that the test purports to measure, rather than reflecting the impaired sensory, manual or speaking skills of the applicant or employee, except if the skills are the factors that the test purports to measure.

G. Notwithstanding any other provision of this article, it is not an unlawful employment practice:

1. For an employer to hire and employ employees, for an employment agency to classify or refer for employment any individual, for a labor organization to classify its membership or classify or refer for employment any individual, or for an employer, labor organization or joint labor-management committee controlling apprenticeship or other training or retraining programs to admit or employ any individual in any such program, on the basis of the individual's religion, sex or national origin in those certain instances when religion, sex or national origin is a bona fide occupational qualification reasonably necessary to the normal operation of that particular business or enterprise.

2. For any school, college, university or other educational institution or institution of learning to hire and employ employees of a particular religion if the school, college, university or other educational institution or institution of learning is in whole or in substantial part owned, supported, controlled or managed by a particular religion or religious corporation, association or society, or if the curriculum of the school, college, university or other educational institution or institution of learning is directed toward the propagation of a particular religion.

3. For an employer to fail or refuse to hire or employ any individual for any position, for an employment agency to fail or refuse to refer any individual for employment in any position or for a labor organization to fail or refuse to refer any individual for employment in any position, if both of the following apply:

    (a) The occupancy of the position or access to the premises in or upon which any part of the duties of the position are performed or are to be performed is subject to any requirement imposed in the interest of the national security of the United States under any security program in effect pursuant to or administered under any statute of the United States or any executive order of the president of the United States.

    (b) The individual has not fulfilled or has ceased to fulfill that requirement.

4. With respect to age, for an employer, employment agency or labor organization:

    (a) To take any action otherwise prohibited under subsection B, C or D of this section if age is a bona fide occupational qualification reasonably necessary to the normal operation of the particular business or if the differentiation is based on reasonable factors other than age.

(b) To observe the terms of a bona fide seniority system or any bona fide employee benefit plan such as a retirement, pension, deferred compensation or insurance plan, which is not a subterfuge to evade the purposes of the age discrimination provisions of this article, except that no employee benefit plan may excuse the failure to hire any individual and no seniority system or employee benefit plan may require or permit the involuntary retirement of any individual specified by §41-1465 because of the individual's age.

(c) To discharge or otherwise discipline an individual for good cause.

H. As used in this article, unlawful employment practice does not include any action or measure taken by an employer, labor organization, joint labor-management committee or employment agency with respect to an individual who is a member of the Communist Party of the United States or of any other organization required to register as a Communist-action or Communist-front organization by final order of the subversive activities control board pursuant to the subversive activities control act of 1950.

I. Notwithstanding any other provision of this article, it is not an unlawful employment practice:

1. For an employer to apply different standards of compensation or different terms, conditions or privileges of employment pursuant to a bona fide seniority or merit system or a system which measures earnings by quantity or quality of production or to employees who work in different locations, provided that these differences are not the result of an intention to discriminate because of race, color, religion, **sex** or national origin. [emphasis added]

2. For an employer to give and act upon the results of any professionally developed ability test provided that the test, its administration or action upon the results is not designed, intended or used to discriminate because of race, color, religion, **sex** or national origin. [emphasis added]

3. For any employer to differentiate upon the basis of **sex** or disability in determining the amount of the wages or compensation paid or to be paid to employees of the employer if the differentiation is authorized by the provisions of § 6(d) or § 14 of the fair labor standards act of 1938, as amended (29 United States Code §206(d)). [emphasis added]

J. Nothing contained in this chapter applies to any business or enterprise on or near an Indian reservation with respect to any publicly announced employment practice of the business or enterprise under which a preferential treatment is given to any individual because the individual is an Indian living on or near a reservation.

K. Nothing contained in this article or article 6 of this chapter 1 requires any employer, employment agency, labor organization or joint labor-management committee subject to this article to grant preferential treatment to any individual or group because of the race, color, religion, **sex** or national origin of the individual or group on account of an imbalance which may exist with respect to the total number or percentage of persons of any race, color, religion, *sex* or national origin employed by any employer, referred or classified for employment by any employment agency or labor organization, admitted to membership or classified by any labor organization or admitted to or employed in any apprenticeship or other training program, in comparison with the total number or percentage of persons of that race, color, religion, *sex* or national origin in any community, state, section or other area, or in the available work force in any community, state, section or other area. [emphasis added]

L. Nothing in the age discrimination prohibitions of this article may be construed to prohibit compulsory retirement of any employee who has attained sixty-five years of age and who, for the two year period immediately before retirement, is employed in a bona fide executive or high policymaking position, if the employee is entitled to an immediate nonforfeitable annual retirement benefit from a pension, profit sharing, savings or deferred compensation plan or any combination of plans of the employer for the employee, which equals, in the aggregate, at least forty-four thousand dollars. In applying the retirement benefit test of this subsection, if any retirement benefit is in a form other than a straight life annuity, with no ancillary benefits, or if employees contribute to the plan or make rollover contributions, the benefit shall be adjusted in accordance with rules adopted by the division so the benefit is the equivalent of a straight life annuity, with no ancillary benefits, under a plan to which employees do not contribute and under which no rollover contributions are made.

M. A covered entity may require that an individual with a disability shall not pose a direct threat to the health or safety of other individuals in the workplace. For the purposes of this subsection, "direct threat" means a significant risk to the health or safety of others that cannot be eliminated by reasonable accommodation.

N. This article does not alter the standards for determining eligibility for benefits under this state's workers' compensation laws or under state and federal disability benefit programs.

O. For the purposes of this section and §41-1481, with respect to employers or employment practices involving a disability, "individual" means a qualified individual.[357]

Birth Certificates

A Bill has been introduced into the Arizona legislature, HB-2867, which, if passed, would do the following:

Section 1. Section 36-337, Arizona Revised Statutes, is amended to read:

36-337. Amending birth certificates

A. The state registrar shall amend the birth certificate for a person who is born in this state when the state registrar receives any of the following:

For a person who has undergone a sex change operation or has a chromosomal count that establishes the sex of the person as different than in the registered birth certificate, both of the following:

(a) A written request for an amended birth certificate from the person or, if the person is a child, from the child's parent or legal guardian.

(b) A written statement by a physician that verifies the sex change operation or chromosomal count.

3. For a person who has undergone gender transition or has a congenital intersex condition, either of the following:

(a) A written request for an amended birth certificate from the person or, if the person is a child, from the child's parent or legal guardian, together with a written statement by a physician that verifies appropriate treatment for permanent gender transition or a congenital intersex condition.

(b) Proof of a legal name change with a written statement from the person or, if the person is a child, from the child's parent or legal guardian, stating that the name change was made for the purpose of affirming the person's gender identity and not for any fraudulent or unlawful purpose.

4. A court order ordering an amendment to a birth certificate.[358]

On November 14, 2020, three Arizona youth filed suit in the U.S. District Court for the District of Arizona to force the Arizona Registrar of Vital Records and the Department of Health Services to change the gender marker on their birth certificates without having to obtain sex reassignment surgery.[359] As stated above, Arizona law requires those who wish to have the gender marker on their birth certificates changed to coincide with their gender identity to first have obtained sex reassignment surgery. Since the plaintiffs, in that case, are between the age of six and thirteen, they are not seeking to obtain sex reassignment surgery.

Driver's Licenses

Arizona does not require that an applicant for a driver's license seek a court order to change the name or gender marker on a driver's license. The University of Arizona, LGBTQ Affairs Office, says:

Wait two days after changing your Social Security records, then visit your local Motor Vehicle Division Office… Once there, tell the intake clerk you wish to change the name on your license. They will give you a number and a form to complete. Complete the form indicating that you want to change both your name and your gender marker. When your number is called, hand the clerk the completed form, a certified copy of your name change order, the original doctor's letter and your current driver's license or ID card. It is likely that the clerk will be unfamiliar with the process for changing your gender marker and will take your documents to a supervisor. Don't panic. If they come back and say they can't do that, refer them to their own Policy 3.1.1 on gender marker changes.[360]

The Southern Arizona Gender Alliance (SAGA) also has information on the process.[361]

Public Accommodation

Arizona law prohibits discrimination in public accommodation because of "sex." The statute in question, Arizona Revised Statutes, §41-1442, states:

41-1442. Discrimination in places of public accommodation; exceptions

A. Discrimination in places of public accommodation against any person because of race, color, religion, *sex*, national origin or ancestry is contrary to the policy of this state and shall be deemed unlawful.

B. No person, directly or indirectly, shall refuse to, withhold from or deny to any person, nor aid in or incite the refusal to deny or withhold, accommodations, advantages, facilities or privileges thereof because of race, color, religion, sex, national origin or ancestry, nor shall distinction be made with respect to any person based on race, color, religion, *sex*, national origin or ancestry in connection with the price or quality of any item, goods or services offered by or at any place of public accommodation.

C. Any person who is under the influence of alcohol or narcotics, who is guilty of boisterous conduct, who is of lewd or immoral character, who is physically violent or who violates any regulation of any place of public accommodation that applies to all persons regardless of race, color, religion, *sex*, national origin or ancestry may be excluded from any place of public accommodation and nothing in this article shall be considered to limit the right of such exclusion.

D. Notwithstanding any other provision of this article and except as required by federal law, it is not an unlawful practice if a person fails to provide a trained and competent bilingual person who is skilled in interpreting a language other than English to assist a person who is seeking services at a place of public accommodation. Notwithstanding any other provision of this article and except as required by federal law, a person who offers a service at a place of public accommodation is not required to provide a person who is seeking the service any form or other documentation in that person's native language.

E. It is not an unlawful practice pursuant to this section for a person to fail to provide service at a place of public accommodation if by providing the service the person offering the service would violate a state or federal law or a rule that is adopted by a state or federal board, commission or agency that has jurisdiction over the person offering the service. [emphasis added]

However, the Arizona Supreme Court, in a case involving a business that creates custom wedding invitations, ruled that an ordinance of the City of Phoenix, which barred discrimination in public accommodations, violated the shop owners' First Amendment rights to free speech and freedom of expression.[362] It should be noted, however, that the Court completely disregarded the City's argument that the ordinance prohibited discrimination in public accommodations on the basis of sex and essentially ruled that Plaintiff's rights to freedom of speech and freedom of expression was more important than the ordinance's prohibition of discrimination because of sex or sexual orientation.

LGBTQ Youth Laws

Since early 2020, Bills have been introduced in state legislatures in Arizona, Florida, West Virginia, Montana, South Carolina, Minnesota, Georgia, Alabama, Mississippi, Kansas, Nebraska, Texas, Oklahoma, Maine, Louisiana, Missouri, Alaska, Wisconsin, Arkansas, North Dakota, North Carolina that would ban participation in school sports by transgender athletes solely on the basis that their stated gender identity or sex is not consistent with their "biological sex." However, since the term "biological sex" is not definitively defined in the medical, psychological, psychiatric, or sociological literature, used in this context, it is a layman's linguistic construct.

Arizona's proposed law, House Bill 2706, the "Save Women's Sports Act," and Senate Bill 1637, the "Equitable Treatment of Women and Girls Sports Act," would ban participation in school sports by transgender youth. As in all the other proposed laws around the country, these two Bills use essentially the same language. They attempt to justify keeping transgender youth out of school sports based on the wrong conclusion that male-to-female trans individuals possess an "unfair advantage" over their cisgender counterparts.

Law Enforcement, Jails, and Prisons

In a report by the UCLA School of Law, the Williams Institute, entitled, "Discrimination and Harassment by Law Enforcement Officers in the LGBTQ community," the authors state:

> Discrimination and harassment by law enforcement officers based on sexual orientation and gender identity continues to be pervasive throughout the United States. For example, a 2014 report on a national survey of LGBT people and people living with HIV found that 73% of respondents had face-to-face contact with the police in the past five years. Of those respondents, 21% reported encountering hostile attitudes from officers, 14% reported verbal assault by the police, 3% reported sexual harassment and 2% reported physical assault at the hands of law enforcement officers. Police abuse, neglect and misconduct were consistently reported at higher frequencies by respondents of color and transgender and gender nonconforming respondents.[363]

In Arizona, in an article by Chase Strangio, Director for Transgender Justice, ACLU LGBT and HIV Project, wrote:

> In Phoenix, Arizona, you can be arrested for repeatedly stopping and engaging a passerby in conversation. This may, under Phoenix law, be evidence that you are "manifesting" an intent to engage in prostitution. Of course, this could also be evidence that you are lost or canvassing for a political group or simply talking about the weather. The difference between "innocent" and "criminal" behavior often comes down to how a person looks.
>
> "Walking while trans" is a saying we use in the trans community to refer to the excessive harassment and targeting that we as trans people experience on a daily basis. "Walking while trans" is a way to talk about the overlapping biases against trans people - trans women specifically - and against sex workers. It's a known experience in our community of being routinely and regularly harassed and facing the threat of violence or arrest because we are trans and therefore often assumed to be sex workers.[364]

This is a classic case of stereotyping behavior simply because of how one looks. Police across the country do this as a means of identifying people who may be committing crimes. It is called profiling. And, as if this were not enough, the American Bar Association has written on this very subject, saying:

> Policing in the U.S. is not neutral. While this issue has been a focus for many communities of color, it is important to understand how it impacts the LGBTQ2I community as well. LGBTQ2I people in many communities are more frequently stopped by police than non-LGBTQ2I people. Police often engage in discriminatory profiling and criminalization of LGBTQ2I people, using loitering, identification, prostitution, lewdness,

and other laws to target them for harassment, arrest, and incarceration. This is a historical and current-day, systemic and nationwide practice.[365]

Health Care and Health Care Benefits

For information on this topic, please see the state data on the MAP website.

Marriage and Parental Rights

For information on this topic, please see the state data on the MAP website. Lease also review the section above under federal laws on marriage.

Religious Exemption Laws

Arizona has a broad religious exemption law. The law states:

Arizona Revised Statutes, Title 41, Article Nine, Section "1493.01. Free exercise of religion protected.

A. Free exercise of religion is a fundamental right that applies in this state even if laws, rules or other government actions are facially neutral.

B. Except as provided in subsection C, government shall not substantially burden a person's exercise of religion even if the burden results from a rule of general applicability.

C. Government may substantially burden a person's exercise of religion only if it demonstrates that application of the burden to the person is both:

1. In furtherance of a compelling governmental interest.

2. The least restrictive means of furthering that compelling governmental interest.

D. A person whose religious exercise is burdened in violation of this section may assert that violation as a claim or defense in a judicial proceeding and obtain appropriate relief against a government. A party who prevails in any action to enforce this article against a government shall recover attorney fees and costs.

E. In this section, the term substantially burden is intended solely to ensure that this article is not triggered by trivial, technical or de minimis infractions.[366]

Arizona Overall Tally

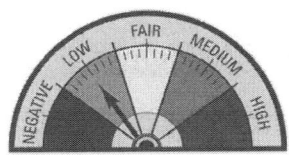

Grand Totals	Sexual Orientation Policy Tally	Gender Identity Policy Tally	Overall Tally
Totals	6.75/20.5	-0.5/22	6.25/42.5
Ratings	FAIR	NEGATIVE	LOW

Arkansas

Arkansas Anti-Discrimination Laws

Arkansas is one of many states that, in 2020 and 2021, has enacted laws that ban transgender athletes from competing in interscholastic and intercollegiate sports and being the first state to ban the provision of transition-related health care to transgender persons under the age of eighteen.

On May 25, 2021, the ACLU filed a suit challenging the law's constitutionality in banning the provision of transition-related health care to transgender minors. In 2017, in House Bill 1894, the Arkansas legislature attempted to prohibit the amendment of birth certificates by those who had undergone sex reassignment surgery. The Bill failed in committee during the *sine die* adjournment, and it appears the issue was not taken up again after that. Current law, A.C.A. § 20-18-307(d), allows for birth certificates to be amended by obtaining a court order showing that the individual has obtained a court-ordered name change and has shown proof of the surgical procedure completed. Transgender persons who are indigent or have an income under the poverty level can request a waiver of the court fees and costs, but the person will need to show proof sufficient for the court to grant *In Forma Pauperis* status. An "In Forma Pauperis Packet" is available.[367]

Birth Certificates

Arkansas requires an applicant for a new birth certificate to obtain a court order changing the registrant's name and designation of sex. The legal fee for amending a birth or death certificate, with or without a court order, is $15. This is in addition to the certificate fee for any replacement certificates that are requested. Birth certificates cost $12 for the first copy and $10 for each additional copy ordered simultaneously.

Arkansas Code (2019) §20-18-307(c) {name change} and (d) {sex change} are the state's authority for requesting an amendment to an existing record.

Arkansas Legal Services has the forms and instructions available on their website to do this independently without the expense of hiring an attorney.[368] They may even be willing to do it for you.

Driver's Licenses

Arkansas has a policy of changing the name on a driver's license if the applicant has obtained a court-ordered name change. The procedure for changing the sex designation on a driver's license is different. All the applicant needs to do is go to the local driver's license office and ask the clerk to change the designation of sex on the license.

Public Accommodation

Arkansas state law does not provide for an explicit prohibition of discrimination in public accommodations. So, anyone who experiences discrimination based on sex in the public accommodation setting will most likely have to rely on federal anti-discrimination statutes, such as the Civil Rights Act of 1964 and the U.S. Constitution, to enforce their rights to be provided with accommodations free from discrimination. In a commentary posted by Professor Jordan Blair Woods, who is a law professor and Faculty Director of the Richard B. Atkinson LGBTQ Law and Policy Program at the University of Arkansas School of Law, Fayetteville, said that Arkansas is one of twenty states that do not have statewide anti-discrimination protections for LGBTQ individuals.[369] The Arkansas legislature went so far as to ban counties and municipalities from enacting their anti-discrimination statutes.

Sports

Arkansas Act 461, the "Fairness in Women's Sports Act, signed by the Arkansas Governor on March 22, 2021, prohibits participation in women's sports by "males" as defined in the Act. A.C.A. Title 6, Chapter 1, Subchapter 1, subsection (c)(1)(1) and 2(A) and (B). As in other laws Arkansas has enacted concerning transgender persons, this law states that sex is defined as one's "biological sex." These laws attempt to redefine that which science has defined through rigorous research.

Act 461, Arkansas Code Title 6, Chapter 1, Subchapter 1, was amended to add a section that reads:

> Section 6-1-107(c) Interscholastic, intercollegiate, intramural, or club athletic teams or sports that a school sponsors shall be expressly designated as one (1) of the following based on biological sex: (1) "Male", "men's", or "boys"; (2)(A) "Female", "women's", or "girls." [line numbers removed for clarity and ease of reading]

Again, as discussed above in the section on Title IX of the Education Amendments of 1972, federal law prohibits discrimination in any educational program or activity based on sex. Arkansas Act 461 discriminates against school students who are trans by attempting to say that since male-to-female trans students were designated as male at birth, they are, therefore, males despite what the medical, psychiatric, and psychological communities have shown through extensive research and should, therefore, be banned from competition. It establishes an irrebuttable presumption that any individual who possesses a penis, is, in fact, male. The reverse applies to females. The proof that this is not true lies in the body of scientific research undertaken over the last 60 years.

Law Enforcement, Jails, and Prisons

According to the U.S. Transgender Survey,[370]

> Respondents experienced high levels of mistreatment and harassment by police. In the past year, of respondents who interacted with police or other law enforcement officers who thought or knew they were transgender, 65% experienced some form of mistreatment.

Health Care and Health Care Benefits

Arkansas Act 626 (SAFE or Save Adolescents from Experimentation Act), introduced in the state Legislature in March 2021 as HB 1570, bans outright any transition-related health care services that may be provided to trans individuals who are under the age of eighteen. Arkansas was the first state in the country to enact such legislation. The law is being challenged in the United States District Court for the Eastern District of Arkansas by four families and two doctors in *Dylan Brandt, et al., v. Leslie Rutledge, et al.* The case was filed on May 25, 2021.

Act 626 says, in part:

> SECTION 3. Arkansas Code Title 20, Chapter 9, is amended to add an additional subchapter to read as follows: Subchapter 15 —Arkansas Save Adolescents from Experimentation (SAFE) Act 1617, 20-9-1501. Definitions. As used in this subchapter: (1) "Biological sex" means the biological indication of male and female in the context of reproductive potential or capacity, such as sex chromosomes, naturally occurring sex hormones, gonads, and nonambiguous

internal and external genitalia present at birth, without regard to an individual's psychological, chosen, or subjective experience of gender.[371]

In signing HB-1570, the Governor of Arkansas, Asa Hutchinson, said:

> "This law simply says that female athletes should not have to compete in a sport against a student of the male sex when the sport is designed for women's competition," Hutchinson said in a statement released by his office. "As I have stated previously, I agree with the intention of this law. This will help promote and maintain fairness in women's sporting events.[372]

In a Supplemental Order filed on August 2, 2021, the United States District Court for the Eastern District of Arkansas, Central Division, in *Dylan Brandt, et al. v. Leslie Rutledge, et al.*, Case No. 4:21-CV00450/JM ruled as follows:

> The Court finds the Act's ban of services and referrals by health care providers is not substantially related to the regulation of the ethics of the medical profession in Arkansas. Gender-affirming treatment is supported by medical evidence that has been subject to rigorous study. Every major expert medical association recognizes that gender-affirming care for transgender minors may be medically appropriate and necessary to improve the physical and mental health of transgender people. Act 626 prohibits most of these treatments. Further, the State's goal of ensuring the ethics of Arkansas healthcare providers is not attained by interfering with the patient-physician relationship, unnecessarily regulating the evidence-based practice of medicine and subjecting physicians who deliver safe, legal, and medically necessary care to civil liability and loss of licensing.
>
> If the Act is not enjoined, health care providers in this State will not be able to consider the recognized standard of care for adolescent gender dysphoria. Instead of ensuring that healthcare providers in the State of Arkansas abide by ethical standards, the State has ensured that its healthcare providers do not have the ability to abide by their ethical standards which may include medically necessary transition-related care for improving the physical and mental health of their transgender patients. The Court finds that Act 626 cannot withstand heightened scrutiny and based on the record would not even withstand rational basis scrutiny if it were the appropriate standard of review. Plaintiffs are, therefore, likely to succeed on the merits of their Equal Protection claim.[373]

Marriage

For information on this topic, please see the state data on the MAP website. Please also review the section above under federal laws on marriage.

LGBTQ Youth Laws

As I discussed above (Sports), Arkansas enacted a new law in 2021 that bans transgender adolescents and youth from participating in interscholastic and intercollegiate sports based on sex. *Brandt, et al. v. Rutledge, et al.*, filed in the U.S. District Court for the District of Eastern Arkansas on May 25, 2021. The Arkansas law, Act 626, bans participation in school sports by trans individuals based on sex.

Religious Exemption Laws

In March 2021, the Arkansas Legislature enacted SJR14, the "Arkansas Religious Freedom Amendment, through a Senate Joint Resolution." The proposed amendment to the state's Constitution would take effect in November 2022 if the state's voters approved.

The proposed amendment states, in relevant part:

> SECTION 4. (a) Except as provided in subsection (b) of this section, government shall not burden a person's freedom of religion even if the burden results from a rule of general applicability.
>
> (b) Government may burden a person's freedom of religion only if the government demonstrates that application of the burden to the person:
>
> (1) Is in furtherance of a compelling government interest; and As Engrossed:
>
> (2) Is the least restrictive means of furthering that compelling government interest. [line numbers and footer removed for clarity and ease of reading].

Arkansas Overall Tally

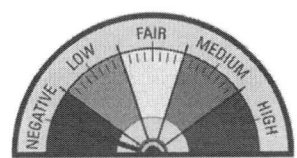

Grand Totals	Sexual Orientation Policy Tally	Gender Identity Policy Tally	Overall Tally
Totals	-0.5/20.5	-5/22	-5.5/42.5
Ratings	NEGATIVE	NEGATIVE	NEGATIVE

California

California Anti-Discrimination Laws

While California is known as a progressive state, it still has laws that provide for a broad religious exemption policy. Other than that, the state's laws treat the transgender and transsexual community well.

California bans discrimination based on sex, sexual orientation, and gender identity in virtually every aspect of life, including employment, housing, public accommodations, and the provision of health care. California bans discrimination based on race, color, religion or creed, national origin or ancestry, sex (including pregnancy, gender, sexual orientation, and gender identity), age, physical or mental disability, and veteran status.[374]

Birth Certificates

To amend an existing birth certificate or record, you need to follow the California Department of Public Health, Vital Records directions.[375] They require that you provide completed Form VS-20 Sworn Statement,[376] Form VS-24 Affidavit to Amend a Record,[377] a certified copy of the Court Order changing your name, and documentation from your physician or surgeon confirming that you have completed sex reassignment surgery, plus the required fees. The process of changing your name is relatively simple in California. Information about the process is available on the California Courts, Judicial Branch of California website.[378,379]

Driver's Licenses

California allows a transgender person to change the designation of sex on their driver's license by filling out a form OLIN 2019-3.[380] You only need to go to court to change your name on your birth certificate.

Public Accommodation Laws

California Civil Code Section 51(b) states:

> (b) All persons within the jurisdiction of this state are free and equal, and no matter what their sex, race, color, religion, ancestry, national origin, disability, medical condition, genetic information, marital status, sexual orientation, citizenship, primary language, or immigration status are entitled to the full and equal accommodations, advantages, facilities, privileges, or services in all business establishments of every kind whatsoever.[381]

Sports

Section 221.5 of the California Education Code[382] prohibits discrimination in K-12 educational programs based on sex. Assembly Bill 1266, signed by the Governor of California on August 12, 2013, states in part:

> a) It is the policy of the state that elementary and secondary school classes and courses, including nonacademic and elective classes and courses, be conducted, without regard to the sex of the pupil enrolled in these classes and courses.

Section 221.5 also states,

f) A pupil shall be permitted to participate in sex-segregated school programs and activities, including athletic teams and competitions, and use facilities consistent with his or her gender identity, irrespective of the gender listed on the pupil's records.

LGBTQ Youth Laws and Policies

For information on this topic, please see the state data on the MAP website.

Law Enforcement, Jails, and Prisons

For information on this topic, please see the state data on the MAP website.

Health Care and Health Care Benefits

In California, transgender individuals can access health care for all health care services related to their gender identity and sex reassignment surgery. In 2012, the California Department of Insurance issued regulations clarifying that insurers are prohibited from denying, canceling, and limiting or refusing insurance coverage based on gender identity, expression, or transgender status. In addition, health insurance policies are prohibited from arbitrarily excluding coverage for gender affirmation services including (but not limited to) hormone therapy, mental health services, and surgical services.[383]

Marriage

For information on this topic, please see the state data on the MAP website. Please also review the section above under federal laws on marriage.

Religion

For information on this topic, please see the state data on the MAP website.

California Overall Tally

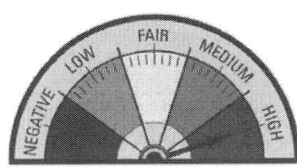

Grand Totals	Sexual Orientation Policy Tally	Gender Identity Policy Tally	Overall Tally
Totals	18.5/20.5	20.75/22	39.25/42.5
Ratings	HIGH	HIGH	HIGH

Colorado

Colorado Non-Discrimination Laws

The Colorado Civil Rights Division enforces Colorado's anti-discrimination laws. Colorado bans discrimination "because of race, creed, color, sex, sexual orientation, religion, age, national origin, or ancestry."[384]

Birth Certificates

The Colorado legislature amended the state's birth certificate and driver's license laws in 2019, under House Bill 19-1039, which went into effect on January 1, 2020. It is named "Jude's Law." The law allows transgender persons to amend their Colorado birth certificate under Colorado Revised Statutes, Section 25-2-113.8. See the One Colorado website of at for information and procedures.[385]

To change your name in Colorado, visit the Colorado Courts website for information and forms.[386]

Driver's Licenses

As above, transgender persons can now obtain a Colorado driver's license, which shows the designation of sex and name that matches the applicant's gender identity by following the procedures outlined in Colorado Revised Statutes Section 25-2-107. See also paragraph 6 on the One Colorado website under "Birth Certificates."

Public Accommodation Laws

Colorado Revised Statutes, Section 24-34-601, prohibits discrimination in places of public accommodation as defined in the statute. The protected classes are defined as disability, race, creed, color, sex, sexual orientation, marital status, national origin, and ancestry. The ACLU of Colorado has published a document entitled, "Know Your Rights: Discrimination in Places of Public Accommodation," that details how to file a complaint should a member of the LGBTQ community face discrimination in public accommodations."[387]

Sports

The Colorado Department of Education issued guidelines for participating in interscholastic and intercollegiate sports, entitled, "Participation of Transgender Athletes in Sport Clubs and Intramural Sports."[388] Essentially, any student who has not yet begun transition-related health care for gender dysphoria is prohibited from participating in school sports. Any student who has begun transition-related health care for gender dysphoria must first complete one year of medically prescribed hormone treatment. Before competing on a men's team, female-to-male trans persons must first obtain written authorization from the "National Governing Body." The reasoning behind this is that testosterone is a banned substance and FtM individuals take testosterone as part of their hormone therapy for gender dysphoria.

Law Enforcement, Jails, and Prisons

For information on this topic, please see the state data on the MAP website.

Health Care and Health Care Benefits

For information on this topic, please see the state data on the MAP website.

Marriage

For information on this topic, please see the state data on the MAP website. Please also review the section above under federal laws on marriage.

Youth Laws and Policies

For information on this topic, please see the state data on the MAP website.

Religious Exemption Laws

For information on this topic, please see the state data on the MAP website.

Colorado Overall Tally

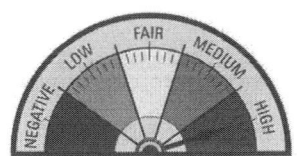

Grand Totals	Sexual Orientation Policy Tally	Gender Identity Policy Tally	Overall Tally
Totals	18.75/20.5	20.75/22	39.5/42.5
Ratings	HIGH	HIGH	HIGH

Connecticut

Connecticut Non-Discrimination Laws

Connecticut Statutes, Volume 12, Title 46a, Chapter 814c, Part II, Section 46a-58(a) states:

> It shall be a discriminatory practice in violation of this section for any person to subject, or cause to be subjected, any other person to the deprivation of any rights, privileges or immunities, secured or protected by the Constitution or laws of this state or of the United States, on account of religion, national origin, alienage, color, race, sex, gender identity or expression, sexual orientation, blindness, mental disability, physical disability or status as a veteran.[389]

Birth Certificates

Connecticut requires that you submit a Name Change Affidavit,[390] along with a copy of a Probate Court Order changing your name to get the new name on your birth certificate. See the Connecticut Department of Public Health website for more information.[391] The Department of Public's website also provides information for changing the designation of sex on your birth certificate to reflect to match your stated gender identity. Additional information is provided on the Connecticut Department of Public Health website.[392]

Essentially, you will need to prepare an affidavit signed under penalty of law, requesting a replacement birth certificate to reflect that your gender differs from the sex designated on your birth certificate. You will also need an affidavit from a licensed physician, a licensed advance practice nurse, or a licensed psychologist, stating that you have undergone surgical, hormonal, or other treatment clinically appropriate for the purpose of gender transition.

You will also need a certified copy of a court order granting a legal name change if you would like your amended birth certificate to reflect a new name.

If you want a copy of your new birth certificate, a "Request for Copy of Birth Certificate" form will need to be submitted to get a certified copy of your amended birth certificate. Along with this form, you will need to send thirty dollars payable to the Treasurer of the State of Connecticut.

Lastly, a photocopy of a valid government issued photo identification card (driver's license, passport) will need to be included with your request.[393]

Driver's Licenses

Connecticut allows transgender applicants to change the sex designation on a driver's license by getting their physician or other approved healthcare professionals to fill out a Gender Designation/Change form B-372. The applicant must submit this form along with any other forms required by the Department of Motor Vehicles.

A Petition for Change of Name, Form PC-901, needs to be filled out and submitted to the Probate Court nearest the petitioner's residence. A fillable pdf form is available.[394] The applicant will have to pay the required fees unless the applicant is indigent and requests permission from the court to proceed *In Forma Pauperis*.

Public Accommodation Laws

Connecticut law states that "places [of accommodation] may not deny full and equal accommodations or discriminate in any way because of a person's gender identity or expression."[395]

Sports

In 2013, The Connecticut Interscholastic Athletic Conference (CIAC) adopted a policy regarding transgender athletes that concludes that:

> It would be fundamentally unjust and contrary to applicable state and federal law to preclude a student from participation on a gender specific sports team that is consistent with the public gender identity of that student for all other purposes.[396]

Law Enforcement, Jails, and Prisons

For information on this topic, please see the state data on the MAP website.

Health Care and Health Care Benefits

For information on this topic, please see the state data on the MAP website.

Marriage

For information on this topic, please see the state data on the MAP website. Please also review the section above under federal laws on marriage.

LGBTQ Youth Laws and Policies

For information on this topic, please see the state data on the MAP website.

Religious Exemption Laws

For information on this topic, please see the state data on the MAP website.

Connecticut Overall Tally

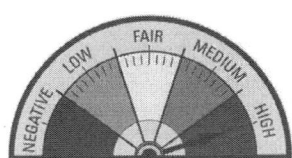

Grand Totals	Sexual Orientation Policy Tally	Gender Identity Policy Tally	Overall Tally
Totals	17.5/20.5	20/22	37.5/42.5
Ratings	HIGH	HIGH	HIGH

Delaware

Delaware Non-Discrimination Laws

In June 2013, Delaware became the seventeenth state to enact protections for the transgender community. The law protects anyone who has or expresses a gender different from their assigned sex at birth from discrimination in housing, employment, state or county government employment, public accommodations, the issuance of insurance policies, or the granting of contracts.[397]

Birth Certificates

In 2017, the Delaware Department of Health and Social Services published new regulations for 16 DE Admin. Code 4205, §10.7 "Amendment of Sex," which states in relevant part:

> 10.7.1 The Registrar shall establish a new certificate of birth that reflects the new sex upon receipt of the following documents:
>
> > 10.7.1.1 An affidavit requesting a new certificate of birth with a sex that differs from the sex listed on the original certificate of birth of the registrant, or if the registrant is a minor, the registrant's parent, guardian, or legal representative; and
> >
> > 10.7.1.2 An affidavit signed by a licensed medical or mental health professional, licensed by a U.S. jurisdiction in a relevant discipline, who has treated or evaluated the registrant, including license number and name of issuing jurisdiction of the professional stating that:
> >
> > > 10.7.1.2.1 The registrant has undergone surgical, hormonal, psychological or other treatment appropriate for the individual for the purpose of gender transition, based on contemporary medical standards; or
> > >
> > > 10.7.1.2.2 The registrant has an intersex condition, and that in the provider's professional opinion, the individual's sex as listed on the original birth certificate should be changed.[398]

To change your name in Delaware, you can download a packet that guides you through the process and provides other information you may need.[399]

Driver's Licenses

Chapter 59, Section 5901, et. seq., of Title 10 of the Delaware Code provides the procedures to be used in petitioning the Delaware courts for a change of name. To change the designation of sex or gender marker on a Delaware Driver's License, you must submit a "Request for Gender Change on Driver's License/I.D. Card" with the medical or social service provider section filled out by your doctor or social service provider.[400]

Public Accommodations

> Delaware Code, Title 6, Chapter 45, Section 4503, provides that"
>
> > All persons within the jurisdiction of this State are entitled to the full and equal accommodations, facilities, advantages and privileges of any place of public accommodation regardless of the race, age, marital status, creed, color, sex, handicap, sexual orientation, gender identity, or national origin of such persons.[401]

Sports

Delaware policy on transgender participation in interscholastic and intercollegiate sports is as follows:

a. A transgender student, defined as a student whose gender identity differs from the student's birth sex, shall be eligible to participate in interscholastic athletics in a manner that is consistent with the student's gender identity, under any of the following conditions:

   i. The student provides an official record, such as a revised birth certificate, a driver's license or a passport, demonstrating legal recognition of the students reassigned sex, or

   ii. A physician certifies that the student has had appropriate clinical treatment for transition to the reassigned sex, or

   iii. A physician certifies that the student is in the process of transition to the reassigned sex.

   iv. The determination of a student's sex-assignment for interscholastic athletics shall be made by the student's school.

   v. The determination of a student's sex-assignment for interscholastic athletics shall remain in effect for the duration of the student's high school eligibility.

b. Any member school may appeal the eligibility of a transgender student on the grounds that the student's participation in interscholastic athletics would adversely affect competitive equity or safety of teammates or opposing players.

c. Any such appeal will be heard by the DIAA Board of Directors.

d. The identity of the student shall remain confidential and at the request of the student's parents the hearing will be confidential.[402]

Law Enforcement, Jails, and Prisons

For information on this topic, please see the state data on the MAP website.

Health Care and Health Care Benefits

For information on this topic, please see the state data on the MAP website.

Marriage

For information on this topic, please see the state data on the MAP website. Please also review the section above under federal laws on marriage.

LGBTQ Youth Laws and Policies

For information on this topic, please see the state data on the MAP website.

Religious Exemption Laws

For information on this topic, please see the state data on the MAP website.

Delaware Overall Tally

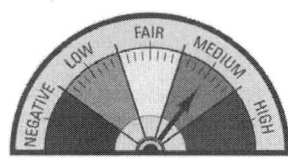

Grand Totals	Sexual Orientation Policy Tally	Gender Identity Policy Tally	Overall Tally
Totals	12.5/20.5	12.75/22	25.25/42.5
Ratings	MEDIUM	MEDIUM	MEDIUM

District of Columbia

District of Columbia Non-Discrimination Laws

The DC Office of Human Rights enforces the DC Human Rights Act, which makes discrimination illegal based on 21 protected traits for people who live, visit, or work in the District of Columbia. The DC Human Rights Act prohibits discrimination in housing, employment, public accommodations, and educational institutions.[403]

Birth Certificates

The District government allows transgender persons to change the name and gender on their birth certificates by using the appropriate forms.[404] Furthermore, DC Code states:

> §7–231.22. New records of live birth for change of gender designation.
>
> > (a) The Registrar shall establish a new record of live birth that reflects the new gender designation and, if applicable, the new name of an individual born in the District upon receipt of the following documents:
> >
> > > (1) A written request, signed under oath or affirmation, for a new record of live birth with a gender designation that differs from the gender designated on the original record of live birth, from the individual or, if the individual is a minor, the individual's:
> > >
> > > > (A) Parent;
> > > > (B) Guardian; or
> > > > (C) Legal representative;
> > >
> > > (2) A statement, signed under oath or affirmation, by a licensed healthcare provider who has treated or evaluated the individual, stating that:
> > >
> > > > (A) The individual has undergone surgical, hormonal, or other treatment appropriate for the individual for the purpose of gender transition, based on contemporary medical standards; or
> > > >
> > > > (B) The individual has an intersex condition, and that in the healthcare provider's professional opinion, the individual's gender designation should be changed; and
> > >
> > > (3) If a change of name listed on the certificate is also being requested, an original or certified copy of the order of the court granting the change of name.[405]

Driver's Licenses

The District also has a form to request that the gender marker on a driver's license be changed.[406]. The form is also available in several other languages on the District's DMV site.[407]

Public Accommodations

DC Municipal Regulations, Title 4, § 801.1, makes it unlawful for anyone to discriminate based on gender identity or expression in housing, employment, public accommodations, educational institutions, and Columbia government district.[408]

Sports

The District of Columbia State Athletic Association (DCSAA) publishes a handbook covering the policies, rules, and regulations governing athletic competition. Section XII Policy Positions, A. Gender Equity, 3 Gender Identity Participation, states:

> No person shall, on the basis of gender, be excluded from participating in, be denied the benefits of, or be treated differently from another person or otherwise be discriminated against in any interscholastic athletics. Pursuant to 5-F DCMR § 102.6, the DCSAA allows for participation for all students in a manner that is consistent with their gender identity and/or expression regardless of the gender listed on the student's birth certificate. All students should have the opportunity to participate in DCSAA activities in a manner that is consistent with their gender identity, irrespective of the gender listed on a student's records or identification documents.[409]

District of Columbia leadership has stated that the District will not follow other states that have enacted laws barring participation in interscholastic sports by transgender students.

Law Enforcement, Jails, and Prisons

For information on this topic, please see the state data on the MAP website.

Health Care and Health Care Benefits

For information on this topic, please see the state data on the MAP website.

Marriage

For information on this topic, please see the state data on the MAP website. Please also review the section above under federal laws on marriage.

LGBTQ Youth Laws and Policies

For information on this topic, please see the state data on the MAP website.

Religious Exemption Laws

For information on this topic, please see the state data on the MAP website.

District of Columbia Overall Tally

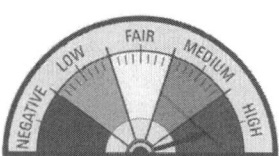

Grand Totals	Sexual Orientation Policy Tally	Gender Identity Policy Tally	Overall Tally
Totals	17/20.5	18.5/22	35.5/42.5
Ratings	HIGH	HIGH	HIGH

Florida

Florida Non-Discrimination Laws

Florida recognizes the significance of the U.S. Supreme Court's decision in *Bostock, supra,* by enacting "TITLE XLIV, CIVIL RIGHTS, CHAPTER 760, DISCRIMINATION IN THE TREATMENT OF PERSONS; MINORITY REPRESENTATION" [caps in the original].[410,411] See also the National Center for Transgender Equity[412] and the Notice published on the Florida Commission on Human Relations website.[413]

Birth Certificates

There is a step-by-step guide[414] on how to get your name changed and your birth certificate amended with the correct name and designation of the sex listed.

Driver's Licenses

As mentioned above (Birth Certificates), step 3 of the step-by-step guide explains how to get your driver's license updated. The Florida Department of Highway Safety and Motor Vehicles website[415] provides additional information.

Public Accommodations

The Florida Civil Rights Act, in Section 760.08, states:

> Discrimination in places of public accommodation—All persons are entitled to the full and equal enjoyment of the goods, services, facilities, privileges, advantages, and accommodations of any place of public accommodation without discrimination or segregation on the ground of race, color, national origin, sex, pregnancy, handicap, familial status, or religion.[416]

Sports

Florida Statutes, Section 1002.20(7) "Nondiscrimination," states:

> All education programs, activities, and opportunities offered by public educational institutions must be made available without discrimination based on race, ethnicity, national origin, gender, disability, religion, or marital status, in accordance with the provisions of s. 1000.05.[417]

Section 1000.05 specifically states:

> Discrimination against students and employees in the Florida K-20 public education system prohibited; equality of access required.
>
>> (1) This section may be cited as the "Florida Educational Equity Act."
>>
>> (2)(a) Discrimination on the basis of race, ethnicity, national origin, gender, disability, religion, or marital status against a student or an employee in the state system of public K-20 education is prohibited. No person in this state shall, on the basis of race, ethnicity, national origin, gender, disability, religion, or marital status, be excluded from participation in, be denied the benefits of, or be subjected to discrimination under any public K-20 education program or activity, or in any employment conditions or practices, conducted

by a public educational institution that receives or benefits from federal or state financial assistance.[418]

Yet, on June 1, 2021, Governor Ron DeSantis signed into law SB1028, The "Fairness in Women's Sports Act," which states, in part:

> that certain athletic teams or sports sponsored by certain educational institutions be designated on the basis of students' biological sex at birth; authorizing athletic teams or sports designated for male students to be open to female students; prohibiting athletic teams or sports designated for female students to be open to male students.[419]

Law Enforcement, Jails, and Prisons

For information on this topic, please see the state data on the MAP website.

Health Care and Health Care Benefits

For information on this topic, please see the state data on the MAP website.

Religious Exemption Laws

For information on this topic, please see the state data on the MAP website.

Marriage

For information on this topic, please see the state data on the MAP website. Please also review the section above under federal laws on marriage.

LGBTQ Youth Laws and Policies

For information on this topic, please see the state data on the MAP website.

Religious Exemption Laws

Florida statutes, Title XLIV, Chapter 761, provides that:

> 1) The government shall not substantially burden a person's exercise of religion, even if the burden results from a rule of general applicability, except that government may substantially burden a person's exercise of religion only if it demonstrates that application of the burden to the person:
>
>> (a) Is in furtherance of a compelling governmental interest; and
>>
>> (b) Is the least restrictive means of furthering that compelling governmental interest.
>
> (2) A person whose religious exercise has been burdened in violation of this section may assert that violation as a claim or defense in a judicial proceeding and obtain appropriate relief.[420]

This law, along with others around the country, is being used to discriminate against the LGBTQ community based on sex by persons who claim that their religious beliefs prevent them from serving LGBTQ individuals in stores and restaurants, and other places of public accommodation, as well in school sports.

Essentially, people with "deeply held religious beliefs" use these laws to become a law unto themselves. But the Supreme Court has yet to rule that religious belief justifies certain behaviors directed toward others, who may not express or share the same religious beliefs. The government has a compelling interest in preventing discrimination. When religious beliefs form the basis of such discrimination, the courts are left to decide which constitutional right carries more weight. All too often, the result is that religious beliefs that discriminate against others are allowed even though the rights of others to be free from discrimination suffer.

Florida Overall Tally

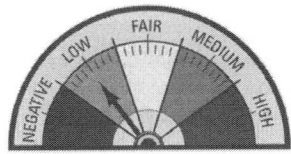

Grand Totals	Sexual Orientation Policy Tally	Gender Identity Policy Tally	Overall Tally
Totals	5.75/20.5	4/22	9.75/42.5
Ratings	FAIR	LOW	LOW

Georgia

Georgia Non-Discrimination Laws

According to one source, Georgia has no specific nondiscrimination laws. A search of the Georgia statutes yielded no results, and the author found no laws relating to non-discrimination.

Birth Certificates

Georgia Code (O.C.G.A.) Title 19, § 19-12-1(h) provides that a petition must be filed with the court to change a person's name. The name change petition form is available from your local County Superior Court. The availability of court forms seems to differ from county to county. In Fulton County, forms are available online.[421]

The Georgia Department of Public Health requires applicants who wish to change the designation of sex on their birth certificate to use the "General Amendments" section of their website. See "Affidavit for Amendment" (Form 3977).[422] Applicants are advised to follow the instructions on page two of the form carefully. Scroll down the Georgia Department of Public Health website[423] to about mid-page to find the "General Amendments" section where the form is located. To change your name in Georgia, you must file a Petition to Change Name of Adult with the Superior Court Family Court Division in the county where you live. To find your local Superior Court, use the interactive map.[424]

Driver's Licenses

Georgia residents who currently possess a Georgia Driver's License can change the name on the license during their original license term. If the applicant's name has changed from the original birth record or passport, the applicant is required to present certified legal documents supporting each name change, such as marriage certificate, divorce decree, adoption papers, or legal name change. NOTE: All name change documents are required for new applicants and new residents. For a gender update, a court order or physician's letter certifying the gender change is required.[425]

Public Accommodations

As stated above (Non-discrimination laws), Georgia has no specific law that bans discrimination in public accommodations. The reader is directed to visit the website for your city or municipality to see if they have a public accommodations law that prohibits discrimination based on sexual orientation or gender identity.

Sports

Republican State Senators in Georgia introduced SB266 in February 2021 entitled the "Save Girls' Sports Act." If the Bill passes and is signed into law by the Governor:

> Title 20 of the Official Code of Georgia Annotated, relating to education, is amended in Code Section 20-2-315, relating to gender discrimination prohibited, authorized separate gender teams, equal athletic opportunity, physical education classes, employee designated to monitor compliance, grievance procedures, and reporting requirements, by adding a new subsection to read as follows:
>
>> (k)(1) As used in this subsection, the term 'gender' shall mean a person's biological sex and shall be solely recognized based on a person's reproductive biology and genetics at birth.[426]

Further, in Section 3 of the Bill, it states:

SECTION 3. Said title is further amended in Part 2 of Article 2 of Chapter 3, relating to University System of Georgia, by adding a new Code section to read as follows:

> 20-3-65.1. 40 (a) As used in this Code section, the term 'sex' refers only to biological distinctions between male and female.
>
> (b) In any intercollegiate athletic activity that is subject to rules, standards, or classifications that provide for student eligibility restrictions in order to ensure, enhance, or promote fair competition, each institution of the University System of Georgia shall make all determinations based on sex and not on gender.[427]

Law Enforcement, Jails, and Prisons

For information on this topic, please see the state data on the MAP website.

Health Care and Health Care Benefits

The Healthcare.gov website has specific information for those seeking gender-related transition services.[428] Georgia's August 1991 State Medicaid Plan (Section 7) explicitly excludes:

> Experimental or investigational services, drugs or procedures which are not generally recognized by the Food and Drug Administration, the U.S. Public Health Service, Medicare and the Department's contracted Peer Review Organization as acceptable treatment.
>
> The following list is representative of non-covered procedures that are considered to be experimental or investigational… Transsexual surgery.[429]

Courts in other states have ruled that to exclude the provision of gender-related treatment for gender dysphoria from coverage under a state's Medicaid Plan is unconstitutional and violates Section 1557 of the ACA.[430] For example, the Iowa Supreme Court, in the case of *Eerieanna Good and Carol Beal v. Iowa Department of Human Services*, Case No 18-1158 (March 8, 2019), found that:

> Given our holding that rule 441—78.1(4)'s exclusion of Medicaid coverage for gender-affirming surgery violates the ICRA as amended by the legislature in 2007, we need not address the other issues raised on appeal.[431]

Marriage

For information on this topic, please see the state data on the MAP website. Please also review the section above on federal laws on marriage.

LGBTQ Youth Laws and Policies

For information on this topic, please see the state data on the MAP website.

Religious Exemption Laws

For information on this topic, please see the state data on the MAP website.

Georgia Overall Tally

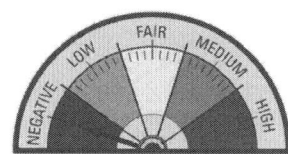

Grand Totals	Sexual Orientation Policy Tally	Gender Identity Policy Tally	Overall Tally
Totals	2.5/20.5	-3/22	-0.5/42.5
Ratings	LOW	NEGATIVE	NEGATIVE

Hawai'i

Hawai'i Non-Discrimination Laws

Article I, Section 5 of the Hawai'i Constitution provides that "no person shall be denied the enjoyment of civil rights or be discriminated against in the exercise thereof because of race, religion, sex or ancestry." The legislature gave meaning to this commitment by creating the Hawai'i Civil Rights Commission (HCRC) and by enacting Act 219 in 1988 and Acts 386 and 387 in 1989.

Birth Certificates

Transgender individuals can use a form to change the sex designation on the Hawai'i Birth Certificate.[432] An explanation of the process and what supporting documents you may need to file with your application to amend your birth certificate can be found on the Vital Records page of the Hawaii Department of Health website.[433]

To change your name in Hawai'i, the website of the State Lieutenant Governor provides information and a link to the online application form and instructions.[434] You do not need to go to court to change your name in the State of Hawai'i.

Driver's Licenses

To change the gender marker on your driver's license, visit the State of Hawai'i Department of Transportation website.[435]

Public Accommodations

Hawai'i statutes, Chapter 489, §489-2 Definitions indicates:

> "Gender identity or expression" includes a person's actual or perceived gender, as well as a person's gender identity, gender-related self-image, gender-related appearance, or gender-related expression, regardless of whether that gender identity, gender-related self-image, gender-related appearance, or gender-related expression is different from that traditionally associated with the person's sex at birth.[436]

Hawai'i statutes, Chapter 489, §489-3 Discriminatory Practices Prohibition states:

> Unfair discriminatory practices that deny, or attempt to deny, a person the full and equal enjoyment of the goods, services, facilities, privileges, advantages, and accommodations of a place of public accommodation based on race; sex, including gender identity or expression; sexual orientation; color; religion; ancestry; or disability, including the use of a service animal, are prohibited. [L 1986, c 292, pt of §1; am L 1990, c 210, §2; am L 1992, c 33, §5; am L 2006, c 76, §3; am L 2018, c 217, §8][437]

Sports

The Hawai'i High School Athletics Association has a policy of inclusion of transgender athletes. The policy was challenged in March 2020 by a coach who felt that transgender athletes presented an unfair advantage over female athletes who were not transgender. Former Hawai'i Representative Tulsi Gabbard introduced a Bill in the U.S. House of Representatives on December 10, 2020, that would have banned transgender athletes from participation in school sports. The Bill was entitled HR8932, the "Protect Women in Sports Act," It appears that the Bill died in committee.

Law Enforcement, Jails, and Prisons

For information on this topic, please see the state data on the MAP website.

Health Care and Health Care Benefits

For information on this topic, please see the state data on the MAP website.

Marriage

For information on this topic, please see the state data on the MAP website. Please also review the section above under federal laws on marriage.

LGBTQ Youth Laws and Policies

For information on this topic, please see the state data on the MAP website.

Religious Exemption Laws and Policies

For information on this topic, please see the state data on the MAP website.

Hawai'i Overall Tally

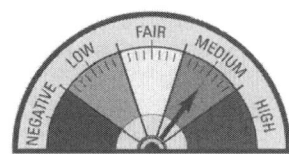

Grand Totals	Sexual Orientation Policy Tally	Gender Identity Policy Tally	Overall Tally
Totals	14.5/20.5	15.5/22	30/42.5
Ratings	MEDIUM	MEDIUM	MEDIUM

Idaho

Idaho Non-Discrimination Laws

There appears to be no general non-discrimination law or policy in Idaho that protects the LGBTQ community from discrimination. The Idaho Human Rights Commission's website states that Idaho prohibits discrimination in various areas, but there is no specific mention of the LGBTQ community. However, Senate Bill 1030, introduced in January 2021 would amend Section 67-5901 of the Idaho Code:

> 67-901. PURPOSE OF CHAPTER. The general purposes of this chapter are: (1) To provide for execution within the state of the policies embodied herein and in the federal Civil Rights Act of 1964, as amended, and the Age Discrimination in Employment Act of 1967, as amended, and Titles I and III of the Americans with Disabilities Act. (2) To secure for all individuals within the state freedom from discrimination because of race, color, religion, sex, sexual orientation, gender identity, or national origin, or disability in connection with employment, public accommodations, and real property transactions, discrimination because of race, color, religion, sex, sexual orientation, gender identity, or national origin in connection with education, discrimination because of age in connection with employment, and thereby to protect their interest in personal dignity, to make available to the state their full productive capacities, to secure the state against domestic strife and unrest, to preserve the public safety, health, and general welfare, and to promote the interests, rights and privileges of individuals within the state.[438]

Birth Certificates

On June 1, 2020, the U.S. District Court for the District of Idaho granted a plaintiff's motion for clarification of the Court's order of March 5, 2018, which granted a permanent injunction ordering the Idaho Department of Health and Welfare to provide a means by which transgender individuals are able to change the designation of sex on their birth certificates.[439]

On March 18, 2020, however, the Idaho Legislature passed, and on March 30, 2020, the Idaho Governor signed into law, House Bill 509 (HB 509) which provides that the sex listed on a birth certificate can be amended in only one of two ways:

1) by filing a notarized affidavit within one year of the filing of the certificate, signed by the requisite persons, declaring the information contained on the certificate "incorrectly represents a material fact at the time of birth," and

2) after one year, a party may challenge the qualitative statistics and material facts on the certificate "in court only on the basis of fraud, duress, or material mistake of fact.[440]

It would appear that the Idaho Legislature and Governor believe that the federal court order can be violated on whim and caprice. One commentator remarked, "The Idaho legislature and Governor seem to think they are above the law." Since the Court did not decide on the constitutionality of HB509, the issue may once again be before the Court once the IDHW decides how to implement the provisions of HB509.

To change your name in Idaho, see the Court Assistance Office, State of the Idaho Judicial Branch.[441]

Driver's Licenses

Transgender individuals can change the designation of sex on their driver's license by using the form found on the Government of Idaho website.[442] Transgender persons can obtain a name change by using the Idaho Judicial Branch Court Assistance Office forms.[443] But the author could not find any specific information for transgender persons wishing to get a new driver's license with the designation of sex that matches their stated gender identity.

Public Accommodations

There are no public accommodations laws at the state level in Idaho. However, at least eleven cities in Idaho have enacted broad employment, housing, and public accommodations ordinances that prohibit discrimination against the LGBTQ community.

Sports

The "Fairness in Women's Sports Act," HB500a, was introduced in the Idaho House of Representatives on February 13, 2020, and signed by the Governor on March 30, 2020. The law bans participation in school sports by persons who are transgender. The law was challenged in U.S. District Court for the District of Idaho and is before the U.S. Court of Appeals for the Ninth Circuit. The oral argument took place on May 3, 2021. A decision by the Ninth Circuit is pending.

Law Enforcement, Jails, and Prisons

The U.S. Supreme Court, on October 13, 2020, denied the Petition for Writ of Certiorari to the U.S. Court of Appeals for the Ninth Circuit in the case of *Adree Edmo v. Idaho Department of Corrections*, 949 F.3d 489 (2020). The agency appealed a ruling of the Ninth Circuit that Idaho had to provide Adree Edmo with sex reassignment surgery, noting that to do otherwise would violate the Eighth Amendment to the United States Constitution's prohibition of Cruel and Unusual punishment.

Health Care and Health Care Benefits

For information on this topic, please see the state data on the MAP website.

Marriage

For information on this topic, please see the state data on the MAP website. Please also review the section above under federal laws on marriage.

LGBTQ Youth Laws and Policies

As noted previously, on March 30, 2020, the Governor of Idaho signed into law HB500, which bans transgender athletes from participating in interscholastic and intercollegiate sports. The law is being challenged in the case of *Lindsey Hecox v. Bradley Little* and is before the U.S. Court of Appeals for the Ninth Circuit, awaiting a decision.

Religious Exemption Laws

For information on this topic, please see the state data on the MAP website.

Idaho Overall Tally

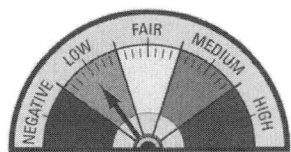

Grand Totals	Sexual Orientation Policy Tally	Gender Identity Policy Tally	Overall Tally
Totals	4.25/20.5	-0.5/22	3.75/42.5
Ratings	LOW	NEGATIVE	LOW

Illinois

Illinois Non-Discrimination Laws

Following is the text from an email I received from the Illinois Human Rights Commission:

> The Illinois Human Rights Commission (Commission) is a quasi-judicial agency and a neutral, impartial forum for the litigation of Complaints filed pursuant to the Illinois Human Rights Act (Act) following the Illinois Department of Human Rights investigation of a charge of discrimination. The Illinois Human Rights Act forbids discrimination based on age (40+), ancestry, arrest record, citizenship status, color, conviction record, disability (physical and mental), familial status (with respect to real estate transactions), gender identity, marital status, military status, national origin, orders of protection, pregnancy, race, religion, sex, sexual harassment, sexual orientation and unfavorable military discharge in the areas of education, employment, access to financial credit, public accommodations, and real estate transactions. The Act also protects against retaliation.
>
> The Act created two separate administrative agencies with distinct functions regarding enforcement of the Act: the Illinois Department of Human Rights (the "Department") to investigate charges of discrimination, and the Illinois Human Rights Commission (the "Commission") to adjudicate complaints of civil rights violations.
>
> To file a charge of discrimination, please visit the Illinois Department of Human Rights website[444] for more information. For more information about the Commission, and the entire process, please visit the Commission website.[445]

Birth Certificates

In Illinois, to obtain a new or corrected birth certificate that shows a new name *and* a change in the designation of sex, you must first go to court to get your name changed. The procedures to be followed can be found on the Illinois Courts website.[446] Make sure you ask the court clerk for at least two additional copies of your records for other government agencies that may request proof of name change before issuing a government I.D.

Once your name has been changed, you can go to the Illinois Department of Public Health website to obtain a new birth certificate with the correct name on it. You will need to follow the procedures set out on their site to get the certificate with your correct name and a change in the designation of sex recorded thereon.[447]

Driver's Licenses

To get a driver's License in Illinois, the reader should read about the REAL ID program[448]. There are links to resources in the gold-colored box at the bottom of the page.

Public Accommodations

Article 1, Section 1-102(A) Freedom from Unlawful Discrimination, states that no person shall be subject to unlawful discrimination based on "'sex', or 'sexual orientation.'"[449] Absent from this statute is "gender identity." The author has reached out to the Illinois Human Rights Commission for comment. As of the date of publication, the author has received no response from the Illinois Secretary of State on this issue.

Sports

The Illinois High School Association has a policy that:

> The student and/or parents shall contact the school administrator or athletic director at their member school notifying them that the student has a different gender identity than listed on the student's school registration card or birth certificate and that the student wishes to participate in athletics/activities in a manner consistent with their gender identity. The school shall collect the following for the participation ruling:
>
> a. Gender identity used for school registration records
>
> b. Medical documentation (hormonal treatments, sexual re-assignment surgery, counseling, medical personnel, etc.)
>
> c. Gender Identity related advantages for approved participation
>
> 2) Once the school administrator has collected the relevant information, the member school shall contact the IHSA office in writing of the request for the ruling, the student's gender identity, and the selected athletics/activities that the student would like the opportunity to participate in if they are selected through the team try-out process.
>
> a. Once the student is approved, participation is granted through the duration of their high school career, it does not need to be annually renewed.[450]

Law Enforcement, Jails, and Prisons

For information on this topic, please see the state data on the MAP website.

Health Care and Health Care Benefits

The state of Illinois Department of Healthcare and Family Services (IHFS) issued a Notice to Providers[451] dated June 29, 2020, which reaffirmed that, in Illinois, discrimination in the provision of health care services to transgender persons is prohibited under Illinois law. The notice was issued after the Trump administration eliminated discrimination based on gender identity and sex stereotyping on June 12, 2020. After he became President of the United States on January 20, 2021, President Joe Biden issued an Executive Order stating, in part,

> People should be able to access healthcare and secure a roof over their heads without being subjected to sex discrimination.[452]

The order effectively bans discrimination based on gender identity through the enforcement of Title VII and other federal laws and regulations that prohibit discrimination based on gender identity.

Marriage

For information on this topic, please see the state data on the MAP website. Please also review the section above under federal laws on marriage.

LGBTQ Youth Laws and Policies

For information on this topic, please see the state data on the MAP website.

Religious Exemption Laws

The Illinois Religious Freedom Restoration Act (RFRA), 775 ILCS 35,[453] allows those who express, demonstrate, or exercise religious beliefs may do so freely. The government may only "burden" a person's free exercise, expression, or demonstration of those beliefs when it can show that there is a compelling government interest that is enforced in the least restrictive means available.

Illinois Overall Tally

Grand Totals	Sexual Orientation Policy Tally	Gender Identity Policy Tally	Overall Tally
Totals	17/20.5	18/22	35/42.5
Ratings	HIGH	HIGH	HIGH

Indiana

Indiana Non-Discrimination Laws

Indiana has no statewide LGBTQ nondiscrimination laws and no prohibition of discrimination against the LGBTQ community on a wide variety of subjects, including marriage, birth certificates and driver's licenses, the provision of health care to persons under the age of eighteen, transgender participation in school sports programs, discrimination in the criminal justice system, housing, and public accommodations. Indiana is among the growing list of states where the legislature has passed laws limiting LGBTQ participation in everyday activities and where laws have been proposed but have not yet been enacted into law.

Two Bills currently before the 2021 Session of the legislature, SB0224 and HB1505, have virtually the same wording, word for word, intended to ban the provision of gender-related health care to persons under eighteen years of age. It is draconian in its approach and scope.

Further, Indiana is among a growing list of states that have, or are considering enacting, state Religious Freedom Restoration laws that allow anyone who claiming to be acting on their "deeply held religious beliefs" to deny services to transgender people.

Birth Certificates

In Indiana, changing the name or gender marker on a birth certificate requires the individual to go to court to obtain an order that the Indiana Department of Health change the name or gender marker. It is one of the most restrictive policies of any of the states regarding changes to birth certificates. Details are available on the Indiana Department of Health website.[454]

Driver's Licenses

Indiana allows changes/amendments to a driver's license to birthdate, address, and gender.[455]

Public Accommodations

Indiana does not have a comprehensive statewide non-discrimination law that protects the LGBTQ community or its members from discrimination in public accommodations. Members of the LGBTQ community who experience discrimination in public accommodations need to rely on federal laws to enforce their rights.

Sports

The Indiana High School Athletic Association (IHSAA) governs how student-athletes may participate in high school sports. A Position Statement on Gender Equity can be found on the IHSAA website.[456]

Law Enforcement. Jails, and Prisons

For information on this topic, please see the state data on the MAP website.

Health Care and Health Care Benefits

For information on this topic, please see the state data on the MAP website.

Marriage

For information on this topic, please see the state data on the MAP website. Please also review the section above under federal laws on marriage.

LGBTQ Youth Laws and Policies

For information on this topic, please see the state data on the MAP website.

Religious Exemption Laws

Indiana has one of the most comprehensive Religious Freedom Restoration Acts (RFRA) in the country, which was signed into law in 2015 by former Governor Mike Pence. The law was widely criticized by businesses and others. An article on the Indiana Democratic Party's website, quoting the International Business Times declares:

> **Indiana experienced an estimated $256 million economic panic following RFRA.** Major businesses boycotting a new religious freedom law in Indiana could cost the state's economy some $256.4 million and counting over the next six years, according to the Center for American Progress.[457]

Indiana Overall Tally

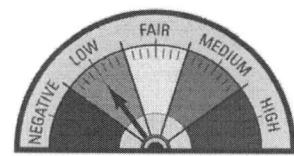

Grand Totals	Sexual Orientation Policy Tally	Gender Identity Policy Tally	Overall Tally
Totals	5.25/20.5	1.25/22	6.5/42.5
Ratings	FAIR	LOW	LOW

Iowa

Iowa Non-Discrimination Laws

Iowa Code, Chapter 216, Section 216.6, states that it is illegal to discriminate in employment:

> Because of the age, race, creed, color, sex, sexual orientation, gender identity, national origin, religion, or disability of such applicant or employee, unless based upon the nature of the occupation.[458]

Iowa also prohibits discrimination because of age, color. creed, familial status, gender identity, marital status, mental disability, national origin, physical disability, race, religion, ancestry, sex, and sexual orientation.[459]

Birth Certificates

Iowa Code §144.39 allows a person to change their name on their birth certificate after receiving an order from an Iowa court to change their name. To find information on how to change your name, you can visit the website of the Iowa Judicial Branch.[460]

In terms of changing the designation of sex on a birth certificate, the Iowa Department of Public Health, Vital Records Section, in Iowa Department of Public Health Rule 641-99.20(144) sets out the requirements and procedures for obtaining a new or amended birth certificate for those who have received treatment for gender dysphoria.[461] The Administrative Notice of Rule Changes can be found on the Iowa Admin Rules website.[462] It is listed under subrule §601.5(7) in the listing. Rule 641-99.20(144) of Chapter 99 Vital Records Modifications provides additional information.[463]

Driver's Licenses

The Iowa Notice of Intended Action outlines the following:

> Subrule 601.5(7) is amended to ensure that the procedure for changing the sex designation on a person's driver's license remains consistent with the requirements of Iowa law and is applied on equal terms to all Iowa driver's license holders, whether born in Iowa or outside of Iowa. Iowa Code section 321.182 requires a driver's license applicant to provide the applicant's sex designation at the time of application, and Iowa Code section 321.189 requires the Department to include the applicant's sex on any driver's license issued. Policy on change of sex designation in Iowa is guided by Iowa Code section 144.23(3), which allows the state registrar to establish a new birth certificate for a person born in Iowa that shows a new sex designation when the person submits a notarized affidavit from a licensed physician and surgeon or osteopathic physician and surgeon stating that by reason of surgery or other treatment, the sex designation of the person has been changed.[464]

Public Accommodations

Iowa Code Chapter 216 Civil Rights Commission, §216.7 Unfair Practices—Accommodations or Services, states:

> 216.7 Unfair practices—accommodations or services. 1. It shall be an unfair or discriminatory practice for any owner, lessee, sublessee, proprietor, manager, or superintendent of any public accommodation or any agent or employee thereof: a. To refuse or deny to any person because of race, creed, color, sex, sexual orientation, gender identity, national origin, religion, or disability the accommodations, advantages,

facilities, services, or privileges thereof, or otherwise to discriminate against any person because of race, creed, color, sex, sexual orientation, gender identity, national origin, religion, or disability in the furnishing of such accommodations, advantages, facilities, services, or privileges.[465]

Sports

The Iowa High School Athletic Association (IHSAA) has a policy of inclusion in interscholastic sports. The policy is modeled after the sections in Iowa Code Section 216, which deal with the transgender athlete population and Iowa's non-discrimination policy. The Iowa High School Athletic Association Transgender Statement can be found on the IHSAA website.[466]

Law Enforcement, Jails, and Prisons

For information on this topic, please see the state data on the MAP website.

Health Care and Health Care Benefits

The Iowa Administrative Code, Human Services Department, Title 441, Chapter 78, Section 78.1(4), pp. 682-683, states:

> For the purposes of this program, cosmetic, reconstructive, or plastic surgery is surgery which can be expected primarily to improve physical appearance or which is performed primarily for psychological purposes or which restores form but which does not correct or materially improve the bodily functions. When a surgical procedure primarily restores bodily function, whether or not there is also a concomitant improvement in physical appearance, the surgical procedure does not fall within the provisions set forth in this subrule. Surgeries for the purpose of sex reassignment are not considered as restoring bodily function and are excluded from coverage.[467]

Marriage

For information on this topic, please see the state data on the MAP website. Please also review the section above under federal laws on marriage.

LGBTQ Youth Laws and Policies

For information on this topic, please see the state data on the MAP website.

Religious Exemption Laws

For information on this topic, please see the state data on the MAP website.

Iowa Overall Tally

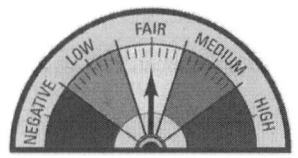

Grand Totals	Sexual Orientation Policy Tally	Gender Identity Policy Tally	Overall Tally
Totals	11/20.5	7/22	18/42.5
Ratings	MEDIUM	FAIR	FAIR

Kansas

Kansas Non-Discrimination Laws

The Kansas Act Against Discrimination (KAAD) was first enacted in 1953 and amended numerous times, the last amendments being enacted in 2012. The Act prohibits discrimination as follows:

> "Unlawful discriminatory practice" means:
>
> (1) Any discrimination against persons, by reason of their race, religion, color, sex, disability, national origin or ancestry:
>
> (A) In any place of public accommodations; or
>
> (B) in the full and equal use and enjoyment of the services, facilities, privileges and advantages of any institution, department or agency of the state of Kansas or any political subdivision or municipality thereof.[468]

The Kansas Human Rights Commission stated the Bostock decision by the U.S. Supreme Court as a principle factor in its decision to change its policy, stating, in part:

> The U.S. Supreme Court ruling in *Bostock* determined that Title VII's "sex" discrimination prohibition includes employment discrimination on the basis of homosexuality and transgender status. Effective today, the Kansas Human Rights Commission will begin accepting complaints of "sex" discrimination in employment, housing, and public accommodations wherein allegations include discrimination based on LGBTQ and all derivates of "sex".[469]

The Commission issued its Guidance document on September 18, 2020. The document can be found on the Commission's website.[470]

Birth Certificates

Kansas Statutes, Chapter 65, Article 24, Section 22a provides for changes to a registrant's name when they have received a court order changing their name. A certified copy of the order is required to be presented along with the application. Kansas has been successfully sued in the Federal Courts to provide registrants with a new birth certificate that shows a change in the designation of sex. The Department of Health and Environment (KDHE) has entered into settlement decrees. The District Court ordered the KDHE secretary and other Kansas government officials to provide accurate birth certificates that reflect a person's sex, consistent with their gender identity. As a result, the office of vital statistics at KDHE will begin allowing a transgender person born in Kansas to obtain a certified copy of their amended birth certificate reflecting a change in sex designation.

To request a birth certificate in Kansas, individuals must submit a sworn statement requesting the change, accompanied by a passport or driver's license reflecting the person's "actual" sex or a certification issued by a health professional or mental health professional with whom the person has a doctor-patient relationship. The certification must document the health professional's opinion of an applicant's true gender identity and that the gender designation will continue into the future.[471]

In a 2019 case in the U.S. District Court for the District of Kansas, Kansas City Division, the Court approved a Consent Judgment that, among other things, says:

> 2. Whereas, a federal court has held that the State of Idaho "violate[d] the Equal Protection Clause by failing to provide an avenue for transgender people to amend the

sex listed on their birth certificates." *F. V. v. Barron*, 286 F. Supp.3d 1131, 1145 (D. Idaho 2018).

3. Whereas, a federal court determined that the Commonwealth of Puerto Rico's birth certificate policy, prohibiting transgender people born in Puerto Rico from obtaining birth certificates reflecting their true sex, consistent with their gender identity, "violate[d] transgender persons' decisional privacy and informational privacy" by forcing them to disclose their transgender status. *Arroyo Gonzalez v. Rossello Nevares*, 305 F. Supp. 3d 327, 333 (D.P.R. 2018). And that "[s]uch forced disclosure of a transgender person's most private information is not justified by any legitimate government interest." *Id.*

4. Whereas, the parties to this litigation desire to resolve the issues raised by Plaintiffs' Complaint and subsequent proceedings without the necessity of further litigation.

5. Whereas, the parties agree to jointly resolve this matter and consent to entry of the following final and binding consent judgment as dispositive of all issues raised in this case; and

6. Whereas, the parties intend this Consent Judgment to benefit all Kansans, including transgender people born in Kansas, and to be binding on Defendants unless and until modified by the Court on motion with proper cause shown under Federal Rule of Civil Procedure 60.[472]

Driver's Licenses

On July 9, 2021, the author received the following email from the Kansas Division of Vehicles.

The name change can be completed by visiting the driver's license office with your license, a proof of current residential address, and the legal name change document.

Listed below are the 3 documents that may be used to change the gender on a Kansas credential.

Lawful presence document showing correct gender (birth certificate, passport, certificate of naturalization, etc.

1. Court order announcing a gender reclassification (cannot be name change document only)
2. Letter from driver's licensing management authorizing the gender change

If you are needing the approval letter from licensing management, please mail a written request to:

Driver Services
PO BOX 2188
TOPEKA, KS66601

The request must include:

1. A photocopy of your Kansas credential.
   a. If you do not have a Kansas credential, you may send in a copy of your lawful presence document instead.
2. A letter from your licensed medical or osteopathic physician stating you have undergone the appropriate clinical treatment for change of sex.

3. A letter requesting the gender change. The letter must include:
   a. Full legal name
   b. Kansas residential address
   c. Gender classification currently on Kansas credential and requested new gender
   d. Requested new name (If applicable)
   e. New address (If applicable)
   f. Phone number and email address.[473]

Public Accommodations

The Kansas Act Against Discrimination (KAAD) prohibits discrimination in public accommodations. Kansas Statutes, Section 44-1002(h) states:

> "Public accommodations" means any person who caters or offers goods, services, facilities and accommodations to the public. Public accommodations include, but are not limited to, any lodging establishment or food service establishment, as defined by K.S.A 36-501 and amendments thereto; any bar, tavern, barbershop, beauty parlor, theater, skating rink, bowling alley, billiard parlor, amusement park, recreation park, swimming pool, lake, gymnasium, mortuary or cemetery which is open to the public; or any public transportation facility. Public accommodations do not include a religious or nonprofit fraternal or social association or corporation.[474]

Similarly, Kansas Statutes, Section 44-1002(i)(1)(A) prohibits discrimination in public accommodations.

Sports

The Kansas High School Athletic Association (KSHSAA) has a policy that allows transgender students to participate in school sports programs. The policy is directed at member schools and intended as guidance on how to proceed with approving a transgender student's participation in a school sports program. The Policy for Transgender Student Participation can be obtained online from the KSHSAA.[475]

Law Enforcement, Jails, and Prisons

For information on this topic, please see the state data on the MAP website.

Health Care and Health Care Benefits

Several representatives in the Kansas legislature have introduced House Bill 2210 in the 2021 Session of the legislature, which, if enacted into law, would ban all transition-related health care services for transgender people under the age of eighteen. The opening paragraph of the Bill reads as follows:

> New Section 1. (a) Unlawful gender reassignment service is knowingly performing, or causing to be performed, any of the following upon a child under 18 years of age for the purpose of attempting to change or affirm the child's perception of the child's sex, if that perception is inconsistent with the child's sex.[476]

The Bill's sponsors are all Republicans, as in the other states with similar legislation pending, and have made public statements about wanting to "protect children." Yet, these Bills will hurt some of the most vulnerable children—those who are gender dysphoric.

Marriage

For information on this topic, please see the state data on the MAP website. Please also review the section above under federal laws on marriage.

LGBTQ Youth Laws and Policies

Religious Exemption Laws

In July 2013, the Kansas legislature passed House Bill 2203, the Kansas Preservation of Religious Freedom Act. The Act has broad protections for "religious freedom" that negatively impact the LGBTQ community. The Act is available on the Kansas Legislature's website.[477] An analysis of the Act by the Kansas Legislative Research Department is also available.[478]

Kansas Overall Tally

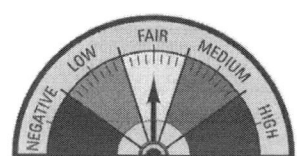

Grand Totals	Sexual Orientation Policy Tally	Gender Identity Policy Tally	Overall Tally
Totals	11/20.5	7/22	18/42.5
Ratings	MEDIUM	FAIR	FAIR

Kentucky

Kentucky Non-Discrimination Laws

The Kentucky Revised Statutes, Chapter 344.020(1)(b), "Purposes and Construction of Chapter," states:

> To safeguard all individuals within the state from discrimination because of familial status, race, color, religion, national origin, sex, age forty (40) and over, or because of the person's status as a qualified individual with a disability as defined in KRS 344.010 and KRS 344.030; thereby to protect their interest in personal dignity and freedom from humiliation, to make available to the state their full productive capacities, to secure the state against domestic strife and unrest which would menace its democratic institutions, to preserve the public safety, health, and general welfare, and to further the interest, rights, and privileges of individuals within the state.[479]

Birth Certificates

The Kentucky Admin. Reg., 901 KAR 5:070, Certificate of Birth Amended, states, in relevant part:

> Section 4. Amendment of Name. A change of name ordered by a court of competent jurisdiction shall be required to change the name as shown on the birth certificate, unless the registrant, parents, legal guardian, or individual responsible for filing the birth certificate presents documentation that the name was incorrectly recorded at the time of registration of the birth and meets the requirements in Section 8 of this administrative regulation.[480]

It should be noted that the author found no regulation in the Cabinet for Health and Family Services Title (901) that provides for the amendment of a birth certificate's designation of sex. Section 6 of the above regulation says that an affidavit must be submitted with the application for all other situations.[481]

The author received an email from the Cabinet for Health and Family Services, Department for Public Health, Office of Vital Statistics, which provided a policy document on Gender Reassignment Requirements.[482] Kentucky Revised Statutes, Section 213.121(5), states:

> Upon receipt of a sworn statement by a licensed physician indicating that the gender of an individual born in the Commonwealth has been changed by surgical procedure and a certified copy of an order of a court of competent jurisdiction changing that individual's name, the certificate of birth of the individual shall be amended as prescribed by regulation to reflect the change.[483]

Driver's Licenses

In Kentucky, you must follow the procedures set out on the website of driver licensing. A "Name Change" section toward the bottom of the web page provides instructions.[484]

Public Accommodations

Kentucky Revised Statutes, Section 344.120 prohibits discrimination in public accommodations based on disability, race, color, religion, and national origin. But sex is not included in the list.

Sports

The Kentucky High School Athletic Association (KHSAA) has a policy document that allows transgender students to participate in school sports programs.[485]

At least one Bill has been introduced in the Kentucky legislature that would ban participation in school sports by transgender persons. SB 114, the "Save Women's Sports Act," was introduced in the Kentucky Senate during the 2020 session of the Kentucky legislature. The Bill, which uses much of the same language as other state's Bills with the same or similar titles, appears to have died in committee.

Law Enforcement, Jails, and Prisons

For information on this topic, please see the state data on the MAP website.

Health Care and Health Care Benefits

For information on this topic, please see the state data on the MAP website.

Marriage

For information on this topic, please see the state data on the MAP website. Please also review the section above under federal laws on marriage.

LGBTQ Youth Laws and Policies

For information on this topic, please see the state data on the MAP website.

Religious Exemption Laws

Section 446.350 of the Kentucky Revised Statutes places a prohibition upon government against substantially burdening an individual's freedom of religion. Under the Act, the government must show a compelling governmental interest in the proposed action. The statute states,

> Government shall not substantially burden a person's freedom of religion. The right to act or refuse to act in a manner motivated by a sincerely held religious belief may not be substantially burdened unless the government proves by clear and convincing evidence that it has a compelling governmental interest in infringing the specific act or refusal to act and has used the least restrictive means to further that interest. A "burden" shall include indirect burdens such as withholding benefits, assessing penalties, or an exclusion from programs or access to facilities.[486]

Like many of these state laws, this law is viewed as a way to "go around" U.S. Supreme Court decisions upholding the rights of the LBGTQ community.

Kentucky Overall Tally

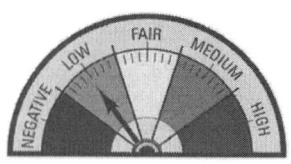

Grand Totals	Sexual Orientation Policy Tally	Gender Identity Policy Tally	Overall Tally
Totals	7.25/20.5	3/22	10.25/42.5
Ratings	FAIR	LOW	LOW

Louisiana

Louisiana Non-Discrimination Laws

After a thorough search, the author found no anti-discrimination laws or policies in place in Louisiana.

Birth Certificates

A Louisiana court-ordered change of name must be obtained to change a person's last name on their birth certificate. A certified copy of the Judgment, Petition, and District Attorney's Answer must be submitted to Vital Records to determine if the court order can be used to amend the birth certificate. The author could not find a link to the court forms necessary to file such a request with the state's trial courts. The state website is not transparent and lacks essential information.

Driver's Licenses

Louisiana Department of Public Safety, Office of Motor Vehicles, Policy 22.00 allows for name changes on a driver's license as follows:

> Complete or partial name change: An applicant must have a judgment signed by a judge and filed with the Clerk of Court's office OR in cases of persons over the age of seventeen (17) being adopted by persons over the age of eighteen (18), the applicant may present a certified copy of a notarial act of adoption as provided by R.S. 9:461 and 462 indicating a name change: This notarial act of adoption must be properly notarized and filed, signed by both adoptive parents and natural parents, and presented together with a certified copy of the corrected birth certificate: Any name changes by religious orders for religious reasons will not be accepted unless legal action has been taken to change their name.[487]

Louisiana Department of Public Safety, Office of Motor Vehicles, Policy 22.01 allows for a change in the designation of sex on a driver's license as follows:

> Definition: If an applicant for or a holder of a Louisiana driver's license/identification card indicates that he has undergone a gender change/reassignment procedure and desires to change the gender identification on his driver's license/ID card, the change will be noted, and a new driver's license/ID card will be issued.
>
> Requirements:
>
> A medical statement signed by a physician stating that the applicant has undergone a successful gender change/reassignment.
>
> In addition, should the applicant or holder of a Louisiana driver's license/ID card seek a name change due to the gender change/reassignment, a certified or true copy of a court order must be presented.[488]

Public Accommodations

According to the Governor of Louisiana's website (LA R.S. 51: 2247),[489] the following is correct.

> It is discriminatory practice for a person to deny an individual the full and equal enjoyment of the goods, services, facilities, privileges, advantages, and accommodations of a place of public accommodation, resort, or amusement, on the grounds of race, creed, color, religion, sex, age, disability or national origin.[490]

Sports

Louisiana's Governor vetoed Senate Bill 156, authored by Louisiana State Senator Beth Mizell. SB156 would have banned participation in interscholastic and intercollegiate sports programs in Louisiana based on the sex of the participant when that participant Is a "biological male" attempting to play in a women's sport. The Bill's text skips right over the fact that Federal Courts have ruled that to discriminate based on sex in school sports violates Title IX. The author of the Bill uses citations to court decisions, such as *United States v Virginia*, 518 U.S. 515 (1996), to support her contention that government cannot bar discrimination based on sex when it comes to sporting events for women. The Virginia case involved Virginia Military Institute, an all-male university. The Supreme Court held that the university could not bar female students from attendance. Other states have cited this case as well. Still, they forget that seven of the eleven U.S. Circuit Courts of Appeal have ruled Title IX bars states from enacting laws prohibiting transgender athletes from participating in school sports. Several court opinions from the circuits applied the Supreme Court's decision last year in *Bostock v. Clayton County, Georgia* to Title IX cases.

Law Enforcement, Jails, and Prisons

For information on this topic, please see the state data on the MAP website.

Health Care and Health Care Benefits

According to the Transgender Legal Defense and Education Fund (TLDEF), six Medicaid coverage plans in Louisiana will pay for transition-related health care.[491]

Marriage

For information on this topic, please see the state data on the MAP website. Please also review the section above under federal laws on marriage.

LGBTQ Youth Laws and Policies

Louisiana is one of the worst states for having laws that fail to protect the LGBTQ Youth community from discrimination. Indeed, the state does not protect its LGBTQ youth from discrimination at all.

Religious Exemption Laws

In 2015, when the Louisiana legislature failed to move a religious freedom Bill out of committee, former Governor Bobby Jindal issued an Executive Order doing what the legislature could not do. The ACLU filed suit to challenge Jindal's authority to issue such an executive order, but while the case was pending, a new governor was elected, and the order was allowed to expire.

Louisiana Overall Score

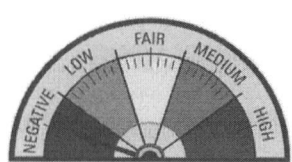

Grand Totals	Sexual Orientation Policy Tally	Gender Identity Policy Tally	Overall Tally
Totals	1/20.5	-3.5/22	-2.5/42.5
Ratings	LOW	NEGATIVE	NEGATIVE

Louisiana's score puts it at the bottom of the list of states examined thus far.

Maine

Maine Non-Discrimination Laws

According to the Maine Revised Statutes, Title 5, Part 12, Chapter 337, Subchapter 1, Section 4552, the policy of the State of Maine is:

> To protect the public health, safety and welfare, it is declared to be the policy of this State to keep continually in review all practices infringing on the basic human right to a life with dignity, and the causes of these practices, so that corrective measures may, where possible, be promptly recommended and implemented, and to prevent discrimination in employment, housing or access to public accommodations on account of race, color, sex, sexual orientation, physical or mental disability, religion, ancestry or national origin; and in employment, discrimination on account of age or because of the previous assertion of a claim or right under former Title 39 or Title 39-A[492] and in housing because of familial status; and to prevent discrimination in the extension of credit on account of age, race, color, sex, sexual orientation, marital status, religion, ancestry or national origin; and to prevent discrimination in education on account of sex, sexual orientation or physical or mental disability.[493]

Birth Certificates

Maine allows people to use either of two different methods to amend their birth records:

> Fill out and mail in your application using the Maine Center for Disease Control and Prevention VS-7 form,[494] or

> Use the online system. Maine has partnered with VitalCheck,[495] to respond to questions about amending birth records.

The Maine Division of Public Health Systems provides additional information.[496]

Driver's Licenses

The Maine Bureau of Motor Vehicles allows changes to the designation of sex on a Maine Driver's License by using the form available on their website.[497] A hyperlink allows you to download the form.

Public Accommodations

Maine Revised Statutes, Title 5 Administrative Procedures and Services, Part 12 Human Rights, Chapter 337 Human Rights Act, Subchapter 5 Public Accommodations, Section 4591 allows:

> The opportunity for every individual to have equal access to places of public accommodation without discrimination because of race, color, sex, sexual orientation, physical or mental disability, religion, ancestry or national origin is recognized as and declared to be a civil right.[498]

Sports

Currently, there are two proposals before the Maine Legislature that would ban transgender athletes from participating in school sports. Maine Republican Representative Beth O'Connor proposed House Bill L.D. 926, entitled, "An Act to Ban Biological Males from Participating in Women's Sports." The Bill's Summary Section states the following:

This bill prohibits any student from joining or participating in an interscholastic or intramural athletic team or sports activity sponsored by an elementary or secondary school or post-secondary institution that is designated for "females," "women" or "girls" except for students of the female gender. A student prohibited from joining or participating in an athletic team or sport activity on the basis that the student is not a female may dispute the denial to the Commissioner of Education with a signed statement from a physician stating that the student is a female based upon the student's internal and external reproductive anatomy and naturally occurring level of testosterone and an analysis of the student's chromosomes.[499]

The second House Bill, L.D. 1401, authored by MaryAnne Kinney, is entitled "An Act To Prohibit Biological Males from Participating in School Athletic Programs and Activities Designated for Females at Schools That Receive Federal Funding." The Bill summary states:

This bill directs a school administrative unit or an elementary school, secondary school or postsecondary educational institution in the State that receives any federal funding to prohibit a person whose biological sex at birth is male from participating in an athletic program or activity that is designated for females.[500]

Law Enforcement, Jails, and Prisons

For information on this topic, please see the state data on the MAP website.

Health Care and Health Care Benefits

For information on this topic, please see the state data on the MAP website.

Marriage

For information on this topic, please see the state data on the MAP website. Please also review the section above under federal laws on marriage.

LGBTQ Youth Laws and Policies

For information on this topic, please see the state data on the MAP website.

Religious Exemption Laws

For information on this topic, please see the state data on the MAP website.

Maine Overall Tally

Grand Totals	Sexual Orientation Policy Tally	Gender Identity Policy Tally	Overall Tally
Totals	18.5/20.5	18.5/22	37/42.5
Ratings	HIGH	HIGH	HIGH

Maryland

Maryland Non-Discrimination Laws

The Maryland Department of Labor Office of Fair Practices Non-Discrimination Statement states, in relevant part:

> All programs, policies, procedures and activities conducted by and through this Department, its employees, contractors and subcontractors shall be conducted without regard to age, ancestry, color, creed, citizenship (where applicable), genetic information/testing, marital status, mental or physical disability, political affiliation, belief or opinion (where applicable), national origin, race, religious affiliation, belief or opinion, sex, (except where age, sex, or disability involves a bonafide occupational qualification), sexual orientation (where applicable) or status as a participant in Workforce Innovation Opportunity Act (WIOA) funded programs (where applicable).[501]

Birth Certificates

Maryland provides an easy method and a direct link on its Department of Health, Vital Records website to correct the designation of sex on a birth certificate of a transgender person.[502] Like many other states, Maryland requires a Court-Ordered change of name Certificate or Order from a Maryland court. A form is available on the Maryland Judiciary website.[503] After obtaining the Court-Ordered name change, you should also correct your Social Security records by following the procedures outlined on the Social Security website.[504]

Driver's Licenses

The Maryland Department of Transportation, Motor Vehicle Administration, handles changes to a Maryland Driver's License. Information on how to change your name and the policy regarding changing the designation of sex on your Maryland Driver's License, is available on the Maryland Department to Transportation Motor Vehicle Administration website.[505]

Public Accommodations

The state of Maryland has a policy prohibiting discrimination in public accommodations "because of race, sex, age, color, creed, national origin, marital status, sexual orientation, gender identity, **or** disability."[506]

Sports

The Maryland Public Secondary Schools Athletic Association (MPSSAA) has a policy that allows transgender students to participate in school sports programs. The policy can be found on the MPSSAA's website,[507] which indicates which counties in Maryland explicitly state that they do not discriminate. See, for example, the Allegany County Public Schools website, where they say declare that:

> Title IX applies to students, school employees, or anyone present on school campus regardless of sexual orientation, gender identity, immigration, or disability status. It includes all of a school's operations, including school-sponsored activities or travel that occurs away from school.[508]

Law Enforcement, Jails, and Prisons

For information on this topic, please see the state data on the MAP website.

Health Care and Health Care Benefits

The State of Maryland website, called the Maryland Health Connection, states that transgender individuals cannot be discriminated against in the provision of transition-related health care services.[509]

Marriage

For information on this topic, please see the state data on the MAP website. Please also review the section above under federal laws on marriage.

LGBTQ Youth Laws and Policies

For information on this topic, please see the state data on the MAP website.

Religious Exemption Laws

For information on this topic, please see the state data on the MAP website.

Maryland Overall Tally

Grand Totals	Sexual Orientation Policy Tally	Gender Identity Policy Tally	Overall Tally
Totals	13.25/20.5	16.5/22	29.75/42.5
Ratings	MEDIUM	HIGH	MEDIUM

Massachusetts

Massachusetts Non-Discrimination Laws

Massachusetts General Laws, Chapter 151B, Section 4 states:

It shall be an unlawful practice:

1. For an employer, by himself or his agent, because of the race, color, religious creed, national origin, sex, gender identity, sexual orientation, which shall not include persons whose sexual orientation involves minor children as the sex object, genetic information, pregnancy or a condition related to said pregnancy including, but not limited to, lactation or the need to express breast milk for a nursing child, ancestry or status as a veteran of any individual to refuse to hire or employ or to bar or to discharge from employment such individual or to discriminate against such individual in compensation or in terms, conditions or privileges of employment, unless based upon a bona fide occupational qualification.[510]

Birth Certificates

The Massachusetts Registry of Vital Records and Statistics will change the name and designation of sex on your Massachusetts Birth Certificate. Information on what is required to initiate the process is available on the Massachusetts government website.[511]

Driver's Licenses

To change your name or the gender marker on your Massachusetts Driver's License, visit the website and follow the directions.[512]

Public Accommodations

Massachusetts has a policy that prohibits discrimination in public accommodations because of "race, color, religious creed, national origin, sex, gender identity, sexual orientation, deafness, blindness, or any physical or mental disability, or ancestry."[513]

Sports

The Massachusetts Interscholastic Athletic Association (MIAA) has a policy that allows transgender students to participate in school sports programs. The MIAA policy can be found on their website.[514]

Law Enforcement, Jails, and Prisons

For information on this topic, please see the state data on the MAP website.

Health Care and Health Care Benefits

For information on this topic, please see the state data on the MAP website.

Marriage

For information on this topic, please see the state data on the MAP website. Please also review the section above under federal laws on marriage.

LGBTQ Youth Laws and Policies

For information on this topic, please see the state data on the MAP website.

158 | The Transgender Compendium

Religious Exemption Laws

Massachusetts does not to have a religious exemption law at the present time.

Massachusetts Overall Tally

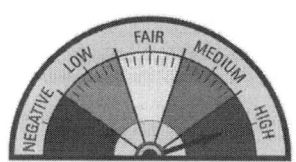

Grand Totals	Sexual Orientation Policy Tally	Gender Identity Policy Tally	Overall Tally
Totals	16.25/20.5	17.25/22	33.5/42.5
Ratings	HIGH	HIGH	HIGH

Michigan

Michigan Non-Discrimination Laws

Michigan has a civil rights law that bans discrimination based on several classifications.

> Sec. 102. (1) The opportunity to obtain employment, housing and other real estate, and the full and equal utilization of public accommodations, public service, and educational facilities without discrimination because of religion, race, color, national origin, age, sex, height, weight, familial status, or marital status as prohibited by this act, is recognized and declared to be a civil right.[515]

Birth Certificates

Michigan has a policy that allows a birth certificate to be amended provided the registrant has undergone sex reassignment. The individual will need to submit proof of surgery from their surgeon.[516] Change of name on a Michigan Birth Certificate is first accomplished by obtaining a court-ordered name change and submitting it with the appropriate form. The Change Name form to petition the court for an order to change your name is available on the State of Michigan Judicial Circuit, Family Division website.[517] You can also visit the website of Michigan Legal Aid at for help.[518]

Driver's Licenses

To change your name on a Michigan Driver's License, you must first get a court order changing your name, a new Social Security Card, and then apply to have your name changed on your Michigan Driver's License.

The author tried numerous times in August 2021 to contact the Michigan Secretary of State's Driver Licensing Office (with no success) to find out what their policy is regarding changing the designation of sex on a driver's license for someone who is transgender. Finally, in an email dated November 16, 2021, the Michigan Department of State sent the following:

> As of Nov. 10, 2021, Michigan residents can denote their sex on their license or state ID as nonbinary (X), female (F), or male (M). Those who would like to correct the sex designation on their license or ID will need visit a Secretary of State office to submit a Sex Designation Form to correct their credential. No additional documentation is required when making this change.

> At the time of your visit, our staff will correct your credential, take a new photo, and issue you a temporary paper credential to use until your corrected card arrives in the mail. A correction fee ($9 for driver's license, $10 for ID) will be due at the time of your visit.

> To schedule your visit, visit Michigan.gov/SOS and select *Schedule an Office Visit* or call 888-SOS-MICH (888-767-6424). Visits may be scheduled up to six months in advance or for the next day. Thousands of office visits are released twice per day at 8 a.m. and noon, every business day.

Public Accommodations

Michigan law prohibits discrimination in employment, education, housing, public accommodations, and public service. The Michigan Department of Civil Rights has the authority to accept complaints based on unlawful consideration of religion, race, color, national origin, arrest record, genetic information, sex, age, height, weight, marital status, and disability. Discrimination based on disability must be related to the person's ability to perform on the job or use facilities which cannot be reasonably altered.[519]

Sports

The Michigan High School Athletics Association (MHSAA) apparently has a policy that allows transgender students to participate in school sports programs, but the author could not find it on their website, and the person the author talked with at the Association was very elusive and only reluctantly provided the policy to the author. In the end, I finally received an email, not from MHSAA, but from someone at the Michigan Department of Education providing me with the State Board of Education's policy statement on transgender student athletes. Part of that statement is reproduced here:

> The State Board of Education (SBE) is committed to promoting a safe, supportive, and inclusive learning environment for all students and ensuring that every student has equal access to educational programs and activities. Due to a variety of factors, the school experience can be significantly more difficult for some students including those with marginalized identities. Students continue to face challenges that threaten their health, safety, and learning opportunities in schools.
>
> Research indicates that LGBTQ students, nationally and in Michigan, are targeted with physical violence and experience a hostile school environment more frequently than their non-LGBTQ peers.

Data from the 2015 Michigan Youth Risk Behavior Survey (YRBS)[520] show that students who identify as lesbian, gay, or bisexual (LGB), representing 8.4% of all high school students, are 2.3 times more likely to be threatened or injured with a weapon on school property than their non-LGB peers. Further, they are 2.3 times more likely to skip school because they feel unsafe. Forty-one percent of LGB students report being bullied on school property, and they are 4.5 times more likely to attempt suicide. Moreover:

- According to a national report, 26 percent of transgender students were physically assaulted, (e.g., punched, kicked, or injured with a weapon) in school in the past year because of their gender expression.
- Overall, LGBTQ students who are bullied and harassed are more likely to experience depression and anxiety, feel excluded from the school community, and experience lower academic achievement and stunted educational aspirations.
- Lesbian, gay, bisexual, and transgender (LGBT) students are over-represented in the unaccompanied homeless youth population, creating significant barriers to health, safety, and school success.
- Not all LGBTQ students are equally affected by these risk factors. LGBTQ students with intersecting, marginalized identities are at greater risk of negative outcomes, including school failure and dropout.
- The adverse health and educational consequences for transgender students are even greater than those for LGB students.

> Supportive environments that acknowledge and affirm a student's identity are protective factors that improve health and educational outcomes [footnotes omitted].[521]

In the Michigan State Senate, Senate Bill 218 was introduced by several Republican Senators on March 10, 2021, concerning transgender students' participation in school sports programs. The text of the Bill states:

A Bill to amend 1976 PA 451, entitled "The revised school code," (MCL 380.1 to 380.1852) by adding section 1146a; and to repeal acts and parts of acts.

THE PEOPLE OF THE STATE OF MICHIGAN ENACT:

Sec. 1146a. (1) The board of a school district or intermediate school district or board of directors of a public-school academy shall ensure that each high school operated by the board or board of directors, as applicable, establishes and maintains a policy that includes both of the following:

(a) If the school designates a team in an interscholastic athletic activity offered to pupils enrolled at the school as a girls', women's, or female team, a requirement that each pupil who competes for a position on that team or who is selected to compete on that team must be female based on biological sex.

(b) If the school designates a team in an interscholastic athletic activity offered to pupils enrolled at the school as a boys', men's, or male team, a requirement that each pupil who competes for a position on that team or who is selected to compete on that team must be male based on biological sex.

(2) As used in this section, "biological sex" means the physical condition of being male or female as determined by an individual's chromosomes and anatomy as identified at birth.

Enacting section 1. Section 1289 of the revised school code, 16 1976 PA 451, MCL 380.1289, is repealed.[522]

The website for the Bill shows that nothing has happened on this Bill since it was introduced.

Law Enforcement, Jails, and Prisons

For information on this topic, please see the state data on the MAP website.

Health Care and Health Care Benefits

For information on this topic, please see the state data on the MAP website.

Marriage

For information on this topic, please see the state data on the MAP website. Please also review the section above under federal laws on marriage.

LGBTQ Youth Laws and Policies

For information on this topic, please see the state data on the MAP website.

Religious Exemption Laws

The Michigan Senate failed to pass SB-4, after the Michigan House passed HB-5958 in 2014. In HB-5958, at Section 2(e), the Bill stated:

In *City of Boerne v P.F. Flores*, 521 U.S. 507 (1997), the United States supreme court held that the religious freedom restoration act of 1993 infringed on the legislative powers reserved to the states under the United States constitution."[523]

It should be noted that in *City of Boerne v. Flores, et al.*, 521 U.S. 507, at 511, the Court ruled:

The case calls into question the authority of Congress to enact RFRA. We conclude the statute exceeds Congress' power.[524]

The High Court went on to state:

> Legislation which alters the meaning of the Free Exercise Clause cannot be said to be enforcing the Clause. Congress does not enforce a constitutional right by changing what the right is. It has been given the power "to enforce," not the power to determine what constitutes a constitutional violation. Were it not so, what Congress would be enforcing would no longer be, in any meaningful sense, the "provisions of [the Fourteenth Amendment].[525]

I should note here that it is my opinion that since the Fourteenth Amendment applies to the state, as discussed in *City of Boerne* (above), the state cannot attempt to legislate that which the Supreme Court ruled that Congress cannot do. States that have altered, or attempted to alter, the right of free exercise in the ways we have seen in the last twenty-four years may be suspect. If a state constitution provides a right to the free exercise of religion similar to that of the U.S. Constitution, state legislatures may not have the authority to alter that right because they don't like what the U.S. Supreme Court or the State Supreme Court has ruled.

Michigan Overall Tally

Grand Totals	Sexual Orientation Policy Tally	Gender Identity Policy Tally	Overall Tally
Totals	7.75/20.5	11.25/22	19/42.5
Ratings	FAIR	MEDIUM	FAIR

Minnesota

Minnesota Non-Discrimination Laws

Minnesota Statutes Chapter 363A.01, et seq., contains the Minnesota Human Rights Act, which states, in relevant part:

363A.02 PUBLIC POLICY.

Subdivision 1. Freedom from discrimination.

(a) It is the public policy of this state to secure for persons in this state, freedom from discrimination:

(1) in employment because of race, color, creed, religion, national origin, sex, marital status, disability, status with regard to public assistance, sexual orientation, and age;

(2) in housing and real property because of race, color, creed, religion, national origin, sex, marital status, disability, status with regard to public assistance, sexual orientation, and familial status;

(3) in public accommodations because of race, color, creed, religion, national origin, sex, sexual orientation, and disability;

(4) in public services because of race, color, creed, religion, national origin, sex, marital status, disability, sexual orientation, and status with regard to public assistance; and

(5) in education because of race, color, creed, religion, national origin, sex, marital status, disability, status with regard to public assistance, sexual orientation, and age.

(b) Such discrimination threatens the rights and privileges of the inhabitants of this state and menaces the institutions and foundations of democracy. It is also the public policy of this state to protect all persons from wholly unfounded charges of discrimination. Nothing in this chapter shall be interpreted as restricting the implementation of positive action programs to combat discrimination.[526]

Birth Certificates

Minnesota allows a birth certificate to be amended to change the certificate's name and correct the designation of sex. The Minnesota Department of Health has a Birth Certificate Amendment Packet available.[527]

Driver's Licenses

The author received an email from the Minnesota Division of Public Safety[528] stating:

A person may request that their gender be changed on their license. Proof of gender reassignment is not required. They simply pay for the duplicate license. However, if they changed their name, they must present certified copies of court records showing the name change.

Name Change on a Minnesota Driver's License

If you have not updated your name change with the Social Security Administration, you must do so prior to applying for a new license or ID.

If you legally change your name, you are required by law to update the name on your driver's license or state ID within 30 days. To do this, go to any Driver's License Office or Driver and Vehicle Services Exam Station and request a duplicate license. The fee for a duplicate is $17. There is an additional $15 fee if you have an enhanced driver's license or ID.

If you complete the Pre-Application for a Driver's License or ID, it will save time at the licensing counter and help ensure that your information is correct. Once at the office, present your current driver's license/ID and a certified marriage certificate, a certified divorce or dissolution of marriage decree specifying the name change, or other certified court order specifying the name change. These requirements are the same for getting a duplicate of the Real and Enhanced ID/Licenses.[529]

Public Accommodations

The Minnesota Human Rights Act, Section 363A.11 PUBLIC ACCOMMODATIONS, states, in relevant part:

Subdivision 1. Full and equal enjoyment of public accommodations.

(a) It is an unfair discriminatory practice:

(1) to deny any person the full and equal enjoyment of the goods, services, facilities, privileges, advantages, and accommodations of a place of public accommodation because of race, color, creed, religion, disability, national origin, marital status, sexual orientation, or sex, or for a taxicab company to discriminate in the access to, full utilization of, or benefit from service because of a person's disability.[530]

The Act states that gender identity is a protected class under the statute.

Sports

As in other states, Minnesota Republicans have introduced two Minnesota House and Senate Bills that use the same language. The Bills would make it a violation of the law for a transgender or male-to-female trans student to play on a girl's or woman's sports team in interscholastic athletics. The main sponsor and author of the Senate Bill, SF96, Carrie Ruud (R-10th Dist.), claims that it is not her intention to discriminate against the trans community, but the Bill's language shows that this is not true. Further, the Bill's title is the exactly the same as that used in many other states' Bills, "The Save Women's Sports Act." Another Bill, HF350, is authored by other Republicans in the Minnesota House of Representatives.

In a Minnesota Court of Appeals decision issued on September 28, 2020, the Court in *N.H., Respondent, and Rebecca Lucero, Commissioner of the Minnesota Department of Human Rights, Plaintiff-Intervenor, Respondent v. Anoka-Hennepin School District No. 11, Appellant*, 950 N.W.2d 553 (Ct. of Appeals 2020), ruled that the Minnesota Human Rights Act protects transgender students from discrimination in schools based on sex. The Court's Opinion can be found on the Minnesota government website.[531] In short, the Court ruled that it was illegal to refuse to allow transgender students to use the restroom or locker room that most closely aligns with their gender identity.

Law Enforcement, Jails, and Prisons

For information on this topic, please see the state data on the MAP website.

Health Care and Health Care Benefits

For information on this topic, please see the state data on the MAP website.

Marriage

For information on this topic, please see the state data on the MAP website. Please also review the section above on federal laws on marriage.

LGBTQ Youth Laws and Policies

For information on this topic, please see the state data on the MAP website.

Religious Exemption Laws

Concerning religious exemptions, the Minnesota Statutes, Chapter 393A.26 states the following:

> 363A.26 EXEMPTION BASED ON RELIGIOUS ASSOCIATION.
>
> Nothing in this chapter prohibits any religious association, religious corporation, or religious society that is not organized for private profit, or any institution organized for educational purposes that is operated, supervised, or controlled by a religious association, religious corporation, or religious society that is not organized for private profit, from:
>
> (1) limiting admission to or giving preference to persons of the same religion or denomination;
>
> (2) in matters relating to sexual orientation, taking any action with respect to education, employment, housing and real property, or use of facilities. This clause shall not apply to secular business activities engaged in by the religious association, religious corporation, or religious society, the conduct of which is unrelated to the religious and educational purposes for which it is organized.[532]

Minnesota Overall Tally

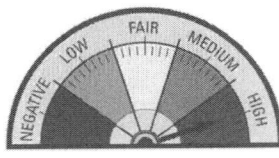

Grand Totals	Sexual Orientation Policy Tally	Gender Identity Policy Tally	Overall Tally
Totals	15.25/20.5	18.25/22	33.5/42.5
Ratings	MEDIUM	HIGH	HIGH

Mississippi

Mississippi Non-Discrimination Laws

As of this writing, Mississippi does not have a non-discrimination law that prohibits discrimination in employment, housing, public accommodations, or any other subject-based on sex.

Birth Certificates

As of the date of publication, the author has not heard from the Mississippi Department of Health Vital Records office regarding what policy, if any, that would allow a transgender person to change the designation of sex on their birth certificate to match their stated gender identity.

Driver's Licenses

Mississippi Code, Title 63, Chapter 1, Article 1, Section 63-1-19(2) and (3) provides that an applicant may change the name on their driver's license by first obtaining a court-ordered name change and filing that with the application. This statute does not address the issue of changing the designation of sex on a driver's license.

Public Accommodations

As above, under "Non-Discrimination," Mississippi has no law that prohibits discrimination in public accommodations.

Sports

The Mississippi Governor signed Senate Bill 2536 into law and took effect on July 1, 2021.

> **SECTION 2. Protection for educational institutions.** A government entity, any licensing or accrediting organization, or any athletic association or organization shall not entertain a complaint, open an investigation, or take any other adverse action against a primary or secondary school or institution of higher education for maintaining separate interscholastic or intramural athletic teams or sports for students of the female sex.[533]

Law Enforcement, Jails, and Prisons

For information on this topic, please see the state data on the MAP website.

Health Care and Health Care Benefits

For information on this topic, please see the state data on the MAP website.

Marriage

For information on this topic, please see the state data on the MAP website. Please also review the section above under federal laws on marriage.

LGBTQ Youth Laws and Policies

For information on this topic, please see the state data on the MAP website.

Religious Exemption Laws

On April 5, 2016, Mississippi's Governor signed into law the "Protecting Freedom of Conscience from Government Discrimination Act," which states, in relevant part:

> **SECTION 2.** The sincerely held religious beliefs or moral convictions protected by this act are the belief or conviction that:

(a) Marriage is or should be recognized as the union of one man and one woman;

(b) Sexual relations are properly reserved to such a marriage; and

(c) Male (man) or female (woman) refer to an individual's immutable biological sex as objectively determined by anatomy and genetics at time of birth.[534]

Mississippi Overall Tally

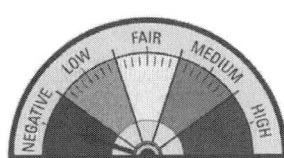

Grand Totals	Sexual Orientation Policy Tally	Gender Identity Policy Tally	Overall Tally
Totals	-0.5/20.5	-3/22	-3.5/42.5
Ratings	NEGATIVE	NEGATIVE	NEGATIVE

Missouri

Missouri Non-Discrimination Laws

Missouri statutes, Title XII Public Health and Welfare, Chapter 213 Human Rights, Section 213.010(6) defines discrimination as:

> conduct proscribed herein, taken because of race, color, religion, national origin, ancestry, sex, or age as it relates to employment, disability, or familial status as it relates to housing.[535]

It should be noted that Chapter 213 does not define "sex," "gender identity," or "transgender."

The author received an email from the Missouri Commission on Human Rights, which states:

> Only the Missouri legislature can revise Missouri statutes, and there have been several proposals in the past to revise the Missouri Human Rights Act (MHRA) to include sexual orientation and gender identity, but they did not passed [sic].

> The *Bostock* decision you referred to was decided under federal law. While state law interpretation in discrimination cases often parallels federal law, it sometimes diverges, as it does with this issue. Missouri has a court of appeals decision (*Pittman v. Cooper Paper Recycling Corp.*) holding that *sex* under the MHRA does not include sexual orientation. However, the Missouri Supreme Court in *Lampley v. Missouri Commission on Human Rights* held that non-conformance with gender stereotypes was sex discrimination under the MHRA. Therefore, MCHR has jurisdiction over complaints involving sexual orientation and gender identity when they are couched in terms of non-conformance with gender stereotypes as sex discrimination.[536]

The email cited above discusses two Missouri cases, *Pittman v. Cooper Paper Recycling Corp.*, 478 S.W.3d 479 (Mo. Ct. App. 2015); 128 Fair. Empl. Prac. Cas. 379, and *Lampley v. Missouri Commission on Human Rights*, 570 S.W.3d 16 (Mo. 2019).

In *Pittman*, the Missouri Court of Appeals stated that because the Missouri statute does not include discrimination based on sexual orientation, his case was properly dismissed by the Missouri District Court, saying:

> Because the Missouri Human Rights Act does not prohibit discrimination on the basis of sexual orientation, we affirm the circuit court's judgment dismissing Pittman's petition for failure to state a claim.[537]

In the second case, the Missouri Supreme Court held that:

> *Pittman*, however, declined to address whether sex discrimination based on sex stereotyping was covered under the Act because that claim was not at issue in *Pittman*. Contrary to the circuit court's suggestion, *Pittman* provides no support for the Commission's decision. Lampley's sexual orientation was merely incidental to the sex discrimination complaints filed. Lampley and Frost specifically stated they were discriminated against on the basis of sex because Lampley did not conform to generally held sexual stereotypes. Because the Commission erroneously characterized their claims as sexual orientation discrimination, the circuit court's reliance on *Pittman* is misplaced.[538]

Legal Aspects | 169

Birth Certificates

Missouri's website for the Department of Health and Senior Services, Vital Records, does not discuss their policy or procedures for correcting or amending a birth certificate for someone who is transgender. Further, it appears that to change your name on a birth certificate, you first must obtain a court order from a court in Missouri to change your name. Once you have done that, you need to notify the Social Security Administration of the change of name. Finally, you must contact the people at the Vital Records section to get your name and designation of sex changed on your birth certificate.

The Missouri State Code of Regulations, Title 19, Division 10, Chapter 10, Section 10-10.110(9) appears to allow a person whose gender marker and "name appears to be that typically used for the opposite sex"[539] to change their name and designation of sex on their birth certificate.

Driver's Licenses

The Missouri Code of State Regulations, Title 12, Division 10, Chapter 24, Driver License Bureau Rules, does not appear to address a transgender person's ability to correct or amend a driver's license after obtaining a court-ordered name change or to change the designation of sex on a driver's license. Likewise, the Missouri Statutes do not seem to address these issues. However, the author did receive an email from the Missouri Department of Revenue, Driver's License Bureau, which states:

> To request a change of the gender designation on your Missouri driver license, non-driver ID, or instruction permit, you must provide one of the following with your application:
>
> - A completed Gender Designation Change Request Form (Form 5532)[540];
> - Medical documentation showing completion of the gender reassignment surgery;
> - A U.S. Passport which reflects the gender designation requested by the applicant;
> - An amended U.S. birth certificate which reflects the gender designation requested by the applicant; or
> - A court order declaring the gender designation requested by the applicant (may be part of a court-ordered name change).

The above requirement is in addition to any standard documents and fees for the transaction.[541]

Public Accommodations

Missouri statutes, Section 213.065, states:

> All persons within the jurisdiction of the state of Missouri are free and equal and shall be entitled to the full and equal use and enjoyment within this state of any place of public accommodation, as hereinafter defined, without discrimination or segregation on the grounds of race, color, religion, national origin, sex, ancestry, or disability.[542]

The statute goes on to state in paragraph 2 that:

> It is an unlawful discriminatory practice for any person, directly or indirectly, to refuse, withhold from or deny any other person, or to attempt to refuse, withhold from or deny any other person, any of the accommodations, advantages, facilities, services, or privileges made available in any place of public accommodation, as defined in section

213.010 and this section, or to segregate or discriminate against any such person in the use thereof on the grounds of race, color, religion, national origin, sex, ancestry, or disability.[543]

Sports

The Missouri State High School Activities Association (MSHSAA) 2019-2020 Official Handbook, Board of Directors Policies, Section 34, pp. 142, "Board Policy on Transgender Participation," was adopted:

> To insure competitive fairness, equity and physical safety of all interscholastic sports and student-athletes. A transgender student is defined as a student whose consistent gender identity or expression does not match the sex assigned to him or her at birth as reflected on the student's birth certificate and school records.[544]

A recent effort by Republicans in the Missouri legislature to ban participation in school sports by transgender athletes failed to proceed through the legislative process.

Law Enforcement, Jails, and Prisons

For information on this topic, please see the state data on the MAP website.

Health Care and Health Care Benefits

It should be noted that Missouri Republican State Representative Suzie Pollack introduced House Bill 33 in the 101st General Assembly. HB 33 would ban the provision of gender-related transition health care to persons under the age of eighteen and provide penalties for those who provided or sought treatment for transition-related health care. The Bill did not receive a vote in the House Children and Families Committee. The text of the Bill can be found on the General Assembly website.[545]

Marriage

For information on this topic, please see the state data on the MAP website. Please also review the section above under federal laws on marriage.

LGBTQ Youth Laws and Policies

For information on this topic, please see the state data on the MAP website.

Religious Exemption Laws

Missouri Statutes, Title I, Chapter 1, Section 1.302 is Missouri's Religious Freedom Restoration Act.

> A governmental authority may not restrict a person's free exercise of religion, unless:
>
> (2) The restriction is in the form of a rule of general applicability, and does not discriminate against religion, or among religions; and
>
> (3) The governmental authority demonstrates that application of the restriction to the person is essential to further a compelling governmental interest and is not unduly restrictive considering the relevant circumstances.[546]

Missouri Overall Tally

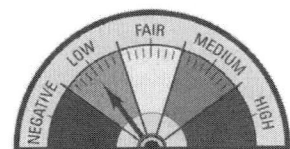

Grand Totals	Sexual Orientation Policy Tally	Gender Identity Policy Tally	Overall Tally
Totals	3.5/20.5	-2.75/22	0.75/42.5
Ratings	LOW	NEGATIVE	LOW

Montana

Montana Non-Discrimination Laws

Montana Code Annotated, Title 49 Human Rights, Chapter 1 Basic Rights, Part 1, Basic Personal Rights, Section 49-1-102, says:

> (1) The right to be free from discrimination because of race, creed, religion, color, sex, physical or mental disability, age, or national origin is recognized as and declared to be a civil right. This right must include but not be limited to:
>
> > (a) the right to obtain and hold employment without discrimination; and
> >
> > (b) the right to the full enjoyment of any of the accommodation facilities or privileges of any place of public resort, accommodation, assemblage, or amusement.
>
> (2) This section does not prevent the nonarbitrary consideration in adoption proceedings of relevant information concerning the factors listed in subsection (1). Consideration of religious factors by a licensed child-placing agency that is affiliated with a particular religious faith is not arbitrary consideration of religion within the meaning of this section.[547]

Birth Certificates

As of the date of publication, the author has not heard from the Montana Department of Public Health, Vital Records Division regarding what policy, if any, allows a transgender person to get the designation of sex on their birth certificate changed to match their stated gender identity.

Driver's Licenses

A name change must be completed at a driver's license exam station. An applicant's full legal name is required on a driver's license or identification card application, including on a renewal application and the license itself. The Identity Confirmation section on the Montana Department of Justice website provides information regarding Social Security Administration requirements.[548]

The name on your application must be the same as the name shown on a primary document[549] unless:

- you submit the required name change documentation
- your last name replaced your middle name before marriage. U.S. or Canadian birth certificates are acceptable proof of prior last name.
- your name has been truncated per policy (Administrative Rules of Montana).[550]

The space provided for recording a full legal name on a driver record or driver's license may not exceed 31 characters, including up to three commas. Titles such as Dr., Rev., Mrs., and Mr. are not allowed. You may include hyphens only if used in your name as it appears in the primary document used as proof of your identity.

Required Documents for a name change:

Applications for name change must be supported by a certified copy of one of the following documents:

- a marriage certificate from the issuing government jurisdiction

- a decree or judgment granting a name change from a court of competent jurisdiction
- a divorce decree or dissolution of marriage specifying change of name
- a U.S. Department of Homeland Security, Citizenship and Immigration Services (USCIS) certificate of naturalization (form N-550, N-570) issued to the applicant
- a declaration of marriage filed with the district court clerk where the declaration was made.[551]

Public Accommodations

Montana Code Annotated, Title 49 Human Rights, Chapter 2 Illegal Discrimination, Part 3 Prohibited Discriminatory Practices, Section 49-2-304 states, in relevant part:

> (1) Except when the distinction is based on reasonable grounds, it is an unlawful discriminatory practice for the owner, lessee, manager, agent, or employee of a public accommodation:
>
> > (a) to refuse, withhold from, or deny to a person any of its services, goods, facilities, advantages, or privileges because of sex, marital status, race, age, physical or mental disability, creed, religion, color, or national origin;
> >
> > (b) to publish, circulate, issue, display, post, or mail a written or printed communication, notice, or advertisement which states or implies that any of the services, goods, facilities, advantages, or privileges of the public accommodation will be refused, withheld from, or denied to a person of a certain race, creed, religion, sex, marital status, age, physical or mental disability, color, or national origin.[552]

It should be noted that the statute does not include sexual orientation or gender identity.

Sports

On May 7, 2021, the Montana Governor signed a measure that bans transgender athletes from participating in school sports. In other states, House Bill 112 has been entitled "The Save Women's Sports Act."[553]

Law Enforcement, Jails, and Prisons

For information on this topic, please see the state data on the MAP website.

Health Care and Health Care Benefits

For information on this topic, please see the state data on the MAP website.

Marriage

For information on this topic, please see the state data on the MAP website. Please also review the section above on federal laws on marriage.

LGBTQ Youth Laws and Policies

For information on this topic, please see the state data on the MAP website.

Religious Exemption Laws

For information on this topic, please see the state data on the MAP website.

Montana Overall Tally

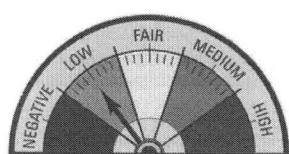

Grand Totals	Sexual Orientation Policy Tally	Gender Identity Policy Tally	Overall Tally
Totals	4.5/20.5	-0.5/22	4/42.5
Ratings	LOW	NEGATIVE	LOW

Nebraska

Nebraska Non-Discrimination Laws

The author received an email from the Nebraska Equal Opportunity Commission (NEOC) stating, "Sexual Orientation falls under our Sex basis for the state of Nebraska, which coincides with the laws established under the federal EEOC guidelines."[554] The email and the state's EOC website do not address whether gender identity is covered by the Nebraska Fair Employment Practice Act, the Nebraska Age Discrimination in Employment Act, the Equal Pay Act of Nebraska, the Nebraska Fair Housing Act, or the Act providing Equal Enjoyment of Public Accommodations.

Birth Certificates

The author received an email from the Nebraska Department of Health and Human Services[555] stating:

> An application for amendment completed with your signature notarized. We will need a copy of a court order that changed your name. A notarized affidavit from the physician that performed (completed) the sex reassignment surgery. The statement must say in effect: "I (name of surgeon) performed the surgery that accomplished the sex reassignment on…" and must also identify the name of the patient. We need the surgeon to attest that he performed the surgery and that it is irreversible and complete and that you went from which gender to which gender. The surgeon must have his signature notarized. Fees $16.00 to complete the amendment and $17.00 for a copy of the birth certificate and a copy of your id.[556]

Driver's Licenses

Name changes can't be updated online. Individuals must apply at any Driver Licensing Office in order to change a name on a driver's license. To apply for a replacement Driver's License, Permit or State Identification Card, a resident must submit the following:

- Acceptable Proof of Identification - Nebraska requires one form of identification that includes name and date of birth to obtain a replacement driver license, permit or State ID Card.
- Evidence of your name change:
    1. Certified documents such as a marriage license, divorce decree or a court order. The documentation that you present must enable the driver licensing staff to tie the two names together.
    2. Note: In order to change any other name, besides the last name, when using a marriage license, the full legal name prior to marriage and the full legal name after marriage must be on the marriage license.
- Complete a data form, Operators License-ID data form at a driver licensing office.
- Two forms of proof of address (If address has not previously been verified, or if you have moved). Acceptable proof of address may be found at: Identification/Address/SS Verification Requirements.
- The appropriate License Fees.
- If applicable, you will also be required to meet DMV vision and medical requirements.

Upon completion of processing and payment of the fee, the County Treasurer or Driver License Service Center will issue you a 30-day receipt, with driving privileges, if appropriate. Your driver license, permit or State ID Card will be mailed to you within 14 business days. If you don't receive your license, permit or ID card within 20 days, contact Driver Licensing Services at 402-471-3861.

Once a replacement document has been issued, the previously issued document is invalid and cannot be used as proof of identification.

The author received an email from the Nebraska Department of Motor Vehicles which stated:

> Currently the DMV does not have a policy to allow a transgender individual to choose a gender other than what is on the birth certificate, however we do allow the gender to be changed if a Doctor/PA or APRN certifies they have undergone the necessary sex reassignment procedures required for social gender recognition, by completing the Certification of Sex Reassignment.

Public Accommodations

As discussed above under "Non-Discrimination Laws," Nebraska has a law prohibiting discrimination in public accommodations, and the Nebraska EOC has determined that it includes sexual orientation under "sex." but does not mention or address gender identity.

Sports

Republican Legislators in Nebraska have proposed laws that would ban transgender athletes from participating in school sports in Nebraska, but the Nebraska School Activities Association (NSAA) currently has the following policy:

> It is the policy of the NSAA and its member schools not to discriminate on the basis of race, religion, gender, disability or national origin in its co-curricular activities. It is also the policy of the Association not to discriminate with any other practices or interactions that are necessary in the daily operation of the organization.[557]

Law Enforcement, Jails, and Prisons

For information on this topic, please see the state data on the MAP website.

Health Care and Health Care Benefits

For information on this topic, please see the state data on the MAP website.

Marriage

For information on this topic, please see the state data on the MAP website. Please also review the section above under federal laws on marriage.

LGBTQ Youth Laws and Policies

For information on this topic, please see the state data on the MAP website.

Religious Exemption Laws

For information on this topic, please see the state data on the MAP website.

Nebraska Overall Tally

Grand Totals	Sexual Orientation Policy Tally	Gender Identity Policy Tally	Overall Tally
Totals	5.25/20.5	-1.25/22	4/42.5
Ratings	FAIR	NEGATIVE	LOW

Nevada

Nevada Non-Discrimination Laws

Nevada statutes, Chapter 613, Section 330, states in part:

Except as otherwise provided in NRS 613.350 Lawful Employment Practices, it is an unlawful employment practice for an employer:

(4) To fail or refuse to hire or to discharge any person, or otherwise to discriminate against any person with respect to the person's compensation, terms, conditions or privileges of employment, because of his or her race, color, religion, sex, sexual orientation, gender identity or expression, age, disability or national origin.[558]

Birth Certificates

A Nevada resident may request that their birth certificate be corrected to show a change of name resulting from a court order pursuant to NRS 440.305. Accordingly, one must first obtain a court-ordered name change.

The legal requirements for adult name changes can be found in NRS Chapter 440 Sections 270-.290.[559] The basic requirements are:

- You must list your current name, the new name you wish to take, and the reasons for the change.

- You must disclose any felony convictions to the court. If you have been convicted of a felony, you must get fingerprinted and submit your fingerprints to the Court with the name change forms. If the name change is granted, the court will submit a copy of the name change order to the Central Repository for Nevada Records of Criminal History for inclusion in your criminal record.

- You must publish a notice of the proposed name change one time in a newspaper in Clark County. (*If you are changing your name for gender identity reasons, you do not have to do this.*) If you believe that publishing your proposed name change would put your safety at risk, you can ask the court to waive the publication requirement.[560]

Nevada Administrative Code Chapter 440, Section 030, Subsection (5)(a), Alteration or Correction of Certificate allows, without limitation, an alteration or correction to gender or sex.[561]

The person requesting the change must submit an affidavit, the first part of which must set forth the facts not correctly stated on the original certificate and the necessary changes needed to correct the certificate.

The second part of the affidavit must provide other verifiable evidence corroborating the facts contained in the first part, which may include, without limitation, a supplementary affidavit if deemed appropriate by the State Registrar.[562]

To get the designation of sex on your birth certificate changed to match your gender identity, you must provide the following:

1. U.S Original Certified Court Order (if it is not certified, they cannot accept it) that states to change name for child.

2. $45 fee for each birth record (includes corrected copy). Additional copies are $25. Please be sure to sign the check/money order and make it payable to the "Office of Vital Records."

3. If the court order does not instruct Vital Records to change your gender, then they will need either a doctor's letter verifying gender/sex change or a supplemental affidavit filled out by someone who has knowledge of the change.

You will not be getting the original certified court order back as the Office of Vital Statistics is required to seal it away with the original birth record.

All documents must be mailed to their office at:

> Nevada Department of Health and Human Services
> Division of Public and Behavioral Health
> Office of Vital Records
> 4150 Technology Way Ste 104
> Carson City, NV 89706

Driver's Licenses

Like many other states, Nevada requires that you must first change your name with the Social Security Administration before you change your name on your driver's license. To change your name with the Social Security Administration, you must have obtained a court order changing your name.

Public Accommodations

Nevada Revised Statutes, NRS 651.070:

> All persons entitled to equal enjoyment of places of public accommodation. All persons are entitled to the full and equal enjoyment of the goods, services, facilities, privileges, advantages and accommodations of any place of public accommodation, without discrimination or segregation on the ground of race, color, religion, national origin, disability, sexual orientation, sex, gender identity or expression.[563]

Sports

In January 2014, The Nevada Interscholastic Activities Association (NIAA) issued a position statement on the participation of transgender athletes in school sports programs, saying, in part:

> A student shall be permitted to participate on a gender specific sports team that is consistent with the public gender identity of that student for all other purposes. In making a determination of eligibility, the NIAA will first refer to the position of the student and his or her local school regarding the student's gender identification.[564]

Law Enforcement, Jails, and Prisons For information on this topic, please see the state data on the MAP website.

For information on this topic, please see the state data on the MAP website.

Health Care and Health Care Benefits

For information on this topic, please see the state data on the MAP website.

Marriage

For information on this topic, please see the state data on the MAP website. Please also review the section above under federal laws on marriage.

LGBTQ Youth Laws and Policies

For information on this topic, please see the state data on the MAP website.

Religious Exemption Laws

For information on this topic, please see the state data on the MAP website.

Nevada Overall Tally

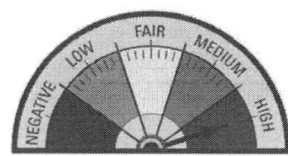

Grand Totals	Sexual Orientation Policy Tally	Gender Identity Policy Tally	Overall Tally
Totals	17.5/20.5	20.5/22	38/42.5
Ratings	HIGH	HIGH	HIGH

New Hampshire

New Hampshire Non-Discrimination Laws

New Hampshire Statutes, Title XXXI, Chapter 354A, Section 6, states:

> The opportunity to obtain employment without discrimination because of age, sex, gender identity, race, creed, color, marital status, physical or mental disability or national origin is hereby recognized and declared to be a civil right. In addition, no person shall be denied the benefits of the rights afforded by this section on account of that person's sexual orientation.[565]

Birth Certificates

On July 19, 2021, the author received an email from the New Hampshire Department of State Division of Vital Records Administration saying:

> New Hampshire requires a certified copy of a court order to amend your gender on your birth record. Statute does require that the individual complete the process medically in order to obtain an order. You will need to provide evidence to the court (usually a letter from the surgeon or your healthcare provider) that all procedures have been completed and that the order would be correcting your gender to the appropriate one. You need only submit the court order and the $10 amendment fee to the city/town clerk in the city/town where you were born to have your record amended.
>
> As a courtesy, we remove marginal notes that are usually standard when a substantive amendment is made to a vital record. A marginal note is a small notation at the bottom of the record describing what change has been made and what the information was prior to the change.[566]

Driver's Licenses

The following is information found on the New Hampshire Department of Safety, Division of Motor Vehicles concerning changing your name and designation of sex on your New Hampshire Driver's License:

> Any New Hampshire driver who changes his or her name is required by law (RSA 263:9) to submit written notification to the DMV within 30 days. Applicants must request an appointment to appear in person at any DMV office with the following:
>
> - A completed and signed Record Change Request
> - Your current New Hampshire Driver License
> - Legal documentation of the name change, such as:
>
>   1. Marriage certificate
>   2. Divorce decree
>   3. Adoption decree
>   4. Name change petition from the court of Probate
>   5. Other court decree authorizing a legal name change.
>
> You must hand in your current New Hampshire driver license and a replacement license with a new photo and signature will be issued at no charge. At the DMV office, you will

be given a 60-day, temporary paper license and the permanent license will be mailed to you.[567]

Under Saf-C 1011.03, an individual may change their gender on an NH Driver License or Non-Driver Identification Card by completing a Change of Gender Designation form which includes a certification by a licensed and qualified Health Care Provider.[568] This change requires an appointment at a DMV office.

A new picture will be taken, and a duplicate NH Driver License or Non-Driver Identification Card will be printed. The fee is $10.00, and the individual's current NH License or Non-Driver Identification card must be surrendered.

Public Accommodations

New Hampshire Revised Statutes, Title XXXI, Chapter 354-A, Section 354-A:17, states:

> It shall be an unlawful discriminatory practice for any person, being the owner, lessee, proprietor, manager, superintendent, agent or employee of any place of public accommodation, because of the age, sex, gender identity, race, creed, color, marital status, physical or mental disability or national origin of any person, directly or indirectly, to refuse, withhold from or deny to such person any of the accommodations, advantages, facilities or privileges thereof; or, directly or indirectly, to publish, circulate, issue, display, post or mail any written or printed communication, notice or advertisement to the effect that any of the accommodations, advantages, facilities and privileges of any such place shall be refused, withheld from or denied to any person on account of age, sex, gender identity, race, creed, color, marital status, physical or mental disability or national origin; or that the patronage or custom thereat of any person belonging to or purporting to be of any particular age, sex, gender identity, race, creed, color, marital status, physical or mental disability or national origin is unwelcome, objectionable or acceptable, desired or solicited. In addition, no person shall be denied the benefit of the rights afforded by this section on account of that person's sexual orientation.[569]

Sports

New Hampshire also protects transgender students' rights to be free from discrimination in education.

> No person shall be excluded from participation in, denied the benefits of, or be subjected to discrimination in public schools because of their age, sex, gender identity, sexual orientation, race, color, marital status, familial status, disability, religion or national origin, all as defined in this chapter.[570]

Law Enforcement, Jails, and Prisons

For information on this topic, please see the state data on the MAP website.

Health Care and Health Care Benefits

For information on this topic, please see the state data on the MAP website.

Marriage

For information on this topic, please see the state data on the MAP website. Please also review the section above under federal laws on marriage.

LGBTQ Youth Laws and Policies

For information on this topic, please see the state data on the MAP website.

Religious Exemption Laws

For information on this topic, please see the state data on the MAP website.

New Hampshire Overall Tally

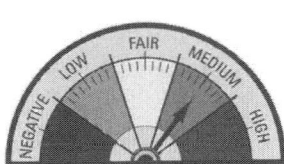

Grand Totals	Sexual Orientation Policy Tally	Gender Identity Policy Tally	Overall Tally
Totals	13.5/20.5	14/22	27.5/42.5
Ratings	MEDIUM	MEDIUM	MEDIUM

New Jersey

New Jersey Non-Discrimination Laws

New Jersey Statutes Annotated, Section 10:5-3 Findings, Declarations, states, in part:

> The Legislature finds and declares that practices of discrimination against any of its inhabitants, because of race, creed, color, national origin, ancestry, age, sex, gender identity or expression, affectional or sexual orientation, marital status, familial status, liability for service in the Armed Forces of the United States, disability or nationality, are matters of concern to the government of the State, and that such discrimination threatens not only the rights and proper privileges of the inhabitants of the State but menaces the institutions and foundation of a free democratic State; provided, however, that nothing in this expression of policy prevents the making of legitimate distinctions between citizens and aliens when required by federal law or otherwise necessary to promote the national interest.[571]

Birth Certificates

New Jersey enacted the Babs Siperstein Law in 2018 to allow transgender people to correct their New Jersey birth certificates. This landmark legislation removed a decades-old requirement that a person submit documentation of gender reassignment surgery to change the sex designation on NJ vital records.

The new law allows individuals (or parents/guardians in, the case of minors, to document gender identity using self-attestation instead of surgery. Sex designation on birth certificates can now be changed more easily to conform to individual gender identities.

Anyone wishing to change the designation of gender on their birth certificate can use this form to change their designation of gender.[572] To change your name on your birth certificate, you must first go to court to get a court-ordered name change order. Information on how to do this is available on the New Jersey Courts website.[573]

Driver's Licenses

To change the designation of sex on your driver's license, use the Declaration of Gender Designation Change form.[574] As above, you will need a court-ordered name change first.

Public Accommodations

The law in New Jersey protects people from discrimination in public accommodations. The New Jersey Law Against Discrimination (LAD)[575] prohibits discrimination in places of public accommodation based on actual or perceived:

- Race or color;
- Religion or creed;
- National origin, nationality, or ancestry;
- Sex, pregnancy, or breastfeeding;
- Sexual orientation;
- Gender identity or expression;
- Disability;
- Marital status or domestic partnership/civil union status;
- Liability for military service.

A place of public accommodation is generally any place that offers goods, services, or facilities to the public, including:

- Schools, colleges, and universities
- Stores and businesses
- Restaurants
- Summer camps
- Hotels and motels
- Medical providers, hospitals, and doctors' offices
- Government offices or agencies

This law means people cannot be denied access to or treated less favorably by a place of public accommodation because of their actual or perceived race, religion, national origin, gender, sexual orientation, disability, gender identity or expression, or other protected characteristic. In addition, employees and agents of places of public accommodation cannot harass patrons or customers. They must take action to stop bias-based harassment if they knew or should have known about it, even if the harassment is perpetrated by a fellow patient, patron, or customer. The website of the New Jersey Attorney General provides additional information.[576]

Sports

New Jersey's State Interscholastic Athletic Association allows transgender athletes to play sports aligned with their gender identity.[577] Nevertheless, Bills have been introduced in the legislature to ban transgender athletes from school sports. Three Republican state lawmakers have introduced a Bill that bans transgender athletes from participating in girls' sports in New Jersey. This effort mirrors conservative-promoted cultural battles playing out in state houses across the country.

State Sen. Mike Testa, R-Cumberland, introduced the Fairness in Women's Sports Act[578] on March 11, 2021. If passed, it would force students to compete under their biological gender at birth, reversing state rules that accommodate transgender athletes. The proposal's chances are "somewhere between zero and less than zero," said Patrick Murray, a Monmouth University political scientist.[579]

Law Enforcement, Jails, and Prisons

For information on this topic, please see the state data on the MAP website.

Health Care and Health Care Benefits

For information on this topic, please see the state data on the MAP website.

Marriage

For information on this topic, please see the state data on the MAP website. Please also review the section above under federal laws on marriage.

LGBTQ Youth Laws and Policies

For information on this topic, please see the state data on the MAP website.

Religious Exemption Laws

For information on this topic, please see the state data on the MAP website.

New Jersey Overall Tally

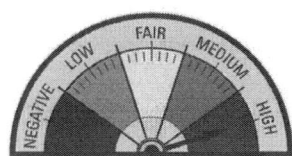

Grand Totals	Sexual Orientation Policy Tally	Gender Identity Policy Tally	Overall Tally
Totals	16.5/20.5	19.5/22	36/42.5
Ratings	HIGH	HIGH	HIGH

New Mexico

New Mexico Non-Discrimination Laws

The Human Rights Bureau in the New Mexico Department of Workforce Solutions is a neutral agency created to enforce the New Mexico Human Rights Act. The Bureau accepts and investigates claims of discrimination based on race, color, national origin, religion, ancestry, sex, age, physical and mental handicap, serious medical condition, spousal affiliation, sexual orientation, and gender identity in the areas of employment, housing, credit or public accommodation. Section 28-1-7 of the New Mexico statutes prohibit discrimination in employment, housing, and public accommodations based on "race, age, religion, color, national origin, ancestry, sex, physical or mental handicap or serious medical condition," or "gender identity."[580]

Birth Certificates

The author received an email from the New Mexico Activities Association on July 20, 2021, saying they follow the New Mexico Department of Health, Epidemiology and Response, Vital Records, and Health Statistics on allowing transgender athletes to participate in school sports. The Department's website says:

> On October 29, 2019, Senate Bill 20 went into effect. Under this law, individuals who were born in New Mexico and want to change the gender designation or the gender designation of their child on the birth certificate to do so by completing the appropriate request form through the Bureau of Vital Records. The new law will allow for Male, Female and X as acceptable options. "X" refers to a gender other than male or female or an undesignated gender.[581]

Also found on their website was the following information:

> The Request to Change Gender Designation on a Birth Certificate: Adult Form[582] must be completed by a person requesting to change the sex designation on their birth certificate. Guardians acting on behalf of an adult must include proof of guardianship appointed under chapter 40-10B NMSA.

> The Request to Change Gender Designation on a Birth Certificate: Adult Form must be signed in the presence of a notary public.

> If your full current legal name is different than the full name listed on your birth certificate, you must provide a certified legal name change court order with the form. If you want your full current legal name amended on your birth certificate, indicate by checking the appropriate box on the request form. Additional proof documentation might be requested.[583]

Driver's Licenses

As of the date of publication, the author has not heard from the New Mexico Department of Motor Vehicles regarding what policy, if any, allows a transgender person to get the designation of sex on their driver's license changed to match their stated gender identity.

Public Accommodations

New Mexico statutes, Section 28-1-7(F) states:

Any person in any public accommodation to make a distinction, directly or indirectly, in offering or refusing to offer its services, facilities, accommodations or goods to any person because of race, religion, color, national origin, ancestry, sex, sexual orientation, gender identity, spousal affiliation or physical or mental handicap, provided that the physical or mental handicap is unrelated to a person's ability to acquire or rent and maintain particular real property or housing accommodation.[584]

In housing, the statute, in Section 28-1-7(G), says:

It is an unlawful discriminatory practice for any person to:

(1) refuse to sell, rent, assign, lease or sublease or offer for sale, rental, lease, assignment or sublease any housing accommodation or real property to any person or to refuse to negotiate for the sale, rental, lease, assignment or sublease of any housing accommodation or real property to any person because of race, religion, color, national origin, ancestry, sex, sexual orientation, gender identity, spousal affiliation or physical or mental handicap, provided that the physical or mental handicap is unrelated to a person's ability to acquire or rent and maintain particular real property or housing accommodation;

(2) discriminate against any person in the terms, conditions or privileges of the sale, rental, assignment, lease or sublease of any housing accommodation or real property or in the provision of facilities or services in connection therewith because of race, religion, color, national origin, ancestry, sex, sexual orientation, gender identity, spousal affiliation or physical or mental handicap, provided that the physical or mental handicap is unrelated to a person's ability to acquire or rent and maintain particular real property or housing accommodation; or

(3) print, circulate, display or mail or cause to be printed, circulated, displayed or mailed any statement, advertisement, publication or sign or use any form of application for the purchase, rental, lease, assignment or sublease of any housing accommodation or real property or to make any record or inquiry regarding the prospective purchase, rental, lease, assignment or sublease of any housing accommodation or real property that expresses any preference, limitation or discrimination as to race, religion, color, national origin, ancestry, sex, sexual orientation, gender identity, spousal affiliation or physical or mental handicap, provided that the physical or mental handicap is unrelated to a person's ability to acquire or rent and maintain particular real property or housing accommodation.[585]

Sports

As noted above, under "Birth Certificates," the New Mexico Activities Association (NMAA), the association of public secondary schools in the state, follows the statutes available on the website of the Department of Health regarding the sex of an athlete. The author visited the website for the New Mexico Activities Association and could find nothing regarding this issue. Since the Department of Health website concerns birth certificates, and the NMAA says they follow the Health Department's statutes, rules, or regulations, it appears that the NMAA *will* allow a transgender student to participate if the student has obtained a birth certificate that says they are female or male. But that could be open to interpretation.

On July 20, 2021, the author received an email from the Transgender Resource Center of New Mexico stating:

> It's my understanding that the current NMAA policy is the one that was adopted in 2013[586]: It's near the bottom of that PDF but in summary:
>
>> A transgender student, defined as a student whose gender identity differs from the student's birth sex, shall be eligible to participate in interscholastic athletics in a manner that is consistent with the student's gender identity, under any of the following conditions:
>>
>> 1. The student provides an official record, such as a revised birth certificate or a passport, demonstrating legal recognition of the student's reassigned sex, or
>> 2. A physician certifies that the student has had appropriate clinical treatment for transition to the reassigned sex.
>
> This was one of the motivating factors in our decision to update the law on changing birth certificates in NM. In 2019, we were instrumental in writing and passing the Vital Records Modernization Act. This law removed the surgical requirement to change the gender on your NM birth certificate (as well as introducing X markers). When the NMAA created this policy, there was no way that a student 18 or under could update their birth certificate. Surgeons almost never perform surgery under the age of 18. The NMAA wrote it this way purposefully, meaning to box trans student athletes into the sex on the original birth certificate.[587]

Law Enforcement, Jails, and Prisons

For information on this topic, please see the state data on the MAP website.

Health Care and Health Care Benefits

For information on this topic, please see the state data on the MAP website.

Marriage

For information on this topic, please see the state data on the MAP website. Please also review the section above under federal laws on marriage.

LGBTQ Youth Laws and Policies

For information on this topic, please see the state data on the MAP website.

Religious Exemption Laws

The New Mexico Religious Freedom Restoration Act, New Mexico Statutes, Chapter 28, Article 22, Section 3, states, in relevant part:

> RELIGIOUS FREEDOM PROTECTED—EXCEPTIONS—A government agency shall not restrict a person's free exercise of religion unless: A. the restriction is in the form of a rule of general applicability and does not directly discriminate against religion or among religions; and B. the application of the restriction to the person is essential to further a

compelling governmental interest and is the least restrictive means of furthering SB 644 Page 2 that compelling governmental interest.[588]

New Mexico Overall Tally

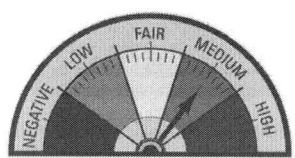

Grand Totals	Sexual Orientation Policy Tally	Gender Identity Policy Tally	Overall Tally
Totals	13.5/20.5	14.5/22	28/42.5
Ratings	MEDIUM	MEDIUM	MEDIUM

New York

New York Non-Discrimination Laws

New York Executive Law, Article 15, Section 296 (1), states the following:

It shall be an unlawful discriminatory practice:

a) For an employer or licensing agency, because of an individual's age, race, creed, color, national origin, sexual orientation, gender identity or expression, military status, sex, disability, predisposing genetic characteristics, familial status, marital status, or [Effective until November 18, 2019: domestic violence victim status] [Effective November 18, 2019: status as a victim of domestic violence], to refuse to hire or employ or to bar or to discharge from employment such individual or to discriminate against such individual in compensation or in terms, conditions or privileges of employment.

b) For an employment agency to discriminate against any individual because of age, race, creed, color, national origin, sexual orientation, gender identity or expression, military status, sex, disability, predisposing genetic characteristics, familial status, or marital status, in receiving, classifying, disposing or otherwise acting upon applications for its services or in referring an applicant or applicants to an employer or employers.

c) For a labor organization, because of the age, race, creed, color, national origin, sexual orientation, gender identity or expression, military status, sex, disability, predisposing genetic characteristics, familial status, or marital status of any individual, to exclude or to expel from its membership such individual or to discriminate in any way against any of its members or against any employer or any individual employed by an employer.[589]

Other sections within the New York Human Rights law are discussed under the appropriate headings below.

Birth Certificates

The State of New York Department of Health, Vital Records Section, has a form that can be used to correct a person's name or gender marker on their birth certificate.[590] There is an information sheet that explains what forms should be used and how to submit them.[591]

Driver's Licenses

You can change or update your legal name and order a new DMV document if

- you have a Social Security Number (SSN) on file with the DMV and you already changed your name with the Social Security Administration.

    Note: the name you request on your new DMV document must exactly match the name on your Social Security Card

- you do not have a commercial driver license (CDL) or commercial learner permit (CLP)

- you do not need to change any other information (for example, height, gender, address, etc.)

To change by mail:

- complete an Application for Name Change Only on Standard Permit, Driver License or Non-Driver ID Card (PDF) (MV-44NC)[592]
    1. your full signature, which will be used on your new license, permit or ID, must be within the signature box (your application will be rejected if your signature touches or crosses the edge of the box)
- provide a copy of your new Social Security Card
    1. the name on your card must exactly match the name requested for your new document
- provide a copy of your current "Standard" New York State license, permit or non-driver ID
- provide a copy of one or more of these proofs of your name change
    1. government issued marriage certificate
    2. government issued court order
    3. amended birth certificate
    4. divorce papers (must indicate name change)
    5. naturalization papers
- provide a check or money order for $12.50 (for license or permit) or $5.00 (non-driver ID) payable to "Commission of Motor Vehicles."

Mail to:

Department of Motor Vehicles
55 Hanson Place, 6th Floor
Brooklyn, NY 11217

If you have had a gender change or you are transgender, bring the following to your local DMV office:

- a completed Application for Permit, Driver License or Non-Driver ID Card (PDF) (MV-44)[593]
- your current learner permit, driver license or non-driver ID
- proof of a gender change

Additional information is available at the New Your State Department of Motor Vehicles website.[594]

Public Accommodations

New York Executive Law, Article 15, Section 296(2)a states:

> It shall be an unlawful discriminatory practice for any person, being the owner, lessee, proprietor, manager, superintendent, agent or employee of any place of public accommodation, resort or amusement, because of the race, creed, color, national origin, sexual orientation, gender identity or expression, military status, sex, disability or marital status of any person, directly or indirectly, to refuse, withhold from or deny to such person any of the accommodations, advantages, facilities or privileges thereof, including the extension of credit, or, directly or indirectly, to publish, circulate, issue, display, post or mail any written or printed communication, notice or advertisement, to the effect that

any of the accommodations, advantages, facilities and privileges of any such place shall be refused, withheld from or denied to any person on account of race, creed, color, national origin, sexual orientation, gender identity or expression, military status, sex, disability or marital status, or that the patronage or custom thereat of any person of or purporting to be of any particular race, creed, color, national origin, sexual orientation, gender identity or expression, military status, sex or marital status, or having a disability is unwelcome, objectionable or not acceptable, desired or solicited.[595]

Sports

The author received an email from the New York Public High School Athletic Association on July 21, 2021, stating:

Our guidelines on transgender student-athletes can be found on page 50 of our handbook.[596]

The Handbook, in Section 32, pp. 50-52, states:

The NYSPHSSAA recognizes the value of participation in interscholastic sports for all student athletes. The NYSPHSAA is committed to providing all students with the opportunity to participate in NYSPHSAA activities in a manner consistent with their gender identity and the New York State Commissioner of Education's Regulations. The Dignity for All Students Act (DASA) prohibits discrimination and/or harassment of students on school property or at school functions by students or employees. The prohibition against discrimination includes discrimination based on a student's actual or perceived sex and gender. Gender includes a person's actual or perceived sex as well as gender identity and expression.

The New York City Department of Education has a policy of inclusion and has devoted a section of its website to the matter.[597]

Law Enforcement, Jails, and Prisons

For information on this topic, please see the state data on the MAP website.

Health Care and Health Care Benefits

For information on this topic, please see the state data on the MAP website.

Marriage

For information on this topic, please see the state data on the MAP website. Please also review the section above under federal laws on marriage.

LGBTQ Youth Laws and Policies

For information on this topic, please see the state data on the MAP website.

Religious Exemption Laws

For information on this topic, please see the state data on the MAP website.

New York Overall Tally

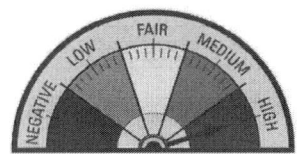

Grand Totals	Sexual Orientation Policy Tally	Gender Identity Policy Tally	Overall Tally
Totals	18.5/20.5	20.5/22	39/42.5
Ratings	HIGH	HIGH	HIGH

North Carolina

North Carolina Non-Discrimination Laws

North Carolina does not appear to have a general non-discrimination law. The State took away the right of cities and municipalities to enact laws that ban discrimination. A proposed law in 2016 attempted to change the wording of the state's non-discrimination wording for "sex" to "biological sex." This would have eliminated whatever protections the LGBTQ community had at the time. The state does ban discrimination in employment based on sex.[598]

Birth Certificates

North Carolina Statutes, Article 4, Section 130A-118(b)(4) allows for the designation of sex on a birth certificate to be changed for those who have undergone sex reassignment surgery.[599] For name changes, Chapter 41H, Section .0801 North Caroline Court Orders, states:

> For court orders changing a name issued under the authority of North Carolina law, and if the name has not been previously changed, the name on the certificate shall be lined out, and the new name entered. The face of the certificate shall be noted, "Name changed by court order" with the date of the change. The register of deeds in the county of occurrence shall be notified.

Driver's Licenses

An individual whose name changes from the name stated on a driver's license or ID must notify the N.C. Division of Motor Vehicles within 60 days after the change occurs and obtain a duplicate card with the new name. NCDMV will confirm the name change with the Social Security Online Verification System, so an individual changing their name must first visit their local Social Security Administration Office at least 24-36 hours before changing their name with NCDMV.

Name changes must be completed at an NCDMV driver license office.[600] You will need to bring:

- A certified marriage certificate issued by a government agency
- Documented proof from the courts or the Register of Deeds establishing that the name change was officially accomplished
- Execution of a notarized DL-101 (obtained from a DMV office)[601]

All documentation must be provided by the appropriate government agency of the United States, Puerto Rico, U.S. territories, or Canada.

The author was unable to find any information on the North Carolina DMV website regarding their policy on changing the designation of sex on a driver's license or the procedures are for changing the gender marker. As North Carolina is one of those states that does not believe in email, attempting to get answers via phone turned out to be an exercise in futility.

Public Accommodations

North Carolina is one of several states that does not have a law prohibiting discrimination in public accommodations for non-disabled persons. So, in North Carolina, LGBTQ people can be denied service because the state does not prohibit it. The only recourse for someone who is transgender is to sue under 42 U.S.C. §1983 for violating your civil rights.

Sports

The North Carolina High School Athletic Association has a policy allowing transgender athletes to participate in school sports. Their website states:

> The NCHSAA allows participation in interscholastic athletics for all students, regardless of gender or gender identification. It is the intent that all students are able to compete on a level playing field in a safe, competitive and friendly environment, free of discrimination. Rules and regulations are intended to provide every student-athlete with equal opportunities to participate in athletics.[602]

Law Enforcement, Jails, and Prisons

For information on this topic, please see the state data on the MAP website.

Health Care and Health Care Benefits

For information on this topic, please see the state data on the MAP website.

Marriage

For information on this topic, please see the state data on the MAP website. Please also review the section above under federal laws on marriage.

LGBTQ Youth Laws and Policies

For information on this topic, please see the state data on the MAP website.

Religious Exemption Laws

The North Carolina Legislature has failed several times to pass a Bill, even though they claim that it is fashioned after the federal RFRA.

North Carolina Overall Tally

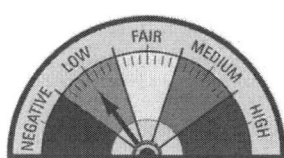

Grand Totals	Sexual Orientation Policy Tally	Gender Identity Policy Tally	Overall Tally
Totals	4.75/20.5	1/22	5.75/42.5
Ratings	LOW	LOW	LOW

North Dakota

North Dakota Non-Discrimination Laws

The North Dakota Department of Labor and Human Rights has issued the following statement on its website:

> On June 15, 2020, the United States Supreme Court issued a ground-breaking Opinion in the case of *Bostock v. Clayton County, Georgia*. Title VII of the Civil Rights of 1964, as amended, protects employees from discrimination based on race, color, national origin, religion, and sex. The Bostock Opinion clarifies what the basis of "sex" means.
>
>> The Court recognized that "sex" has traditionally referred to the biological distinctions between males and females. Through the Bostock Opinion, the Court has now confirmed that the basis of sex also provides protections for homosexual and transgender employees. The Court stated, in part: "An employer who fires an individual for being homosexual or transgender fires that person for traits or acquisitions it would not have questioned in members of a different sex. Sex plays a necessary and undisguisable role in the decision, exactly what Title VII forbids."
>>
>> It is the Department's opinion the Bostock definition of sex, may and should be applied to the North Dakota Human Rights Act, as amended, and the Housing Discrimination Act, as amended. Therefore, effective June 15, 2020, the Department will be accepting and investigating complaints of discrimination, based on sexual orientation and gender identity, in all human rights laws the Department enforces, including employment, public services, public accommodations, credit transactions, and housing. The Department is in the process of updating all of its intake forms and educational material, to reflect the Bostock decision.[603]

It should be noted that North Dakota Code, Section 14-02.4-02 (6) states:

> "Discriminatory practice" means an act or attempted act which because of race, color, religion, **sex**, national origin, age, physical or mental disability, status with regard to marriage or public assistance, or participation in lawful activity off the employer's premises during nonworking hours which is not in direct conflict with the essential business-related interests of the employer results in the unequal treatment or separation or segregation of any persons, or denies, prevents, limits, or otherwise adversely affects, or if accomplished would deny, prevent, limit, or otherwise adversely affect, the benefit of enjoyment by any person of employment, labor union membership, public accommodations, public services, or credit transactions. The term "discriminate" includes segregate or separate and for purposes of discrimination based on sex, it includes sexual harassment. Sexual harassment includes unwelcome sexual advances, requests for sexual favors, sexually motivated physical conduct or other verbal or physical conduct or communication of a sexual nature when:
>
>> a. Submission to that conduct or communication is made a term or condition, either explicitly or implicitly, of obtaining employment, public accommodations or public services, or education;

b. Submission to or rejection of that conduct or communication by an individual is used as a factor in decisions affecting that individual's employment, public accommodations or public services, education, or housing; or

c. That conduct or communication has the purpose or effect of substantially interfering with an individual's employment, public accommodations, public services, or educational environment; and in the case of employment, the employer is responsible for its acts and those of its supervisory employees if it knows or should know of the existence of the harassment and fails to take timely and appropriate action.[604] [emphasis added]

Under 14-02.4-02(18), Sex is defined thusly:

Sex" includes pregnancy, childbirth, and disabilities related to pregnancy or childbirth.[605]

Birth Certificates

If you, or your child, were born in North Dakota and you wish to have your name updated on the birth record following a name change, you must provide the Vital Records office with the following:

1. Certified copy of the Court Order changing you or your child's name.
2. Certified copy of the court's Confidential Information Form, if one was created.
3. Dated/Signed letter from you requesting our office update you or your child's birth record based on the court order.
4. The $15 amendment fee made payable to the: North Dakota Department of Health.
5. A legible, non-expired, copy of your photo ID.

The author received an email from the North Dakota Department of Health, Vital Records Section, which states:

The requirements to change a name and sex on a birth record filed in North Dakota are listed below.

We need a written request from you listing all your birth information (name, date, place of birth and parents' names). You need to specify what changes are to be made to the birth record and what they are to be changed to. Your request must be dated and signed by you, and you must include a copy of a valid photo ID.

Our office requires a notarized affidavit from the physician that performed the sex conversion operation. The notarized affidavit must state the patient's name and date of birth; that the sex conversion operation was performed on that individual and list the date of the operation. The notarized affidavit would also need to list, that by reason of the sex conversion operation the sex designation of the person is to be changed on their birth record from male to female or female to male. The notarized affidavit should be printed on their letterhead. We require the original notarized affidavit.

In order for us to update a name change, we require a certified copy of the court order name change. There is a $15 amendment fee to make the changes to the birth record. If you would like a certified copy of your birth record, you can return the birth request form with the proper fees and ID.[606]

Driver's Licenses

To change your name on your North Dakota Driver License, you will be required to bring in person certified documentation of the change, such as your: Marriage certificate, Divorce decree, or Court order to any ND Driver's License site.[607]

The author received an email from the North Dakota Driver's License Division stating:

> North Dakota currently uses the gender male/female designated on your legal presence documents. In the event there is a change in gender designation SFN 61146[608] would be completed and presented to a ND Drivers License Division in order to change the gender on your current ND drivers license, permit, or identification card. There would be an application and fee to this process.[609]

Public Accommodations

A privately-owned business may not unlawfully discriminate (see list of protected categories[610]) against a person in the provision of "public accommodation"—the services and facilities it offers. See the website of the North Dakota Department of Labor and Human Rights for more information.[611]

Sports

The North Dakota High School Athletic Association (NDHSAA) has the following regulations regarding participation in sports by transgender persons.

> A transgender student will be defined as a student whose gender identity does not match the sex assigned to him or her at birth.
>
> Any transgender student who is not taking hormone treatment related to gender transition may participate in a sex-separated interscholastic contest in accordance with the sex assigned to him or her at birth.
>
> The following email from the NDHSAA clarifies participation in sex-separated interscholastic contests of transgender students undergoing hormonal treatment for gender transition:
>
> - A trans male (female to male) student who has undergone treatment with testosterone for gender transition may compete in a contest for boys but is no longer eligible to compete in a contest for girls.
>
> - A trans female (male to female) student being treated with testosterone suppression medication for gender transition may continue to compete in a contest for boys but may not compete in a contest for girls until completing one calendar year of documented testosterone-suppression treatment.[612]

Law Enforcement, Jails, and Prisons

For information on this topic, please see the state data on the MAP website.

Health Care and Health Care Benefits

For information on this topic, please see the state data on the MAP website.

Marriage

For information on this topic, please see the state data on the MAP website. Please also review the section above under federal laws on marriage.

LGBTQ Youth Laws and Policies

For information on this topic, please see the state data on the MAP website.

Religious Exemption Laws

North Dakota's is one of almost 20 religious freedom Bills to be introduced in legislatures around the country. However, the North Dakota Bill goes much further in giving people, who claim a religious exemption, even greater opportunities to discriminate. The Act states:

> a. Substantially burden the exercise of religion by an offender in the custody of the correctional facility unless the burden is in furtherance of a compelling governmental interest and is the least restrictive means of furthering that compelling governmental interest;
>
> b. Treat religious conduct more restrictively than any comparable secular conduct unless the correctional facility demonstrates the disparate treatment is necessary to further a compelling penological interest and is the least restrictive means of furthering that compelling penological interest.[613]

Along with other states, North Dakota is using this, or very similar language, in various Bills and Statutes. They have adopted the language from the Federal RFRA, which was found unconstitutional by the U.S. Supreme Court in *City of Boerne v. Flores*, 521 U.S. 507 (1997). They have been using this language as a model for legislation in state legislatures. These laws will allow anyone, who doesn't like a law prohibiting discrimination against a protected class of individuals, to claim a religious exemption.

North Dakota Overall Tally

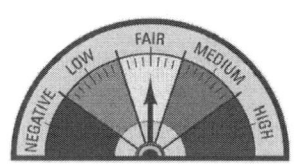

Grand Totals	Sexual Orientation Policy Tally	Gender Identity Policy Tally	Overall Tally
Totals	7.5/20.5	4.25/22	11.75/42.5
Ratings	FAIR	LOW	FAIR

Ohio

Ohio Non-Discrimination Laws

The Ohio Revised Code, Title 41, Chapter 4112, Section 4112.01 Definitions (16)(a), states that:

> Except as provided in division (A)(16)(b) of this section, "physical or mental impairment" includes any of the following:
>
> > (a)(i) Any physiological disorder or condition, cosmetic disfigurement, or anatomical loss affecting one or more of the following body systems: neurological; musculoskeletal; special sense organs; respiratory, including speech organs; cardiovascular; reproductive; digestive; genito-urinary; hemic and lymphatic; skin; and endocrine;
> >
> > (ii) Any mental or psychological disorder, including, but not limited to, intellectual disability, organic brain syndrome, emotional or mental illness, and specific learning disabilities;
> >
> > (iii) Diseases and conditions, including, but not limited to, orthopedic, visual, speech, and hearing impairments, cerebral palsy, autism, epilepsy, muscular dystrophy, multiple sclerosis, cancer, heart disease, diabetes, human immunodeficiency virus infection, intellectual disability, emotional illness, drug addiction, and alcoholism.
>
> (b) "Physical or mental impairment" does not include any of the following:
>
> > (i) Homosexuality and bisexuality;
> >
> > (ii) Transvestism, transsexualism, pedophilia, exhibitionism, voyeurism, gender identity disorders not resulting from physical impairments, or other sexual behavior disorders;
> >
> > (iii) Compulsive gambling, kleptomania, or pyromania;
> >
> > (iv) Psychoactive substance use disorders resulting from the current illegal use of a controlled substance or the current use of alcoholic beverages.[614]

It should be noted here that the statute *specifically* excludes homosexuality, bisexuality, transvestism, transsexualism, pedophilia, exhibitionism, voyeurism, gender identity disorders, or other sexual behavior disorders from inclusion in the Act.

Birth Certificates

When a legal name change has been granted to a person whose birth occurred in Ohio, the Vital Statistics office will accept a certified copy of the court-ordered legal name change to update the birth record. A U.S. court must have granted the court order. Some courts may send the certified copy directly to the Vital Statistics office, while some may require the petitioner to do so.

Once the Vital Statistics office accepts the legal name change, a footnote will appear on the birth record indicating that a legal name change is on file. In addition, the new name exactly as listed on the court order is the name that will be reflected in the updated birth record.

The Ohio Revised Code states this somewhat differently:

> When a legal change of name of a person whose birth occurred in this state has been granted by a court, the office of vital statistics shall receive and file a certified copy of the court order legally changing the name. The court order shall be cross-referenced with the original birth record and the office of vital statistics shall issue a certification of birth containing the new name. Such certification shall disclose information that a legal change of name has been granted by a court.
>
> Provided, if the original birth record was filed prior to the establishment of the division of vital statistics, a certified copy of the court order legally changing the name shall be received and filed with the probate court of the county wherein the birth occurred, instead of with the office of vital statistics. The court order shall be cross-referenced with the original birth record and upon request the probate court shall issue a birth record containing the new name. Such record shall disclose information that a legal change of name has been granted by the court.[615]

As for getting the designation of sex changed on an Ohio Birth Certificate, the author received a somewhat delayed response from the State of Ohio in the form of an email from the Ohio Department of Health, Bureau of Vital Statistics on July 27, 2021, that reads as follows:

> In order to comply with the court decision in *Ray v. McCloud*, Case # 2:18-cv-00272, the Ohio Department of Health will make changes to the sex marker on a birth certificate with a probate court order. You will need to contact your local probate court or the Ohio probate court in the county you were born in to get a court order.
>
> Once a certified court order has been received by our office, we will update the birth record. After that time a new birth record can be purchased.[616]

In the case cited by The Bureau of Vital Statistics, above, *Ray v. McCloud*, U.S. District Court for the Southern District, Eastern Division, Case No. 2:18-cv-272, Opinion, and Order dated 12/16/2020, the Court ruled that:

> This Policy resembles the sort of discrimination-based legislation struck down under the equal protection clause in *Romer v. Evans* [*Romer, et al., v. Evans, et al.* 517 U.S. 620 (1996)] as nothing more than a Policy "born of animosity toward the class of person affected" that has "no rational relation to a legitimate government purpose." 517 U.S. 620, 634 (1996). Indeed, when an almost identical policy (interpreting a similar neutral statute) in Idaho was challenged, the state defendants conceded that "no rational basis exist[ed] to support the categorical denial of requests to amend sex-assigned birth on the basis of correcting it to match one's gender identity.[617]

Indeed, the Court held that Ohio's policy was unconstitutional and issued a Permanent Injunction barring further enforcement of the policy.

Even with the decision in *Ray, supra*, the Ohio Department of Health, Bureau of Vital Statistics is not making it easy for transgender individuals to obtain a new birth certificate. As they state above, an applicant must go to probate court in the county where they were born to get a court order instructing the Department of Health, Bureau of Vital Statistics to change the designation of sex on the certificate. Because the transgender population often suffers from extreme financial hardship and may not be able to follow these procedures to get a new birth certificate, they will remain adversely impacted by the state's "new" policy. The implied level of hostility directed at transgender people by the state is hard to miss. It should also be noted that when the above case was heard in the Federal Court, Ohio was only one of two states that prohibited changes to the gender marker on birth records.

Driver's Licenses

The Ohio Bureau of Motor Vehicles has the following policy and procedures to get a new driver's license to be used by transgender individuals:

> A licensed, qualified medical professional must attest that the transition is being conducted per the guidelines set forth by the World Professional Association for Transgendered Health's Standard of Care. Only made as part of a permanent full-time gender transition.

> The completed gender change form can be faxed to License Control at (614) 752-7306. The completed form can also be mailed back to License Control at the address below. Allow 7-10 business days for processing. Ohio Bureau of Motor Vehicles Attn: License Control PO Box 16784 Columbus, Ohio 43216-6784.

> If the gender identification is marked transitional, a new form must be submitted for each driver license/ID renewal until gender identification is complete. If the form is not submitted at renewal, the gender marker will revert back to the original gender. Each individual is limited to changing the gender back to the original gender on the driver license/ID card one time. Send inquiries on the status of the form through the phone log to License Control. The applicant will be notified in writing if the gender change is approved and will receive documentation that can be presented at any Deputy Registrar. The applicant must then surrender the current driver license and will be mailed the new corrected card for a duplicate fee of $24.50.[618]

Public Accommodations

Ohio Revised Code, Title 41, Chapter 4112, Section 4112.02(G) provides that:

> For any proprietor or any employee, keeper, or manager of a place of public accommodation to deny to any person, except for reasons applicable alike to all persons regardless of race, color, religion, sex, military status, national origin, disability, age, or ancestry, the full enjoyment of the accommodations, advantages, facilities, or privileges of the place of public accommodation. Place of public accommodation is defined as:

>> "Place of public accommodation" means any inn, restaurant, eating house, barbershop, public conveyance by air, land, or water, theater, store, other places for the sale of merchandise, or any other place of public accommodation or amusement of which the accommodations, advantages, facilities, or privileges are available to the public.[619]

The reader will note that sexual orientation or transgender are not among the list of protected classifications.[620]

Sports

The Ohio High School Athletics Association (OHSAA) has the following information in its Handbook:

A male to female (MTF) transgender student may participate on girls' teams as long as she is compliant with the OHSAA transgender policies. Please see the OHSAA policies on the Transgender Student.[621]

Law Enforcement, Jails, and Prisons

For information on this topic, please see the state data on the MAP website.

Health Care and Health Care Benefits

For information on this topic, please see the state data on the MAP website.

Marriage

For information on this topic, please see the state data on the MAP website. Please also review the section above under federal laws on marriage.

LGBTQ Youth Laws and Policies

For information on this topic, please see the state data on the MAP website.

Religious Exemption Laws

For information on this topic, please see the state data on the MAP website.

Ohio Overall Tally

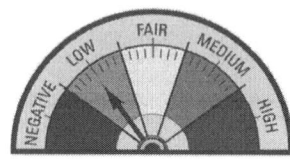

Grand Totals	Sexual Orientation Policy Tally	Gender Identity Policy Tally	Overall Tally
Totals	5.5/20.5	2.25/22	7.75/42.5
Ratings	FAIR	LOW	LOW

Oklahoma

Oklahoma Non-Discrimination Laws

Oklahoma has no general anti-discrimination statutes: however, the state's non-discrimination statutes cover different areas of discrimination. Oklahoma's non-discrimination statutes can be found in the Oklahoma Statutes Citationized, Title 25 Definitions and General Provisions, Chapter 21, Articles 3 through 5.[622]

The Oklahoma State Department of Health (OSDH) complies with applicable Federal civil rights laws. It does not discriminate against any individual or group because of race, religion, age, national origin, color, marital status, genetic information, sex, sexual orientation, gender identity or expression, political beliefs or disability.

Under Oklahoma law, employers may not discriminate based on race, color, religion, sex, national origin, age, genetic information, or disability, unless the employer can demonstrate that accommodation for the disability would impose an undue hardship on the operation of the business.

Oklahoma Statutes Citationized, Title 25 Definitions, and General Provisions, Chapter 21 Discrimination, Article 3 Discrimination in Employment, Section 1301 Definitions, Section 1301(6), states:

> "Sex", "because of sex" or "based on sex" includes, but is not limited to, pregnancy, childbirth, or related medical conditions; women affected by pregnancy, childbirth or related medical conditions shall be treated the same for all employment-related purposes as other persons not so affected but similar in their ability or inability to work.[623])

Section 1452 of Article 4A prohibits discrimination in housing because of "race, color, religion, gender, national origin, age, familial status, or disability.[624]

The statute that covers discrimination in public accommodations is discussed below.

Birth Certificates

A legal change of information on your driver's license can be requested online.[625]. A convenience fee will be charged for online applications or if priority shipping is requested.

To request a legal change of information by mail, you must complete a birth application[626] and mail it along with a copy of the applicant's photo ID,[627] applicable fees, a certified copy of the court order (see below), and a brief note explaining what action is being requested. The Birth and Death Certificate Amendments website indicates that:

> Specific instructions will be provided on a case-by-case basis as to what documents are recommended and whether a court order can be obtained through the OSDH Administrative Law Judge (ALJ) or if it must be obtained from a district court. District Court orders must be issued by either a U.S. Court or recognized tribal court. [Note: If sex was recorded correctly in the attendant's opinion but was actually incorrect due to a condition which made it difficult to determine, we will require a physician's statement to amend. Please contact our office for the form which needs to be completed by your physician.]

> The court order must identify the subject of the record by full current legal name, full legal name at time of birth (if different), and date and place of birth.

The order should identify what name should be shown as after amendment. [Note: If name is being amended, there should be no abbreviations or omissions in the final name. The name on the final record will be reflected exactly as indicated in the order.] [hyperlinks removed][628]

Driver's Licenses

As of the date of publication, the author has not heard from the Oklahoma Department of Public Safety regarding what policy, if any, allows a transgender person to get the designation of sex on their driver's license changed to match their stated gender identity.

Public Accommodations

The Oklahoma statutes declare that it is a discriminatory practice for a person to deny any individual the full and equal enjoyment of the goods, services, facilities, privileges, advantages, and accommodations of a "place of public accommodation" because of race, color, religion, sex, national origin, age, or disability.[629]

Sports

The Oklahoma Secondary Schools Activities Association (OSSAA) holds to the following policy regarding participation in school sports by transgender athletes:

> **LVII. TRANSGENDER STUDENTS PARTICIPATING IN ATHLETIC ACTIVITIES**
>
> A. The following guidelines should be applied by a member school in determining the gender-specific athletic teams on which a transgender student is permitted to participate:
>
> (1) A female-to-male who is not taking testosterone may choose to participate on either boys or girls teams. Once that choice is made, the student must consistently participate as that gender in any athletic activities at the secondary school level.
>
> (2) A female-to-male student taking testosterone may only compete on boys teams.
>
> (3) A male-to-female student who is not taking hormone therapy, or who has been taking hormone therapy for less than one year, may only participate on boys teams.
>
> (4) A male-to-female who has completed one year or more of hormone therapy may participate on girls teams.
>
> (5) A transgender student seeking to participate on a school team for the gender with which the student identifies must submit documentation to the member school demonstrating that the student is under the care of a licensed physician. If the student is taking hormone or testosterone therapy, then documentation must be submitted to the member school demonstrating that the therapy has been prescribed by the student's licensed physician, and how long the prescribed therapy has been administered. The member school should consider any other relevant information submitted in support of the request. The member school will then determine, pursuant to the guidelines

and requirements above, whether the student should be permitted to participate as requested.

B. The member school should notify OSSAA when the school determines that a transgender student will be permitted to participate on a school team for the gender with which the student identifies. In the interest of preserving the student's privacy, the member school should not disclose the identity of the student, or any of the other information relating to the request, to OSSAA.

C. If a member school decides not to permit a transgender student to participate as the gender requested by the student, that decision may be appealed to OSSAA's Board of Directors. The identity of the transgender student, and all discussions and written documentation submitted concerning the transgender athlete, will be maintained as confidential by OSSAA unless the information already has been publicly disclosed or the student has consented to disclosure.[630]

It should be noted, however, that the Oklahoma State Senate has before it SB331, otherwise known as SB2, the "Save Women's Sports Act." It is illustrative that the proposed legislation classifies students into one of three categories, "boys," "girls," and "mixed." It says boys should play in boys' sports and girls should play in girls' sports as determined by their "biological sex," but never defines what is meant by that term. One is left to guess, I guess. As of July 2021, the Bill had not progressed beyond obtaining cosponsors and coauthors.

Law Enforcement, Jails, and Prisons

For information on this topic, please see the state data on the MAP website.

Health Care and Health Care Benefits

An Oklahoma State Senator, Senator Warren Hamilton (R-Dist. 7), in January 2021, introduced SB 676, which would make it a criminal felony offense for any health care provider to provide gender-affirming transition-related care to anyone under the age of twenty-one and would penalize parents who sought such care for an under twenty-one-year-old son or daughter. As of July 2021, the Bill had not progressed further than obtaining additional sponsors.

Marriage

For information on this topic, please see the state data on the MAP website. Please also review the section above under federal laws on marriage.

LGBTQ Youth Laws and Policies

For information on this topic, please see the state data on the MAP website.

Religious Exemption Laws

For information on this topic, please see the state data on the MAP website.

Oklahoma Overall Tally

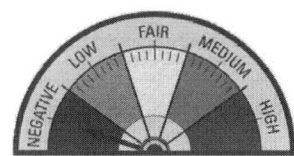

Grand Totals	Sexual Orientation Policy Tally	Gender Identity Policy Tally	Overall Tally
Totals	2/20.5	-4/22	-2/42.5
Ratings	LOW	NEGATIVE	NEGATIVE

Oregon

Oregon Non-Discrimination Laws

Oregon Revised Statutes, Chapter 659A, Section 659A.006 prohibits discrimination:

> (1) It is declared to be the public policy of Oregon that practices of unlawful discrimination against any of its inhabitants because of race, color, religion, sex, sexual orientation, national origin, marital status, age, disability or familial status are a matter of state concern and that this discrimination not only threatens the rights and privileges of its inhabitants but menaces the institutions and foundation of a free democratic state.[631]

It's illegal for your employer, public businesses, places of housing, or other "public accommodations" to treat you differently because of your sex, sexual orientation, or gender. You are protected both at work and outside of work.

Federal civil rights laws and the Equal Employment Opportunity Commission also protect you from discrimination based on sex, gender identity, including transgender status, or sexual orientation. Additional information is available on the Bureau of Labor and Industries, Civil Rights website.[632]

Birth Certificates

The following is taken from the website of the Oregon Health Authority, Oregon Center for Health Statistics:

> Oregon law provides two methods to change a person's designated sex on their birth certificate: administratively or by court judgment. By either method, Oregon Vital Records will change the recorded sex of a registrant (person named on an Oregon birth record) if the proper documents and fees are submitted.
>
> For more information on the new process to change designated sex without a court order, visit our page on House Bill 2673.[633]
>
> A court judgment of change of sex is not required to correct a typographical error in the sex of a child. Please see the Correcting Birth Record Information page[634] for instructions.
>
> How to change a birth record with a court order of change of sex
>
>> Oregon Revised Statute (ORS) 33.460,[635] effective January 1, 2014, states:
>>
>> 1. A court that has jurisdiction to determine an application for change of name of a person under ORS 33.410 and 33.420 may order a legal change of sex and enter a judgment indicating the change of sex of a person if the court determines that the individual has undergone surgical, hormonal, or other treatment appropriate for that individual for the purpose of gender transition and that sexual reassignment has been completed.
>>
>> 2. The court may order a legal change of sex and enter the judgment in the same manner as that provided for a change of name of a person under ORS 33.410 and 33.420.
>>
>> 3. If a person applies for a change of name under ORS 33.410 and 33.420 at the time the person applies for a legal change of sex under this section, the court

may order change of name and legal change of sex at the same time and in the same proceeding.

Once you have an original certified copy of the court order of change of sex, submit the following in person (our office location)[636] or by mail.[637]

1. Original certified copy of the court order showing the original seal and signature of the court clerk. (Our office will keep this document in a sealed file.)

2. If the court order changes the legal name as well as the sex of a person named on an Oregon birth certificate, send a signed statement[638] from the person named on the record if that person is 18 or older, or from the parent requesting that the birth record name be changed. Use the signed statement to clarify whether there are two first, middle, or last names if the court order does not specify this information about the new name. If the birth record is for a child under the age of 18, then a parent named on the birth record, the legal guardian, or the parent who has sole legal custody of the child may sign the request to change the birth certificate name. This signed request statement is not required when only submitting a change of sex by court order.

3. A completed birth record order form.[639] The order form will provide the mailing address and information on how to pay the fee. If you are ordering a full image/long form certificate for a birth occurring prior to 2008, please use this full image birth record order form.[640]

4. $35 amendment fee[641]

5. Fees for new birth certificate copies.[642] Short form certificates or any certificate for a birth occurring in 2008 or later is $25 for each copy. Full image/long form birth certificates are $30 for each copy.

6. Fees for replacement certificates.[643] You may return one original birth certificate issued in the last year for a free replacement. If you return more than one record for replacement, there is a $5 fee per certificate.[644]

Driver's Licenses

The procedure in Oregon to change the designation of sex on your driver's license is as follows:

To change the sex identifier on your driver license or ID card:

- Make an appointment at a DMV office;[645]
- Request a card with the desired indicator;
- Meet the requirements for issuance of a renewal or replacement license or ID card; and
- Pay the renewal or replacement fee.[646]

You may also change your name as part of this request.[647]

Public Accommodations

All Oregonians have the right to full and equal accommodations, advantages, facilities, and privileges of any place of public accommodation, without any distinction, discrimination, or restriction on account of race, color, religion, sex, sexual orientation, national origin, marital status or age (above 18).

> A place of public accommodation includes, but is not limited to, any place or service offering to the public accommodations, advantages, facilities, or privileges whether like goods, services, lodgings, amusements, transportation, or otherwise.
>
> A place of public accommodation does not include Department of Corrections institutions and state hospitals, youth correctional facilities, or institutions, bona fide clubs, or a place of accommodation that is in its nature distinctly private.
>
> It's illegal for your employer, public businesses, places of housing, or other "public accommodations" to treat you differently because of your sex, sexual orientation, or gender.
>
> You are protected both at work and outside of work.
>
> Federal civil rights laws and the Equal Employment Opportunity Commission also protect you from discrimination based on sex, gender identity, including transgender status, or sexual orientation.[648]

Sports

The Oregon Schools Activities Association has the following policy regarding participation in school sports by transgender students:

> The OSAA endeavors to allow students to participate for the athletic or activity program of their consistently asserted gender identity while providing a fair and safe environment for all students. As with Rule 8.2 regarding Duration of Eligibility/Graduation, rules such as this one promotes harmony and fair competition among member schools by maintaining equality of eligibility and increase the number of students who will have an opportunity to participate in interscholastic activities.[649]

Law Enforcement, Jails, and Prisons

For information on this topic, please see the state data on the MAP website.

Health Care and Health Care Benefits

For information on this topic, please see the state data on the MAP website.

Marriage

For information on this topic, please see the state data on the MAP website. Please also review the section above under federal laws on marriage.

LGBTQ Youth Laws and Policies

For information on this topic, please see the state data on the MAP website.

Religious Exemption Laws

For information on this topic, please see the state data on the MAP website.

Oregon Overall Tally

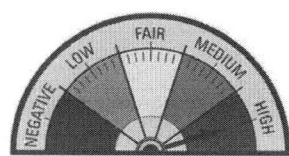

Grand Totals	Sexual Orientation Policy Tally	Gender Identity Policy Tally	Overall Tally
Totals	17/20.5	19.5/22	36.5/42.5
Ratings	HIGH	HIGH	HIGH

Pennsylvania

Pennsylvania Non-Discrimination Laws

Pennsylvania's Human Relations Act prohibits discrimination and states in Section 2:

> (a) The practice or policy of discrimination against individuals or groups by reason of their race, color, familial status, religious creed, ancestry, age, sex, national origin, handicap, or disability, use of guide or support animals because of the blindness, deafness or physical handicap of the user or because the user is a handler or trainer of support or guide animals is a matter of concern of the Commonwealth. Such discrimination foments domestic strife and unrest, threatens the rights and privileges of the inhabitants of the Commonwealth, and undermines the foundations of a free democratic state.[650]

Birth Certificates

Pennsylvania allows a birth certificate to be amended showing that a transgender person has completed their transition. The form and instructions can be found on the Pennsylvania website.[651] You will be required to file documentation of your completed transition with the application.

Driver's Licenses

The Pennsylvania Driver's License Application, Form DL-180,[652] allows you to select the gender that matches your gender identity most accurately.

If you are requesting a name change, you must provide the Pennsylvania Department of Transportation with a certified copy of the court order changing your name. Pennsylvania law allows you to file with a court in Pennsylvania by following the procedures set out in Title 54, Chapter 7 Judicial Name Change, Section 701(a1).[653]

Public Accommodations

Pennsylvania prohibits discrimination based on someone's race, color, sex, ancestry, national origin, religious creed, handicap or disability, the use, handling, or training of a guide or support animal for disability, or relationship to a person with a disability.[654]

Sports

The Pennsylvania Interscholastic Athletics Association (PIAA) has the following policies in force as of July 2021:

> **EQUAL OPPORTUNITY AND TREATMENT POLICY**
>
> The Pennsylvania Interscholastic Athletic Association, Inc. (PIAA) is committed to the principles of equal opportunity and treatment for all individuals involved in interscholastic athletics. PIAA believes that all boys and girls, Coaches, Contest officials, and athletic administrators should have equal opportunity to participate in, Coach, officiate, and administer at all levels of interscholastic athletics and receive equal treatment, without regard to race, color, religion, gender, age, national origin, or ethnic background.
>
> Alleged violations of this Equal Opportunity and Treatment Policy should be reported to the Executive Director, who will attempt to resolve the matter informally, either directly or through a designee. Any person dissatisfied with the efforts of the Executive Director

may seek relief from the District Committee having jurisdiction over the matter. Appeals of District Committee decisions may be taken to the Board of Directors.

TRANSGENDER POLICY

Where a student's gender is questioned or uncertain, the decision of the Principal as to the student's gender will be accepted by PIAA.[655]

Law Enforcement, Jails, and Prisons

For information on this topic, please see the state data on the MAP website.

Health Care and Health Care Benefits

For information on this topic, please see the state data on the MAP website.

Marriage

For information on this topic, please see the state data on the MAP website. Please also review the section above under federal laws on marriage.

LGBTQ Youth Laws and Policies

For information on this topic, please see the state data on the MAP website.

Religious Exemption Laws

Pennsylvania Statutes, RELIGIOUS FREEDOM PROTECTION ACT of December 9, 2002, P.L. 1701, No. 214, Section 2, states:

> The General Assembly finds and declares as follows:
>
> (1) Laws and governmental actions which are facially neutral toward religion, as well as laws and governmental actions intended to interfere with religious exercise, may have the effect of substantially burdening the free exercise of religion. However, neither State nor local government should substantially burden the free exercise of religion without compelling justification.[656]

Many organizations and business entities consider these laws harmful to the state's economy and have urged that they be repealed.

Pennsylvania Overall Tally

Grand Totals	Sexual Orientation Policy Tally	Gender Identity Policy Tally	Overall Tally
Totals	6.25/20.5	9.25/22	15.5/42.5
Ratings	FAIR	FAIR	FAIR

Rhode Island

Rhode Island Non-Discrimination Laws

The Rhode Island statutes prohibit discrimination in employment and public accommodations. The statutes prohibit discrimination based on race, color, sex (including pregnancy and sexual harassment), disability, ancestral origin, religion, sexual orientation, gender identity/expression, and age. In addition to prohibiting discrimination on these bases, the credit statute also prohibits discrimination based on marital status, familial status, military status, and association with members of a protected class. The housing statute covers all of the previously mentioned areas and status as a victim of domestic abuse, housing status, and lawful source of income.[657]

Birth Certificates

Title 216, Chapter 10, Subchapter 10, Part 1 of the Rhode Island Code of Regulations, Sections 1.37 and 1.38 determine the requirements and procedures for amending a Rhode Island birth certificate. The Regulations can be found on the Department of Health website.[658] The author could find no specific text relating to transgender persons or gender identity. But you can assume they will want a letter from your surgeon or other physician stating you have completed transitioning from one gender or sex to another.

Driver's Licenses

Rhode Island requires the following to change your name on your driver's License: [659]

You must first update your records with the Social Security Administration after obtaining a court-ordered name change.

Bring your current Rhode Island license with you to the nearest DMV Branch Location.

You need to complete and sign the License/ID/Permit Application.[660]

One document showing your correct name. Refer to the third page of the License/ID/Permit Application for a list of documents needed to perform this transaction.

Applicants requesting a change of the gender designation on their driver's license or identification card from that showing on their identity proof documents must:

- Surrender any current state-issued license or identification card.
- Submit a completed Gender Designation form.[661]
- Pay applicable fees for a new or updated license or identification card. The applicant shall have a new photograph taken.

Name changes related to gender are completed via submitting appropriate court documents and must be reflected on the Social Security card.[662] Please refer to the RI DMV Document Checklist - License and ID Cards.[663]

Public Accommodations

Rhode Island statutes, Title 11, Chapter 11-24, Section 11-24-1 prohibits discrimination in public accommodations:

All persons within the jurisdiction of this state shall be entitled to the full and equal accommodations, advantages, facilities, and privileges of any place of public accommodation, resort or amusement, subject only to the conditions and limitations established by law and applicable alike to all persons.[664]

Sections 11-24-2 and 11-24-2.2 add sex and sexual orientation, respectively, to the prohibition.

Sports

The Rhode Island Interscholastic League (RIIL) has a policy that states:

> The RIIL recognizes the value of participation in interscholastic sports for all member school student athletes. The RIIL is committed to providing all student-athletes with equal opportunities to participate in RIIL athletic programs consistent with their gender identity. This policy addresses eligibility determinations for students who have a gender identity that is different from the gender listed on their official birth certificates.[665]

Law Enforcement, Jails, and Prisons

For information on this topic, please see the state data on the MAP website.

Health Care and Health Care Benefits

For information on this topic, please see the state data on the MAP website.

Marriage

For information on this topic, please see the state data on the MAP website. Please also review the section above on federal laws on marriage.

LGBTQ Youth Laws and Policies

For information on this topic, please see the state data on the MAP website.

Religious Exemption Laws

For information on this topic, please see the state data on the MAP website.

Rhode Island Overall Tally

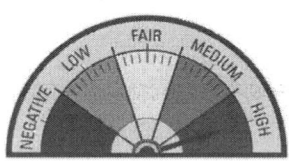

Grand Totals	Sexual Orientation Policy Tally	Gender Identity Policy Tally	Overall Tally
Totals	16.5/20.5	16/22	32.5/42.5
Ratings	HIGH	MEDIUM	HIGH

South Carolina

South Carolina Non-Discrimination Laws

South Carolina has no general non-discrimination statute. However, it does have statutes that prohibit discrimination in employment, housing, and public accommodations based on a person's race, color, religion, sex, national origin, physical or mental handicaps. Sex discrimination is defined as discrimination against an individual who is transgender and is considered discrimination because of sex in violation of Title VII. It is also known as gender identity discrimination. In addition, lesbian, gay, and bisexual individuals may bring sex discrimination claims. These may include, for example, allegations of sexual harassment or other kinds of sex discrimination, such as adverse actions taken because of the person's non-conformance with sex stereotypes. The EEOC has provided additional resources about sexual orientation and gender identity workplace rights. See "Protections Against Employment Discrimination Based on Sexual Orientation or Gender Identity" on the U.S. Equal Employment Opportunity Commission website.[666]

Sex-based discrimination also includes both "sexual harassment" and pregnancy discrimination. Sexual harassment can include unwelcome sexual advances, requests for sexual favors, and other verbal or physical harassment of a sexual nature. Pregnancy discrimination involves treating a woman unfavorably because of pregnancy, childbirth, or a medical condition related to pregnancy or childbirth.[667]

Birth Certificates

The author received an email on July 29, 2021, from the South Carolina Division of Vital Records, S.C. Dept. of Health and Environmental Control, stating that:

> South Carolina statutes and regulations do not speak directly to gender change; however, we look for the following elements as those needed to make a gender change on a birth record (other than correction of a mistaken entry at birth):
>
> 1. A physical change related to the individual's sex;
> 2. A physical change that has been completed, with the result that the individual is now a different gender from the gender at birth, understood as biological sex at birth, either male or female, and is not merely in the process of transitioning (although additional procedures or treatment may still be continuing and life-long, or anticipated later);
> 3. A permanent physical change; and
> 4. A physical change that is made with the intent to change gender permanently and for all purposes.
>
> To amend the gender marker on your birth record, we require an order from a court of competent jurisdiction, supported by a licensed physician's statement, finding sufficient evidence to establish each of these elements.
>
> If you do obtain a court order to establish a gender change, please send the following items to my attention at the address below:
>
> 1. Certified, True Copy of the Final Order, with the Clerk's seal or stamp;

2. A completed and signed application for an amended birth certificate (blank form attached or available as a fillable PDF)[668];

3. A photocopy of government-issued photo identification of the applicant/signatory; and

4. A check or money order is payable to SCDHEC for $27.

5. $3 for each additional copy of the amended certificate. The fee above entitles you to one amended copy of the certificate.

You may show this email to the court as a statement of DHEC's position. I request that you send me a copy of any proposed final order before the judge signs it to prevent any processing delays that may occur as a result of insufficient language in the order.

Mail to:

DHEC Vital Records
2600 Bull Street
Columbia, SC 29201

Driver's Licenses

You may change your name at an SCDMV branch[669] and buy a new beginner's permit, driver's license, or identification card if you do all of the following:

- Complete the Application for Name or Address Change (SCDMV Form 4057),[670]
- Complete the Application for a Driver's License, Beginner's Permit, or Identification Card (SCDMV Form 447-NC),[671]
- Present proper documentation.

You must change your name with the Social Security Administration at least 48 hours before visiting the SCDMV to change your name.

The proper documentation includes any of the following:

- Marriage license
- Court order (issued by your county's family court)

It's $10 for a new license that reflects your updated name unless you're interested in a REAL ID. Your first REAL ID is $25 since it's considered to be renewing your license. You must have all required documents to purchase a REAL ID[672] to be eligible for this card.

Public Accommodations

Section 45-9-10: States that every person is entitled to the full enjoyment of described services and accommodations without discrimination on account of race, color, religion, or national origin and defines places of public accommodation.

Sports

The South Carolina legislature has failed to pass legislation that would ban transgender students from participating in school athletic programs. The last measure was defeated in April 2021.

Law Enforcement, Jails, and Prisons

For information on this topic, please see the state data on the MAP website.

Health Care and Health Care Benefits

For information on this topic, please see the state data on the MAP website.

Marriage

For information on this topic, please see the state data on the MAP website. Please also review the section above under federal laws on marriage.

LGBTQ Youth Laws and Policies

For information on this topic, please see the state data on the MAP website.

Religious Exemption Laws

For information on this topic, please see the state data on the MAP website.

South Carolina Overall Tally

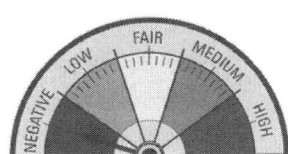

Grand Totals	Sexual Orientation Policy Tally	Gender Identity Policy Tally	Overall Tally
Totals	1/20.5	-1.5/22	-0.5/42.5
Ratings	LOW	NEGATIVE	NEGATIVE

South Dakota

South Dakota Non-Discrimination Laws

The South Dakota Human Relations Act of 1972 currently does not cover gender identity or sexual orientation. In an email the author received from the South Dakota Human Rights Commission, dated August 2, 2021, the agency referred the author to the Equal Employment Opportunity Commission (EEOC) for more information.[673]

Birth Certificates

The South Dakota Department of Health, Vital Records, will amend a birth record pursuant to 44:09:05:02. Requirements for amending vital records of the South Dakota Administrative Rules.

> Unless otherwise provided in this chapter or in statute, the Department of Health shall make all amendments to vital records. The following information is required:
>
> (1) An affidavit of correction setting forth the following:
>
> (a) Information to identify the certificate;
>
> (b) The incorrect data as it is listed on the certificate; and
>
> (c) The correct data as it should appear; or
>
> (2) An order from a court of competent jurisdiction which directs that the record be amended and provides the following information:
>
> (a) Information to identify the certificate;
>
> (b) The incorrect data as it is listed on the certificate; and
>
> (c) The correct data as it should appear.
>
> **Source:** SL 1975, Ch 16, § 1; 6 SDR 93, effective July 1, 1980; 24 SDR 60, effective November 13, 1997; 26 SDR 89, effective January 9, 2000.
>
> **General Authority:** SDCL 34-25-51.
>
> **Law Implemented:** SDCL 34-25-51.[674]

Driver's Licenses

For a duplicate/replacement license or ID card, you may be able to apply online,[675] or you can schedule an appointment[676] to visit a driver licensing location. Only U.S. citizens and permanent residents can apply online. The documents you'll need are:

- A completed application form (in English or in Spanish).

- Two documents to prove your residential/physical address (cannot be handwritten documents). Documents must show your name and be less than one year old; this could include a utility bill, paystub, rent receipt, phone bill, bank statement, mortgage document, homeowner's policy, or tax document.

- If your name has changed, you'll need to provide proof of the name change with a marriage certificate, divorce decree, or court order (applicants with name changes must apply at a Driver Licensing location).[677] No photocopies! We can only accept original documents.

- If you are not a U.S. Citizen or were not when you last applied, you will need to provide a Certificate of Citizenship/Naturalization, a Permanent Resident Card, an Employment Authorization Card, or a Foreign Passport with a valid U.S. Visa/I-94.[678]

As for changing the designation of sex on your South Dakota Driver's License, an agent with the agency told the author that, they require a letter or some documentation from your attending physician or surgeon that you have completed all the requirements for sex reassignment surgery and the date that surgery was completed. They also require you to submit a certified copy of your amended birth certificate.

Public Accommodations

No person can be denied the right to the full and equal use of any public accommodation or public service in South Dakota because of race, color, creed, religion, sex, ancestry, disability, or national origin.

A public accommodation is any place that offers facilities, goods, or services to the general public. Private clubs that do not serve the general public are not included. If a private club occasionally offers such facilities, goods, or services to the public, it is considered a public accommodation only during that period.

Public services include hospitals, police, welfare, and all departments, agencies, boards, or commissions owned, operated, or managed by or for the State of South Dakota or any political subdivision.[679]

Sports

Governor Kristi Noem signed an Executive Order dated March 29, 2021, which bans participation in school sports at the interscholastic and intercollegiate levels for transgender athletes.

Law Enforcement, Jails, and Prisons

For information on this topic, please see the state data on the MAP website.

Health Care and Health Care Benefits

For information on this topic, please see the state data on the MAP website.

Marriage

For information on this topic, please see the state data on the MAP website. Please also review the section above under federal laws on marriage.

LGBTQ Youth Laws and Policies

For information on this topic, please see the state data on the MAP website.

Religious Exemption Laws

On March 29, 2021, Governor Kristi Noem signed into law the following Religious Exemption law:

1-1A-4. Government authority--Limitations related to the exercise of religion.

Notwithstanding any other provision of law, no state agency, political subdivision, or any elected or appointed official or employee of this state or its political subdivisions may:

(1) Substantially burden a person's exercise of religion unless applying the burden to that person's exercise of religion in a particular situation is essential to further

a compelling governmental interest and is the least restrictive means of furthering that compelling government interest;

(2) Treat religious conduct more restrictively than any secular conduct of reasonably comparable risk; or

(3) Treat religious conduct more restrictively than comparable secular conduct because of alleged economic need or benefit.

This section constitutes a general law of the state within the meaning of S.D. Const., Article IX, § 2 and supersedes any contrary provision in a home rule charter. Any person aggrieved by a violation of this section may file an action for damages, injunctive relief, or other appropriate redress in circuit court, or may assert such violation as a defense in a judicial or administrative proceeding. The plaintiff, if the prevailing party, may also recover reasonable attorney's fees and costs.[680]

South Dakota Overall Tally

Grand Totals	Sexual Orientation Policy Tally	Gender Identity Policy Tally	Overall Tally
Totals	-0.5/20.5	-4/22	-4.5/42.5
Ratings	NEGATIVE	NEGATIVE	NEGATIVE

Tennessee

Tennessee Non-Discrimination Laws

The Tennessee Human Rights Act and Tennessee Disability Act prohibit discrimination related to employment actions, including Advertisement, Benefits, Discipline, Compensation, Discharge, Harassment, Hiring, Layoff, Leave, Promotion, Suspension, and Training. It is illegal for employers to discriminate in employment actions based on age (40+), Color, Creed, Disability, National Origins, Race, Religions, and Sex. The law applies to any Tennessee employer, prospective employer, employment agencies, or labor organization with eight or more employees. Only one employee is required in complaints alleging retaliation.[681]

The Tennessee Code, Title 4, Chapter 21, Section 102(4) states that:

> "Discriminatory practices" means any direct or indirect act or practice of exclusion, distinction, restriction, segregation, limitation, refusal, denial, or any other act or practice of differentiation or preference in the treatment of a person or persons because of race, creed, color, religion, sex, age or national origin.[682]

Birth Certificates

The Tennessee Code Annotated, Title 68, Chapter 3, Part 2, Section 203(d), states:

> The sex of an individual shall not be changed on the original certificate of birth as a result of sex-change surgery.[683]

For name changes on birth certificates, the agency requires that an applicant follows the procedure of obtaining a court order first, then get the name changed with the Social Security Administration, and finally file the appropriate paperwork with the agency.[684]

Driver's Licenses

The Tennessee Department of Safety and Homeland Security, Driver Services, does not provide the information you need on their website. The author called and, after several menus, got an agent who said:

- You need to have a Valid Tennessee Regular Driver's License
- A Letter from your physician or surgeon detailing that you have completed your transition, including any surgery performed.
- A copy of your birth certificate
- A copy of your Social Security Card
- If you do not have a valid license, you will need to provide two proofs of Tennessee residence.

The author does not know if a form needs to be filled out, and the agent who provided the above information did not know either.

Public Accommodations

It is illegal for a place of public accommodations to refuse or deny the full and equal enjoyment of goods, facilities, and accommodations based on age (40+), color, creed, national origin, race, religion, and sex. The law applies to any business, accommodation, refreshment, entertainment, recreation, or transportation facility, licensed or not, whose goods, services, facilities, and privileges are extended, offered, sold, or otherwise made available to the public.

The reader will note that sexual orientation and gender identity are not listed as being protected pursuant to Tennessee Code 4-21-102(4). This law includes prohibitions on publishing, circulation or displaying any material that communicates that any person is unwelcome on the basis of unlawful discrimination. The preceding information was confirmed in an email the author received from the Tennessee Human Rights Commission staff on August 3, 2021, which states:

> The state statute does not cover sexual orientation or gender identity. However, EEOC does cover those issues.[685] Go to the menu on the right-hand side of the page.

Sports

In March 2021, Tennessee became the third state to pass its version of the "Save Women's Sports" Act, banning transgender athletes from participating in interscholastic sports programs. Previously, Idaho and Mississippi had passed the same legislation. No transgender person has come forward thus far to challenge the law.

Law Enforcement, Jails, and Prisons For information on this topic, please see the state data on the MAP website.

Health Care and Health Care Benefits

For information on this topic, please see the state data on the MAP website.

Marriage

For information on this topic, please see the state data on the MAP website. Please also review the section above under federal laws on marriage.

LGBTQ Youth Laws and Policies

For information on this topic, please see the state data on the MAP website.

Religious Exemption Laws

For information on this topic, please see the state data on the MAP website.

Tennessee Overall Tally

Grand Totals	Sexual Orientation Policy Tally	Gender Identity Policy Tally	Overall Tally
Totals	-0.25/20.5	-5.75/22	-6/42.5
Ratings	NEGATIVE	NEGATIVE	NEGATIVE

Texas

Texas Non-Discrimination Laws

There is no general non-discrimination law in Texas, although Texas does have a law that prohibits discrimination in employment:

> Sec. 21.051. DISCRIMINATION BY EMPLOYER. An employer commits an unlawful employment practice if because of race, color, disability, religion, sex, national origin, or age the employer:
>
> (1) fails or refuses to hire an individual, discharges an individual, or discriminates in any other manner against an individual in connection with compensation or the terms, conditions, or privileges of employment; or
>
> (2) limits, segregates, or classifies an employee or applicant for employment in a manner that would deprive or tend to deprive an individual of any employment opportunity or adversely affect in any other manner the status of an employee.
>
> Acts 1993, 73rd Leg., ch. 269, Sec. 1, eff. Sept. 1, 1993.[686]

Texas also prohibits discrimination in housing[687] and rehabilitation services under Federal law[688] in any program or activity that receives State or Federal funding. Nevertheless, the author could not find any provisions in State law that prohibited discrimination because of sexual orientation or gender identity.

Birth Certificates

To change your name on a Texas birth certificate, you must first obtain a court order from a court in Texas. Then, you submit that court order with your application to correct your birth certificate. The form to use is the VS-170.[689]

Driver's Licenses

The author received an email from the Texas Department of Public Safety which says:

> Any modifications are required to be completed at the driver license office. You must provide original documentation to prove the modification such as a Court Order.

The email did not go into detail about the process. The reader may want to go to the nearest Driver License Office to get more information, but in all likelihood, you will need to obtain a court order that changes both your name and sex. You may also need to present proof of surgery.

Public Accommodations

Texas currently has no statewide law prohibiting discrimination because of race, color, religion, sex, national origin, sexual orientation, gender identity/ expression, age, or physical disability.

Sports

The website of the Texas Interscholastic League has the following policy:

> Section 360: NON-DISCRIMINATION POLICY
>
> Failure to comply with the provisions of this subchapter constitutes an act or omission that is a violation of the Constitution. Except as provided for below, no student otherwise eligible under Subchapter M of the Constitution shall be denied, because of disability,

race, color, gender, religion or national origin, the equal opportunity to try out for and, if selected, participate in the Academic, Music, and Athletic Plan contests offered by the member school districts.

> (a) Member schools may not permit boys to try out for or participate under the Jr. High School or High School Athletic Plans designated for girl's teams."

And in Subsection (h) states the following:

> (h) Gender shall be determined based on a student's birth certificate. In cases where a student's birth certificate is unavailable, other similar government documents used for the purpose of identification may be substituted.[690]

Law Enforcement, Jails, and Prisons

For information on this topic, please see the state data on the MAP website.

Health Care and Health Care Benefits

For information on this topic, please see the state data on the MAP website.

Marriage

For information on this topic, please see the state data on the MAP website. Please also review the section above under federal laws on marriage.

LGBTQ Youth Laws and Policies

For information on this topic, please see the state data on the MAP website.

Religious Exemption Laws

Texas law provides for sweeping Religious Freedom.

> **CIVIL PRACTICE AND REMEDIES CODE**
>
> **TITLE 5. GOVERNMENTAL LIABILITY**
>
> **CHAPTER 110. RELIGIOUS FREEDOM**
>
> The following section was amended by the 87th Legislature. Pending publication of the current statutes, see H.B. 1239,[691] 87th Legislature, Regular Session, for amendments affecting the following section.
>
>> Sec. 110.001. DEFINITIONS. (a) In this chapter:
>>
>> (1) "Free exercise of religion" means an act or refusal to act that is substantially motivated by sincere religious belief. In determining whether an act or refusal to act is substantially motivated by sincere religious belief under this chapter, it is not necessary to determine that the act or refusal to act is motivated by a central part or central requirement of the person's sincere religious belief.
>>
>> (2) "Government agency" means:
>>
>>> (A) this state or a municipality or other political subdivision of this state; and
>>>
>>> (B) any agency of this state or a municipality or other political subdivision of this state, including a department, bureau, board, commission, office, agency, council, or public institution of higher education.

(b) In determining whether an interest is a compelling governmental interest under Section 110.003,[692] a court shall give weight to the interpretation of compelling interest in federal case law relating to the free exercise of religion clause of the First Amendment of the United States Constitution.[693]

Texas Overall Tally

Grand Totals	Sexual Orientation Policy Tally	Gender Identity Policy Tally	Overall Tally
Totals	2.75/20.5	-2.25/22	0.5/42.5
Ratings	LOW	NEGATIVE	LOW

Utah

Utah Non-Discrimination Laws

Utah statutes prohibit discrimination in employment. The statute states, in relevant part:

> 34A-5-106. Discriminatory or prohibited employment practices -- Permitted practices.
>
> (1) It is a discriminatory or prohibited employment practice to take an action described in Subsection (1)(a) through (g).
>
>> (a)(i) An employer may not refuse to hire, promote, discharge, demote, or terminate a person, or to retaliate against, harass, or discriminate in matters of compensation or in terms, privileges and conditions of employment against a person otherwise qualified, because of:
>>
>>> (A) race,
>>> (B) color,
>>> (C) sex,
>>> (D) pregnancy childbirth, or pregnancy related conditions,
>>> (E) age, if the individual is 40 years or age or older,
>>> (F) religion,
>>> (G) national origin,
>>> (H) disability,
>>> (I) sexual orientation, or
>>> (J) gender identity.[694]

Birth Certificates

Utah allows transgender persons to amend their birth certificates to show their gender after completing transition-related health care services.[695]

> A court order is required if the individual has undergone treatment to transition from one gender to another. The court order must state the child's full name, the gender that is currently on the birth record and the gender that will be corrected on the birth record. Submit the certified court order with Court Order Amendment Form, a Birth Certificate Application, a copy of the requester's ID, and check or money order for the correct fees.
>
> All amendments become part of the record unless the court order states that the changes are to be sealed. If the record is to be sealed, the fee is $60 instead of $25."[696]
>
> For information regarding a typographically error to the gender field at the time of birth see "Change Other Birth Information."[697]

Driver's Licenses

The author spoke with an agent with the Utah Department of Public Safety, Driver License Division and found that, in Utah, residents must first get a Court-Ordered change of sex and name,[698] then apply for a new birth certificate with the designation of sex and name having been changed. You then present the Court Order and the new Birth Certificate to the DMV office near you, and they will issue a new Driver's License with the correct name and sex listed.

Public Accommodations

The following is from the Utah Code, Title 13, Chapter 7 Civil Rights:

13-7-1 Policy and purposes of act.

It is hereby declared that the practice of discrimination on the basis of race, color, sex, pregnancy, religion, ancestry, or national origin in business establishments or places of public accommodation or in enterprises regulated by the state endangers the health, safety, and general welfare of this state and its inhabitants; and that such discrimination in business establishments or places of public accommodation or in enterprises regulated by the state, violates the public policy of this state. It is the purpose of this act to assure all citizens full and equal availability of all goods, services and facilities offered by business establishments and places of public accommodation and enterprises regulated by the state without discrimination because of race, color, sex, pregnancy, religion, ancestry, or national origin. The rules of common law that statutes in derogation thereof shall be strictly construed has no application to this act. *This act shall be liberally construed with a view to promote the policy and purposes of the act and to promote justice.* The remedies provided herein are not exclusive but are in addition to any other remedies available at law or equity. [emphasis added] [699]

Sports

The Utah High School Activities Association (UHSAA) Handbook, in UHSAA By-Laws and Interpretations and Guidelines, Article 1 Eligibility of Players, in Section 1.1.4 Interps and Guidelines, Transgender Participation, the Handbook states:

This policy addresses eligibility determinations for students who have a gender identity that is different from the gender listed on their official birth certificates. For the protection of competitive balance and the integrity of women's sports, the UHSAA will review athletic eligibility decisions based on gender assignment of trans gender student athletes in accordance with its approved policies and appeals procedures. If a sport is offered for both boys and girls, girls must play on the girls team and boys must play on the boys team. If a school sponsors only a single team in a sport:

b. Girls are eligible to play on boys teams.
c. b. Boys are not eligible to play on girls teams.[700]

Law Enforcement, Jails, and Prisons

For information on this topic, please see the state data on the MAP website.

Health and Health Care Benefits

For information on this topic, please see the state data on the MAP website.

Marriage

For information on this topic, please see the state data on the MAP website. Please also review the section above under federal laws on marriage.

LGBTQ Youth Laws and Policies

For information on this topic, please see the state data on the MAP website.

Religious Exemption Laws

Utah Code Annotated, 63L-5-101 to 63L-5-403 (2008) states:

63L-5-101. Title, This chapter is known as the "Utah Religious Land Use Act," Renumbered and Amended by Chapter 382, 2008 General Session:

63L-5-102. Definitions.

As used in this chapter:

(1) "Free exercise of religion" means an act or refusal to act that is substantially motivated by sincere religious belief, whether or not the act or refusal is compulsory or central to a larger system of religious belief, and includes the use, building, or conversion of real property for the purpose of religious exercise.

(2) "Government entity" means the state, a county, a municipality, a higher education institution, a local district, a special service district, any other political subdivision of the state, or any administrative subunit of any of them.

(3) "Land use regulation" means any state or local law or ordinance, whether statutory or otherwise, that limits or restricts a person's use or development of land or a structure affixed to land.

(4) "Person" means any individual, partnership, corporation, or other legal entity that owns an interest in real property. Renumbered and Amended by Chapter 382, 2008 General Session

63L-5-201. Protection of land use as religious exercise.

(1) Except as provided in Subsection (2), a government entity may not impose or implement a land use regulation in a manner that imposes a substantial burden on a person's free exercise of religion.

(2) A government entity may impose or implement a land use regulation in a manner that imposes a substantial burden on a person's free exercise of religion if the government can establish that the imposition of the burden on that person:

a) is in furtherance of a compelling governmental interest; and

b) is the least restrictive means of furthering that compelling governmental interest.[701]

Utah Overall Tally

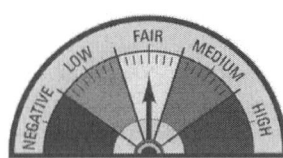

Grand Totals	Sexual Orientation Policy Tally	Gender Identity Policy Tally	Overall Tally
Totals	8/20.5	7.25/22	15.25/42.5
Ratings	FAIR	FAIR	FAIR

Vermont

Vermont Non-Discrimination Laws

The Vermont Human Rights Commission's website states that:

> Vermont's anti-discrimination laws protect people from discrimination based on race, color, sex, sexual orientation, religion, national origin, ancestry or place of birth, mental or physical disability, age, marital status and credit history (though the categories apply differently to housing, employment, and public accommodations - see our Jurisdiction page[702] for details). In addition, you may not be denied housing because you have minor children in your family or because you receive public assistance. Notwithstanding any other provision of law, a mother may breastfeed a child in any place of public accommodation where the mother and child would otherwise have the legal right to be. Vermont's laws do not protect individuals from discrimination based on criminal record, poor credit rating, or any other category not listed above.[703]

Birth Certificates

Vermont Statutes, Title 18, Chapter 104, Section 5112, allows transgender people to obtain a new birth certificate. The process is outlined in the text of the section. See the Vermont Statutes Online website[704] for more information or to fill out an application form.[705]

For both birth certificates and driver's licenses, transgender persons will first need to change their name by a court order. You can fill out a Petition of Adult to Change Name form[706] and submit it to the court where you live. Once you have the name change accomplished, you can then show the Vital Records Division and the Driver's License Division that documentation.

Driver's Licenses

You must apply in person to have your name changed on your license or non-driver ID card. To obtain a corrected license, please provide the following documentation:

- Documentation of your new name in the form of:
    1. An original or certified copy of a marriage license/ certificate
    2. Civil union certificate, or
    3. Court order clearly stating your new name
- Completed Name/Address Change Form (Form #VL-040)[707]

NOTE: If your License or ID is Real ID compliant, we must verify your name and date of birth via Social Security Online Verification (SSOLV).[708] You must update your records with the Social Security Administration[709] before processing a name change at DMV. Before a license or ID can be issued in the new name, SSA records must be updated.

Public Accommodations

Vermont Statutes, Title 9, Chapter 139, Section 4502 Public Accommodations states:

> (a) An owner or operator of a place of public accommodation or an agent or employee of such owner or operator shall not, because of the race, creed, color, national origin, marital status, sex, sexual orientation, or gender identity of any person, refuse,

withhold from, or deny to that person any of the accommodations, advantages, facilities, and privileges of the place of public accommodation.[710]

Sports

The Vermont Principals' Association (VPA) recognizes the value of participation in interscholastic sports for all student athletes. The VPA is committed to providing all students with the opportunity to participate in VPA activities in a manner consistent with their gender identity as is outlined in the Vermont Agency of Education Best Practices For Schools For Transgender And Gender Nonconforming Students. Vermont's Public Accommodations Act (9 V.S.A. 4502) and VPA policies prohibits discrimination and/or harassment of students on school property or at school functions by students or employees. The prohibition against discrimination includes discrimination based on a student's actual or perceived sex and gender. Gender includes a person's actual or perceived sex as well as gender identity and expression.[711]

Law Enforcement, Jails, and Prisons

For information on this topic, please see the state data on the MAP website.

Health and Health Care Benefits

For information on this topic, please see the state data on the MAP website.

Marriage

For information on this topic, please see the state data on the MAP website. Please also review the section above under federal laws on marriage.

LGBTQ Youth Laws and Policies

For information on this topic, please see the state data on the MAP website.

Religious Exemption Laws

For information on this topic, please see the state data on the MAP website.

Vermont Overall Tally

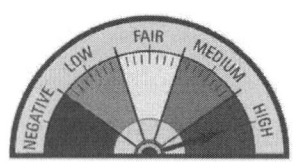

Grand Totals	Sexual Orientation Policy Tally	Gender Identity Policy Tally	Overall Tally
Totals	17.5/20.5	18.5/22	36/42.5
Ratings	HIGH	HIGH	HIGH

Virginia

Virginia Non-Discrimination Laws

Virginia Human Rights Act, Section 2.2-3900 Declaration of Policy has an inclusive policy that states:

> It is the policy of the Commonwealth to:
>
> 1. Safeguard all individuals within the Commonwealth from unlawful discrimination because of race, color, religion, national origin, sex, pregnancy, childbirth or related medical conditions, age, marital status, sexual orientation, gender identity, military status, or disability in places of public accommodation, including educational institutions and in real estate transactions;
>
> 2. Safeguard all individuals within the Commonwealth from unlawful discrimination in employment because of race, color, religion, national origin, sex, pregnancy, childbirth or related medical conditions, age, marital status, sexual orientation, gender identity, disability, or military status;
>
> 3. Preserve the public safety, health, and general welfare;
>
> 4. Further the interests, rights, and privileges of individuals within the Commonwealth; and
>
> 5. Protect citizens of the Commonwealth against unfounded charges of unlawful discrimination.[712]

Birth Certificates

Virginia Code, Title 32.1, Section 261, Subsection A, Paragraph 5, states:

> Upon request of a person and in accordance with requirements of the Board, the State Registrar shall issue a new certificate of birth to show a change of sex of the person and, if a certified copy of a court order changing the person's name is submitted, to show a new name. Requirements related to obtaining a new certificate of birth to show a change of sex shall include a requirement that the person requesting the new certificate of birth submit a form furnished by the State Registrar and completed by a health care provider from whom the person has received treatment stating that the person has undergone clinically appropriate treatment for gender transition. Requirements related to obtaining a new certificate of birth to show a change of sex shall not include any requirement for evidence or documentation of any medical procedure.[713]

Driver's Licenses

The Virginia Code, Title 46.2, Chapter 3, which covers driver's licenses, has no provision that addresses the ability of a transgender driver to get a new driver's license where the designation of sex matches the person's stated gender identity. Furthermore, the author was unable to locate information on the Virginia DMV's website, which necessitated a call to the agency's FOIA contact requesting the information rather than submitting an official FOIA Request. The agency's website also did not provide a general email address where questions of a general nature could be sent.

Public Accommodations

The Code of Virginia, Title 2.2 Administration of Government, Subtitle II, Part B, Chapter 39, Section 2.2 3904, Nondiscrimination in Places of Public Accommodation, Definitions States the following:

> A. As used in this section:
>
> "Age" means being an individual who is at least 18 years of age.
>
> "Place of public accommodation" means all places or businesses offering or holding out to the general public goods, services, privileges, facilities, advantages, or accommodations.
>
> B. It is an unlawful discriminatory practice for any person, including the owner, lessee, proprietor, manager, superintendent, agent, or employee of any place of public accommodation, to refuse, withhold from, or deny any individual, or to attempt to refuse, withhold from, or deny any individual, directly or indirectly, any of the accommodations, advantages, facilities, services, or privileges made available in any place of public accommodation, or to segregate or discriminate against any such person in the use thereof, or to publish, circulate, issue, display, post, or mail, either directly or indirectly, any communication, notice, or advertisement to the effect that any of the accommodations, advantages, facilities, privileges, or services of any such place shall be refused, withheld from, or denied to any individual on the basis of race, color, religion, national origin, sex, pregnancy, childbirth or related medical conditions, age, sexual orientation, gender identity, marital status, disability, or military status.[714]

Sports

The Virginia High School League (YHSL) Handbook and Policy Manual, 2021-2022, Section 28A-8-1 Transgender Policy (12-14), states:

> Students who wish to participate in a VHSL gender-specific sports team that is different from the gender identity listed on the student's official birth certificate or school records are advised to address the gender identification issue with the local school district well in advance of the deadline for athletic eligibility determinations for a current sports season. Students should not be permitted to participate in practices or to try out for gender-specific sports teams that are different from their publicly identified gender identity at the time or to try out simultaneously for VHSL sports teams of both genders.
>
> When a school identifies a transgender student who seeks to participate in VHSL sports and/or activities, the school principal should submit a letter requesting an appeal to the district chairman and the VHSL executive director. The letter should be responsive to the conditions in the policy below…
>
> VHSL rules and regulations allow transgender student-athlete participation under the following conditions:
>
> 1. The student/or parents shall contact the school principal or athletic director indicating that the student has a consistent gender identity different than the gender listed on the student's official birth certificate or school registration

records, and that the student desires to participate in activities in a manner consistent with his/her gender identity.[715]

Law Enforcement, Jails, and Prisons

For information on this topic, please see the state data on the MAP website.

Health and Health Care Benefits

For information on this topic, please see the state data on the MAP website.

Marriage

For information on this topic, please see the state data on the MAP website. Please also review the section above under federal laws on marriage.

LGBTQ Youth Laws and Policies

For information on this topic, please see the state data on the MAP website.

Religious Exemption Laws

The Code of Virginia, Title 57 Religious and Charitable Matters, Chapter 1 Religious Freedom, Section 02, states:

> A. As used in this section:
>
> "Demonstrates" means meets the burdens of going forward with the evidence and of persuasion under the standard of clear and convincing evidence.
>
> "Exercise of religion" means the exercise of religion under Article I, Section 16 of the Constitution of Virginia, the Virginia Act for Religious Freedom (§ 57-1 et seq.), and the First Amendment to the United States Constitution.
>
> "Government entity" means any branch, department, agency, or instrumentality of state government, or any official or other person acting under color of state law, or any political subdivision of the Commonwealth and does not include the Department of Corrections, the Department of Juvenile Justice, and any facility of the Department of Behavioral Health and Developmental Services that treats civilly committed sexually violent predators, or any local, regional or federal correctional facility.
>
> "Prevails" means to obtain "prevailing party" status as defined by courts construing the federal Civil Rights Attorney's Fees Awards Act of 1976, 42 U.S.C. § 1988.
>
> "Substantially burden" means to inhibit or curtail religiously motivated practice.
>
> B. No government entity shall substantially burden a person's free exercise of religion even if the burden results from a rule of general applicability unless it demonstrates that application of the burden to the person is (i) essential to further a compelling governmental interest and (ii) the least restrictive means of furthering that compelling governmental interest.[716]

Virginia Overall Tally

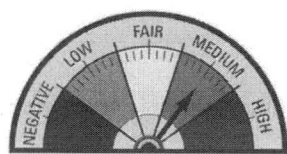

Grand Totals	Sexual Orientation Policy Tally	Gender Identity Policy Tally	Overall Tally
Totals	10.5/20.5	13.5/22	24/42.5
Ratings	MEDIUM	MEDIUM	MEDIUM

Washington

Washington Non-Discrimination Laws

The Revised Code of Washington RCW 49.60.030, Freedom from discrimination—Declaration of civil rights states:

> (1) The right to be free from discrimination because of race, creed, color, national origin, citizenship or immigration status, sex, honorably discharged veteran or military status, sexual orientation, or the presence of any sensory, mental, or physical disability or the use of a trained dog guide or service animal by a person with a disability is recognized as and declared to be a civil right.[717]

Birth Certificates

The Washington state Department of Health website, Vital Records, directs people who were born in Washington State and want to change their sex designation on their birth certificate to reflect their gender identity, to complete the Request to Change Sex Designation on a Birth Certificate for an Adult form.[718] The new rule allows "X" as a third sex designation option, which designates a gender that is not exclusively male or female, including, but not limited to, intersex, agender, amalgagender, androgynous, bigender, demi gender, female-to-male, genderfluid, genderqueer, male-to-female, neutrois, nonbinary, pangender, third sex, transgender, transsexual, Two-Spirit, and unspecified. Since January 27, 2018, a court order or letter from your physician will no longer be accepted.

For Adults (over 18 years of age or an emancipated minor)

- The Request to Change Sex Designation on a Birth Certificate for an Adult form must be completed by a person requesting to change the sex designation on their birth certificate. Emancipated minors must include proof of legal emancipation under chapter 13.64 RCW (i.e., certified court order). Guardians acting on behalf of an adult must include proof of guardianship appointed under chapter 11.92 RCW.

- The Request to Change Sex Designation on a Birth Certificate for an Adult form must be signed in the presence of a Notary Public.

- Suppose your full current legal name is different than the full name listed on your birth certificate. In that case, you must provide a certified legal name change court order with the form). If you want your full current legal name amended on your birth certificate, indicate by checking the appropriate box. Additional proof documentation might be requested.[719]

Driver's Licenses

Washington Administrative Code, Title 308, Chapter 104, Section 0150 states:

WAC 308-104-0150 Changing sex designation on a driver's license, instruction permit, or identification card.

> (1) Persons may change the sex designation on a driver's license, instruction permit, or identification card by means of completing a sex designation change application signed under penalty of perjury pursuant to chapter 9A.72 RCW.

(2) For the purposes of this section, "X" means a sex that is not exclusively male or female. [Statutory Authority: RCW 46.01.110. WSR 19-21-022, § 308-104-0150, filed 10/7/19, effective 11/12/19][720]

Public Accommodations

The Revised Code of Washington, RCW 49.60.215, states the following:

Unfair practices of places of public resort, accommodation, assemblage, amusement—Trained dog guides and service animals.

It shall be an unfair practice for any person or the person's agent or employee to commit an act which directly or indirectly results in any distinction, restriction, or discrimination, or the requiring of any person to pay a larger sum than the uniform rates charged other persons, or the refusing or withholding from any person the admission, patronage, custom, presence, frequenting, dwelling, staying, or lodging in any place of public resort, accommodation, assemblage, or amusement, except for conditions and limitations established by law and applicable to all persons, regardless of race, creed, color, national origin, citizenship or immigration status, sexual orientation, sex, honorably discharged veteran or military status, status as a mother breastfeeding her child, the presence of any sensory, mental, or physical disability, or the use of a trained dog guide or service animal by a person with a disability: PROVIDED, That this section shall not be construed to require structural changes, modifications, or additions to make any place accessible to a person with a disability except as otherwise required by law: PROVIDED, That behavior or actions constituting a risk to property or other persons can be grounds for refusal and shall not constitute an unfair practice.[721]

Sports

Discrimination in Washington state's public schools is prohibited. RCW 28A.642.010, Discrimination Prohibited, Section 010—Definitions.

Discrimination in Washington public schools on the basis of race, creed, religion, color, national origin, honorably discharged veteran or military status, sexual orientation including gender expression or identity, the presence of any sensory, mental, or physical disability, or the use of a trained dog guide or service animal by a person with a disability is prohibited. The definitions given these terms in chapter 49.60[722] RCW apply throughout this chapter unless the context clearly requires otherwise.[723]

Further, the Revised Code of Washington, RCW 28A.642.080 Transgender Student Policy and Procedure, also states:

(1)(a) By January 31, 2020, each school district must adopt or amend if necessary policies and procedures that, at a minimum, incorporate all the elements of the model transgender student policy and procedure described in subsection (3) of this section.

(b) School districts must share the policies and procedures that meet the requirements of (a) of this subsection with parents or guardians, students, volunteers, and school employees in accordance with rules adopted by the office of the superintendent of public instruction.

(c)(i) Each school district must designate one person in the school district as the primary contact regarding the policies and procedures relating to transgender students that meet the requirements of (a) of this subsection. In addition to any other duties required by law and the school district, the primary contact must:

- (A) Ensure the implementation of the policies and procedures relating to transgender students that meet the requirements of (a) of this subsection;

- (B) Receive copies of all formal and informal complaints relating to transgender students;

- (C) Communicate with the school district employees responsible for monitoring school district compliance with this chapter, and the primary contact regarding the school district's policy and procedure prohibiting harassment, intimidation, and bullying under RCW 28A.600.477[724]; and

- (D) Serve as the primary contact between the school district, the office of the education ombuds, and the office of the superintendent of public instruction on policies and procedures relating to transgender students that meet the requirements of (a) of this subsection.

  - (ii) The primary contact from each school district must attend at least one training class as provided in RCW 28A.600.477, once this training is available.

  - (iii) The primary contact may also serve as the primary contact regarding the school district's policy and procedure prohibiting harassment, intimidation, and bullying under RCW 28A.600.477.

(2) As required by the office of the superintendent of public instruction, each school district must provide to the office of the superintendent of public instruction its policies and procedures relating to transgender students that meet the requirements of subsection (1)(a) of this section.

(3)(a) By September 1, 2019, and periodically thereafter, the Washington state school directors' association must collaborate with the office of the superintendent of public instruction to develop and update a model transgender student policy and procedure.

(b) The elements of the model transgender student policy and procedure must, at a minimum: Incorporate the office of the superintendent of public instruction's rules and guidelines developed under RCW 28A.642.020[725] to eliminate discrimination in Washington public schools on the basis of gender identity and expression; address the unique challenges and needs faced by transgender students in public schools; and describe the application of the model policy and procedure prohibiting harassment, intimidation, and bullying, required under RCW 28A.600.477, to transgender students.

(c) The office of the superintendent of public instruction and the Washington state school directors' association must maintain the model policy and procedure on each agency's web site at no cost to school districts.

(4)(a) By December 31, 2020, the office of the superintendent of public instruction must develop online training material available to all school staff based on the model transgender student policy and procedure described in subsection (3) of this section and the office of the superintendent of public instruction's rules and guidance as provided under this chapter.

(b) The online training material must describe the role of school district primary contacts for monitoring school district compliance with this chapter prohibiting discrimination in public schools, RCW 28A.600.477 related to the policies and procedures prohibiting harassment, intimidation, and bullying, and this section related to policies and procedures relating to transgender students.

(c) The online training material must include best practices for policy and procedure implementation and cultural change that are guided by school district experiences.

(d) The office of the superintendent of public instruction must annually notify school districts of the availability of the online training material.[726]

Finally, the Washington Interscholastic Activities Association (WIAA) Handbook, Appendix 1, states:

> The Washington Interscholastic Activities Association does not and shall not discriminate on the basis of race, color, religion, gender, gender expression, age, natural origin, disability, marital, sexual orientation or military status, in any of its activities or operations.[727]

See also Appendix 6—Gender Identity, which provides a discussion of commonly used language.

Law Enforcement, Jails, and Prisons

For information on this topic, please see the state data on the MAP website.

Health and Health Care Benefits

For information on this topic, please see the state data on the MAP website.

Marriage

For information on this topic, please see the state data on the MAP website. Please also review the section above under federal laws on marriage.

LGBTQ Youth Laws and Policies

For information on this topic, please see the state data on the MAP website.

Religious Exemption Laws

Article 1, Section 11 of the Washington state Constitution says:

> Absolute freedom of conscience in all matters of religious sentiment, belief and worship, shall be guaranteed to every individual, and no one shall be molested or disturbed in person or property on account of religion; but the liberty of conscience hereby secured shall not be so construed as to excuse acts of licentiousness or justify practices inconsistent with the peace and safety of the state. No public money or property shall be appropriated for or applied to any religious worship, exercise or instruction, or the support of any religious establishment: PROVIDED, HOWEVER, That this article shall

not be so construed as to forbid the employment by the state of a chaplain for such of the state custodial, correctional, and mental institutions, or by a county's or public hospital district's hospital, health care facility, or hospice, as in the discretion of the legislature may seem justified. No religious qualification shall be required for any public office or employment, nor shall any person be incompetent as a witness or juror, in consequence of his opinion on matters of religion, nor be questioned in any court of justice touching his religious belief to affect the weight of his testimony.[728]

Washington Overall Tally

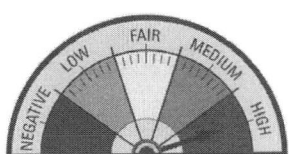

Grand Totals	Sexual Orientation Policy Tally	Gender Identity Policy Tally	Overall Tally
Totals	16.75/20.5	20/22	36.75/42.5
Ratings	HIGH	HIGH	HIGH

West Virginia

West Virginia Non-Discrimination Laws

West Virginia Code, Chapter 5, Article 11, Section 9(2) states:

> For any employer, employment agency or labor organization, prior to the employment or admission to membership, to: (A) Elicit any information or make or keep a record of or use any form of application or application blank containing questions or entries concerning the race, religion, color, national origin, ancestry, sex or age of any applicant for employment or membership; (B) print or publish or cause to be printed or published any notice or advertisement relating to employment or membership indicating any preference, limitation, specifications or discrimination based upon race, religion, color, national origin, ancestry, sex, disability or age; or (C) deny or limit, through a quota system, employment or membership because of race, religion, color, national origin, ancestry, sex, age, blindness or disability.[729]

Birth Certificates

According to Chapter 16, Article 5, Section 25(d) of the West Virginia Code, an individual must obtain a court order to change their name on their birth certificate. Chapter 48, Article 25, Section 101 governs legal name changes in West Virginia.[730]

To change the designation of sex on your birth certificate, you can try calling them, but the author's experience was that the call was never answered. There is no statutory provision specifically addressing how a transgender person may request that their birth record be amended to reflect their stated gender identity. Also, there is no information on the West Virginia Department of Health and Human Resources, Health Statistics Center about any policies or procedures that may be in force to allow a transgender person to amend or correct their information in their birth record.

Driver's Licenses

The West Virginia Department of Motor Vehicles form DMV-99-RO[731] allows a transgender applicant to apply for a driver's license with the designation of sex that reflects their stated gender identity. You will also need to provide documentation from your physician detailing that you have completed your transition.

Public Accommodations

The West Virginia Human Rights Commission says discrimination in public accommodations is prohibited on the basis of a person's race, religion, color, national origin, ancestry, sex, age (40 and above), blindness, or disability.

Sports

Earlier in 2021, the West Virginia Legislature passed HB 3293, which the Governor signed. The law became effective on July 1, 2021, as codified in the West Virginia Code, at Chapter 18, Article 2, Section 25(d), which clarifies "participation for sports events to be based on biological sex of the athlete at birth."[732]

(a) The Legislature hereby finds:

(1) There are inherent differences between biological males and biological females, and that these differences are cause for celebration, as determined by the Supreme Court of the United States in *United States v. Virginia* (1996);

(2) These inherent differences are not a valid justification for sex-based classifications that make overbroad generalizations or perpetuate the legal, social, and economic inferiority of either sex. Rather, these inherent differences are a valid justification for sex-based classifications when they realistically reflect the fact that the sexes are not similarly situated in certain circumstances, as recognized by the Supreme Court of the United States in *Michael M. v. Sonoma County, Superior Court* (1981) and the Supreme Court of Appeals of West Virginia in *Israel v. Secondary Schools Act. Com'n* (1989);

(3) In the context of sports involving competitive skill or contact, biological males and biological females are not in fact similarly situated. Biological males would displace females to a substantial extent if permitted to compete on teams designated for biological females, as recognized in *Clark v. Ariz. Interscholastic Ass'n* (9th Cir. 1982);

(4) Although necessarily related, as concluded by the United States Supreme Court in *Bostock v. Clayton County* (2020), gender identity is separate and distinct from biological sex to the extent that an individual's biological sex is not determinative or indicative of the individual's gender identity. Classifications based on gender identity serve no legitimate relationship to the State of West Virginia's interest in promoting equal athletic opportunities for the female sex; and

(5) Classification of teams according to biological sex is necessary to promote equal athletic opportunities for the female sex.

(b) Definitions. As used in this section, the following words have the meanings ascribed to them unless the context clearly implies a different meaning:

(1) "Biological sex" means an individual's physical form as a male or female based solely on the individual's reproductive biology and genetics at birth.

(2) "Female" means an individual whose biological sex determined at birth is female. As used in this section, "women" or "girls" refers to biological females.

(3) "Male" means an individual whose biological sex determined at birth is male. As used in this section, "men" or "boys" refers to biological males.

(c) Designation of Athletic Teams.

(1) Interscholastic, intercollegiate, intramural, or club athletic teams or sports that are sponsored by any public secondary school or a state institution of higher education, including a state institution that is a member of the National Collegiate Athletic Association (NCAA), National Association of Intercollegiate Athletics (NAIA), or National Junior College Athletic Association (NJCAA), shall be expressly designated as one of the following based on biological sex:

(A) Males, men, or boys;

(B) Females, women, or girls; or

(C) Coed or mixed.

(2) Athletic teams or sports designated for females, women, or girls shall not be open to students of the male sex where selection for such teams is based upon competitive skill or the activity involved is a contact sport.

(3) Nothing in this section shall be construed to restrict the eligibility of any student to participate in any interscholastic, intercollegiate, or intramural athletic teams or sports designated as "males," "men," or "boys" or designated as "coed" or "mixed": *Provided*, that selection for a team may still be based on those who try out and possess the requisite skill to make the team.

(d) Cause of Action.

(1) Any student aggrieved by a violation of this section may bring an action against a county board of education or state institution of higher education alleged to be responsible for the alleged violation. The aggrieved student may seek injunctive relief and actual damages, as well as reasonable attorney's fee and court costs, if the student substantially prevails.

(2) In any private action brought pursuant to this section, the identity of a minor student shall remain private and anonymous.

(e) The State Board of Education shall promulgate rules, including emergency rules, pursuant to §29A-3B-1 et. seq. of this code to implement the provisions of this section. The Higher Education Policy Commission and the Council for Community and Technical College Education shall promulgate emergency rules and propose rules for legislative approval pursuant to §29A-3A-1 et. seq. of this code to implement the provisions of this section.

On May 26, 2021, B.P.J., an 11-year-old transgender girl, filed suit against the West Virginia Board of Education, challenging the above statute by and through her mother. On July 21, 2021, the Judge in the U.S. District Court for the Southeastern District, Charleston Division, in West Virginia, issued a preliminary injunction halting enforcement of the statute until the case can be heard at trial.

Law Enforcement, Jails, and Prisons

For information on this topic, please see the state data on the MAP website.

Health and Health Care Benefits

For information on this topic, please see the state data on the MAP website.

Marriage

For information on this topic, please see the state data on the MAP website. Please also review the section above under federal laws on marriage.

LGBTQ Youth Laws and Policies

For information on this topic, please see the state data on the MAP website.

Religious Exemption Laws

For information on this topic, please see the state data on the MAP website.

West Virginia Overall Tally

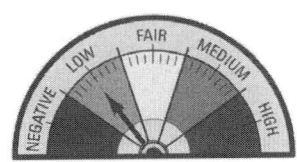

Grand Totals	Sexual Orientation Policy Tally	Gender Identity Policy Tally	Overall Tally
Totals	5.5/20.5	-1.5/22	4/42.5
Ratings	FAIR	NEGATIVE	LOW

Wisconsin

Wisconsin Non-Discrimination Laws

The Wisconsin Fair Employment Law prohibits employers, employment agencies, labor unions, and licensing agencies from discriminating against employees and job applicants because of any of the following:

- Age
- Arrest and/or Conviction Record
- Ancestry, Color, National Origin or Race
- Creed
- Disability
- Genetic Testing
- Honesty Testing
- Marital Status
- Military Service
- Pregnancy or Childbirth
- Sex
- Sexual Orientation
- Use or nonuse of lawful products off the employer's premises during nonworking hours.[733]

Birth Certificates

For information on obtaining a legal name change, contact the court clerk in the county where you currently live.[734]

Once a legal name change court order has been issued, submit a certified copy of the court order to our office, along with a Birth Certificate Application form[735] if you are requesting copies of the birth certificate. "Certified" means the document contains an original court seal. The certified court order will be returned to you once the name change has been processed. There is a fee for filing a legal name change court order, which does not include a certified copy of the amended birth certificate. Applications should be mailed to the

> Wisconsin Vital Records
> ATTN: Legal Name Changes
> P.O. Box 309
> Madison, WI 53701[736]

To amend the sex on a birth certificate following a sex change, our office requires the following:

- A certified copy of a court order from a court in the United States or Canada that orders the sex designation on the birth certificate to be changed.
- A fee to file the court order does not include a certified copy of the new certificate.

Driver's Licenses

For existing Wisconsin customers who want to change the sex on their driver record must apply for a driver license or ID card with one of the following documents:

- An affidavit or statement from a medical doctor or director of a facility specializing in sex change

OR
- Court order

Customers who also change their names will need to provide acceptable proof of name change, such as a court-ordered name change or valid passport and will also need to have their name changed with the Social Security Administration at least 24-48 hours before applying for a product with the Wisconsin DMV.

First-time Wisconsin customers applying for a driver's license or ID card do not need to provide additional documentation for sex change if their driver's license or ID card from the other state/jurisdiction lists sex not listed on their proof of name and date of birth document.

Public Accommodations

Chapter 106, Subchapter 3, Section 106.52(3)(a)(1), Public Place of Accommodation or Amusement, of the Wisconsin statutes states, in part:

> No person may do any of the following:
>
> 1. Deny to another or charge another a higher price than the regular rate for the full and equal enjoyment of any public place of accommodation or amusement because of sex, race, color, creed, disability, sexual orientation, national origin or ancestry.[737]

Sports

The Wisconsin Interscholastic Athletic Association has a policy that allows transgender students to participate in school sports programs. The organization claims that its policy was derived from other interscholastic athletic associations or leagues.[738]

On June 16, 2021, the Wisconsin State Assembly passed a Bill to ban transgender athletes from participating in school sports programs. The Senate, which the Republicans control, will take up the measure next. Governor Tony Evers has said that he intends to veto the Bill if it gets to his desk.

Law Enforcement, Jails, and Prisons

For information on this topic, please see the state data on the MAP website.

Health and Health Care Benefits

For information on this topic, please see the state data on the MAP website.

Marriage

For information on this topic, please see the state data on the MAP website. Please also review the section above under federal laws on marriage.

LGBTQ Youth Laws and Policies

For information on this topic, please see the state data on the MAP website.

Religious Exemption Laws

The Wisconsin State Constitution states, in Article 1, Section 18:

> The right of every person to worship Almighty God according to the dictates of conscience shall never be infringed; nor shall any person be compelled to attend, erect or support any place of worship, or to maintain any ministry, without consent; nor shall

any control of, or interference with, the rights of conscience be permitted, or any preference be given by law to any religious establishments or modes of worship; nor shall any money be drawn from the treasury for the benefit of religious societies, or religious or theological seminaries.[739]

This statute generally follows the text of many of the other Religious Freedom Bills that have been introduced in legislatures all across the country since the U.S. Supreme Court's decision in *City of Boerne v. Flores, Archbishop of San Antonio, et al.* 521 U.S. 507 (1997), where the High Court ruled the Religious Freedom Restoration Act of 1993, 107 Stat. 1488, 42 U. S. C. § 2000bb et seq., known as the "RFRA," to be an unconstitutional overreach by Congress, exceeding its authority. Republican members of State legislatures almost immediately began introducing Bills to, as they said, protect the First Amendment right to freedom of religion and freedom to exercise "deeply-held" religious beliefs. The language that was found unconstitutional in *Boerne* has become a model for legislation in many States.

Wisconsin Overall Tally

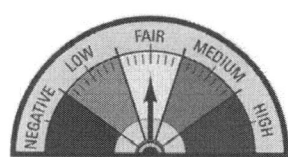

Grand Totals	Sexual Orientation Policy Tally	Gender Identity Policy Tally	Overall Tally
Totals	12.75/20.5	5.25/22	18/42.5
Ratings	MEDIUM	LOW	FAIR

Wyoming

Wyoming Non-Discrimination Laws

Wyoming has no explicit non-discrimination laws or policies that prohibit discrimination based on or because of sex, sexual orientation, or gender identity.

However, in Title 27, Chapter 9, Section 105, the state does prohibit discrimination in employment as follows:

> (a) It is a discriminatory or unfair employment practice:
>
>> (i) For an employer to refuse to hire, to discharge, to promote or demote, or to discriminate in matters of compensation or the terms, conditions, or privileges of employment against, a qualified disabled person or any person otherwise qualified, because of age, sex, race, creed, color, national origin, ancestry, or pregnancy.[740]

Birth Certificates

The Wyoming Department of Health, Vital Statistics Services will change your name on your birth certificate as follows:

1. Obtain a certified copy of the court order that stipulates the name change from the court that issued the change.
2. Complete the Application for Correction Form.[741]
3. Send the certified copy of the court order, the application, a photocopy of your current ID (such as a driver's license) and a $55 fee to our office. The fee can be made via a personalized check (third party checks are not accepted) or money order made payable to Vital Statistics Services. The fee also includes one certified copy of the record. We must keep the certified copy of the order, so be sure to make a copy for yourself.
4. Send to:
   Vital Statistics Services—Attn: Birth Corrections
   2300 Capitol Avenue
   Hathaway Building
   Cheyenne, WY 82002
5. Vital Statistics Services will review the documentation submitted to ensure accuracy. If there are no discrepancies, we will move forward with the processing of the name change. If we do find errors, you will be contacted to address these errors prior to filing.
6. Once the court order has been processed, we will not be able to make any additional changes to the certificate without another court order. It is very important the court order submitted is correct.
7. If the event did not occur in Wyoming, we will not be able to process your request.[742]

Wyoming Administrative Rules, Department of Health, Vital Records Services, Chapter 10, Section 4e) Sex as Stated on Birth Certificate, (iii), requires that:

> When the sex of an individual has been changed, a court order shall be required to amend the birth certificate.[743]

Driver's Licenses

The Wyoming Department of Transportation Driver Services has a form you can use to obtain a new driver's license with the designation of sex changed to match your stated gender identity. Your primary care physician or the physician treating you for gender-related issues must fill out the bottom half of the form. You then take the form with your identification to the nearest driver's license office to get the change accomplished.

Public Accommodations

Wyoming prohibits discrimination in public accommodations according to Wyoming Statutes, Title 6, Chapter 9, Section 101 as follows:

> (a) All persons of good deportment are entitled to the full and equal enjoyment of all accommodations, advantages, facilities and privileges of all places or agencies which are public in nature, or which invite the patronage of the public, without any distinction, discrimination or restriction on account of race, religion, color, sex or national origin.
>
> (b) A person who intentionally violates this section commits a misdemeanor punishable by imprisonment for not more than six (6) months, a fine of not more than seven hundred fifty dollars ($750.00), or both.[744]

Wyoming prohibits discrimination in housing under Wyoming Statutes, Title 40, Chapter 26, Section 103 as follows:

> (a) A person may not refuse to sell or rent, after the making of a bona fide offer, refuse to negotiate for the sale or rental of, or in any other manner make unavailable or deny a dwelling to an individual because of race, color, religion, sex, disability, familial status, or national origin.
>
> (b) A person may not discriminate against an individual in the terms, conditions, or privileges of sale or rental of a dwelling or in providing services or facilities in connection with a sale or rental of a dwelling because of race, color, religion, sex, disability, familial status or national origin.
>
> (c) This section does not prohibit discrimination against an individual because the individual has been convicted under federal law or the law of any state of the illegal manufacture or distribution of a controlled substance.[745]

Sports

The Wyoming High School Activities Association Handbook, 6.0.0 Participant Eligibility Rules and Regulations, Section 6.8.0 Gender Identity Participation has the following policy on participation in interscholastic sports programs by transgender athletes:

> Please refer to Appendix B for Philosophy and Definitions for Gender Identity.
>
> After consideration of the WHSAA Philosophy set forth in Appendix B, all students should be considered for the opportunity to participate in Wyoming High School Activities Association activities in a manner that is consistent with their gender identity, irrespective of the gender listed on a student's records. Should any bona fide questions arise whether a student's school gender records to participate in a sex-segregated activity is consistent with his or her gender identity, a student may seek review of his or

her eligibility for participation through the procedure set forth below. Once the student has been granted eligibility to participate in the activity consistent with his/her gender identity, the eligibility is granted for the duration of the student's participation and does not need to be renewed every activity season or school year.

Privacy: All discussion and documentation will be kept confidential, and the proceedings will be sealed unless the student and family make a specific request.[746]

It should be noted that some legislators in Wyoming are attempting to pass legislation that would ban transgender athletes from participating in school sports programs.

Law Enforcement, Jails, and Prisons

For information on this topic, please see the state data on the MAP website.

Health and Health Care Benefits

For information on this topic, please see the state data on the MAP website.

Marriage

For information on this topic, please see the state data on the MAP website. Please also review the section above under federal laws on marriage.

LGBTQ Youth Laws and Policies

For information on this topic, please see the state data on the MAP website.

Religious Exemption Laws

In 2015, the Wyoming Legislature passed HB83, a Bill that very broadly expands upon the state's religious exemption law. The author was unable to find out if this Bill ever became law.

Wyoming Overall Tally

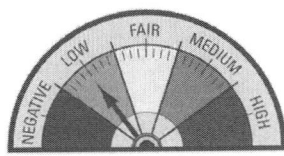

Grand Totals	Sexual Orientation Policy Tally	Gender Identity Policy Tally	Overall Tally
Totals	2.5/20.5	-0.75/22	1.75/42.5
Ratings	LOW	NEGATIVE	LOW

United States Territories and Possessions

As of the date of publication, the author has not heard from any of the U.S. Territories regarding any of the subjects covered in the sections of the book dedicated to the individual States. The author contacted the United States Department of State, Bureau of Consular Affairs to obtain the information, and even though their website said it could take three to five days for them to respond to the request, after day five the author still had not received a response. The tables below come from the MAP website

American Samoa

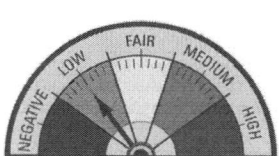

Grand Totals	Sexual Orientation Policy Tally	Gender Identity Policy Tally	Overall Tally
Totals	1.5/20.5	-1/22	0.5/42.5
Ratings	LOW	NEGATIVE	LOW

Commonwealth of the Northern Mariana Islands

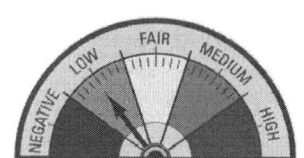

Grand Totals	Sexual Orientation Policy Tally	Gender Identity Policy Tally	Overall Tally
Totals	4.5/20.5	-1/22	3.5/42.5
Ratings	LOW	NEGATIVE	LOW

Guam

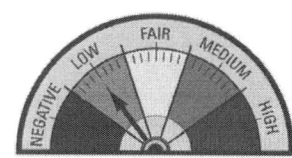

Grand Totals	Sexual Orientation Policy Tally	Gender Identity Policy Tally	Overall Tally
Totals	7.5/20.5	-0.75/22	6.75/42.5
Ratings	FAIR	NEGATIVE	LOW

Puerto Rico

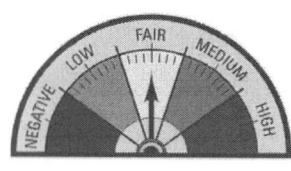

Grand Totals	Sexual Orientation Policy Tally	Gender Identity Policy Tally	Overall Tally
Totals	10/20.5	10/22	20/42.5
Ratings	FAIR	FAIR	FAIR

The U.S. District Court for the District of Puerto Rico, in *Gonzalez, et. al. v. Nevares, et al.*, Case No. 3:17-cv-01457/CCC, decided on April 20, 2018, that the Commonwealth of Puerto Rico violated the Autonomy Branch of the Fourteenth Amendment by forcing transgender people to disclose their gender identity even though they had lawfully changed their names through the courts. The Court found that:

Puerto Rico categorically requires that birth certificates reflect the sex assigned at birth and prohibits transgender persons from correcting the gender marker in their birth certificates so that these accurately reflect the persons' sex, as determined by their gender identity.[747]

The Court further held that:

> The Demographic Registry of the Commonwealth of Puerto Rico SHALL ADOPT the criteria of the Department of Transportation and Public Work's "Request to Change Transgender Persons' Gender Marker," DTOP-DIS-324 Form, as the application form to be submitted by transgenders and which shall be accepted as the first step towards the issuance of their new birth certificates, in compliance with the Court's mandate.[748]

United States Virgin Islands

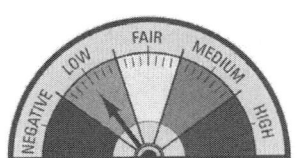

Grand Totals	Sexual Orientation Policy Tally	Gender Identity Policy Tally	Overall Tally
Totals	4.5/20.5	0/22	4.5/42.5
Ratings	LOW	LOW	LOW

SUMMARY

This final table provides MAP narrative categories (high, medium, fair, low, and negative) for Sexual Orientation, Gender Identity, and Overall Tally for each individual state. The Final Score and Percent columns provide numerical scores (out of a total 42.5 points) and proportions (out of 100%) ranked from highest to lowest. These data provide a clear overview of the policy climate across the U.S. and its territories and possessions generally and within each individual state. Lower scores indicate a preponderance of harmful or discriminatory policies, while higher scores indicate a higher proportion of LGBTQ-inclusive or protective laws.

Summary of State Scores for Sexual Orientation, Gender Identity and Overall Tally
Source: Movement Advancement Project (MAP

State	Sexual Orientatio	Gender Identity	Overall Tally	Final Score	Percent
Colorado	High	High	High	39.5/42.5	92.94%
California	High	High	High	39.25/42.5	92.35%
New York	High	High	High	39/42.5	91.76%
Nevada	High	High	High	38/42.5	89.41%
Connecticut	High	High	High	37.5/42.5	88.24%
Maine	High	High	High	37/42.5	87.06%
Washington	High	High	High	36.75/42.5	86.47%
Oregon	High	High	High	36.5/42.5	85.88%
Vermont	High	High	High	36/42.5	84.71%
New Jersey	High	High	High	36/42.5	84.71%
District of Columbia	High	High	High	35.5/42.5	83.53%
Illinois	High	High	High	35/42.5	82.35%
Minesota	Medium	High	High	33.5/42.5	78.82%
Massachusetts	High	High	High	33.5/42.5	78.82%
Rhode Island	High	Medium	High	32.5/42.5	76.47%
Hawai'i	Medium	Medium	Medium	30/42.5	70.59%
Maryland	Medium	High	Medium	29.75/42.5	70.00%
New Mexico	Medium	Medium	Medium	28/42.5	65.88%
New Hampshire	Medium	Medium	Medium	27.5/42.5	64.71%
Delaware	Medium	Medium	Medium	25.25/42.5	59.41%
Virginia	Medium	Medium	Medium	24/42.5	56.47%

Puerto Rico	Fair	Fair	Fair	20/42.5	47.06%
Michigan	Fair	Medium	Fair	19/42.5	44.71%
Wisconsin	Medium	Low	Fair	18/42.5	42.35%
Kansas	Medium	Fair	Fair	18/42.5	42.35%
Iowa	Medium	Fair	Fair	18/42.5	42.35%
Alaska	Fair	Fair	Fair	17.75/42.5	41.76%
Pennsylvania	Fair	Fair	Fair	15.5/42.5	36.47%
Utah	Fair	Fair	Fair	15.25/42.5	35.88%
North Dakota	Fair	Low	Fair	11.75/42.5	27.65%
Kentucky	Fair	Low	Low	10.25/42.5	24.12%
Florida	Fair	Low	Low	9.75/42.5	22.94%
Ohio	Fair	Low	Low	7.75/42.5	18.24%
Guam	Fair	Negative	Low	6.75/42.5	15.88%
Indiana	Fair	Low	Low	6.5/42.5	15.29%
Arizona	Fair	Negative	Low	6.25/42.5	14.71%
North Carolina	Low	Low	Low	5.75/42.5	13.53%
Virgin Islands	Low	Low	Low	4.5/42.5	10.59%
West Virginia	Fair	Negative	Low	4/42.5	9.41%
Nebraska	Fair	Negative	Low	4/42.5	9.41%
Montana	Low	Negative	Low	4/42.5	9.41%
Idaho	Low	Negative	Low	3.75/42.5	8.82%
Mariana Islands	Low	Negative	Low	3.5/42.5	8.24%
Wyoming	Low	Negative	Low	1.75/42.5	4.12%
Missouri	Low	Negative	Low	.75/42.5	1.76%
Texas	Low	Negative	Low	.5/42.5	1.18%
American Samoa	Low	Negative	Low	.5/42.5	1.18%
South Carolina	Low	Negative	Negative	-0.5/42.5	-1.18%
Georgia	Low	Negative	Negative	-.5/42.5	-1.18%
Oklahoma	Low	Negative	Negative	-2/42.5	-4.71%
Louisiana	Low	Negative	Negative	-2.5/42.5	-5.88%
Mississsppi	Negative	Negative	Negative	-3.5/42.5	-8.24%
Alabama	Negative	Negative	Negative	-4/42.5	-9.41%
South Dakota	Negative	Negative	Negative	-4.5/42.5	-10.59%
Arkasas	Low	Negative	Negative	-5.5/42.5	-12.94%
Tennessee	Negative	Negative	Negative	-6/42.5	-14.12%

ACKNOWLEGEMENTS

The author thanks two very good friends and close colleagues, Joanna M. Clark and Jude Patton, PA-C, for their guidance and scrutiny of this work. The immensity of their contribution cannot be underestimated or overstated. I also want to thank my partner, Yaly Rivero, for the support she was able to provide during the time I was working on the manuscript. Yaly designed the cover image for the book by colorizing Lady Justice. Additionally, I want to thank my publisher for her input and guidance. Her expertise in publishing was invaluable to me.

I recognize the singular and collective contributions the LGBTQ community has made, not directly in the publication of this work, but on a much larger scale in the long fight we have been engaged in to secure our rights guaranteed by the United States Constitution to Equality Under the Law. The list of names is too long to include here, but a few whose struggle was so extraordinary must be given recognition. Not necessarily in any order of significance, they are Anna Mosten, Christine Jorgensen, Karen Ulane, Joanna Clark, Renee Richards, Jude Patton, Carol Katz, Vicky Hernández, Andrea González, Cecy Caricia Ixpata, Kael McKenzie, Reed Erickson, Joy Shaffer, Theresa Sparks, Stu Rasmussen, Candice Brown, Chaz Bono, Paula Grossman, Alan Turing, Lynn Conway, Dr. Marci Bowers, Brandon Teena, Phyllis Frye, Rita Hester, Gwen Araujo, Angie Zapata, Aleshia Brevard, Wendy Carlos, Amanda Simpson, Jennifer Finney Boylan, Gavin Grimm, Dylan Brandt, Darcy Corbitt, Lindsey Hecox, Aiden Stockman, Marylin Rae Baskin, Jamison Green, Aaron Devor, Dallas Denney, and Susan Stryker.

ABOUT THE AUTHOR

Diane Saunders has been involved in trans rights advocacy for nearly 40 years, first when she lived in Central Coastal California, then in Los Angeles, California, while working as a legal assistant with the ACLU Foundation of Southern California. Diane has associate degrees in Respiratory Care and Emergency Management and Homeland Security and is an Emergency Manager Certified in Minnesota. Diane worked as a Respiratory Therapist in Minnesota and Wisconsin for over 21 years in the private sector and with the Federal Government.

Diane first became involved with advocating for transsexual rights when she was transitioning in the 1980s, prosecuting her case against the California Department of Rehabilitation to obtain services that helped her gain employment. It was during this time that Diane and Joanna Clark became friends. In 1980, Diane was a Founding Member of the ACLU Transsexual Rights Committee along with Joanna Clark, Jude Patton, Carol Katz, Candice Brown, and Joy Schaffer.

After Diane obtained surgery in the 1990s, she focused mainly on her career in healthcare and did little to no advocacy work. However, she kept up to date on what was happening in the medical community, constantly reviewing research journals to locate scholarly articles on transsexualism (her designation of choice). Diane also maintains a deep interest in many areas of terrorism, such as bioterrorism, chemical terrorism, and other areas. Diane was also a volunteer Emergency Medical Technician from the 1980s to 2000, and, while she was in school for emergency management, she wrote two papers on terrorism and emergency management.

Diane began work for this book in 2018, performing an additional review of the research in the disciplines mentioned in the book. Most of the writing for the book began during the SARS-CoV-2 virus outbreak, which became a worldwide pandemic in February 2020, while Diane was self-quarantined at home, starting in March 2020 through May 2021, then to September 2021, after she became fully vaccinated.

Diane is an avid amateur radio operator and can often be heard on local VHF, UHF, and sometimes on HF frequencies. She volunteers for several county-level amateur radio emergency communications organizations.

DEFINITIONS

The reader is cautioned that the language used by and within the trans community is fluid and since this book was first published, and throughout its several versions, the terminology has changed significantly. The definitions offered in this section are those developed by the author and explain how she has used them throughout this volume. They may (or may not) conform to the ways in which other members of the trans community understand and/or use these terms. A number of websites listed in the terminology section (see "Early Research" above) provide alternative descriptions. Sources for entries below include: WPATH Standards of Care, Merriam-Webster Dictionary online, MedlinePlus, WebMD.

Ally
Noun: someone who supports equal civil rights, gender equality, and LGBTQ+ social movements; advocates on behalf of others; and challenges fear and discrimination in all its forms.

Cisgender
Adjective: anyone who seeks relationships with others of the opposite sex; denoting or relating to a person whose sense of personal identity and gender corresponds with their birth sex.

Asexual, or ace
Adjective: someone who experiences little or no sexual attraction, or who experiences attraction but doesn't feel the need to act out that attraction sexually. Many people who are asexual still identify with a specific sexual orientation.

Binary/Non-Binary
Noun: the belief is that such things as gender identity have only two distinct, opposite, and disconnected forms.; in other words, they believe in the gender binary, that only male and female genders exist; in rejection of this belief, many people embrace a non-binary gender identity (see "Gender Nonconforming").

Bisexual, or bi
Adjective: someone who is attracted to those of the same gender and those of different gender (for example, a woman who is attracted to both women and men); some people use the word "bisexual" as an umbrella term to describe individuals attracted to more than one gender; in this way, the term is closely related to pansexual, or omnisexual, meaning someone attracted to people of any gender identity.

Butch, or masc (short for masculine)
Adjective: someone whose gender expression is masculine; "butch" is sometimes a derogatory term for lesbians, but it can also be claimed as an affirmative identity label; in many communities of color in the United States, words like "stud" and "aggressive" are used instead.

Other gender expressions include androgynous (or androgyne, someone who presents as neither male nor female, mixed, or neutral) and stemme (derived from the words "stud" and "femme" used in the lesbian community to describe a woman who is boyish but in a very feminine way), or stem (someone whose gender expression is both masculine and feminine) (see also "Femme, or fem").

Coming Out
Verb, noun: the process through which a person accepts their sexual orientation or gender identity as part of their overall identity; for many, this involves sharing that identity with others, which makes it more of a lifetime process rather than just a one-time experience.

Crossdresser

Noun: someone who wears clothes associated with a different gender; a form of gender expression not always undertaken for entertainment purposes; many crossdressers may not wish to present as a different gender all of the time. NOTE: Avoid using the term "transvestite."

Drag

Noun, adjective: the act of performing a gender or presenting as a different gender, usually for entertainment (i.e., drag kings and queens); many people who do drag may not wish to present as a different gender all of the time.

Femme, or fem

Adjective: someone whose gender expression is feminine.

Other gender expressions include androgynous (or androgyne, presenting as neither male nor female, mixed, or neutral) and stemme (or stem), gender expressions that are masculine and feminine (see also "Butch, or masc" above).

Gay

Adjective: someone who is attracted to those of the same gender; often used as an umbrella term but more specifically to describe men attracted to men. (NOTE: Avoid using the term "homosexual"; the clinical history of the word causes many feel that the term suggests that gay people are somehow diseased or psychologically/emotionally disordered.)

Gender Affirmation Surgery

Noun: some individuals elect to undergo medical procedures to change their physical appearance to more closely resemble how they view their gender identity. [Note: This term is not uniformly used to describe surgery.]; also "sex reassignment surgery" [see below].

Gender Dysphoria

Noun: discomfort or distress caused by a discrepancy between a person's gender identity and sex assigned at birth (including associated gender roles and/or primary and secondary sex characteristics); only some gender-nonconforming people experience gender dysphoria at some point in their lives; gender dysphoria and gender-non-conforming are not the same.

See the WPATH discussion on page 5 of the Standards of Care related to Diagnoses Related to Gender Dysphoria.

Gender Role/Expression

Noun: physical and behavioral manifestations of one's gender identity; also, characteristics of personality, appearance, and behavior in a given cultural and historical period designated as masculine or feminine.

Gender Identity

Noun: a person's internal sense of being male, female, some combination of male and female, or neither.

Gender Nonconforming

Adjective: someone whose gender identity or gender expression does not conform to the cultural or social expectations of a specific gender; an umbrella term for many identities including, but not limited to:

Agender, (also neutrois, gender-neutral, or genderless), someone who has little or no personal connection with gender;

Bigender, someone who identifies with both male and female genders, or as a third gender;

Genderfluid, someone whose gender identity or expression varies over time;

Genderqueer (or third gender), someone whose gender identity or expression falls between or outside of male and female;
Intergender, someone whose identity is between genders or a combination of gender identities and expressions.
Pangender, someone whose identity is comprised of all or many gender identities and expressions.

Hermaphrodite
Noun: someone who possesses both male and female reproductive organs, tissue, or structures; in ovotesticular disorder, XX is the most common (55-80% of cases); most individuals with this form are SRY negative; next most common is XX/XY (20-30% of cases) and XY (5-15% of cases); the remainder are a variety of other chromosomal anomalies and mosaicisms; some degree of mosaicism is present in about 25%; encountered karyotypes include 46XX/46XY, or 46XX/47XXY or XX and XY with SRY mutations, mixed chromosomal anomalies or hormone deficiency/excess disorders, 47XXY; less than 1% have XX/XY chimerism.

Hormone Therapy
Noun: (also endocrine therapy) begins with prepubertal hormone suppression after girls and boys first exhibit the physical changes of puberty; in adults, hormone therapy typically begins with evaluating the adult person's medical health, then sex steroids are administered and maintained in the normal range for the affirmed gender; the purpose of hormone therapy is to either feminize or masculinize the external physical characteristics, which for male-to-female trans people often results in the growth of breast tissue, a marked reduction in the production of testosterone, atrophy of the testes and prostate, and loss of some muscle tissue; in the female-to-male trans people, hormone therapy often results in increased body hair growth, some lowering of the voice, increased muscle mass, and atrophy of the ovaries.

Intersex
Adjective: someone who, due to a variety of factors, has reproductive or sexual anatomy that does not seem to fit the typical definitions for the female or male sex; some may identify with the gender assigned to them at birth, while many others do not.

Lesbian
Adjective, noun.: a woman who is attracted to other women; some lesbians prefer to identify as "gay women."

LGBT+/LGBTQ+
Adjective: acronym for "lesbian, gay, bisexual, and transgender" (sometimes seen as "GLBT"); the plus sign represents the many communities that expand the acronym to include other identities; for example, while it is common in the United States to see "LGBT" or "LGBTQ" (Q for queer), it is more common to see "LGBTI" (I for intersex) in Europe.

Marginalization
Noun: to relegate to an unimportant or powerless position within a society or group; the process of marginalizing a person or group, or community; marginalization is central to discrimination. Marginalization can be either explicit or implicit.

Queer
Adjective: in a fundamental sense, anyone who is not heterosexual or cisgender; considered, in the past, to be a negative or pejorative term for people who are gay and, thus sometimes disliked; increasingly being used to describe all identities and politics that go against normative beliefs; as such, valued by many LGBTQ+ people for its defiance and by others who find it to be an appropriate term to describe a more fluid identity.

Questioning

Noun, verb: a time of questioning or experimenting with gender expression, gender identity, or sexual orientation; unique to everyone; for some lasting a lifetime or repeated many times throughout a lifetime.

Sex
Noun: either of the two primary forms that occur in many species and that are distinguished respectively as female or male, mainly based on reproductive organs and structures; the words "sex" and "gender" have a long and intertwined history.

In the 15th century, "gender" expanded from its use as a term for a grammatical subclass to join "sex" in referring to either of the two primary biological forms of a species, a meaning "sex" has had since the 14th century; phrases like "the male sex" and "the female gender" are both grounded in uses established for more than five centuries. In the 20th century, the terms "sex" and "gender" acquired new uses. "Sex" developed its "sexual intercourse" meaning in the early part of the century (now, its more familiar meaning), and, a few decades later, "gender" gained meaning to refer to the behavioral, cultural, or psychological traits typically associated with one sex, as in "gender roles." Later in the century, "gender" also came to have application in two closely related compound terms: "gender identity" refers to a person's internal sense of being male, female, some combination of male and female, or neither male nor female; "gender expression" refers to the physical and behavioral manifestations of one's gender identity. By the end of the century, "gender" by itself was being used as a synonym of *gender identity.*

Among those who study gender and sexuality, a clear delineation between "sex" and "gender" is typically prescribed, with "sex" as the preferred term for biological forms and "gender" limited to meanings involving behavioral, cultural, and psychological traits. The terms "male" and "female" relate only to biological forms (i.e., "sex"), while "masculine/masculinity," "feminine/femininity," "woman/girl," and "man/boy" relate only to psychological and sociocultural traits (i.e., "gender"). This delineation also tends to be observed in technical and medical contexts. The term "sex" refers to biological forms in such phrases as sex hormones, sex organs, and biological sex. But in nonmedical and nontechnical contexts, there is no clear delineation, and the status of the words remains complicated. When comparisons explicitly between male and female people are made, we see the term "gender" employed. That term dominates in such collocations as gender differences, gender gap, gender equality, gender bias, and gender relations. Gender is likely applied in such contexts because of its psychological and sociocultural meanings, the word's duality making it dually useful. The fact remains that it is often applied in such cases against the prescribed use.

Usage of "sex" and "gender" is by no means settled. For example, while discrimination was far more often paired with sex from the 1960s through the 20th century and into the 21st, gender discrimination has steadily increased since the 1980s. It is on track to become the dominant collocation. Both terms are currently employed with their intended synonymy made explicit: sex/gender discrimination and gender (sex) discrimination.

Sexual Orientation
Noun: a person's sexual identity or self-identification as bisexual, straight, gay, pansexual, etc.; the state of being bisexual, straight, gay, pansexual, etc.

Sex Reassignment Surgery (SRS)
Noun: refers to the surgical procedures used to alter the external or internal genitalia and surrounding structures in males and females more closely match the individual's gender identity; in male-to-female trans individuals, this sometimes also refers to "top" surgery or breast implantation or breast enhancement surgery; in female-to-male trans individuals, this aspect refers to breast removal surgery.

Straight or heterosexual
Adjective: women who are attracted to men and men who are attracted to women; not exclusive to those who are cisgender; for example, some transgender men identify as straight because they are attracted to women.

Stereotyping
Noun: a fixed general image or set of characteristics that people generally believe to represent a particular type of person or thing; if someone is stereotyped in a particular way, people form a fixed generalized idea or image of the person, so that it is assumed that they will behave in a particular way; sex or gender stereotyping is a generalized view or a preconceived view of the attitudes, behaviors, characteristics, or societal roles that are, or should be, possessed or performed by men or women; stereotypes become the basis of discrimination based on the sex (male or female) or the gender of a person, which may (or may not)coincide with the person's perception of self. Stereotyping can be either explicit or implicit.

Stigmatization
Stigmatization is the action of describing or regarding someone or something as worthy of disgrace or great disapproval or the act of unfairly by publicly opprobrious terms. Stigmatization of the LGBTQ community is particularly pernicious in the harm it causes members of this segment of society. Also, the denoting, labeling or ruining of an identity, which leads to ostracism, marginalization, discrimination, and abuse. Stigma is a process of labeling, stereotyping, and denying human variations as a form of social control.

They/Them/Their/Her/She/Him/His
Pronouns: one of many sets of gender-neutral singular pronouns in English that can be used as an alternative to he/him/his or she/her/hers; becoming more and more prevalent, particularly within the LGBTQ+ community.

Transgender, or trans
Adjective: someone whose gender identity differs from the sex that was assigned to them at birth. Many trans people identify as either male or female, while others see transgender as an umbrella term and identify that includes gender non-conforming or queer; gender is individualistic, as is transition; by and large, do not seek sex reassignment surgery.

Transition
Noun: process by which some transgender people change their gender expression to resemble more closely their gender identity; can include personal, medical, and legal steps, such as using a different name and pronouns, dressing differently, changing one's name or sex on legal documents; hormone therapy, or gender affirmation surgery; some may not choose to make these changes or may only make a few of them; an individual one, there is no right or wrong way to transition.

Transsexual
Noun: someone, either male or female, diagnosed by a professional in one of several medical or social science disciplines with gender dysphoria syndrome or gender identity disorder; someone for whom surgery to bring their genitals into conformity with their perception of gender is the most appropriate treatment.

Transvestite
Noun: someone who wears clothes designed for the opposite sex; a cross-dresser.

Turner Syndrome
Noun: a chromosomal disorder that affects development in females; results when a female's cells have one normal X chromosome and the other sex chromosome is either missing or structurally altered (females without Turner syndrome have two normal X chromosomes in each cell, males have one X and one Y chromosome); signs and symptoms may include short stature, premature ovarian failure, a "webbed" neck, a low hairline at the back of the neck, and swelling (lymphedema) of the hands and feet; some with Turner syndrome have skeletal abnormalities, kidney problems, and/or a congenital heart defect; most have average intelligence; some have developmental delays, learning disabilities, or behavior problems; typically not inherited, but it can be in rare cases; treatment may include growth hormone therapy for short stature and estrogen therapy to help stimulate

sexual development; although often infertile, assisted reproductive techniques may help some women become pregnant.

REFERENCES

Periodicals

Almazan, A.N., B.A., and Keuroghlian, A.S., M.D., MPH. (2021). "Association Between Gender-Affirming Surgeries and Mental Health Outcomes." *JAMA Surgical E1-E8 doi:10.1001/jamasurg.2021.0952.*

Anton, B.S. (2010). "Proceedings of the American Psychological Association for the legislative year 2009: Minutes of the annual meeting of the Council of Representatives and minutes of the meetings of the Board of Directors." *American Psychologist,* 65:385–475. doi:10.1037/a0019553.

Arriola, E.R. (1998). "The penalties for puppy love: Institutionalized violence against lesbian, gay, bisexual, and transgender youth." *The Journal of Gender, Race, and Justice,* 429:1-43.

Auer, M.K., Liedl, A., Fuss, J., Fuss, J., Nieder, T., Briken, P., Stalla, G.K., Hilderbrandt, T., Biedermann, S.V., and Sievers, C. (2017). "High impact of sleeping problems on quality of life in transgender individuals: A cross-sectional multicenter study." *PLoS one* 12(2):1-18. doi:10.1371/journal.pone.0171640.

Bartoli, E., & Gillem, A.R. (2008). "Continuing to depolarize the debate on sexual orientation and religious identity and the therapeutic process." *Professional Psychology: Research and Practice,* 39:202-209.

Beach, R.K., Boulter, S., Felice, M.E., Gottlieb. E.M., Greydanus, D.E., Hoyle, J.C., and Shenker, I.R., Committee on Adolescence. (1993). "Homosexuality and Adolescence." *Pediatrics* 92(4):631-634. ISSN:0031-4005.

Beckstead, A.L., & Morrow, S.L. (2004). "Mormon clients' experiences of conversion therapy: The need for a new treatment approach." *The Counseling Psychologist,* 32:651-690.

Benjamin, H., and Ihlenfeld, C.L., "Transsexualism." *Am. J Nursing* 73:457-461 (3/1973).

Benjamin, H., "Transvestism and Transsexualism in the Male and Female." *Journal of Sexual Research,* 3(2):107-127 (1967); Benjamin, H., "Clinical Aspects of Transsexualism in the Male and Female." *American Journal of Psychotherapy* 18(3):458-469 (1964). See also, *The Transsexual Phenomenon,* Julian Press 1966.

Benjamin, H., "Should Surgery Be performed on Transsexuals," *American Journal of Psychotherapy* 25:74-76 (1971).; Foreman, M., Hare, L., York, K., et. Al., "Genetic Link Between Gender Dysphoria and Sex Hormone Signaling," *Journal of Clinical Endocrinology and Metabolism,* 4(2):390-396, 2/2019, published 9/21/18; Graves, J., "How Genes and Evolution Shape Gender—and Transgender—Identity," *theconversation.com,* January 24, 2019.

Bermon, S., Garnier, P.Y., Hirschberg, A.L., Robinson, N., Giraud, S., Nicoli, R., Baume, N., Saugy, M., Fénichel, P., Bruce, S.J., Henry, H., Dollé, G., and Ritzen, M. (2014). "Serum Androgen Levels in Elite Female Athletes." *Journal of Clinical Endocrinology and Metabolism* 99(11):4328-4335. doi:10.1210/jc.2014-1391.

Birk, L., Huddleston, W., Miller, E., and Cohler, B. (1971). "Avoidance conditioning for homosexuality." *Archives of General Psychiatry,* 25:314-323.

Block, N.L., and Tessler, A.N., "Transsexualism and Surgical Procedures," *Surgery, Gynecology, Obstetrics* Mar;132(3):517-25 (2/1971) PMID: 4925941; Kroger, M.J., McAninch, J. W., Weiner, S.R., "Self-Performed Bilateral Orchiectomy in Transsexuals," *Journal of Clinical Psychiatry,* 43(7):292-293 (1982); Lowy, F.H., Kolivais, T.L., "Auto-Castration by a Male Transsexual," *Canadian Psychiatric Association. Journal,* 16(5):3499-405 (110/1971).

Bolin, A. "Transsexualism and the Limits of Traditional Analysis." *American Behavioral Scientist,* 31(1):41–65 (1987). doi:10.1177/000276487031001004.

Bollinger, A., "Pennsylvania Radio Host calls Trans Health Secretary a "freak show" in Disgusting On-Air Tirade." December 15, 2020 *LGBTQ Nation,* https://www.lgbtqnation.com/2020/12/pennsylvania-radio-host-calls-trans-health-secretary-freak-show-disgusting-air-tirade/.

Brown, L.S. (2006). The neglect of lesbian, gay, bisexual, and transgendered clients. In J. C. Norcross, L. E. Beutler & R. F. Levant (eds.), *Evidence-based practices in mental health: Debate and dialogue on the fundamental questions,* pp. 346-353. Washington, DC: American Psychological Association.

Bullough, V.L. "A nineteenth-century transsexual." *Archives of Sexual Behavior* 16:81–84 (1987). https://doi.org/10.1007/BF01541843.

Bullough, V.L. (1976). *Sexual variance in society and history.* Chicago: University of Chicago Press.

Burstein, "Dr. Money Explains the Why and How of People Who Want to Change Their Sex," *People Magazine*, September 20, 1976, pp. 63; Greene, R., "What Makes A Person Want To Change Sexes." *The National Observer*, October 16, 1976, pp. 1; Liddick, B., "Most Transsexuals Search For Happiness In Vain," *Pittsburgh Press*, October 19, 1976, pp. 13.

Coleman, D., Navratilova, K;M. et al., "Pass the Equality Act, But Don't Abandon Title IX." *Washington Post*, April 29, 2019, https://wapo.st/2VKlNN1.

Connolly,M.D., Zervos, M. J., Barone, C. J., Johnson, C. C., Joseph, C. L. M. (2016). "The Mental Health of Transgender Youth: Advances in Understanding," *Journal of Adolescent Health* 59(5):489-495, ISSN 1054-139X, https://tinyurl.com/9c9ym9s.

D'Augelli, A.R. (2003). "Lesbian and bisexual female youths aged 14 to 21: Developmental challenges and victimization experiences." *Journal of Lesbian Studies,* 7(4):9-29.

D'Augelli, A.R., Hershberger, S. L., & Pilkington, N. W. (1998). "Lesbian, gay, and bisexual youth and their families: Disclosure of sexual orientation and its consequences." *American Journal of Orthopsychiatry,* 68(3):361-371.

Davison, G.C. (1976). *Homosexuality: The ethical challenge. Journal of Consulting and Clinical Psychology,* 44(2):157-162.

Davies, G., MB, BS, DPM, and Parkinson, J.P., BA, MB, BS, DPM. (2007) "Klinefelter's Syndrome and Gender Identity." *Australian and New Zealand Journal of Psychiatry* 41:A70-A70.

Dowshen, N. Meadows, R., Byrnes, M., Hawkins, L., Eder, J., and Noonan, K., (2016). "Policy Perspective: Ensuring Comprehensive Care and Support for Gender Nonconforming Children and Adolescents," *Transgender Health*, 1(1). DOI https://doi.org/10.1089/trgh.2016.0002.

Drescher, J. (2003). "The Spitzer study and the culture wars." *Archives of Sexual Behavior*, 32(5):431-432.

Duke, S., (1976) "Transsexual Wars With the Army." *Los Angeles Times*, September 14, `1977, at C-1; "Sex Changed Teacher Wants Her Job Back." *Los Angeles Times*, November 27.

Eisenberg, M.E., Gower, A.L., McMorris, B.J., Rider, G.N., Shea, G., and Coleman, E., (2017). "Risk and Protective Factors in the Lives of Transgender/Gender Nonconforming Adolescents," *Journal of Adolescent Health* 61(4): 521-526. ISSN 1054-139X, https://tinyurl.com/3nyazyk9.

Fernandez, R., et. Al., (2014). "Association Study of ERβ, AR, and CYP19A1 and Miff Transsexualism." *Journal of Sexual Medicine* 11:2986-2994.

Forman, M., Hare, L., York, K., Balakrishnan, K., Sánchez, F.J., Harte, F., Erasmus, J., and Harley, V. (2019). "Genetic Link Between Gender Dysphoria and Sex Hormone Signaling." *Journal of Clinical Endocrinology and Metabolism* 104(2):390-396. doi:10.1210/jc.2018-01105.

Frazier, S.H., and Carry, A.C. (1974). *An Introduction to Psychopathology*. New York. Jason Aronsson.

Frigerio, A., Ballerini, L., and Valdés-Hernandez, M. (2021). "Structural, Functional, and Metabolic Brain Differences as a Function of Gender Identity or Sexual Orientation: A Systematic Review of the Human Neuroimaging Literature." *Archives of Sexual Behavior.* https://doi.org/10.1007/s10508-021-02005-9.

Glassgold, J. M. (2008). "Bridging the divide: Integrating lesbian identity and Orthodox Judaism." *Women and Therapy*, 31(1):59-73.

Goodenow, C., Szalacha, L., & Westheimer, K. (2006). "School support groups, other school factors, and the safety of sexual minority adolescents." *Psychology in the Schools*, 43(5):573-589.

Gooren, L.G., and Bunck, C.M. (2004). "Transsexuals and competitive sports." *European Journal of Endocrinology* 151:425-429. ISSN: 0804-4643.

Gooren, L. (2011). "The Significance of testosterone for fair participation of the female sex in competitive sports." *Asian Journal of Andrology* 13:653-654. doi:10.1038/aja.2011.91.

Grossman, A.H., D'augelli, A.R. & Frank, J.A. (2011). "Aspects of Psychological Resilience among Transgender Youth," *Journal of LGBT Youth*, 8:2:103-115, DOI: https://tinyurl.com/47h63j9d.

Haldeman, D. C. (1994). "The practice and ethics of sexual orientation conversion therapy." *Journal of Consulting and Clinical Psychology*, 62:221-227.

Haldeman, D. C. (2002). Gay rights, patient rights: The implications of sexual orientation conversion therapy. Professional Psychology: Research and Practice, 33:200-204.

Haldeman, D. C. (2004). "When sexual and religious orientation collide: Considerations in working with conflicted same-sex attracted male clients." *The Counseling Psychologist,* 32:691-715.

Herek, G. M. & Garnets, L. D. (2007). "Sexual orientation and mental health." *Annual Review of Clinical Psychology*, 3:353-375.

James, S. (1978). "Treatment of homosexuality II. Superiority of desensitization/arousal as compared with anticipatory avoidance conditioning: Results of a controlled trial." *Behavior Therapy*, 9:28-36.

Jones, B.A., Arcelus, J., Bouman, W.P., and Haycraft, E. (2017). "Sport and Transgender People: A Systematic Review of the Literature Relating to Sport Participation and Competitive Sport Policies." *Sports Med* 47:701-716. doi:10.1007/s40279-016-0621-y.

Kennedy, R., (1976). "She'd Rather Switch-and fight." *Sports Illustrated*, September 6, pp. 16

Kruijver, F.P.M., Zhou, J-N., Pool, C.W., Hoifman, M.A., Gooren, L.J.G., and Swaab, D.F. (2000). "Male-to-Female Transsexuals Have Female Neuron Numbers in a Limbic Nucleus." *Journal of Clinical Endocrinology and Metabolism* 85(5):2034-2041. Doi:10.1210/jcem.85.5.6564.

Lasser, J. S., & Gottlieb, M. C. (2004). "Treating patients distressed regarding their sexual orientation: Clinical and ethical alternatives." *Professional Psychology: Research and Practice*, 35:194-200.

Martell, C. R., Safren, S. A., & Prince, S. E. (2004). *Cognitive-behavioral therapies with lesbian, gay, and bisexual clients*. New York: Guildford.

McCarn, S. R., & Fassinger, R. E. (1996). "Revisioning sexual minority identity formation: A new model of lesbian identity and its implications for counseling and research." *The Counseling Psychologist*, 24:508-534.

McConaghy, N. (1969). "Subjective and penile plethysmograph responses following aversion-relief and Apomorphine aversion therapy for homosexual impulses." *British Journal of Psychiatry*, 115:723-730.

McConaghy, N. (1976). "Is a homosexual orientation irreversible?" *British Journal of Psychiatry*, 129:556-563.

McConaghy, N., Proctor, D., & Barr, R. (1972). "Subjective and penile plethysmography responses to aversion therapy for homosexuality: A partial replication." *Archives of Sexual Behavior*, 2(1):65-79.

Molnar, B. E. (1997). "Juveniles and psychiatric institutionalization: Toward better due process and treatment review in the United States." *Health and Human Rights*, 2(2):98-116.

Morrow, S. L., & Beckstead, A. L. (2004). "Conversion therapies for same-sex attracted clients in religious conflict: Context, predisposing factors, experiences, and implications for therapy." *The Counseling Psychologist*, 32:641–650.

Nahata, L., Quinn, G.P., Caltabellotta, N.M., and Tishelman, A.C., (2017). "Mental Health Concerns and Insurance Denials Among Transgender Adolescents." *LGBT Health*, 4(3). https://www.liebertpub.com/doi/abs/10.1089/lgbt.2016.0151.

Nazarian, C., (2018). "How Renaissance-Era Sexism Connects the Fights for Gender Equality and Trans Liberation." March 28, *MS. Magazine* article, https://msmagazine.com/2018/03/28/renaissance-era-sexism-connects-fights-gender-equality-trans-liberation/

Nguyen, H.B., Loughead, J., Lipner, E., Hantsoo, L., Kornfield, S.L., and Epperson, C.N. (2019). "What has sex got to do with it? The role of hormones in the transgender brain." *Neuropsychopharmacology* 44:22-37. doi:10.1038/s41386-018-0140-7.

Nicolosi, J., Byrd, A. D., & Potts, R. W. (2000). "Retrospective self-reports of changes in homosexual orientation: A consumer survey of conversion therapy clients." *Psychological Reports*, 86:1071-1088.

Pampati, S., Andrzejewski, J., Steiner, R.J., Rasberry, C.N., Adkins, S.H., Lesesne, C.A., Boyce, L., Grose, R.G., Johns, M.M., (2021). "We Deserve Care and We Deserve Competent Care: Qualitative Perspectives on Health Care from Transgender Youth in the Southeast United States." *Journal of Pediatric Nursing* 56: 54-59, ISSN 0882-5963, https://tinyurl.com/en87hxdk. (https://tinyurl.com/rdzavs4m.

Pauly, I.B. (1981). "Outcome of Sex Reassignment Surgery for Transsexuals." *Australia and New Zealand Journal of Psychiatry* 15(1):45-51. doi: 10.3109/00048678109159409.

Pitsiladis, Y., Harper, J., Betancurt, J.O., Martinez-Patino, M-J., Parisi, A., Wang, G., and Pigozzi, F. (2016). "Beyond Fairness: The Biology of Inclusion for Transgender and Intersex Athletes." *Current Sports Medicine Reports* 15(6):386-388. doi:10.1249/JSR.0000000000000314.

Ponticelli, C. M. (1999). "Crafting stories of sexual identity reconstruction." *Social Psychology Quarterly*, 62(2):157-172.

Remafedi, G., Farrow, J. A., & Deisher, R. W. (1991). "Risk factors of attempted suicide in gay and bisexual youth." *Pediatrics* 87:869–875.

Rider, G.N., McMorris, B.J., Gower, A.L., Coleman, E., and Eisenberg, M.E. (2017). "Health and Care Utilization of Transgender and Gender Nonconforming Youth: A Population-Based Study." *Pediatrics* 141(3). doi:10.1542/peds.2017-1683.

Ryan, C. & Futterman, D. (1997). "Lesbian and gay youth: Care and counseling." *Adolescent Medicine: State of the Art Reviews*, 8(2):207-374.

Ryan, C., Huebner, D., Diaz, R. M., & Sanchez, J. (2009). "Family rejection as a predictor of negative health outcomes in White and Latino lesbian, gay, and bisexual young adults." *Pediatrics* 129(1):346-352.

Savin-Williams, R. C. (1989). "Parental influences on the self-esteem of gay and lesbian youths: A reflected appraisals model." *Journal of Homosexuality* 17(1/2):93-109.

Savin-Williams, R. C. (1994). "Verbal and physical abuse as stressors in the lives of lesbian, gay male, and bisexual youths: Associations with school problems, running away, substance abuse, prostitution, and suicide." *Journal of Consulting and Clinical Practice* 62:261–269.

Schaeffer, K. W., Hyde, R. A., Kroencke, T., McCormick, B., & Nottebaum, L. (2000). "Religiously motivated sexual orientation change." *Journal of Psychology and Christianity*,19:61-70.

Schneider, M. S., Brown, L., & Glassgold, J. (2002). "Implementing the resolution on appropriate therapeutic responses to sexual orientation: A guide for the perplexed. Professional Psychology:" *Research and Practice* 33:265-276.

Shidlo, A., & Schroeder, M. (2002). "Changing sexual orientation: A consumer's report." *Professional Psychology: Research and Practice* 33:249-259.

Smith, E.S., Junger, J., Derntl, B., and Habel, U. (2015). "The transsexual brain—A review of findings on the neural basis of transsexualism." *Neuroscience and Behavioral Reviews* 59:251-266. doi:10.1016/j.neubiorev.2015.09.008.

Spitzer, R. L. (2003). "Can some gay men and lesbians change their sexual orientation? Two hundred participants reporting a change from homosexual to heterosexual orientation." *Archives of Sexual Behavior*, 32:403–417.

Srinivasan, S. P., & Chandrasekaran, S. (2020). "Transsexualism in Hindu Mythology." *Indian Journal of Endocrinology and Metabolism*, 24(3):235–236. doi:10.4103/ijem.IJEM-152-20.

Swaab, D.F. (2004). "Sexual differentiation of the human brain: relevance for gender identity, transsexualism and sexual orientation." *Gynecological Endocrinology* 19:301-312. doi:10.1080/0951390400018231.

Tanner, B. A. (1974). "A comparison of automated aversive conditioning and a waiting list control in the modification of homosexual behavior in males." *Behavior Therapy* 5:29-32.

Tanner, B. A. (1975). "Avoidance training with and without booster sessions to modify homosexual behavior in males." *Behavior Therapy* 6:649-653.

Thibault, V., et al., (2010). "Women and Men in Sport Performance: The Gender Gap has not Evolved since 1983," Journal of Sports Science and Medicine 9:214, 219.

West-Sell, S.A., Van Ness, J.M., and Ciccoletta, M.E. (2019). "Law, Policy, and Physiology as Determinants of Fairness for Transgender Athletes." *PEPOnline* 22(2). ISSN: 1099-5862. American Association of Exercise Physiologists, www.asep.org.

Weston, K. (1993). "Lesbian/Gay Studies in the House of Anthropology." *Annual Review of Anthropology*. Social and Behavioral Sciences, Arizona State University West, Phoenix, AZ, 22:339-367.

Wolkomir, M. (2001). "Emotion work, commitment, and the authentication of the self: The case of gay and ex-gay Christian support groups." *Journal of Contemporary Ethnography* 30:305-334.

Zubiaurre-Elorza, L. Ph.D., Junque, C., Ph.D., Gomez-Gil, E., M.D., Ph.D., and Guillamon, A., M.D., Ph.D. (2014). "Effects of Cross-Sex Hormone Treatment on Cortical Thickness in Transsexual Individuals." *Journal of Sexual Medicine* 11(5):1248-6. doi:10.1111/jsm.12491.

Books

Beckstead, L., & Israel, T. (2007). Affirmative counseling and psychotherapy focused on issues related to sexual orientation conflicts. In K. J. Bieschke, R. M. Perez, & K. A. DeBord (Eds.), *Handbook of counseling and psychotherapy with lesbian, gay, bisexual, and transgender clients* (2nd ed.), pp. 221-244. Washington, DC: American Psychological Association.

Bell, A. P., Weinberg, M. S., & Hammersmith, S. K. (1981). *Sexual preference: Its development in men and women.* Bloomington, IN: Indiana University Press.

Blumenfeld, W. J. (1992). Introduction. In W. J. Blumenfeld (ed.), *Homophobia: How we all pay the price* (pp. 1-19). New York: Beacon Press.

Denny, D., (ed.) (1998). *Current Concepts in Transgender Identity*, Garland Publishing, Inc., Chapter 1, "Mythological, Historical, and Cross-Cultural Aspects of Transsexualism, Green, R., M.D., J.D. (see https://tinyurl.com/b5e9uf32 for more information about Dr. Green's experience). See also, Susan Stryker, *Transgender History: The Roots of Today's Revolution*, Second Edition (2017) Seal Press. ISBN: 9781580056908.

Drescher, J., and Zucker, K. J. (eds.). (2006). *Ex-gay research: Analyzing the Spitzer study and its relation to science, religion, politics, and culture.* New York: Harrington Park Press.

Kinsey, A. C., Pomeroy, W. B., & Martin, C. E. (1948). *Sexual behavior in the human male.* Philadelphia: W.B. Saunders.

Kinsey, A. C., Pomeroy, W. B., Martin, C. E., & Gebhard, P. (1953). *Sexual behavior in the human female.* Philadelphia: Saunders.

McIntyre, L. (2015). *respecting TRUTH—willful ignorance in the internet age.* New York: Routledge ISBN 978-1-138-88881-4, pp. 4.

Nicolosi, J. (1991). *Reparative therapy of male homosexuality.* Northvale, NJ: Jason Aronson.

Norcross, J. C. (2002). *Psychotherapy relationships that work: Therapist contributions and responsiveness to patients.* New York: Oxford University Press.

Perrin, E. C. (2002). *Sexual orientation in child and adolescent health care.* New York: Kluwer/Plenum.

Socarides, C. W. (1968). *The overt homosexual.* New York: Grune & Stratton.

Ullerstam, L. (1966). *The erotic minorities: A Swedish view.* New York: Grove.

Clinical Practice Guidelines

American Academy of Child and Adolescent Psychiatry, Clinical Guidelines and Training for Providers and Professionals, and Trainees, https://www.aacap.org/AACAP/Member_Resources/SOGIIC/Clinical_Guidelines_Training_Providers_Professionals_Trainees.aspx#gender.

American Academy of Child and Adolescent Psychiatry, (2012). "Practice Parameter on Gay, Lesbian, or Bisexual Sexual Orientation, Gender Nonconformity, and Gender Discordance in Children and Adolescents," *Journal of the. American Academy of Child and Adolescent Psychiatry* 51:957.

American Psychiatric Association Transgender and Gender Non-Conforming Guidelines, https://www.psychiatry.org/psychiatrists/cultural-competency/education/transgender-and-gender-nonconforming-patients.

Caring for Transgender and Gender-Diverse Persons: What Clinicians Should Know. American Family Physicians website, https://www.aafp.org/afp/2018/1201/p645.html.

Endocrine Treatment of Gender Dysphoric/Gender-Incongruent Persons: An Endocrine Society Clinical Practice Guideline, https://academic.oup.com/jcem/article/102/11/3869/4157558.

Guidelines for Psychological Practice with Transgender and Gender-Non-Conforming People, https://www.apa.org/practice/guidelines/transgender.pdf.

Wilber, S., Ryan, C., & Marksamer, J. (2006). CWLA, Best practice guidelines. Washington, DC: Child Welfare League of America. The Best Practice Guidelines, https://www.aacap.org/AACAP/Member_Resources/SOGIIC/Clinical_Guidelines_Training_Providers_Professionals_Trainees.aspx#gender.

World Professional Association for Transgender Health (WPATH) Standards of Care, 8th Edition, https://www.wpath.org/soc8.

Organization Policy Statements

American Medical Association Position on Transgender Health Care. (2021). https://www.ama-assn.org/press-center/press-releases/ama-states-stop-interfering-health-care-transgender-children.

Burack, C., & Josephson, J. J. (2005). *A report from "Love won out: Addressing, understanding, and preventing homosexuality" Minneapolis, Minnesota,* September 18, 2004. New York: National Gay and Lesbian Task Force Policy Institute.

Cianciatto, J. & Cahill, S. (2006). *Youth in the crosshairs: The third wave of ex-gay activism.* New York: National Gay and Lesbian Task Force Policy Institute.

Daniel, Hilary, and Renee Butkus, For the Health and Public Policy Committee of the American College of Physicians. (2015). *Lesbian, Gay, Bisexual, and Transgender Health Disparities: Executive Summary of a Policy Position Paper From the American College of Physicians.* Annals of Internal Medicine (21 July 2015) 163:2 135-148.

Joint Statement Opposing State Legislation Targeting Transgender Youth. Freedom for All Americans, https://freedomforallamericans.org/joint-statement-opposing-state-legislation-targeting-transgender-youth/.

Marra, Janelle, and Conlon, Elizabeth. (2021). Clinical Considerations in Caring for Transgender Athletes. *American Family Physician* 103(9):518-520.

NCAA Board of Governors Statement on Transgender Participation, https://www.ncaa.org/about/resources/media-center/news/general-board-receives-equity-report-reaffirms-transgender-participation.

Pediatricians Say State Bills Would Harm Transgender Youths. American Association of Pediatrics News, https://publications.aap.org/aapnews/news/12780.

United States Professional Association for Transgender Health (USPATH) Statement on the Surge of Anti-trans Legislation Occurring Within the U.S. https://www.wpath.org/policies.

Reports

Fisk, N., "Gender Dysphoria Syndrome: The How, What and Why of a Disease." *Proceedings of the Second Interdisciplinary Symposium on Gender Dysphoria Syndrome,* pp. 7; Paperback Edition, Stanford University Medical Center (1973)

Grant, Jaime M., Lisa A. Mottet, Justin Tanis, Jack Harrison, Jody L. Herman, and Mara Keisling (2011). *Injustice at Every Turn: A Report of the National Transgender Discrimination Survey, Washington, D.C.* National Center for Transgender Equality and National Gay and Lesbian Task Force.

Herek, G. M. (2009). Sexual stigma and sexual prejudice in the United States: A conceptual framework. In D. A. Hope (ed.), *Contemporary perspectives on lesbian, gay, & bisexual identities: The 54th Nebraska symposium on motivation,* pp. 65-111. New York: Springer.

Sears, Brad, Mallory, Christy, Flores, Andrew R., and Conron, Kerith J. *LGBT People's Experiences of Workplace Discrimination and Harassment.* September 2021. Williams Institute of the UCLA School of Law.

Southern Poverty Law Center. (2005, Spring). A mighty army. Intelligence Report, Issue 117, accessed May 14, 2009, http://www.splcenter.org/intel/intelreport/article.jsp?aid=524.

Constitutional Provisions
United States Constitution, First Amendment

United States Constitution, Fourteenth Amendment

Laws of the United States
21 U.S.C. §§ 811-812

Age Discrimination Act of 1975 (42 U.S.C. §6101)

Fair Housing Act of 1968 (42 U.S.C. §3601, et seq.)

Patient Protection and Affordable Care Act (42 USC §18116) ("ACA") - Nondiscrimination

Rehabilitation Act of 1973 (29 U.S.C. §794), Section 504

Title VI of the Civil Rights Act of 1964 (42 U.S.C. §2000)

Title VII of the Civil Rights Act of 1964, as amended (Pub. L. 88-352) (42 U.S.C. §2000e)

Title IX of the Education Amendments of 1972 (20 U.S.C. §1681)

Title 42 U.S.C. §2000a, et seq. Discrimination in Public Accommodations

Federal Religious Freedom Restoration Act (RFRA) of 1993, Title 42 U.S.C. Section 2000bb, et seq.

Code of Federal Regulations
Title 24 CFR Part 100 – Fair Housing Discrimination

Title 34 CFR Chapter 1 – Department of Education Office of Civil Rights

Title 42 CFR Chapter 21 – Civil Rights

Title 42 CFR Chapter 21B – Religious Freedom

Title 45 CFR §86.31 – Title IX of the Education Amendments of 1972 Regulations

Title 49 CFR Subtitle B, Chapter VI, Part 601, Subpart A, §601.3(d) Office of Civil Rights

U.S. Departmental Policies
Department of Defense DoD Instruction 6130.03 Volume 1, "Medical Standards for Military Service, Appointment, Enlistment, or Induction," dated April 30, 2021

VHA Directive 1341(2), issued May 23, 2018

Legal Cases
Federal Courts
United States Supreme Court
Baker v. *Nelson*, 409 U.S. 810 (1972)

Bostock v. *Clayton County GA*, 590 U.S. ____ (2020)

Bowers v. *Hardwick*, 478 U.S. 186 (1986)

Burwell, Secretary of Health and Human Services et al., v. *Hobby Lobby Stores, Inc., et al.* 573 U.S. 682 (2014)

City of Boerne v. *Flores, Archbishop of San Antonio, et al.*, 521 U.S. 507 (1997)

Davis v. *Ermold*, 592 U.S. ____ (2020)

Eisenstadt v. *Baird*, 405 U.S. 438, 453 (1972)

Employment Division, Department of Human Resources of Oregon, et al., v. Alfred L. Smith, et al., 494 U.S. 872, 110 S.Ct. 1595, 108 L.Ed.2d 876 (1990)

Griswold v. *Connecticut*, 381 U.S. 479, 484–486 (1965)

Kirchberg v. *Feenstra*, 450 U.S. 455, 460–461 (1981)

Lawrence v. *Texas*, 539 U. S. 558, 575 (2003)

Loving v. *Virginia*, 388 U.S. 1, 12 (1967)

M. L. B. v. *S. L. J.*, 519 U. S. 102, 120–121 (1996)

Maynard v. *Hill*, 125 U.S. 190, 211 (1888)

Obergefell v. Hodges, 576 U.S. 644 (2015)

Oncale v. Sundowner Offshore Services, Inc., 523 U.S. 75 (1998)

Pierce v. *Society of Sisters*, 268 U.S. 510 (1925)

Price Waterhouse v. Hopkins, 490 U.S. 228 (1989)

Tanzin v, Tanvir, 19-71 (Slip Opinion) (2020) affirming 894 F. 3d 449

Turner v. *Safley*, 482 U.S. 78, 95 (1987)

United States v. Virginia, 518 U.S. 515, 24 533 (1996)

United States v. *Windsor*, 570 U.S. 744 (2012)

University of Tex. Southwestern Medical Center v. *Nassar,* 570 U. S. 338, 350 (2013)

Washington v. *Davis,* 426 U. S. 229, 241 (1976)

Watson v. *Fort Worth Bank & Trust*, 487 U. S. 977, 986 (1988)

Zablocki v. *Redhail,* 434 U.S. 374 (1978)

United States Circuit Courts of Appeals

Dodds v. U.S. Department of Education, 845 F. 3d 217 (6th Cir. 2016)

Doe v. Boyertown, 897 F.3d 518 (3rd Cir. 2018)

G.G. ex rel. Grimm v. Gloucester County. School Bd., 822 F.3d 709, 729 (4th Cir. 2016)

Gavin Grimm v. Gloucester County School Board, 822 F.3d 709 (USCA 4th 2016)

Glenn v. Brumby, 663 F.3d 1312, 1316 (11th Cir. 2011)

Michelle Nichols v. Azteca Restaurant Enterprises, Inc, 256 F.3d 864 (9th Cir. 2001)

Smith v. City of Salem, 378 F.3d 566, (6th Cir. 2004)

Torbin H. Brenden, et al., v. Independent School District, 342 F.Supp. 1224 (D.Minn. 1972); 477 F.2d 1292 (8th Cir. 1973)

Vandiver Elizabeth GLENN, f.k.a. Glenn Morrison v. Sewell R. BRUMBY, 663 F.3d 1312 (11th Cir. 2011)

United States District Courts

Evancho v. Pine-Richland School District, et al., 237 F.Supp.3d 267 (2017) (USDC Western Dist. PA)

Finkle v. Howard County MD, 12 F.Supp.3d 780 (USDC Dist. MD 2014)

Hecox, et al., v. Little, et al., Case 1:20-cv-00184-DCN U.S. District Court (Dist. Idaho 2020); *see above under* U.S. Courts of Appeals.

Joaquín CARCAÑO, et al., Plaintiffs, v. Patrick McCrory, 203 F.Supp.3d 615 (USDC MD North Carolina 2016)

Johnston v. University of Pittsburgh, 97 F.Supp.3d 657 (2015) (USDC Western Dist. PA)

Lindsay Hecox, et al. v. Bradley Little, et al. Case No. 1:20-cv-00184-DCN (USDC D.Idaho 2020); the case is on appeal to the U.S. Court of Appeals for the Ninth Circuit, Lindsay Hecox, et al, Plaintiffs-Appellees v. Bradley Little, et al., Defendants-Appellants, and Madison Kenyon, et al., Intervenor-Appellants, Case Nos. 20-35813, 20-35815.

Morrison II v. Board of Education of Boyd County, Kentucky, 419 F.Supp.2d 937 (USDC E.D. Kentucky (2006))

Parents for Privacy, et al. v. Dallas School District, 326 F.Supp.3d 1075 (USDC D.Or 2018)

Reynolds, et al. v. Talberg, et al., (USDC W.D. Mich. S. Dist. October 30, 2020)

Law Review Articles

Doriane Lambelet Coleman, "Sex in Sport," 80 LAW & CONTEMP. PROBS. 63, 74 (2017)

Doriane Lambelet Coleman & Wickliffe Shreve, "Comparing Athletic Performances: The Best Elite Women to Boys and Men," DUKE LAW CTR. FOR SPORTS LAW AND POLICY.

Ventrell-Monsees, C., "Proving 'Because of but/for Cause' – A 'Generous' Causation Standard." ABA Section on Labor and Employment Law, 13th Annual Labor and Employment Law Conference, New Orleans, LA (November 7, 2019), pp. 3. https://tinyurl.com/ynsv72e

State Courts

Kleczek v. R.I. Interscholastic League, Inc., 612 A.2d 734, 738 (R.I. 1992)

Petrie v. Ill. High Sch. Ass'n, 394 N.E.2d 855, 861 (Ill. App. Ct. 1979)

Additional Cases Not Cited

California v. Texas, 19-840 (2021) slip opinion

Employment Division, Department of Human Resources of Oregon v. Smith, 494 U.S. 872 (1990)

Transgender Law Center, https://transgenderlawcenter.org/.

NOTES

[1] Lee McIntyre, Respecting Truth: Willful Ignorance in the Internet Age, Routledge Publishing, 2015, ISBN 978-1-138-88880-7, hardbound edition, pp. 4.

[2] https://www.sbc.net/resource-library/resolutions/on-transgender-identity/.

[3] https://www.sbc.net/resource-library/resolutions/on-transgender-identity/.

[4] Aaron Devor "Legitimizing Trans: Reed Erickson (1917-1992) and the Erickson Educational Foundation," in Dallas Denny, Jamison Green, Kyan Lynch, and Carolyn Wolf-Gould (eds), *From Margins to Mainstream: A History of Transgender Medicine in the United States*, SUNY Press (in press).

[5] There is some confusion regarding the publication date of this version. Some sources indicate a publication date of 1978, while others indicate 1979 or 1980 as the publication date.

[6] Srinivasan, S. P., and Chandrasekaran, S. (2020). "Transsexualism in Hindu Mythology," *Indian Journal of Endocrinology and Metabolism*, 24(3), 235–236, https://doi.org/10.4103/ijem.IJEM_152_20.

[7] See https://en.wikipedia.org/wiki/Metamorphoses, where in *Metamorphoses* Ovid describes various metamorphoses or transformations, "Ovid raises the significance of transformation explicitly in the opening lines of the poem: *In nova fert animus mutatas dicere formas / corpora;* (I intend to speak of forms changed into new entities). Nowhere in the text does the poem specifically speak of being trans, nor is there even vague reference to it. Nevertheless, some scholars have taken Ovid's treatise on transformations and applied it to the situation of trans people.

[8] Nazarian, C., "How Renaissance-Era Sexism Connects the Fights for Gender Equality and Trans Liberation," March 28, 2018, *MS. Magazine*, https://msmagazine.com/2018/03/28/renaissance-era-sexism-connects-fights-gender-equality-trans-liberation/.

[9] Bullough, V.L. "A nineteenth-century transsexual," *Archives of Sexual Behavior* 16, 81–84 (1987), https://doi.org/10.1007/BF01541843.

[10] Bolin, A. "Transsexualism and the Limits of Traditional Analysis," *American Behavioral Scientist*, 31(1), 41–65 (1987), https://tinyurl.com/429prvmr.

[11] Weston, K., "Lesbian/Gay Studies in The House of Anthropology," *Annual Review of Anthropology* 22:339-367 (10/1993), https://tinyurl.com/wx5jy2jh.

[12] See note 1.

[13] Denny, D., "Mythological, Historical, and Cross-Cultural Aspects of Transsexualism," *Current Concepts in Transgender Identity, (Garland Gay and Lesbian Studies Book 11)*, 1998, Chapter 1, ISBN: 978-1138967137, with Green, R., M.D., J.D. (see https://tinyurl.com/b5e9uf32 for information about Dr. Green). See also, Susan Stryker, *Transgender History: The Roots of Today's Revolution*, Second Edition (2017), Seal Press. ISBN: 9781580056908.

[14] The term "sex reassignment surgery" is described by the World Professional Association for Transgender Health (WPATH) as the surgical process of modifying the primary and/or secondary sex characteristics to establish greater congruence with the person's gender identity. See WPATH Standards of Care, copyright 2012, pp. 54-55.

[15] "Ex-GI Becomes Blonde Beauty," *New York Daily News*, December 1, 1952, pp. 1.

[16] Kennedy, R., "She'd Rather Switch-and fight," *Sports Illustrated*, September 6, 1976, pp. 16. The story about Dr. Renee Richards and professional tennis.

[17] See, e.g., Burstein, "Dr. Money Explains the Why and How of People Who Want to Change Their Sex," *People Magazine*, September 20, 1976, at pp. 63; Greene, R., "What Makes a Person Want To Change Sexes," *The National Observer*, October 16, 1976, at pp. 1; Liddick, B., "Most Transsexuals Search For Happiness In Vain," *Pittsburgh Press*, October 19, 1976, at pp. 13.

[18] http://transascity.org/joanna-clark-warrior-woman/.

[19] Duke, S., "Transsexual Wars With the Army," *Los Angeles Times*, September 14, 1977, at C-1; "Sex Changed Teacher Wants Her Job Back," *Los Angeles Times*, November 27, 1976.

[20] Benjamin, H., "Transvestism and Transsexualism in the Male and Female," *Journal of Sex Research*, 3(2):107-127 (1967); Benjamin, H., "Clinical Aspects of Transsexualism in the Male and Female," *American Journal of Psychotherapy* 18(3) 458-469 (1964). See also, "The Transsexual Phenomenon," Harry Benjamin, *Julian Press* 1966.

[21] The Harry Benjamin International Gender Dysphoria Association (HBIGDA) *Standards of Care*.

[22] See http://web.uvic.ca/~erick123/ for information on symposia sponsored by the Reed Erickson Educational Foundation.

[23] https://www.digitaltransgenderarchive.net/files/ws859f79d.

[24] https://www.wpath.org/about/history/international-symposia.

[25] WPATH History of International Symposia, www.wpath.org/about/history/international-symposia. The 3rd International Symposium on Gender Identity, sponsored by the Erikson Education Foundation (EEF), was held at the Hotel Libertas in Dubrovnik, Yugoslavia, Sept 8-10, 1973. It featured talks by John Money, Vern Bullough, Thomas Kando, Harold Christianson, Ira Pauly, Anke Ehrhardt, Leo Wollman, Donald Laub, Thomas Mazur, and Zelda Suplee, among others. It was the last of the conferences convened by the EEF.

[26] See https://www.wpath.org/education/upcoming-conferences.

[27] "Gender Dysphoria Syndrome is a descriptive term, encompassing selective clinical situations or a set of psychosocial symptoms and/or behaviors that have been reported by a group of deeply troubled, often desperate patients seeking gender reorientation, including surgical sex conversion," Fisk, N., "Gender Dysphoria Syndrome: The How, What and Why of a Disease," *Proceedings of the Second Interdisciplinary Symposium on Gender Dysphoria Syndrome*, at pp. 7; paperback Edition, Stanford University Medical Center (1973).

[28] "From all available evidence in the field of psychology, as well as physiology, I feel that no one is justified at this time in saying categorically that transsexuals are *made*, not born. The opposite may also be true. More than one cause can bring on—say—convulsions, and more than one cause is probably responsible for the transsexual syndrome," Benjamin, H., Should Surgery Be Performed on Transsexuals?" *American Journal of Psychotherapy* 25:74, 76 (1971).

[29] Fernandez, R., et. Al., "Association Study of ERβ, AR, and CYP19A1 and Miff Transsexualism," *Journal of Sexual Medicine* 11:2986-2994 (2014).

Benjamin, H., "Should Surgery Be performed on Transsexuals," *American Journal of Psychotherapy* 25:74-76 (1971).; Foreman, M., Hare, L., York, K., et. Al., "Genetic Link Between Gender Dysphoria and Sex Hormone Signaling," *J of Clinical Endocrinology and Metabolism*, v. 4, Issue 2, 2/2019, pp. 390-396, published 9/21/18; Graves, J., "How Genes and Evolution Shape Gender—and Transgender—Identity," theconversation.com, January 24, 2019.

[30] Hare, L., Bernard, P., Sánchez, F.J., Baird, P.N., Vilain, E., Kennedy, T., Harley, V.R., "Androgen Receptor Repeat Length Polymorphism Associated with Male-to-Female Transsexualism," Biological Psychiatry, Volume 65, Issue 1, 2009, Pages 93-96, ISSN 0006-3223, DOI.10.1016%2Fj.biopsych.2008.08.033, https://tinyurl.com/5v64se68.

[31] Dr. Ira Pauly said, "The suffering of the transsexual is beyond belief," Luff, D.N., "Genes, Gender and Gender Reversal," *Medical World News* 18(8):45-58, at pp. 56, 4/18/1977. See also, Baker, H.J., and Green, R., "Treatment of Transsexualism," *Current Psychiatric Therapies*, 10:88-99 (1970) PMID: 5469117; Mason, N., "The Transsexual Dilemma: Being A Transsexual," *J Medical Ethics* 6(2):85-89 (June 1980) DOI 10.2307/27715862.

[32] *G.B. v. Lackner*, 145 Claret. 555 (Cal. Ct. of Appeal 1978); 80 Cal. App. 64; Levine, S.B., "Suicide by a Transsexual (letter), *Archives of Sex Behavior* 13(3):287-289 (6/1984) DOI 10.1007/BF01541655; Huxley, P.J., Kenna, J.C., Brandon, S., "Partnership In Transsexualism, Part 1: Paired and non-paired Groups," *Archives of Sex Behavior* 10(2):133-141 (45/1981) DOI 10.1007/bf01542174; Danto, B.M., "Violent Sex and Suicide," *Mental Health and Society* 5(1-2):1-13 (1978) PMID: 750873.; Herschkowitz, S., Kickers, R., "Suicide Attempts in a female-to-male Transsexual," *American Journal of Psychiatry* 135(3):368-369 (3/1978) DOI 10.1176/ajp.135.3.368.

[33] Block, N.L., and Tessler, A.N., "Transsexualism and Surgical Procedures," *Surgery Gynecology Obstetrics*, Mar;132(3):517-25 (2/1971) PMID: 4925941; Kroger, M.J., McAninch, J. W., Weiner, S.R., "Self-Performed Bilateral Orchiectomy in Transsexuals," *Journal of Clinical Psychiatry*, 43(7):292-293 (1982); Lowy, F.H., Koliva is, T.L., "Auto-Castration by a Male Transsexual," *Canadian Psychiatric Association Journal*, 16(5):3499-405 (110/1971).

See also, A confidential memorandum dated July 1, 1981, written by the Chief of Surgery at the Colorado State Hospital, Dr. T.J. Fogel, contains a concise history of plaintiff up to that date:

> "The patient has made six attempts to emasculate himself over a period of years... On the 29th of June, he incised and removed a portion of his scrotum, placed string and rubber bands about the spermatic cords bilaterally and this was found the next day and the constricting bands removed... He stated categorically that he would not allow any treatment if it did not involve the removal of his testicles. He made this truly clear. He was quite rational. He was seen by Dr. Huffaker, the Colorado State Hospital psychiatrist, who in a truly clear evaluation felt that he was in every regard a true transsexual," *Supre v. Ricketts*, 596 F.Supp. 1532 (CO 1984), reversed 792 F.2d 958 (10th Cir. 1986).

Appeal was on awarding of attorney's fees and administration of hormones in the correctional environment.

[34] Pauly, I., "Outcome of Sex Reassignment Surgery for Transsexuals," *Australian and New Zealand Journal Psychiatry* 15(1):45-51 (1981); Pauly, I., "The Current Status of the Change of Sex Operation," *Journal of Nervous and Metal Disease* 147:460 (1968).

[35] Original in Clark, J., "The Legal Aspects of Transsexualism," 1990. The pamphlet was a revision of what had been produced earlier by the Erickson Educational Foundation.

> The Brooklyn-based technical writer Harriet Slavits researched and wrote the pamphlets, which Erickson then scrutinized for accuracy and to ensure that they always maintained a positive tone. (Devor in press)

This information is based on an interview that Aaron Devor did with Sarah Santana in 1997. Originally, there were 8 titles in the series. The two that are pertinent to this book are *Some Legal Aspects of Transsexualism* (1970) and *Legal Aspects of Transsexualism and Information on Administrative Procedures* (1971 and 1973)]

[36] Benjamin, H., and Ihlenfeld, C.L., "Transsexualism," *American Journal of Nursing* 73:457-461 (3/1973).

[37] "It has frequently said that the term 'transsexualism' has come to encompass a variety of conditions that under other circumstances that might be labelled as extremely effeminate homosexuality, transvestism (particularly conscience ridden transvestism), schizoid or borderline personality disorder, polymorphous perverse psychopathy, as well as individuals who apparently have manifested cross-gender drives—the classical "transsexual," Other types of patients occasionally found among applicants for sex reassignment are obsessional neurotics with profound masochistic trends, notoriety seekers, vocationally motivated homosexual prostitutes, borderline patients, and the overtly psychotic," *Proceedings of the Second* Interdisciplinary *Symposium on Gender Dysphoria Syndrome*, at pp. 32; paperback edition, Stanford University Medical Center (1973).

[38] Frazier, S.H., and Carry, A.C. *An Introduction to Psychopathology*. New York. Jason Aronsson (1974).

[39] Herman, J.L., Brown, T.N.T., and Haas, A.P., "Suicide Thoughts and Attempts among Transgender Adults: Findings from the 2015 U.S. Transgender Survey," UCLA School of Law, Williams Institute, September 2019.

[40] "While there are a few people suffering with transsexualism, regular psychotherapy is not effective, and these patients are often hurt by other people" Hynix, J., "Treatment of Transsexualism," V. 44, Abstract No. 16739: Dialog 44-16739; *Smith v. Liberty Mutual Insurance Co.,* 569 F.Supp. 1068 (D.GA 1975), *Aff'd.* 569 F.2d 325 (5th Cir. 1978), *Grossman v. Bernardus Township*, 316 A.2d 39 (1974); *Aff'd.* 538 F.2d 319 (3rd Cir. 1976), *Cert. Denied,*429 U.S. 181 (1976); *Voyles v. Ralph K. Davies Medical Center*, 403 F.Supp. 456 (N.D> CA 1975), *Aff'd. without Opinion,* 570 F.2d 354 (9th Cir. 1977); *Powell v. Reads*, 436 F.Supp. 369 (D. MD 1977); *Holloway v. Arthur Anderson Co.,* 556 F.2d 659 (9th Cir. 1977); *Kirkpatrick v. Seligman and Lantz, Inc.,* 75 F.Supp. 145 M.D. FL 1979); *Sommers v. Budget Marketing,* 667 F.2d 748 (8th Cir. 1980); *Sommers v. Iowa Civil Rights Commission,* 337 N.W.2d 470 (1983); *Ulane v. Eastern Airlines,* 581 F.Supp. 821 N.D. IL 1983), *Revved.* 742 F.2d 1081 (7th Cir. 1984), *Cert. Denied,* 471 U.S. 1017, 85 L. Ed. 2d 304, 105 S. Ct. 2023 (1985), 53 U.S.L.W. 3730 (4/16/1985); Goerth, C.R., "Ulane Case Highlights Issues of Sex Discrimination Lawsuits," *Occ. Health and Safety*, 54-55 (May 1984).

[41] "Could not the time and effort of talented researchers be put to better use, to more legitimate challenges? If a glamorous challenge is insisted upon, we suggest that brain transplanting be preferred to castrating altering 'sick' males," Letter from Nicole J. Michaud and Elliot Bold, G.F. Strong Laboratory for Medical Research, to the editor, *American Journal of Obstetrics and Gynecology* 135(1):163 (9/1/1979).

[42] Pew Research Center, https://tinyurl.com/js2rrdd6. "The number of Americans who had a favorable view of gay men stands at 55%, an 18-percentage point increase compared to a decade earlier; 58% had a favorable opinion of lesbians, a 19 percentage point increase over the same time span.

The Arc of Social Acceptance

% of all LGBT adults saying

■ More accepting ■ No different ■ Less accepting

Compared with 10 years ago, society is now ... of people who are LGBT

10 years from now, society will be ... of people who are LGBT

Notes: Based on all LGBT (N=1,197). Those who didn't answer are not shown.

PEW RESEARCH CENTER   LGBT/54,55

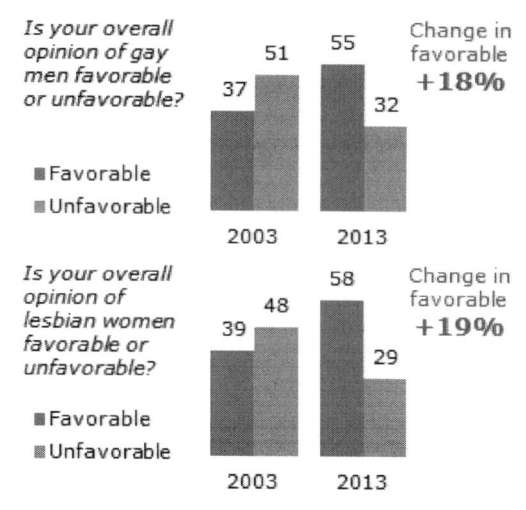

A March-April survey of the general public also showed that, in recent years, there has been a decline in the percentage of Americans who think that more gays and lesbians raising children is a bad thing for American society. Currently, 35% view this as a negative trend for society. While that is unchanged from 2011, it represents a 15-point decline since 2007 (from 50%)," Pew Research Center website 2013 posting, accessed in April 2021.

[43] See also, https://tinyurl.com/r4hu9n5c.

[44] Bollinger, A., "Pennsylvania Radio Host calls Trans Health Secretary a 'freak show' in Disgusting On-Air Tirade," December 15, 2020 LGBTQ Nation, https://www.lgbtqnation.com/2020/12/pennsylvania-radio-host-calls-trans-health-secretary-freak-show-disgusting-air-tirade/.

[45] Marla E. Eisenberg, Amy L. Gower, Barbara J. McMorris, G. Nicole Rider, Glynis Shea, Eli Coleman, "Risk and Protective Factors in the Lives of Transgender/Gender Nonconforming Adolescents," Journal of Adolescent Health, Volume 61, Issue 4, 2017, pp. 521-526, ISSN 1054-139X, https://tinyurl.com/3nyazyk9.

[46] Maureen D. Connolly, Marcus J. Zervos, Charles J. Barone, Christine C. Johnson, Christine L.M. Joseph, "The Mental Health of Transgender Youth: Advances in Understanding," Journal of Adolescent Health, Volume 59, Issue 5, 2016, Pages 489-495, ISSN 1054-139X, https://tinyurl.com/9c9ym9s.

[47] G. Nicole Rider, Barbara J. McMorris, Amy L. Gower, Eli Coleman, and Marla E. Eisenberg, "Health and Care Utilization of Transgender and Gender Nonconforming Youth: A Population-Based Study," Pediatrics, March 2018, 141 (3) e20171683; DOI: https://tinyurl.com/276kra5h.

[48] Arnold H. Grossman, Anthony R. D'augelli and John A. Frank (2011) Aspects of Psychological Resilience among Transgender Youth, Journal of LGBT Youth, 8:2, 103-115, DOI: https://tinyurl.com/47h63j9d.

[49] Dowshen, et al., "Policy Perspective: Ensuring Comprehensive Care and Support for Gender Nonconforming Children and Adolescents," Transgender Health, Vol. 1.1, 2016, https://tinyurl.com/4d7mm636.

[45] Sanjana Pampati, Jack Andrzejewski, Riley J. Steiner, Catherine N. Rasberry, Susan H. Adkins, Catherine A. Lesesne, Lorin Boyce, Rose Grace Grose, Michelle M. Johns, "We Deserve Care and We Deserve Competent Care: Qualitative Perspectives on Health Care from Transgender Youth in the Southeast United States, Journal of Pediatric Nursing, Volume 56, 2021, Pages 54-59, ISSN 0882-5963, https://tinyurl.com/en87hxdk. (https://tinyurl.com/rdzavs4m).

[51] Leena Nahata, Gwendolyn P. Quinn, Nicole M. Caltabellotta, and Amy C. Tishelman, Mental Health Concerns and Insurance Denials Among Transgender Adolescents, LGBT Health, 4(3), https://tinyurl.com/3nsw477m.

[52] Rider, GN, McMorris, BJ, Gower, AL, et al. "Health and Care Utilization of Transgender and Gender Nonconforming Youth: A Population-Based Study," Pediatrics. 2018;141(3): e20171683.

[53] The Georgetown University National Center for cultural Competence (NCCC) defines conscious bias "in its extreme is characterized by overt negative behavior that can be expressed through physical and verbal harassment or through more subtle means such as exclusion," https://nccc.georgetown.edu/bias/module-3/1.php.

54 See the discussion about conscious and unconscious bias, https://pediaa.com/what-is-the-difference-between-conscious-and-unconscious-bias/.

55 The Merriam-Webster Online Dictionary defines "marginalize" as "to relegate to an unimportant or powerless position within a society or group," https://www.merriam-webster.com/dictionary/marginalize.

56 Merriam-Websters Online Dictionary defines "stigmatize" as "to describe or identify in opprobrious terms." https://www.merriam-webster.com/dictionary/stigmatization#other-words.

57 Implicit stigmatization is implied, not plainly expressed, stigmatization; explicit stigmatization is overt or intentional as defined above.

58 https://www.merriam-webster.com/dictionary/marginalize.

59 Collins JC, McFadden C, Rocco TS, Mathis MK. The Problem of Transgender Marginalization and Exclusion: Critical Actions for Human Resource Development. *Human Resource Development Review*. 2015;14(2):205-226. DOI:10.1177/1534484315581755.

60 UN Office of the High Commissioner for Human Rights, https://www.ohchr.org/EN/Issues/SexualOrientationGender/Pages/struggle-trans-gender-diverse.aspx.

61 National Transgender Discrimination Survey, Executive Summary, 2012, https://transequality.org/issues/resources/national-transgender-discrimination-survey-executive-summary.

62 See "Frontline," https://www.pbs.org/wgbh/frontline/article/introduction-2/.

63 https://journalofethics.ama-assn.org/article/sex-gender-and-why-differences-matter/2008-07.

64 Wizemann, T.M., and Pardue, Mary-Lou, Editors, Committee on Understanding the Biology of Sex and Gender Differences, Board on Health Sciences Policy. Exploring the Biological Contributions to Human Health: Does Sex Matter? ISBN: 0-309-51190-9, 288 pages, 6 x 9, (2001) This PDF is available from the National Academies Press. http://www.nap.edu/catalog/10028.html.

65 De Cuypere G, T'Sjoen G, Beerten R, Selvaggi G, De Sutter P, Hoebeke P, Monstrey S, Vansteenwegen A, Rubens R. Sexual and physical health after sex reassignment surgery. Archives of Sexual Behavior 2005 Dec;34(6):679-90, DOI: 10.1007/s10508-005-7926-5. PMID: 16362252.

66 Grant, J.M., Mottet, L.A., Tanis, J., Harrison, J., Herman, J.L., and Keisling. M. (2011) Injustice at Every Turn: A Report of the National Transgender Discrimination Survey. Washington: National Center for Transgender Equality and National Gay and Lesbian Task Force.

67 Flores, A.R. (2014) National Trends in Public Opinion on LGBT rights in the United States. *UCLA School of Law, The Williams Institute*, https://williamsinstitute.law.ucla.edu/wp-content/uploads/Public-Opinion-LGBT-US-Nov-2014.pdf.

68 World Professional Association for Transgender Health (WPATH/USPATH); Hembree, W.C., Cohen-Kettenis, P.T., Gooren, L.G., Hannema, S.E., Meyer, W.J., Murad, M.H., Rosenthal, S.M., Safer, J.D., Tangpricha, V., and T'Sjoen, G.G. (2014) Endocrine Treatment of Gender-Dysphoric/Gender-Incongruent Persons: An Endocrine Society* Clinical Practice Guideline. *Journal of Clinical Endocrinology and Metabolism* (11/2017) 102(11):3869-3093, DOI:10.1210/jc.2017-01658.

69 Rafferty, J. COMMITTEE ON PSYCHOSOCIAL ASPECTS OF CHILD AND FAMILY HEALTH, COMMITTEE ON ADOLESCENCE, SECTION ON LESBIAN, GAY, BISEXUAL, AND TRANSGENDER HEALTH AND WELLNNESS (2018) Ensuring Comprehensive Care and Support for Transgender and Gender-Diverse Children and Adolescents. *Pediatrics* 142(4). https://pediatrics.aappublications.org/content/142/4/e20182162.

70 James, S. E., Herman, J. L., Rankin, S., Keisling, M., Mottet, L., and Anafi, M. (2016). *The Report of the 2015 U.S. Transgender Survey*. Washington, DC: National Center for Transgender Equality; Executive Summary, pp. 10.

71 James, S. E., Herman, J. L., Rankin, S., Keisling, M., Mottet, L., and Anafi, M. (2016). *The Report of the 2015 U.S. Transgender Survey*, Washington, DC: National Center for Transgender Equality; Executive Summary, pp. 10.

72 Genny Beemyn, Trans Bodies, Trans Selves, edited by Laura Erickson-Schroth. Oxford University Press, 1st Ed., June 10, 2014, https://www.umass.edu/stonewall/sites/default/files/Infoforandabout/transpeople/genny_beemyn_transgender_history_in_the_united_states.pdf.

73 Beemyn, G., *Transgender History in the United States*," Introduction," pp. 1. *Trans Bodies, Trans Selves*, edited by Laura Erickson-Schroth. Oxford University Press, 1st Ed., June 10, 2014, https://www.umass.edu/stonewall/sites/default/files/Infoforandabout/transpeople/genny_beemyn_transgender_history_in_the_united_states.pdf.

74 Stryker, S., *Transgender History: The Roots of Today's Revolution*, November 2017, Seal Press, pp. 8.

75 https://tinyurl.com/3ew6m5jd.

76 History Channel, "Stonewall Riots," May 31, 2017, updated June 26, 2020, https://tinyurl.com/3ew6m5jd.

77 Byrnes, H., "13 counties where being gay is punishable by death," *USA Today*, June 20, 2019, https://www.usatoday.com/story/money/2019/06/14/countries-where-being-gay-is-legally-punishable-by-death/39574685/.

78 Eschner, K., "England's Witch Trials Were Lawful," *Smithsonian Magazine*, August 18, 2017, https://www.smithsonianmag.com/smart-news/englands-witch-trials-were-lawful-180964514/.

79 Matthew Shepard Foundation, https /www.matthewshepard.org/.

80 GLAAD, www.glaad.org/tdor.

81 Human Rights Campaign/Trans People of Color Coalition publication, "A Time to Act: Fatal Violence Against Transgender People in America 2017" Human Rights Campaign, http://www.hrc.org. See also, "Dismantling A Culture of Violence—Understanding Anti-transgender Violence and Ending the Crisis," Human Rights Campaign website.

82 Brammer, J.P., "Billy Graham Leaves Painful Legacy for LGBTQ People," February 22, 2018, *NBCNews*, https://www.nbcnews.com/feature/nbc-out/billy-graham-leaves-painful-legacy-lgbtq-people-n850031.

83 https://tinyurl.com/rsksb3ep.

84 Foote, S., *The Civil War: A Narrative*. Volumes 1-3, New York, Random House 1974.

85 For a discussion about transgender or transsexualism and Christian biblical writings, and how they are interpreted today, see "What Does the Bible Say About Transgender People?" Human Rights Campaign, https://tinyurl.com/9j4dhzuv.

86 Declaration of the Global Interfaith Commission, https://globalinterfaith.lgbt/declaration/.

87 Other countries are also instituting bans on the practice, including Canada, see CNN, https://www.cnn.com/2021/12/09/americas/canada-conversion-therapy-ban/index.html.

88 The clinic was found to be in violation of state health regulations, https://tinyurl.com/4bkuv2sr. Another article by *ABC News*, also covered the practice methods in their clinic, https://tinyurl.com/uvprk364.

89 Southern Poverty Law Center, https://tinyurl.com/ahyjcp27.

90 www.scholar.google.com.

91 www.loc.gov.

92 www.nlm.nih.gov.

93 www.hih.gov.

94 www.archives.gov.

95 www.nap.edu.

96 www.lgbtmap.org.

97 www.wpath.org.

98 www.ama-assn.org.

99 www.psychiatry.org.

100 www.apa.org.

101 www.aafp.org.

102 www.aap.org.

103 www.facs.org.

104 www.acep.org.

105 www.socialworkers.org.

106 www.aclu.org.

107 www.transequality.org.

108 www.nclr.org.

109 www.endocrine.org.

[110] https://transequality.org/.

[111] https://www.hrc.org/.

[112] https://egale.ca/.

[113] https://pflag.org/.

[114] https://www.glaad.org/reference.

[115] https://qmunity.ca/resources/queer-glossary/.

[116] https://lgbta.fandom.com/wiki/Special:Search?query=LGBTA_Wiki.

[117] David, T., "Assumptions Made About Gender Roles," *Sociological Inquiry*, Vol. 45, Issue 2-3, April 1975. https://tinyurl.com/48fhyyf5.

[118] Saleem, F., and Rizvi, S. W., "Transgender Associations and Possible Etiology: A Literature Review," *Cureus*, 9(12), e1984, published online 2017, https://doi.org/10.7759/cureus.1984.

[119] Williams, C., "Tracking Transgender: The Historical Truth," 2012, first published in *Transgender Studies Quarterly* and *Present Tense* journals.

[120] Proceedings of the Second Interdisciplinary Symposium on Gender Dysphoria Syndrome, at pp. 7, 1972.

[121] *G.B. v. Lackner* (1978, 1st District) 145 Cal. Rptr. 555, 557; Levine, S.B., "Suicide by Transsexual (letter)" 13(3) *Archives of Sexual Behavior* 278-9 (6/1984); Huxley, P.J., Kenna, J.C., Brandon, S., "Partnership in Transsexualism, Pate 1: Paired and Non-Paired Groups," 10(2) *Archives of Sexual Behavior* 133-41 (4/1981); Danto, B.M., "Violent Sex and Suicide," 5(1-2) *Mental Health Soc.* 1-13 (1978); Herschkowitz, S., Dickes, R., "Suicide Attempts in a Female-to-Male Transsexual," *American Journal of Psychiatry*, 135: 368-9 (3/1978).

[122] Stryker, S., *Transgender History: The Roots of Today's Revolution*, 2nd Ed. 11/2017), Chapter 2, "A Hundred Plus Years of Transgender History," pp.45-77 Seal Press.

[123] Rosario, V.A., M.D., Ph.D. and Interviewer and Joanne Meyerowitz Ph.D. "Transforming Sex: An Interview with Joanne Meyerowitz, Ph.D., author of *How Sex Changed: A History of Transsexuality in the United States*," *Studies in Gender and Sexuality*, 5:4, 473-483, 2004. DOI: 10.1080/15240650509349260.

[124] Benjamin, H., and Ihlenfeld, C.L., "Transsexualism," *American Journal of Nursing* 73 :457-461, 3/1973.

[125] "It has frequently been said here that the term 'transsexualis" 'has come to encompass a variety of conditions that under other circumstances might be labelled extremely effeminate homosexuality, transvestism (particularly conscience-ridden transvestism), schizoid or borderline personality disorder, polymorphous perverse psychopathy, as well as individuals who apparently have manifested cross-gender drives—the classical 'transsexual.' Other types of patients occasionally found among applicants for sex reassignment are obsessional neurotics with profound masochistic trends, notoriety seekers, vocational motivated homosexual prostitutes, borderline patients, and the overtly psychotic," Meyer, J.K., "Some Thoughts on Nosology and Motivation Among Transsexuals," [125] *Proceedings of the Second Interdisciplinary Symposium on Gender Dysphoria Syndrome*, pp. 32, 1972.

[126] Frazier, S.H., and Carr, A.C., *An Introduction to Psychopathology*, New York. Jason Aronson, 1974.

[127] Note, *supra*, pp. 41.

[128] Dhejne, C., Vlerken, R.V., Heylens, G., and Arcelus, J. "Mental health and gender dysphoria: A review of the literature, *International Review of Psychiatry*," 28:1, 44-57, 2016, DOI: 10.3109/09540261.2015.1115753.

[129] See, e.g., Green, R., M.D., "Family Cooccurrence of "Gender Dysphoria": Ten Sibling or Parent-Child Pairs, *Archives of Sexual Behavior*. 29 (5), 2000; Pauly, I.B., M.D., "Outcome of Sex Reassignment Surgery for Transsexuals," *Australian and New Zealand Journal of Psychiatry*, 15:45-51, 1981; Bockting, W., M.D., "Developmental Stages of the Trans-gender Coming Out Process: Toward an Integrated Identity," in *Principles of Transgender Medicine and Surgery*, Chapter 9, Rutledge, 2013; Bockting, W, and Coleman, E., A Comprehensive Approach to the Treatment of Gender Dysphoria, Journal of Psychology and Human Sexuality, 5:4, 131-155, 1993, DOI: 10.1300/J056v05n04_08 ; Green, R., and Money, J., "Transsexualism and Sex Reassignment," *Journal of Plastic and Reconstructive Surgery*, 45(6): 604-605, 1970, https://journals.lww.com/plasreconsurg/Citation/1970/06000/Transsexualism_and_Sex_Reassignment.17.aspx.

[130] "While there are few people suffering with transsexualism, regular psychotherapy is not effective, and these patients are often hurt by other people," Hynie, J., Treatment of Transsexualism, Vol. 44, Abstract No. 16739:DIALOG 44-16739; *Smith v. Liberty Mutual Insurance Co.*, 569 F.Supp. 1098 (D.C. GA 1975), aff'd. *Smith v. Liberty Mut. Ins. Co.*, 569 F.2d 325 (5th Cir. 1978); *Grossman v. Bernards Township*, 316 A.2d 39 (1974), aff'd. 538 F.2d 319 (1975), cert den. 429 U.S. 181 (1976); *Voyles v. Ralph K. Davies Medical Center*, 403 F.Supp. 456 (N.D.Ca 1975), aff'd. w/o op. 570 F.2d 354 (9th Cir. 1977); *Powell v. Reeds*, 439 F.Supp. 369 (D.C. MD 1977) ; *Holloway v. Arthur Anderson and Co.*, 556 F.2d 659 (9th Cir. 1977); *Kirkpatrick v. Seligman Latz, Inc.*, 475 F.Supp. 145 (M.D. FL 1979); *Sommers v. Budget Marketing*, 667 F.2d 748 (8th Cir.

1980); *Sommers v. Iowa Civil Rights Commission*, 337 N.W.2d 470 (1983); *Ulane v. Eastern Airlines*, 581 F.Supp. 821 (N.D. IL 1983), rev'd. 742 F.2d 1081 (7th Cir. 1984); cert. den. 53 U.S.L.W. 3730 (4/16/1985), 105 S.Ct. 2023 (1985); Goerth, C.R., "Ulane Case Highlights Issues of Sex Discrimination Lawsuits," *Occupational Health and Safety*, 54-5, May 1984 (original references found in "Introduction to Gender Dysphoria Syndrome," Sister Mary Elizabeth, posted 1990, http://dallasdenny.com/Writing/2013/05/08/introduction-to-gender-dysphoria-syndrome-sister-mary-elizabeth-1990/).

[131] "There are few, if any, other attorneys in this community who would have undertaken this unusual representation," Supre, *supra*, "Few, if any, attorneys will accept transsexual cases," Letter from Paul Hoffman, Legal Director, ACLU Foundation of Southern California, dated March 1985.

[132] Green and Stoller, *supra*, Note 44. "The primary deterrent to physician involvement in the transsexual problem is a self-protective one, namely fear of censure and considerations regarding reputation," Hoopes, J.E., Knorr, N.J., and Wolf, S.R., "Transsexualism: Considerations Regarding Sexual Reassignment" 147(5) *Journal of. Nervous and Mental Disease* 147(5), 510-516, 1968; Baker and Green, *infra*, at Note 88-90.

[133] "Could not find the time and effort of such talented researchers be put to better use, to more legitimate challenges? If a glamourous challenge be insisted upon, we suggest that brain transplanting be preferred to castrating and altering sick males," Letter from Nicole J. Michaud Elliot Bold, G.F. Strong Laboratory for Medical Research to the Editor, *American Journal. of Obstetrics and Gynecology* 163, 9/1/1979.

[134] Benjamin, H., *supra*.

[135] Money, J., and Ehrhart, A., *Man and Woman, Boy and Girl*, Baltimore, Johns Hopkins University Press (1971); "From animal work it is evident that at least in some species there exists a period of behavioral sexual differentiation in response to male hormone exposure, well as a period of genital differentiation, and that these two critical time periods may be separate," Green, R., *Sexual Identity Conflict in Children and Adults* (1972) at 36. (Citing Wales, Peck, and LoPiccolo, 1966).

[136] Seyler, E.L., Canalis, E., Spare, S., et. Al., "Abnormal Gonadotropin secretory responses to LRH in Transsexual Women after Diethylstilbestrol Priming," *Journal of Endocrinological Metabolism,* 1978.

[137] See also, Foreman, M., Hare, L., York, K., Balakrishnan, K., Sánchez, F.J., Harte, F., Erasmus, J., Vilain, E., Harley, V.R., "Genetic Link Between Gender Dysphoria and Sex Hormone Signaling," *The Journal of Clinical Endocrinology and Metabolism*, 104 (2):390–396, February 2019, https://doi.org/10.1210/jc.2018-01105.

[138] Gooren, L., "The endocrinology of transsexualism: A review and commentary," *Psychoneuroendocrinology*, 15 (1): 3-14, 1990, ISSN 0306-4530, https://doi.org/10.1016/0306-4530(90)90041-7.

[139] Madeleine Foreman, Lauren Hare, Kate York, Kara Balakrishnan, Francisco J Sánchez, Fintan Harte, Jaco Erasmus, Eric Vilain, Vincent R Harley, "Genetic Link Between Gender Dysphoria and Sex Hormone Signaling," *Journal of Clinical Endocrinology and Metabolism,* 104(2):390–396, February 2019, https://doi.org/10.1210/jc.2018-01105.

[140] Ettner, R., Monstrey, S., and Coleman, E. (Eds.). (2007). *Principles of Transgender Medicine and Surgery* (1st ed.), Routledge, https://doi.org/10.4324/9780203822579. Chapter 1, "The Etiology of Transsexualism," written by Randi Ettner, at pp. 10.

[141] Tortora, G.J., and Anagnostakos, N.P., *Principles of Anatomy and Physiology*, 5th Ed. 1987; Chapter 28 "The Reproductive Systems," pp. 712. Harper and Row Publishers ISBN: 0-06-046669-3.

[142] *Principles of Anatomy and Physiology*, *supra*, pp. 722.

[143] See also, Finkelstein JS, Lee H, Burnett-Bowie SA, Pallais JC, Yu EW, Borges LF, Jones BF, Barry CV, Wulczyn KE, Thomas BJ, Leder BZ. "Gonadal steroids and body composition, strength, and sexual function in men," *New England Journal of Medicine*, 369(11):1011-22, September 12, 2013; DOI: 10.1056/NEJMoa1206168. PMID: 24024838; PMCID: PMC4142768 and De Cuypere G, T'Sjoen G, Beerten R, Selvaggi G, De Sutter P, Hoebeke P, Monstrey S, Vansteenwegen A, Rubens R., "Sexual and physical health after sex reassignment surgery," *Archives of Sexual Behavior*,34(6):679-90, December 2005, DOI: 10.1007/s10508-005-7926-5. PMID: 16362252.

[144] Hembree, W.C., Cohen-Kettenis, P.T., and Gooren. L., et al., "Endocrine Treatment of Gender -Dysphoric/Gender-Incongruent Persons: An Endocrine Society Clinical Practice Guideline,*" Journal of Clinical Endocrinology and Metabolism,* 102(11):3869-3903, November 2017, DOI:10.1210/jc.2017-01658.

[145] Frank P. M. Kruijver, Jiang-Ning Zhou, Chris W. Pool, Michel A. Hofman, Louis J. G. Gooren, Dick F. Swaab, "Male-to-Female Transsexuals Have Female Neuron Numbers in a Limbic Nucleus, "*Journal of Clinical Endocrinology and Metabolism*, 85(5):2034–2041, 1 May 2000, https://doi.org/10.1210/jcem.85.5.6564.

[146] Hoenig, J., Kenna, J.C., and Youd, A., "Surgical Treatment for Transsexualism," 47 *Acta Psy. Scandiaevics*, 106, 1971.

[147] "There are no mental or psychological tests which successfully differentiate the transsexual from the so-called normal population," *Proceedings of the Second Interdisciplinary Symposium on Gender Dysphoria Syndrome*, pp. 16, 1972.

[148] Gooren, L.J.G., and Bunck, M.C.M., "Transsexuals and Competitive Sports," *European Journal of Endocrinology* 151;425-429; 2004, ISSN 0804-4643.

[149] Harper, J., "Race Times for Transgender Athletes," *Journal of Sporting Cultures and Identities* 6(1):1-9, 2015, ISSN 2381-6678.

[150] Delemarre-van de Waal, H.A., and Cohen-Kettenis, P.T., "Clinical management of gender identity disorder in adolescents: A protocol on psychological and pediatric endocrinology aspects," *European Journal of Endocrinology* 155 S131–S137, 2006, ISSN 0804-4643.

[151] Moore, E., Wisniewski, A., and Dobs, A., "Endocrine Treatment of Transsexual People: A Review of Treatment Regimins, Outcomes and Adverse Effects," *Journal of Endocrinology and Metabolism* 88(8) 3467-3473, 8/2003, DOI: 10.1210/jc.2002-021967.

[152] Walter Meyer III M.D. (Chairperson), Walter O. Bockting Ph.D, Peggy Cohen-Kettenis Ph.D, Eli Coleman Ph.D., Domenico Diceglie M.D., Holly Devor Ph.D., Louis Gooren M.D., Ph.D., J. Joris Hage M.D., Sheila Kirk M.D., Bram Kuiper Ph.D., Donald Laub M.D., Anne Lawrence M.D., Yvon Menard M.D., Jude Patton PA-C, Leah Schaefer EdD, Alice Webb DHS and Connie Christine Wheeler Ph.D., "The Harry Benjamin International Gender Dysphoria Association's Standards of Care for Gender Identity Disorders," Sixth Version, *Journal of Psychology and Human Sexuality*, 13(1)1-30, 2002, DOI: 10.1300/J056v13n01_01.

[153] The Gender Dysphoria Program of Orange County, California, Inc., located in San Juan Capistrano, which closed in 2006, referred less than four percent of their applicants for sex reassignment surgery; ninety-six percent of the applicants made the decision not to have surgery, a clear indication of the value of private and group therapy to the decision-making process. Interview the Gender Dysphoria Program of Orange County director, William G. Heard Ph.D., "Surgery does not make a poor candidate for surgery into a good one; surgery should come at the end of the rehabilitative process," (Author's note: both Joanna Clark and Jude Patton were staff members of the program since its inception, until closing). Dushoff, I.M., "Economic, Psychologic and Social Rehabilitation of Male and Female Transsexuals Prior to Surgery," Proceedings of the Second Interdisciplinary Symposium on Gender Dysphoria Syndrome, pp. 199, 1972; Pauly, I., "Outcome of Sex Reassignment Surgery for Transsexuals, *Australian and New Zealand Journal of Psychiatry* 15(1):45-51, 1981.

[154] Coleman, E., Bockting, W, Botzer, M., et al., "Standards of Care for the Health of Transsexual, Transgender, and Gender-Nonconforming People," World Professional Association for Transgender Health (WPATH), 7th version, published in the *Journal of Transgenderism* 13(4):165-232, 2012, DOI: 10.1080/15532739.2011.700873.

[155] Selvaggi,G.,1 Dhejne, C.,2 Landen, M.,3 and Elander, A.1 (1 Department of Plastic and Reconstructive Surgery, Sahlgrenska University Hospital, SE-41345 Gothenburg, Sweden; 2 Division of Psychiatry, Department of Clinical Neuroscience, Karolinska University Hospital Huddinge, SE 14186 Stockholm, Sweden; 3 Institute of Neuroscience and Physiology, Sahlgrenska University Hospital, Gothenburg, Sweden). Hindawi Publishing Corporation (3/2012); *Advances in Urology*, Volume 2012, Article ID 581712,13 pages. DOI:10.1155/2012/581712.

[156] Fisk, 1974; Knudson, De Cuypere, and Bockting, 2010b, SOC, pp. 2.

[157] WPATH Standards of Care, Chapter VI, pp.10-11.

[158] WPATH Standards of Care, Chapter VI, pp. 11.

[159] MONEY J, HAMPSON JG, HAMPSON JL. Imprinting and the Establishment of Gender Role. *AMA Archives of Neurology and Psychiatry*. 1957;77(3):333–336, DOI:10.1001/archneurpsyc.1957.02330330119019.

[160] Tyson P. A Developmental Line of Gender Identity, Gender Role, and Choice of Love Object, *Journal of the American Psychoanalytic Association*, 30(1):61-86, 1982, DOI:10.1177/000306518203000103.

[161] Kleeman, J.A. "The establishment of core gender identity in normal girls,". I.(a) introduction; (b) development of the ego capacity to differentiate, *Archives of Sexual Behavior* 1:103–116, 1971, https://doi.org/10.1007/BF01541055.

[162] Barlow, D.H., Abel, G.G., Blandchard, E.B., "Gender Identity Change in A Transsexual: An Exorcism," *Archives of Sexual Behavior,* 6(5):387-95, 9/1977.

[163] Money, J., and Ehrhart, A., *supra*, "Man and Woman, Boy and Girl," Baltimore, Johns Hopkins University Press, 1971.

[164] Any discussion of the treatment of transsexualism and the current status of the change of sex operation must begin with one simple fact. Psychotherapy has not proved helpful in allowing the transsexual to accept that gender identity which is consistent with his genital anatomy," Pauly, I., "The Current Status of the Change of Sex Operation," *Journal of Nervous and Mental Disease,* 147, 460, 465, 1968, (citing 19 sources for the statement); This conclusion was recently confirmed by two psychiatrists who suggest, however, that conscientious psychotherapy may benefit the gender dysphoric who is *not a true* transsexual. Kirkpatrick and Friedman, "Treatment of requests for sex change surgery With Psychotherapy," *American Journal of Psychiatry* 133:1194, 1976.

[165] Wein and Remmers, "Employment Protection and Gender Dysphoria Syndrome," *Hastings Law Journal*, 30(4):1075, note 8, pp. 1077, 1977, *citing* Laub. D., Fisk, N., "A Rehabilitation Program for Gender Dysphoria Syndrome by Surgical Sex

Change," *Plastic and Reconstructive Surgery* 53:388-403, 1974, see also, Money and Schwartz, "Public Opinion and Social Issues in Transsexualism: A Case Study in Medical Sociology," in Green and Money, *Transsexualism and Sex Reassignment*, Baltimore, Johns Hopkins University Press, 1969.

[166] It is doubtful if "cure" is an appropriate word, as there are few references to the word "cure" in the literature. Benjamin's comment, "Sex Change Surgery: The Great Debate," *Sexual Medicine Today* 3(11):18-19, 11/1979, is most descriptive and on point, i.e., "Surgery is Not a Cure for Transsexualism. But no one ever claimed that it was, any more than insulin is a cure for diabetes. What both accomplish is the preservation of the life of the patient. Otherwise, many of the people would commit suicide."

[167] Wein and Remmers, *supra*, Note 67, pp. 1078-9 and nn. 16-19.

[168] Edgerton, M.T., "The Surgical Treatment of Male Transsexuals," *Clinics in Plastic Surgery* 1(2):285, 315, 4/1974.

[169] "Clearly impossible to conclude that transsexual [is] cosmetic surgery, even using the definition relied upon by the director," *G.B. v. Lackner*, 1978, 1st District) 145 Cal. Rptr. 555, 557; 80 Cal.App.3d 64, "As we stated in *G.B. v. Lackner*, we do not believe, in the wildest imagination, that such surgery can reasonably and logically be characterized as cosmetic," *J.D. v. Lackner*, (CA 1st Dist. 1978), 80 Cal.App.3d 90. 95, 145 Cal.Rptr. 570, 572; "radical sex conversion surgery is the only medical treatment available to relieve or solve the problems of a <u>true</u> transsexual," *Pineke v. Prisser*, 623 F.2d 546, 548 (8th Cir. 1980); "Cosmetic surgery is surgery which is deemed optional or elective… The surgery which is lengthy, requires extensive modifications and realignment of the human body. It is requested rarely and done even more infrequently. It is performed to correct a psychological defect and not to improve muscle tone or physical appearance… While many seem appalled by such surgery, it nevertheless has demonstrated proven benefits for its recipients although psychological in nature… From all the above the court concludes that the treatment and surgery involved in the sex change operation is of a medical nature and is feasible and required for the health and well-being of the plaintiff," *Victoria L. Davidson v. Aetna Life and Casualty Ins. Co.* 101 Misc.2d 1, 420 N.Y.S.2d 450 (Sup. Ct. 1979).

[170] Human Rights Campaign (HRC), https://www.hrc.org/resources/the-lies-and-dangers-of-reparative-therapy.

[171] See also, https://www.apa.org/about/policy/sexual-orientation. "Resolution on Appropriate Affirmative Responses to Sexual Orientation Distress and Change Efforts."

[172] *APsaA Position Statement*, https://apsa.org/content/2012-position-statement-attempts-change-sexual-orientation-gender-identity-or-gender, June 2012.

[173] American Medical Association position statement, https://www.ama-assn.org/system/files/2019-12/conversion-therapy-issue-brief.pdf.

[174] Tim Alger, "Adoption Case Raises Issue of Transsexuals Legal Rights," *Orange County Register*, 84, February 2, 1983.

[175] https://tinyurl.com/25dae3zt, International Journal of Transgenderism, 4(1), January-March 2000, the International Journal of Transgenderism is published by WPATH.

[176] Almazan, A.N., B.A., and Keuroghlian, A.S., M.D., MPH, "Association Between Gender-Affirming Surgeries and Mental Health Outcomes," *American Medical Association Journal of Surgery (JAMA Surgery)*, E1-E8, April 28, 2021, DOI:10.1001/jamasurg.2021.0952.

[177] Heylens, G., M.D., Verroken, C., De Cock, S., T'Sjoen, G., M.D., Ph.D., and De Guypere, M.D., Ph.D.., "Effects of Different Steps in Gender Reassignment Therapy on Psychopathology: A Prospective Study of Persons with a Gender Identity Disorder," *Journal of Sexual Medicine*, 11:119-126, 2014); DOI:10.1111/jsm.12363.

[178] Verbeek, M.J.A., Hommes, M.A., Stutterheim, S.E., et. al., "Experiences with stigmatization among transgender individuals after transition: A qualitative study in the Netherlands," *International Journal of Transgender Health*, 21(2):220-233, 2020.

[179] https://en.wikipedia.org/wiki/Social_stigma. "Social stigma is the disapproval of, or discrimination against, a person based on perceivable social characteristics that serve to distinguish them from other members of a society. Social stigmas are commonly related to culture, gender, race, age, sexual orientation, intelligence, and health. Stigma can also be against oneself, stemming from a negatively viewed personal attribute that results in a "spoiled identity" (i.e., self-stigma.)."

[180] Mueller, S.C., Ph.D.., Guypere, G.D., M.D., Ph.D.., and T'Sjoen, G.T., M.D., "Transgender Research in the 21st Century: A Selective Critical Review From a Neurocognitive Perspective," *American Journal of Psychiatry* 174(12): 1155-1162, December 2017.

[181] Hughto, J.M.W., MPH, Reisner, S.L., ScD, and Pachankis, J.E., Ph.D., "Transgender Stigmas and Health: A Critical Review of Stigma Determinants, Mechanisms, and Interventions," Social Science and Medicine 147:222–231, 12/2015, , https://doi.org/10.1016/j.socscimed.2015.11.010.

[182] https://www.psychiatry.org/patients-families/stigma-and-discrimination.

[183] Cannon, Y., Speedlin, S., Avera, J., Robertson, D., Ingram, M., and Prado, A., "Transition, Connection, Disconnection, and Social Media: Examining the Digital Lived Experiences of Transgender Individuals," *Journal of LGBT Issues in Counseling* 11(2):68-872017, https://tinyurl.com/55c3zneu.

[184] Singh, A.A., Hays, D.G., and Watson, L.S., "Strength in the face of Adversity: Resilience Strategies of Transgender Individuals," *Journal of Counseling and Development* 80:20-28, Winter 2011.

[185] Claman, E.E. (2007) "An Examination of the Predictors of Attitudes Toward Transgender Individuals," Doctoral Dissertation, Ohio State University, Columbus, OH USA, https://tinyurl.com/y3smphjr.

[186] Budge, S.L., Tebbe, E.N., and Howard, K.A.S., "The Work Experiences of Transgender individuals: Negotiating the Transition and Career Decision-Making Processes," *Journal of Counseling Psychology*, pp. 1-17, 2010.

[187] Su, D., Irwin, J.A., Fisher, C., Ramos, A., Kelley, M., Mendoza, D.A.R., and Coleman, J.D., Su, D., Irwin, J.A., Fisher, C., Ramos, A., Kelley, M., Mendoza, D.A.R., and Coleman, J.D., "Mental Health Disparities Within the LGBT Population: A Comparison Between Transgender and Nontransgender Individuals," *Transgender Health*, 1(1):12-24, 2016, DOI:10.1089/trgh.2015.0001.

[188] Simbar, M., Nazarpour, S., Mirzababaie, M., Ali Emam Hadi, M., Tehrani, F.R., and Majd, H.A., "Quality of life and Body Image of individuals with Gender Dysphoria," *Journal of Sex and Marital Therapy* 0(0):1-10, 2018, DOI:10.1080/0092623X.2017.1419392.

[189] [12] and [14], shown here respectively, Colozzi, M., Costa, R., Todarello, O., "Transsexual patients' psychiatric comorbidity and positive effect of cross-sex hormonal treatment on mental health; results from a longitudinal study," *Psychoneuroendocrinology* 39:65-73, 2014; Heylens, G., M.D., Verroken, C., De Cock, S., T'Sjoen, G., M.D., Ph.D.., and De Guypere, M.D., Ph.D.., "Effects of Different Steps in Gender Reassignment Therapy on Psychopathology: A Prospective Study of Persons with a Gender Identity Disorder," *Journal of Sexual Medicine* 11:119-126, 2014; DOI:10.1111/jsm.12363.

[190] Barbir, L.A., MS, Vandervender, A.W., MS, and Cohn, T.J., Ph.D.., "Friendship, attitudes, and behavioral intentions of cisgender heterosexuals toward transgender individuals," *Journal of Gay and Lesbian Mental Health*, pp. 2-17; 2016, DOI:10.1080/19359705.2016.1273157.

[191] *Id.*, pp. 13.

[192] Smith, E.S., Junger, J., Derntl, B., Habel, U., "The transsexual brain—A Review of findings on the neural basis of transsexualism," *Neuroscience and Biobehavioral Reviews* 29:251-266, 2015.

[193] Frigerio, A., Ballerini, L. and Valdés Hernández, M. "Structural, Functional, and Metabolic Brain Differences as a Function of Gender Identity or Sexual Orientation: A Systematic Review of the Human Neuroimaging Literature," *Archives of Sexual Behavior*, 2021, DOI: 10.1007/s10508-021-02005-9.

[194] A. Manzouri, K. Kosidou, I. Savic, "Anatomical and Functional Findings in Female-to-Male Transsexuals: Testing a New Hypothesis," *Cerebral Cortex* 27(2):998–1010, February 2017, https://doi.org/10.1093/cercor/bhv278.

[195] Mueller S, C, Landré L, Wierckx K, T'Sjoen G: "A Structural Magnetic Resonance Imaging Study in Transgender Persons on Cross-Sex Hormone Therapy," *Neuroendocrinology* 105:123-130, 2017; DOI: 10.1159/000448787.

[196] Guillamon, A., Junque, C., and Gómez-Gil, E. (2016). A Review of the Status of Brain Structure Research in Transsexualism, *Archives of sexual behavior*, 45(7), 1615–1648. DOI.org/10.1007/s10508-016-0768-5.

[197] Fernandez, R., Ph.D. (Departamento de Psicología. Área Psicobiología; Universidad de A Coruña, A Coruña, Spain), Estevia, I., M.D. (Unidad de Transexualidad e Identidad de Género, Hospital Carlos Haya, Málaga, Spain), Gomez-Gill, E., M.D. (Unidad de Identidad de Género, Hospital Clinic, Barcelona, Spain), Rumbo, T., Ph.D. (Departamento de Psicología. Área Psicobiología; Universidad de A Coruña, A Coruña, Spain), Almaraz, M.C., Ph.D. Unidad de Identidad de Género, Hospital Clinic, Barcelona, Spain), Roda, E., Ph.D. (Unidad de Identidad de Género, Hospital Clinic, Barcelona, Spain), Haro-Mora, J.J., Ph.D. (Unidad de Transexualidad e Identidad de Género, Hospital Carlos Haya, Málaga, Spain), Guillamón, A., M.D. (Departamento de Psicobiología, UNED, Madrid, Spain), and Pásaro, E., Ph.D. (Departamento de Psicología. Área Psicobiología; Universidad de A Coruña, A Coruña, Spain), "The Genetics of Transsexualism," *Gender Identity*, Miller, B.L. (ed), Ch. 6, 122-143; Nova Science Publishers, 2014.

[198] Garcia-Falgueras, A., and Swaab, D.E., "A sex difference in the hypothalamic uncinate nucleus: relationship to gender identity," *Brain* 131:3132-3146, 2008, Oxford University Press, DOI:10.1093/brain/awn276.

[199] Swaab, D.F., "Sexual differentiation of the human brain: relevance for gender identity, transsexualism and sexual orientation," *Gynecological Endocrinology* 19:301-312, 2004, Pantheon Publishing. DOI:10.1080/09514590400018231.

[200] Gooren, L.J.G., and Bunck, M.C.M., "Transsexuals and Competitive Sports," *European Journal of Endocrinology* 151:425–429, 2004, in particular pp. 428, ISSN 0804-4643.

[201] Gottlieb, B., Ph.D. and Trifiro, M.A., M.D., "Androgen Insensitivity Syndrome," March 24, 1999 [Updated May 11, 2017]. in Adam MP, Ardinger HH, Pagon, RA, et al. (eds) *GeneReviews®* [Internet]. Seattle (WA): University of Washington, Seattle; 1993-2021.

[202] For more information see the article on DSD, https://my.clevelandclinic.org/health/diseases/16324-disorders-of-sex-differentiation.

[203] https://www.nature.com/scitable/definition/allele-48/.

[204] Rametti, G., Carrillo, B., Gómez-Gil, E., Elorza, C.J.L.C., Segovia, S., Gomez, A., Guillamon, A., "The microstructure of white matter in male to female transsexuals before cross-sex hormonal treatment. A DTI study," *Journal of Psychiatric Research* 45(7):949-954, 2011, ISSN 0022-3956, https://doi.org/10.1016/j.jpsychires.2010.11.007. *"Our results show that the white matter microstructure pattern in untreated MtF transsexuals falls halfway between the pattern of male and female controls. The nature of these differences suggests that some fasciculi do not complete the masculinization process in MtF transsexuals during brain development."*

[205] European Society of Endocrinology. "Transgender brains are more like their desired gender from an early age," *ScienceDaily,* 24 May 2018, www.sciencedaily.com/releases/2018/05/180524112351.htm.

[206] Hulshoff Pol, H.E., Cohen-Kettenis, P.T., Van Haren, N.E.M., Peper, J.S., Brans, R.G.H., Cahn, W., Schnack, H.G., Gooren, L.J.G., and Kahn, R.S., "Changing your sex changes your brain: influences of testosterone and estrogen on adult human brain structure," *European Journal of Endocrinology* 155 S107-S114, 2006, DOI:10.1530/eje.1.02248.

[207] Fuss, J., Hellweg, R., Van Caenegem, E., Briken, P., Stalla, G.K., T'Sjoen, G., and Auer, M., "Cross-sex hormone treatment in male-to-female transsexual persons reduces serum brain-derived neurotropic factor (BDNF)," *European neuropsychopharmacology* 25:95-99; 2015, DOI: 10.1016/j.euroneuro.2014.11.019.

[208] WPATH SOC, pp. 37-38.

[209] Shumer, D., M.D., MPH, Nokoff, N.J., M.D., and Spack, N.P., M.D., "Advances in the Care of Transgender Children and Adolescents," *Advances in Pediatrics* 63(1):79-102, 2016, DOI: 10.1016/j.yapd.2016.04.018.

[210] Green, R., M.D., "Family Cooccurrence of 'Gender Dysphoria': Ten Sibling or Parent-Child Pairs [1]," Questia.com/PM.qst?action=print&docId=5001086072.

[211] Green, R., "'Spelling "Relief" for Transsexuals: Employment Discrimination and the Criteria of Sex," *Yale Law and Policy Review,* 4:125, 1985.

[212] Lucas-Carr, C.B., and Krane, V., "What is the T in LGBT? Supporting Transgender Athletes Through Sport Psychology," *The Sport Psychologist* 25:532-548, 2011.

[213] Beemyn, B., "Serving the Needs of Transgender College Students," *Journal of Gay and Lesbian Issues in Education*, Fall 2003.

[214] Beemyn, above, pp. 2.

[215] https://www.plannedparenthood.org/learn/gender-identity/sex-gender-identity.

[216] Jones, B.A., Arcelus, J., Bouman, W.P., and Haycraft, E., "Sport and Transgender People: A Systematic Review of The Literature Relating to Sport Participation and Competitive Sport Policies," *Sports Medicine* 47:701–716, 2017, DOI 10.1007/s40279-016-0621-y.

[217] Gooren, L., "The Significance of Testosterone for Fair Participation of the Female Sex in Competitive Sports," *Asian Journal of Andrology* 13:653–654, 2011, DOI:10.1038/aja.2011.9.

[218] Pitsilsadis, Y., MMedSci, Ph.D., FACSM; Harper, J., M.S.; Betancurt, J.O., et al., "Beyond Fairness: The biology of Inclusion for Transgender and Intersex Athletes," *American College of Sports Medicine* 15(6):386-388, November/December 2016.

[219] https://tinyurl.com/2ww3v9nx.

[220] Cornell University Public Policy Research Portal, "What does the Scholarly research say about the effect of gender transition on transgender well-being," https://tinyurl.com/2ww3v9nx.

[221] *Diagnostic and Statistical Manual of Mental Disorders* (DSM-5), Fifth edition, American Psychiatric Association, 2013, https://www.psychiatry.org/psychiatrists/practice/dsm.

[222] The American Psychiatric Association, https://tinyurl.com/ht2ycnjn.

[223] See the following references from the APA website:

> The American Academy of Child and Adolescent Psychiatry, "Conversion Therapy," 2018, https://www.aacap.org/AACAP/Policy_Statements/ 2018/Conversion_Therapy.aspx. Accessed November 7, 2020.

Turban, J. L., Beckwith, N., Reisner, S. L., and Keuroghlian, A. S., "Association between recalled exposure to gender identity conversion efforts and psychological distress and suicide attempts among transgender adults," *JAMA Psychiatry*, 77(1), 68-76, 2020, https://pubmed.ncbi.nlm.nih.gov/31509158/. .

Durwood, L., McLaughlin, K. A., and Olson, K. R. (2017), "Mental health and self-worth in socially transitioned transgender youth," *Journal of the American Academy of Child and Adolescent Psychiatry*, 56(2):116-123, https://www.ncbi.nlm.nih.gov/pmc/articles/PMC5302003/.

Olson, K. R., Durwood, L., DeMeules, M., and McLaughlin, K. A., "Mental health of transgender children who are supported in their identities," *Pediatrics*, 137(3), 2016, https://publications.aap.org/pediatrics/article-abstract/137/3/e20153223/81409/Mental-Health-of-Transgender-Children-Who-Are?redirectedFrom=fulltext.

Scheim, A. I., Perez-Brumer, A. G., and Bauer, G. R., "Gender-concordant identity documents and mental health among transgender adults in the USA: a cross-sectional study," *The Lancet Public Health,* 5(4):E196-E203, 2020,. https://www.thelancet.com/journals/lancet/article/PIIS2468-2667(20)30032-3/fulltext.

Hembree, W. C., Cohen-Kettenis, P. T., Gooren, L., Hannema, S. E., Meyer, W. J., Murad, M. H., Rosenthal, S.M., Safer, J.D., Tangpricha, V., T'Sjoen, G.G., "Endocrine treatment of gender-dysphoric/gender-incongruent persons: an endocrine society clinical practice guideline," *The Journal of Clinical Endocrinology and Metabolism*, 102(11), 3869-3903, 2017, https://academic.oup.com/jcem/article/102/11/3869/4157558.

Coleman, E., Bockting, W., Botzer, M., Cohen-Kettenis, P., DeCuypere, G., Feldman, J., Fraser, L., Green, J., Knudson, G., Meyer, W. J., Monstrey, S., Adler, R.K., Brown, G.R., Devor, A.H., Ehrbar, R., Ettner, R., Eyler, E., Garofalo R., Karasic, D.H., Lev, A.E., Mayer, G., Meyer-Bahlburg, H., Hall, B.P., Pfaefflin, F., Rachlin, K., Robinson, B. Schechter, L.S., Tangpricha, V., van Trotsenburg, M., Vitale, A., Winter, S., Whittle, S., Whylie, K.R., Zucker, K., "Standards of care for the health of transsexual, transgender, and gender-nonconforming people, version 7," *International Journal of Transgenderism*, 13(4), 165-232, 2012, https://www.tandfonline.com/doi/abs/10.1080/15532739.2011.700873.

Klein, A., and Golub, S. A., "Family rejection as a predictor of suicide attempts and substance misuse among transgender and gender nonconforming adults," *LGBT health*, 3(3), 193-199, 2016, https://www.liebertpub.com/doi/abs/10.1089/lgbt.2015.0111?journalCode=lgbt.

Reisner, S. L., Poteat, T., Keatley, J., Cabral, M., Mothopeng, T., Dunham, E., Holland, C. E., Ryan, M, Baral, S. D., "Global health burden and needs of transgender populations: a review," *The Lancet*, 388(10042), 412-436, 2016, https://www.thelancet.com/journals/lancet/article/PIIS0140-6736(16)00684-X/fulltext. .

James, S., Herman, J., Rankin, S., Keisling, M., Mottet, L., and Anafi, M. A. (2016). "The Report of the 2015 US Transgender Survey," http://www.ustranssurvey.org/reports, accessed November 7, 2020.

Perzanowski, E. S., Ferraiolo, T., and Keuroghlian, A. S., "Overview and Terminology." in Forcier, M., VanSchalkwyk, G., and Turban, J.L. (eds.), *Pediatric Gender Identity: Gender-affirming Care for Transgender and Gender Diverse Youth,* Springer Nature, (pp. 1-13). 2020.

[224] Zucker, K.J., "Gender Dysphoria," in *Handbook of Developmental Psychopathology*: Third Edition, pp:683-702, 2014/03/03, DOI:10.1007/978-1-4614-9608-3_35.

[225] Byne, W., Bradley, S.J., Coleman, E., Eyler, A.E., Green, R., Menvielle, E.J., Meyer-Bahlburg, H.F.L., Pleak, R.,R., and Tompkins, D.A., "Report of the American Psychiatric Association Task Force on Treatment of Gender Identity Disorder," *Archives of Sexual Behavior,* 41:759-796, 2012, DOI:10.1007/s10508-012-9975-x. Youth and Adolescent treatment recommendations are also included in the report.

[226] "Guidelines for Psychological Practice with Transgender and Gender Nonconforming People," American Psychological Association, *American Psychologist* 70(9):832-864, 2015, DOI:10.1037/a0039906.

[227] James, S.E., Herman, J.L., et. Al., "Executive Summary of the Report of the 2015 U.S. Transgender Survey," Washington, D.C., National Center for Transgender Equality, 2015, www.ustransgendersurvey.org.

[228] "U.S. Transgender Survey," Executive Summary, pp. 2.

[229] Galupo, M.P., Pulice-Farrow, L., and Kindley, L., "Understanding the social context for gender dysphoria," *Stigma and Health* 5(2):10, 2019, DOI:10.1037/sah0000189.

[230] Galupo, M.P., Pulice-Farrow, L., and Kindley, L., "Understanding the social context for gender dysphoria," *Stigma and Health* 5(2):11, 2019, DOI:10.1037/sah0000189.

[231] WPATH Standards of Care, Version 7, pp. 23-2, 2012, https://www.wpath.org/publications/soc.

[232] Haldeman, D. C., "Gay Rights, Patient Rights: The Implications of Sexual Orientation Conversion Therapy" (PDF), *Professional Psychology: Research and Practice,* 33(3):260–264, June 2002, DOI: 10.1037/0735-7028.33.3.260.

[233] See the Legal section that follows for more information.

[234] The full statement on the American Psychiatric Association, https://tinyurl.com/9uh8686b.

[235] www.thetrevorproject.org.

[236] The Trevor Project, "About Conversion Therapy," www.thetrevorproject.org.

[237] See https://globalinterfaith.lgbt/ for more information on signatories.

See also, https://www.nytimes.com/2020/12/16/world/conversion-therapy-pledge.html for their coverage on the declaration.

[238] Greenwald, A.G., and Banaji, M. R., "Implicit social cognition: Attitudes, self-esteem, and stereotypes," *Psychological Review*, 102(1): 4-27, Jan 1995.

[239] Stanford University, Stanford Encyclopedia of Philosophy, https://plato.stanford.edu/entries/implicit-bias/.

[240] Von der Malsburg, T., Poppels, T., and Levy, R.P., "Implicit Gender Bias in Linguistic Descriptions for Expected Events: The cases of the 2016 United States and 2017 United Kingdom Elections," *Psychological Science*, 31(2):115 -128, 2020.

[241] Amodio D, Ratner K. "A memory systems model of implicit social cognition," *Current Directions in Psychological Science* 20(3):143-14, 2011; Smith ER, DeCoster J. "Dual-process models in social and cognitive psychology: conceptual integration and links to underlying memory systems," *Personality and Social Psychological Review* 4(2):108-131; 2000; and Bobula KA. "This is your brain on bias (or the neuroscience of bias)," Faculty lecture series presented at: Clark College; May 3, 2011; Vancouver, Washington. Developing brains: ideas for parenting and education from the new brain science. http://www.developingbrains.org, accessed September 19, 2012, Georgetown University, National Center for Cultural Competence, Conscious and Unconscious Biases in Health Care, Module 3 Bias and Well-Meaning People, "Two Types of Biases," https://nccc.georgetown.edu/bias/module-3/1.php.

[242] See, for example, "Understanding Bias: A Resource Guide," United States Department of Justice, Community Relations Service, https://www.justice.gov/crs/file/836431/download.

[243] Merriam-Webster Dictionary online, https://www.merriam-webster.com/dictionary/stereotype.

[244] NBC News reporting a story by the Associated Press, "First openly transgender Olympians are competing in Tokyo, July 25, 2021, https://www.nbcnews.com/nbc-out/out-news/first-openly-transgender-olympians-are-competing-tokyo-rcna1507.

[245] IAAF Medical Manual, Chapter 13, Special Issues of Female Athletes, Part 2, https://www.worldathletics.org/about-iaaf/documents/health-science. It should be noted that the IAAF, the International Association of Athletics Federations, changed its name to World Athletics in 2019. Any reference to the IAAF should be treated as World Athletics.

[246] Jones, B.A., Arcelus, J., Bouman, W.P., and Haycraft, E. "Sport and Transgender People: A Systematic Review of the Literature Relating to Sport Participation and Competitive Sport Policies. *Sports Medicine* 47:701-716, 2017, DOI: 10.1007/s40279-016-0621-y.

[247] Jones, at al., *supra*, pp. 701.

[248] "IAAF Publishes briefing notes on Q&A on female eligibility regulations," World Athletics, https://www.worldathletics.org/news/press-release/questions-answers-iaaf-female-eligibility-reg.

[249] ELIGIBILITY REGULATIONS FOR THE FEMALE CLASSIFICATION (ATHLETES WITH DIFFERENCES OF SEX DEVELOPMENT) EXPLANATORY NOTES/Q&A (All Caps in original), available in the Health and Science Documents Section, under "Eligibility for the Female Classification—Related Documents, https://www.worldathletics.org/about-iaaf/documents/health-science.

[250] Bermon, S., Garnier, P.Y., and Hirschberg, A.L., Robinson, N., Giraud, S., Nicoli, R., Baume, N., Saugy, M. Fenichel, P., Bruce, S. J., Henry, H., Dolte, G., Ritzen, M., "Serum Androgen Levels in Elite Female Athletes," *Journal of Clinical Metabolism*, 99(11):4328-4335, specifically pp. 4332, November 2014.

[251] Bermon, et al., *supra*, pp. 4331.

[252] Jones, et al., *supra*, pp. 706.

[253] Entries are transcribed from the website as they were available at the time of publication, https://tinyurl.com/4fcmrbvt

[254] https://www.law.cornell.edu/constitution/amendmentxiv.

[255] Grant, J.M., Ph.D., Mottet, L.A., J.D., and Tanis, J., D.Minn., et al., "Injustice at Every Turn: A Report of the National Transgender Discrimination Survey," Washington: National Center for Transgender Equality, the National Gay and Lesbian Task Force, 2011, https://transequality.org/sites/default/files/docs/resources/NTDS_Report.pdf..

[256] Grant et al., *supra*, pp. 3-6

[257] Title VII of the Civil Rights Act of 1964, as amended; (Pub. L. 88-352) (42 U.S.C. §2000e, Et. Seq.). Title VII prohibits employment discrimination based on race, color, religion, sex and national origin. The Civil Rights Act of 1991 (Pub. L. 102-166) (CRA) and the Lily Ledbetter Fair Pay Act of 2009 (Pub. L. 111-2) amend several sections of Title VII. In addition, section 102 of the CRA amends the Revised Statutes by adding a new section following section 1977 (42 U.S.C. 1981), to provide for the recovery of compensatory and punitive damages in cases of intentional violations of Title VII, the Americans with Disabilities Act of 1990, and section 501 of the Rehabilitation Act of 1973.

[258] *Obergefell, et al. v. Hodges, Director, Ohio Department of Health, et al.*, 772 F. 3d 388, reversed, 576 U.S. 6, 135 S. Ct. 2584 (2015).

[259] *Obergefell, supra*, pp. 3–10.

[260] *Obergefell, supra*, pp. 3–6.

[261] *Obergefell, supra*, pp. 6–10.

[262] *Obergefell, supra*, pp. 10–27.

[263] *Obergefell, supra*, pp. 10–12.

[264] *Obergefell, supra*, pp. 12–18.

[265] *Obergefell, supra*, pp. 18–22.

[266] *Obergefell, supra*, pp. 22–23.

[267] *Obergefell, supra*, pp. 23–27.

[268] *Bostock v. Clayton County, GA*, 590 U.S. ____ (2020) No. 17–1618. Argued October 8, 2019—Decided June 15, 2020. Slip Opinion, pp. 1-4

[269] *Bostock, supra*, pp. 4–33.

[270] *Bostock, supra*, pp.4–12.

[271] *Bostock, supra*, pp. 4–9.

[272] *Bostock, supra*, pp. 9–12."

[273] *Price Waterhouse v. Hopkins*, 490 U.S. 228 Section IIC) (1989).

[274] See https://www.eeoc.gov/prohibited-employment-policiespractices on the EEOC's "Prohibited Employment Policies/Practices,"

[275] EEOC, https://www.eeoc.gov/prohibited-employment-policiespractices, https://www.eeoc.gov/filing-charge-discrimination.

[276] The Office of Civil Rights is responsible for ensuring public transit providers comply with all nondiscrimination requirements. The office oversees the implementation of laws and regulations that prohibit discrimination on the basis of race, color, national origin, religion, sex, disability, and age in the provision of services to the public. The office provides technical assistance and training and conducts complaint investigations and onsite compliance reviews to ensure public transit providers fulfill civil rights requirements. Major programs the office implements include:
Title VI of the Civil Rights Act of 1964
Americans with Disabilities Act of 1990
Disadvantaged Business Enterprise program
Equal Employment Opportunity program

For more information, https://www.transit.dot.gov/regulations-and-guidance/civil-rights-ada/civil-rightsada.

[277] Patient Protection and Affordable Care Act (42 USC 18116), Section 1557.

On June 15, 2020, the U.S. Supreme Court held that Title VII of the Civil Rights Act of 1964 (Title VII)'s prohibition on employment discrimination based on sex encompasses discrimination based on sexual orientation and gender identity. *Bostock v. Clayton County, GA*, 140 S. Ct. 1731 (2020). The *Bostock* majority concluded that the plain meaning of "because of sex" in Title VII necessarily included discrimination because of sexual orientation and gender identity. *Id.* at 1753-54.

Since *Bostock*, two federal circuits have concluded that the plain language of Title IX of the Education Amendments of 1972's (Title IX) prohibition on sex discrimination must be read similarly. *See Grimm v. Gloucester Cnty. Sch. Bd.*, 972 F.3d 586, 616 (4th Cir. 2020), *as amended* (Aug. 28, 2020), *reh'g en banc denied*, 976 F.3d 399 (4th Cir. 2020), *petition for cert. filed*, No. 20-1163 (Feb. 24, 2021); *Adams v. Sch. Bd. of St. Johns Cnty.*, 968 F.3d 1286, 1305 (11th Cir. 2020), *petition for reh'g en banc pending*, No. 18-13592 (Aug. 28, 2020). In addition, on March 26, 2021, the Civil Rights Division of the U.S. Department of Justice issued a memorandum to Federal Agency Civil Rights Directors and General Counsel concluding that the Supreme Court's reasoning in *Bostock* applies to Title IX of the Education Amendments of

1972. As made clear by the Affordable Care Act, Section 1557 prohibits discrimination "on the grounds prohibited under...Title IX," 42 U.S.C. § 18116(a).

Consistent with the Supreme Court's decision in *Bostock* and Title IX, beginning May 10, 2021, OCR will interpret and enforce Section 1557's prohibition on discrimination on the basis of sex to include: (1) discrimination on the basis of sexual orientation; and (2) discrimination on the basis of gender identity. This interpretation will guide OCR in processing complaints and conducting investigations but does not itself determine the outcome in any particular case or set of facts.

In enforcing Section 1557, as stated above, OCR will comply with the Religious Freedom Restoration Act, 42 U.S.C. § 2000bb et seq., and all other legal requirements. Additionally, OCR will comply with all applicable court orders that have been issued in litigation involving the Section 1557 regulations, including *Franciscan Alliance, Inc. v. Azar*, 414 F. Supp. 3d 928 (N.D. Tex. 2019); *Whitman-Walker Clinic, Inc. v. U.S. Dep't of Health and Hum. Servs.*, 485 F. Supp. 3d 1 (D.D.C. 2020); *Asapansa-Johnson Walker v. Azar*, No. 20-CV-2834, 2020 WL 6363970 (E.D.N.Y. Oct. 29, 2020); and *Religious Sisters of Mercy v. Azar*, No. 3:16-CV-00386, 2021 WL 191009 (D.N.D. Jan. 19, 2021).

OCR applies the enforcement mechanisms provided for and available under Title IX when enforcing Section 1557's prohibition on sex discrimination. 45 C.F.R. § 92.5(a). Title IX's enforcement procedures can be found at 45 C.F.R. § 86.71 (adopting the procedures at 45 C.F.R. §§ 80.6 through 80.11 and 45 C.F.R. Part 81). See https://www.hhs.gov/civil-rights/for-individuals/section-1557/index.html for further information.

[278] https://www.justice.gov/crt/title-ix.

[279] 477 F.2d 1292 (1973), https://www.upress.umn.edu/book-division/images/other-images/equality-for-women-in-high-school-sports_2.

[280] *Id.*, at pp. 1292. The Court of Appeals affirmed the lower court's ruling at 342 F.Supp. 1224 (D.Minn. 1972).

[281] *William Dodds, Superintendent; Highland Local School District; Shawn Winkelfoos, Principal; Board of Education of the Highland Local School District, Third Party Defendants-Appellants, v. UNITED STATES DEPARTMENT OF EDUCATION; John King, Secretary of Education; Loretta E. Lynch, Attorney General; United States Department of Justice; Vanita Gupta, Principal Deputy Assistant Attorney General, Defendants*, Jane Doe, a minor by and through her legal guardians Joyce and John Doe, Intervenor-Third Party Plaintiff-Appellee, 845 F.3d 217 (2016), Sixth Circuit.

[282] *Id.*, pp. 87.

[283] *Doe v. Boyertown*, Case 17-3113 USCA 3rd (2021); *G.G. v. Gloucester County School Board*, Case 15-2056 USCA 4th (2016); *Smith v. City of Salem, at al.*, Case 03-3399 USCA 6th (2004); *Whitaker v. Kenosha Unified School District*, Case 16-3522 USCA 7th (2017); and *Hively v. Ivy Tech Community College of Indiana*, Case 15-1720 USCA 7th 853 F.3d 339 (2017). The U.S. Supreme Court has not yet addressed the issue of transgender students participating in interscholastic or intercollegiate sports programs.

[284] *Id.*, pp. 28-29.

[285] Compl., ECF No. 1 Ex. B.

[286] United States Department of Health and Human Services, Office of Civil Rights, https://tinyurl.com/56knw3b5.

[287] See *Bostock*, 140 S. Ct. at 1743, 1748–50.

[288] Federal Register, Vol. 86, No. 117/Tuesday, June 22, 2021, pp. 32367, 34 CFR Chapter I, https://www.govinfo.gov/content/pkg/FR-2021-06-22/pdf/2021-13058.pdf.

[289] The Dear Educator letter, https://www2.ed.gov/about/offices/list/ocr/correspondence/stakeholders/educator-202106-tix.pdf.

[290] (800) 669-9777

[291] www.truecolorsfund.org.

[292] Twitter #40toNone.

[293] https://www.hud.gov/LGBT_resources.

[294] *Dent v. West Virginia*, 129 U.S. 114 (1889), at pp. 121-122.

[295] *DAVID ERMOLD, et al., Plaintiffs, v. KIM DAVIS*, individually and in her official capacity, Defendant, , United States District Court, E.D. Kentucky, Northern Division, Ashland. September 15, 2017.

[296] *April MILLER, et al., Plaintiffs v. Kim DAVIS*, individually and in her official capacity, et al., Defendants. Civil Action No. 15-44-DLB. United States District Court, E.D. Kentucky, Northern Division. at Ashland. Signed July 21, 2017.

[297] Schaefer, A.G., Iyengar, R.K., et al., "Assessing Implications of Allowing Transgender Service Members to Serve Openly," Rand Corporation, Rand National Defense Research Institute, March 2016.

[298] "DEPARTMENT OF DEFENSE REPORT AND RECOMMENDATIONS ON MILITARY SERVICE BY TRANSGENDER PERSONS," pp. 32. February 2018. It should be noted that this report does not cite the authors of the report. It is designated as U/FOUO.

[299] "Executive Order on Enabling All Qualified Americans to Serve Their Country in Uniform," dated January 25, 2021, https://tinyurl.com/5hy5x6a3.

[300] DOD INSTRUCTION 1300.28 IN-SERVICE TRANSITION FOR TRANSGENDER SERVICE MEMBERS, effective April 30, 2021, https://tinyurl.com/yd33x8bj.

[301] DOD INSTRUCTION 6130.03, VOLUME 1 MEDICAL STANDARDS FOR MILITARY SERVICE: APPOINTMENT, ENLISTMENT, OR INDUCTION, April 30, 2021, https://tinyurl.com/37twdhbs.

[302] https://tinyurl.com/c8asnz62.

[303] https://tinyurl.com/y9cxshfv.

[304] Mallory, C., Hasenbush, A., and Sears, B., "Discrimination and Harassment by Law Enforcement Officers in the LGBT Community," UCLA School of Law, Williams Institute, March 2015.

[305] Burns, C., Graham, K.C., and Menefee-Libey, S., "Gay and Transgender Discrimination in the Public Sector: Why It's a Problem for State and Local Governments, Employees, and Taxpayers," Center for American Progress, August 30, 2012, https://tinyurl.com/4tamym6s.

[306] https://faq.ssa.gov/en-us/Topic/article/KA-01453.

[307] https://www.patientcare.va.gov/lgbt/.

[308] See directive https://www.patientcare.va.gov/lgbt/va_lgbt_policies.asp.

[309] Title 42 U.S.C. §2000bb-1(a) and (b), Public Law 103-141, November 16, 1993; 107 Stat. 1448.

[310] United States Constitution, Fourteenth Amendment, Section 1.

[311] This quote is from the website of the University of Notre Dame, https://tinyurl.com/2rwfv66n.

[312] Matthew 22:37-40

[313] Namely, Title 42 U.S. Code, Section 2000bb-1(b)(1) and (2) as follows:

(b) Exception

Government may substantially burden a person's exercise of religion only if it demonstrates that application of the burden to the person

(1) is in furtherance of a compelling governmental interest; and

(2) is the least restrictive means of furthering that compelling governmental interest,"

[314] *City of Boerne v. Flores, Archbishop of San Antonio, et al.* 521 U.S. 507, 532, 117 S. Ct. 2157, 2180 (1997).

[315] *Boerne v. Flores, supra*, 533-535.

[316] https://www.statesidelegal.org/lso.

[317] www.lgbtmap.org.

[318] *Id.*, 166-167.

[319] *Boerne v. Flores, Archbishop of San Antonio*, 521 U.S. 507 (1997), U.S. Supreme Court, www.supremecourt.gov under Opinions.

[320] United States Constitution, Fourteenth Amendment, Section 5, https://tinyurl.com/x7xz3sc.

[321] *Boerne v. Flores, Archbishop of San Antonio*, 521 U.S. 507 at pp. 512.

[322] *Id.* 888.

[323] *Id.* 534.

[324] Edward J. W. Blatnik. (1998). No RFRAF Allowed: The Status of the Religious Freedom Restoration Act's Federal Application in the Wake of *City of Boerne v. Flores, Columbia Law Review* 98(6), 1410-1460, DOI:10.2307/1123302

[325] Alabama Amendment 622, approved by voters in the November 1998 elections, Section III.

[326] Corporate Equality Index 2015, Rating American Workplaces on Lesbian, Gay, Bisexual, and Transgender Equality, Human Rights Campaign, https://assets2.hrc.org/files/documents/CEI-2015-rev.pdf.

[327] American Academy of Pediatrics (AAP) News and Journals Gateway, https://tinyurl.com/2yyubz65. The Academy has issued the following statement about the bills being introduced into state legislatures:

> By: Lee Savio Beers, M.D., FAAP, President, American Academy of Pediatrics
>
> With alarm and dismay, pediatricians have watched bills advance through state legislatures across the country with the sole purpose of threatening the health and well-being of transgender youth.
>
> The American Academy of Pediatrics has long been on the record in support of affirmative care for transgender children through our clinical policy. Today, we are going on the record to oppose public policies that would allow for the opposite.
>
> Several state legislatures have introduced bills that would prohibit gender-affirming care for gender-diverse and transgender youth and forbid transgender youth from participating on sports teams according to their gender identity. These bills are dangerous. If left unchallenged, there will be transgender teens in certain zip codes who will be unable to access basic medical care, and pediatricians in certain zip codes who would be criminalized for providing medical care. And transgender youth would be denied the ability to participate in sports according to their gender identity.
>
> We are in the middle of a pandemic that has led to staggering rises in mental health concerns among children and teens. Transgender children had statistically higher rates of depression and suicidal ideation before the pandemic: around half of transgender youth consider suicide, and a third attempt it.
>
> The American Academy of Pediatrics recommends that youth who identify as transgender have access to comprehensive, gender-affirming, and developmentally appropriate health care that is provided in a safe and inclusive clinical space. We also recommend that playing on sports teams helps youth develop self-esteem, correlates positively with overall mental health, and appears to have a protective effect against suicide.
>
> These bills not only ignore these recommendations, they undermine them. Instead, the legislation would allow policymakers rather than pediatricians to determine the best course of care for our patients, and in some medically underserved states, it could mean losing an already limited number of pediatric practitioners who care for transgender youth. Forcing transgender children to play on teams according to their sex assigned at birth, rather than the gender they live in, also puts their physical and mental health at risk.
>
> Evidence-based medical care for transgender and gender diverse children is a complex issue. Pediatricians are best able to determine what care is necessary and appropriate for these children, but these bills interfere in the physician-patient-family relationship and would cause undue harm.
>
> Politics has no place here. Transgender children, like all children, just want to belong. We will fight state by state, in the courts and on the national stage to make sure they know they do, https://tinyurl.com/wt8vx82a.

[328] Peters, J.W., "Why Transgender Girls Are Suddenly in the G.O.P.'s Culture-Wars," *New York Times Online* https://www.nytimes.com/2021/03/29/us/politics/transgender-girls-sports.html, March 29, 2021.

[329] https://www.psychologytoday.com/us/blog/hide-and-seek/201207/the-battle-the-sexes?amp.

[330] https://web.law.duke.edu/sports/sex-sport/comparative-athletic-performance/, accessed Feb. 10, 2020.

[331] Arizona Senate Bill 1637, introduced by Senator Wendy Rogers (R-Sixth District), 55th Legislature, 1st Regular Session, 2021.

[332] *Nassar*, 570 U. S., 346, 360, *Bostock, supra*, pp. 5.

[333] Hazen Paper Biggins, 507 U.S. 604, 610 (1993), referenced in Ventrell-Monsees, C., "Proving 'Because of but/for Cause'—A 'Generous' Causation Standard," ABA Section on Labor and Employment Law, 13th Annual Labor and Employment Law Conference, New Orleans, LA (November 7, 2019), pp. 3, https://tinyurl.com/ynsv72e.

[334] See the full statement, https://tinyurl.com/bukh5fxf.

[335] Brody, D., and Bickford, S., "Discriminatory Denial of Service: Applying State Public Accommodation Laws to Online Commerce," Lawyers Committee for Civil Rights Under Law, January 2020, Version 1.0.

[336] Data used with permission, www.tgbtmap.org.

[337] https://www.mapresearch.org/state-policy-tally-faq.

[338] https://www.lgbtmap.org/equality_maps/profile_state/AL.

[339] See fn. 336 above.

[340] https://www.mapresearch.org/equality_maps/profile_state/AL.

[341] https://www.lgbtmap.org/equality-maps/.

[342] Based on U.S. Census data, https://tinyurl.com/ysfchhvu.

[343] https://law.justia.com/codes/alabama/2006/17654/22-9a-19.html.

[344] https://eforms.com/name-change/al/.

[345] *Darcy Corbitt, et al. v. Hal Taylor*, CIVIL ACTION NO. 2:18cv91-MHT (WO) (M.D. Ala. Jan. 15, 2021) January 15, 2021, https://www.aclu.org/cases/corbitt-v-taylor. The case is currently with the U.S. Court of Appeals for the Eleventh Circuit as Case No. 21-10486. Amicus briefs were filed in early August, and it is unknown as of the date of publication when oral argument will be scheduled.

[346] https://codes.findlaw.com/al/title-21-handicapped-persons/al-code-sect-21-4-1.html and following.

[347] Chandler, K., "Alabama Governor Ivy Signs Ban on Transgender Athletes," *Associated Press*, https://tinyurl.com/3tk88k4f.

[348] Chandler, K., "Alabama Governor Ivy Signs Ban on Transgender Athletes," *Associated Press*, https://tinyurl.com/3tk88k4f.

[349] *2015 U.S. Transgender Survey, supra*, Alabama State Report, pp. 2.

[350] www.lbgtmap.org.

[351] Alabama Amendment 622, approved by voters in the November 1998 elections, Section III.

[352] Alaska Human Rights Law, Title 18, Chapter 80, Article 4, Section 18.80.210.

[353] See https://transequality.org/documents/state/alaska for more information. Data obtained May 21, 2021.

[354] http://www.courts.alaska.gov/shc/family/shcname.htm.

[355] See https://transequality.org/documents/state/alaska for more information. Data obtained May 21, 2021.

[356] Alaska Statutes, Title 18, Chapter 80, Article 4, Section 18.80.230.

[357] Arizona Revised Statutes, Title 41 State Government, Chapter 9 Civil Rights, Article 4 Discrimination in Employment, Section 1463 Discrimination; Unlawful Practices; Definition, https://www.azleg.gov/arsDetail/?title=41.

[358] The full text of the Bill, https://www.azleg.gov/legtext/54leg/2r/bills/hb2867p.htm.

[359] *D.T., et al. v. Christ, et al.*, United States District Court for the District of Arizona, Case No. 4:20-cv-00484/JAS, complaint filed 11/4/2020, https://www.nclrights.org/our-work/cases/d-t-v-christ/.

[360] See https://lgbtq.arizona.edu/name-and-gender-change for more information from the LGBTQ Affairs Office of the University of Arizona.

[361] https://sagatucson.org/files/documents/name_and_gender_change_guide.pdf.

[362] *Brush and Nib, LLC, et al., v. City of Phoenix, et al.*, 448 P.3d 890 (2019) Arizona Supreme Court Opinion.

[363] Mallory, C., Hasenbush, A., and Sears, B., "Discrimination and Harassment by Law Enforcement Officers in the LGBT Community," UCLA School of Law, Williams Institute, March 2015, pp. 1-2.

[364] https://tinyurl.com/5akf72pt.

[365] "The Impact of Incarceration and Policing in Our Community," American Bar Association, https://tinyurl.com/2v8ar3ua. July 29, 2019.

[366] Arizona Revised Statutes, Title 41, Article 9, Section 1493.01, https://tinyurl.com/6z56mfu8.

[367] arlegalservices.org.

[368] https://www.arlegalservices.org/namechange.

[369] Jordan Blair Woods, "Arkansas Passes Sweeping and Draconian Law Targeting Transgender Youth," JURIST – Academic Commentary, April 12, 2021, https://www.jurist.org/commentary/2021/04/jordan-blair-woods-arkansas-law-targets-transgender-youth/.

[370] See https://transequality.org/sites/default/files/docs/usts/AR%20State%20Report%20FINAL.pdf for more information from their report on Arkansas.

[371] Arkansas SAFE Act, https://tinyurl.com/y4urxzjj.

[372] DeMillo, A., "Arkansas Governor signs Transgender Sports ban into law," *Associated Press* (AP), March 25, 2021, https://apnews.com/article/arkansas-asa-hutchinson-kristi-noem-gender-identity-62fb40814df14f67780f1b57c8d522db.

[373] *Dylan Brandt, et al. v. Leslie Rutledge, at al.*, Case No. 4:21-CV00450/JM, U.S. District Court for the Eastern District of Arkansas, Central Division, "Supplemental Order" dated August 32, 2021, https://www.aclu.org/sites/default/files/field_document/brandt_supplemental_pi_order.pdf.

[374] California Fair Employment and Housing Act of 1959, codified as California Government Code §§12900 – 12996, https://leginfo.legislature.ca.gov/faces/codes_displayText.xhtml?lawCode=GOV&division=3.&title=2.&part=2.8.&chapter=6.&article=1.

[375] California Department of Public Health, Vital Records information page on amending a birth record as to your name and sex, https://www.cdph.ca.gov/Programs/CHSI/Pages/Correcting-or-Amending-a-Birth-Certificate-After-a-Sex-Change-Reassignment.aspx.

[376] https://www.cdph.ca.gov/Programs/CHSI/SiteAssets/Pages/Sworn-Statement/VS20_Sworn%20Statement.pdf.

[377] https://www.cdph.ca.gov/CDPH%20Document%20Library/ControlledForms/VS24.pdf.

[378] https://www.courts.ca.gov/selfhelp-namechange.htm?rdeLocaleAttr=en.

[379] https://www.courts.ca.gov/22489.htm.

[380] https://tinyurl.com/4rzd7wck.

[381] California Department of Fair Employment and Housing, https://www.dfeh.ca.gov/unruh/.

[382] https://leginfo.legislature.ca.gov/faces/codes_displaySection.xhtml?lawCode=EDC&sectionNum=221.5.

[383] http://www.insurance.ca.gov/01-consumers/110-health/60-resources/upload/Economic-Impact-Assessment-Gender-Nondiscrimination-In-Health-Insurance.pdf.

[384] Colorado Statutes, Title 24 Government—State, Article 34 Department of Regulatory Agencies, Part 4 Employment Practices, Section 402(1)(a), https://tinyurl.com/d2mnaur8.

[385] https://one-colorado.org/.

[386] https://www.courts.state.co.us/Self_Help/namechange/.

[387] ACLU of Colorado, "Know Your Rights: Discrimination in Places of Public Accommodation," https://tinyurl.com/9d77vx6.

[388] Colorado Department of Education "Participation of Transgender Athletes in Sport Clubs and Intramural Sports," https://tinyurl.com/u9kzsj63.

[389] Connecticut Statutes, Vol. 12, Title 46a Human Rights, Chapter 814c Human Rights and Opportunities, Part II Discriminatory Practices, Section 46a-58(a), https://www.cga.ct.gov/current/pub/chap_814c.htm#sec_46a-58.

[390] https://portal.ct.gov/-/media/Departments-and-Agencies/DPH/hisr/VR/My-name-change-affidavit.pdf.

[391] https://portal.ct.gov/DPH/Vital-Records/Corrections-and-Amendments.

[392] https://portal.ct.gov/DPH/Vital-Records/Gender-Change.

[393] For more information, send an email maria.d.colon@ct.gov.

[394] http://www.ctprobate.gov/Forms/PC-901.pdf.

[395] Conn. Gen. Stat. secs. 46a-64(a) (1) & (2).

[396] http://ciacsports.com/site/?p=14124.

[397] See Section 1. Amend § 4501, Title 6, Delaware Code.

[398] DE Admin. Code 4205, Section 10.7, February 11, 2017, Secretary of the Delaware Department of Health and Social Services (DSS), https://tinyurl.com/uh2u7wkn.

[399] https://courts.delaware.gov/forms/download.aspx?id=16858.

[400] https://tinyurl.com/7vy4c8hs.

[401] 6 Del. C. 1953, § 4503; 54 Del. Laws, c. 181, § 1; 58 Del. Laws, c. 133, § 1; 58 Del. Laws, c. 386, § 1; 65 Del. Laws, c. 377, § 2; 70 Del. Laws, c. 350, § 1; 77 Del. Laws, c. 90, § 3; 79 Del. Laws, c. 47, § 4., https://legis.delaware.gov/SessionLaws/Chapter?id=29676.

[402] See www.transathlete.com/K-12 under "Delaware,"

403 DC Human Rights Act protections https://ohr.dc.gov/sites/default/files/dc/sites/ohr/publication/attachments/protectedcategories_111319.pdf

404 https://tinyurl.com/2ewmy27r.

405 District of Columbia Code Section 7-231.22, "New Records for Live Birth for Change of Gender Designation," https://code.dccouncil.us/dc/council/code/sections/7-231.22.html.

406 https://tinyurl.com/4unrkjjs.

407 https://dmv.dc.gov/node/135972.

408 See http://dcrules.elaws.us/dcmr/4-801 for more information.

409 "DCSSA Policies, Rules, and Regulations Governing Athletics—A Handbook for Members," May 5, 2020, District of Columbia State Athletic Association, https://tinyurl.com/p9mfx6f4.

410 "TITLE XLIV, CIVIL RIGHTS, CHAPTER 760, DISCRIMINATION IN THE TREATMENT OF PERSONS; MINORITY REPRESENTATION," It is the Florida Civil Rights Act of 1992, https://tinyurl.com/uyv3md6c.

411 https://tinyurl.com/vu2ver6y.

412 National Center for Transgender Equality, www.transequality.org.

413 https://tinyurl.com/2mjss3wr.

414 www.floridanamechange.org.

415 https://tinyurl.com/jh5w3b3f.

416 Florida Human Rights Act, Section 760.08, https://tinyurl.com/ys9m6t4u.

417 Florida Statutes, Section 20, Chapter 1002, Subsection 1002.20(7) "Nondiscrimination," https://tinyurl.com/rwpp2p5r.

418 Florida Statutes, Title XLVIII, Chapter 1000, Section 05, Subsection (1) and (2)(a) https://tinyurl.com/49k9tmfb.

419 Senate Bill 1028, signed into law by Florida Governor Ron DeSantis on June 1, 2021. As of June 18, 2021, the bill had not yet been codified in Florida Statutes, Title XLVIII, Chapter 1006, Section 20, https://www.flsenate.gov/Session/Bill/2021/1028/BillText/er/PDF.

420 Florida Statutes, Chapter 761, Section 761.03, https://tinyurl.com/fcxptehb.

421 https://tinyurl.com/zfrbmr77.

422 file:///C:/Users/mwmoo/AppData/Local/Temp/Affidavit%20for%20Amendment%20(Form%203977)2019.pdf

423 https://dph.georgia.gov/ways-request-vital-record/birth.

424 https://georgiasuperiorcourts.org/find-my-local-superior-court/.

425 Information obtained from the Georgia Department of Driver Services, https://tinyurl.com/4dmwcn9b.

426 The full text of SB266, Georgia Legislature, https://tinyurl.com/b2k25t9w.

427 SB266, Georgia General Assembly, https://tinyurl.com/b2k25t9w pp.2-3.

428 www.healthcare.gov/transgender_health-Care

429 Georgia State Medicaid Plan, as revised August 1991, pp. 4, https://tinyurl.com/5edpa83s.

430 See, e.g., *Cody Flack, et al. v. Wisconsin Department of Health Services*, 395 F.Supp. 1001 (USDC Western District.WI (2019).

431 *EERIEANNA GOOD and Carol Beal v. Iowa Department of Health Services*, Case No 18-1158 (2019), t https://tinyurl.com/ahschh76.

432 https://tinyurl.com/4uvd654c.

433 https://health.hawaii.gov/vitalrecords/amendments/new-birth-certificate-for-sex-designation-change/.

434 https://namechange.ehawaii.gov/public/welcome.html.

435 https://tinyurl.com/53k8dfvh.

436 https://tinyurl.com/4ufsnpv2.

437 https://www.capitol.hawaii.gov/hrscurrent/Vol11_Ch0476-0490/HRS0489/HRS_0489-0003.htm.

438 Idaho Senate Bill 1030, https://tinyurl.com/3hhm8rnz.

[439] *F.V. and Dani Martin v. David Jeppesen, et al.*, Case No. 1:17-CV-00170-CWD, 446 F.Supp.3d 1110, U.S. District Court for the District of Idaho (2018), https://tinyurl.com/vnefs5j9.

[440] https://legislature.idaho.gov/statutesrules/idstat/title39/t39ch2/sect39-245a/.

[441] https://courtselfhelp.idaho.gov/Forms/name.

[442] https://itd.idaho.gov/wp-content/uploads/2017/03/3533Fill.pdf.

[443] https://courtselfhelp.idaho.gov/Forms/name.

[444] https://www2.illinois.gov/dhr/Pages/default.aspx.

[445] https://www2.illinois.gov/sites/ihrc/Rights/Pages/default.aspx, email dated June 29, 2021.

[446] https://www.illinoiscourts.gov/documents-and-forms/approved-forms/circuit-forms/name-change.

[447] https://dph.illinois.gov/topics-services/birth-death-other-records/birth-records/correct-birth-certificate.html.

[448] https://realid.ilsos.gov/.

[449] Illinois Statutes, 775 ILCS 5/ Article 1 General Provisions, Section 1-102(A) Freedom from Unlawful Discrimination, https://tinyurl.com/4a8tju49.

[450] Illinois High School Association, https://tinyurl.com/8wb4hp98. Scroll down and click on the Policy and Procedures Section to number 34, which opens a document that can be saved in pdf format. Number 34 is the policy and school recommendations for transgender participation.

[451] https://www2.illinois.gov/hfs/MedicalProviders/notices/Pages/prn200629a.aspx.

[452] Presidential Executive Order dated January 20, 2021, and signed by Joseph Biden, President of the United States, White House, https://tinyurl.com/nbeus9e5. The order also states:

> It is the policy of my Administration to prevent and combat discrimination on the basis of gender identity or sexual orientation, and to fully enforce Title VII and other laws that prohibit discrimination on the basis of gender identity or sexual orientation. It is also the policy of my Administration to address overlapping forms of discrimination.

[453] https://www.ilga.gov/legislation/ilcs/ilcs3.asp?ActID=2272&ChapterID=64.

[454] https://www.in.gov/health/vital-records/corrections-and-amendments/correctamend-a-birth-certificate/.

[455] https://www.in.gov/bmv/licenses-permits-ids/learners-permits-and-drivers-licenses-overview/drivers-license/amending-your-drivers-license-or-identification-card/.

[456] https://www.ihsaa.org/About-IHSAA/Current-Information/Gender-Equity.

[457] https://tinyurl.com/64h6ewfz, the full text of the RFRA can be accessed at https://tinyurl.com/npv9j3a8.

[458] Iowa Code, Chapter 216 Civil Rights Commission, Section 216.6 Unfair Employment Practices, Paragraph 1(a), https://www.legis.iowa.gov/DOCS/ACO/IC/LINC/Chapter.216.pdf.

[459] Protected Classes table, https://icrc.iowa.gov/your-rights/protected-classes.

[460] https://www.iowacourts.gov/for-the-public/representing-yourself/name-change.

[461] Iowa Code §144.23(3) says, "A notarized affidavit by a licensed physician and surgeon or osteopathic physician and surgeon stating that by reason of surgery or other treatment by the licensee, the sex designation of the person has been changed. The state registrar may make a further investigation or require further information necessary to determine whether a sex change has occurred," https://tinyurl.com/mxtdy8c.

[462] https://rules.iowa.gov/Notice/Details/3307C.

[463] https://www.legis.iowa.gov/docs/ACO/chapter/641.99.pdf.

[464] ARC 3307C TRANSPORTATION DEPARTMENT [761] Notice of Intended Action, https://rules.iowa.gov/Notice/Details/3307C.

[465] Iowa Code Chapter 216, Section 216.7, https://tinyurl.com/2apkwytb.

[466] https://tinyurl.com/dy284upj.

[467] Iowa Administrative Code, Title 441, Chapter 78, Section 78.1(4). Subsection b(2)-(4), c, and d(1)-(17) specifically exclude from coverage any and all procedures and surgical services related to the transsexual community and list 17 "cosmetic, reconstructive, or plastic surgery procedures," as not covered under the [Medicaid] program, https://www.legis.iowa.gov/docs/iac/agency/441.pdf.

[468] Kansas Act Against Discrimination, Kansas Statutes, Section 44-1002, https://tinyurl.com/yuhjx77r.

[469] "Kansas Human Rights Commission Concurs with the U.S. Supreme Court's *Bostock* Decision," August 21, 2020, https://tinyurl.com/wbw5jmc4.

[470] https://tinyurl.com/va9w5adk.

[471] Topeka-Capital Journal, https://tinyurl.com/29kj37nr.

[472] *Nyla Foster, et al. v. Jeff Anderson, et al.*, U.S. District Court for the District of Kansas, Kansas City Division, Case No. 2:18-cv-02552-DDC-KGG, 6/21/2019, pp. 21,

[473] Email received from the Kansas Division of Vehicles in its entirety:

"Good morning,

The name change can be completed by visiting the driver's license office with your license, a proof of current residential address, and the legal name change document. Listed below are the 3 documents that may be used to change the gender on a Kansas credential.

1. Lawful presence document showing correct gender (birth certificate, passport, certificate of naturalization, etc.....)
2. Court order announcing a gender reclassification (cannot be name change document only)
3. Letter from driver's licensing management authorizing the gender change

If you are needing the approval letter from licensing management, please mail a written request to: Driver Services, PO BOX 2188, TOPEKA, KS66601. The request must include:

1. A photocopy of your Kansas credential.
    a. If you do not have a Kansas credential, you may send in a copy of your lawful presence document instead
2. A letter from your licensed medical, osteopathic physician stating you have undergone the appropriate clinical treatment for change of
3. A letter requesting the change in gender. The letter must include:
    a. Full legal name
    b. Kansas residential address
    c. Gender classification currently on Kansas credential and requested new gender
    d. Requested new name (If applicable)
    e. New address (If applicable)
    f. Phone number and email address

All medical records provided to the Division of Vehicles will be held in strict confidence per K.S.A 2010 Supp. 45-221(a)(1) and the Federal Driver's Privacy Protection Act, section 2721 et seq.

Beginning May 3rd, 2023, state issued credentials must have the REAL ID indicator to be used to board federally regulated commercial aircrafts, enter certain designated federal facilities, and enter nuclear power plants. Please visit https://www.ksrevenue.org/dovrealid.html for more information.

Thank you,

Division of Vehicles
Zibell Building
785-296-3671

[474] Kansas Statutes, Chapter 44, Article 10, Section 44-1002, et seq., https://tinyurl.com/6w5kc8r9.

[475] https://tinyurl.com/54u2ux62.

[476] Kansas House of Representatives, House Bill 2210, 2021 Session, Section 1(a), http://www.kslegislature.org/li/b2021_22/measures/documents/hb2210_00_0000.pdf.

[477] https://tinyurl.com/a9kbcyv3..

[478] http://rfraperils.com/wp-content/uploads/2014/01/summary_hb_2203_2013.pdf.

[479] Kentucky Revised Statutes, Chapter 344, Section 344.020(1)(b), https://apps.legislature.ky.gov/law/statutes/statute.aspx?id=32602.

[480] Kentucky Administrative Regulations, Title 901, Chapter 5, Section 070, https://tinyurl.com/4ah432uf.

[481] See section 6, https://apps.legislature.ky.gov/law/kar/901/005/070.pdf.

[482] http://www.transkentucky.com/wp-content/uploads/2018/03/VS-15GR.pdf.

[483] Kentucky Revised Statutes, Title XVIII Public Health, Chapter 213 Vital Statistics, Section 121(5), https://apps.legislature.ky.gov/law/statutes/statute.aspx?id=8741.

[484] https://tinyurl.com/267akmmf.

[485] https://khsaa.org/common_documents/handbook/policies/policies-transgenderpolicy.pdf.

[486] Kentucky Revised Statutes, Section 446.350, the Kentucky Religious Freedom Act, https://tinyurl.com/nybva862.

[487] Louisiana Department of Public Safety, Office of Motor Vehicles, Policy 22.00, https://public.powerdms.com/ladpsc/documents/368302.

[488] Louisiana Department of Public Safety, Office of Motor Vehicles, Policy 22.01 https://public.powerdms.com/ladpsc/documents/368304.

[489] https://tinyurl.com/86cd2d8m.

[490] Louisiana Revised Statutes, Chapter 51, Section 2247, https://tinyurl.com/5bpw3s2j.

[491] See the TLDEF for further information, https://transhealthproject.org/resources/medicaid-regulations-and-guidance/louisiana/explicit-coverage/.

[492] https://www.mainelegislature.org/legis/statutes/39/title39ch0sec0.html.

[493] Main Revised Statutes, Title 5 Administrative Procedures and Services, Part 12 Human Rights, Chapter 337 Human Rights Act, Subchapter 1 General Provisions, Section 4552 Policy, https://www.mainelegislature.org/legis/statutes/5/title5sec4552.html.

[494] https://www.maine.gov/dhhs/mecdc/public-health-systems/data-research/vital-records/documents/pdf-files/VS7.pdf.

[495] https://vitalchek.com/amendments/home/me.

[496] https://tinyurl.com/fuzdab8r.

[497] https://www.maine.gov/sos/news/2018/genderdesignationdlid.html.

[498] Maine Revised Statutes, Title 5 Administrative Procedures and Services, Part 12 Human Rights, Chapter 337 Human Rights Act, Subchapter 5 Public Accommodations, Section 4591, https://legislature.maine.gov/legis/statutes/5/title5sec4591.html.

[499] Maine Legislative Document Number 926, introduced on March 8, 2021, https://tinyurl.com/3yhn6cxw.

[500] Maine Legislative Document Number 1401, introduced on April 7, 2021, https://tinyurl.com/28f4mmct.

[501] https://www.dllr.state.md.us/oeope/ndiscrim.shtml.

[502] https://health.maryland.gov/vsa/Pages/gender.aspx.

[503] https://www.courts.state.md.us/sites/default/files/court-forms/ccdr060.pdf.

[504] https://faq.ssa.gov/en-us/Topic/article/KA-01981.

[505] https://mva.maryland.gov/drivers/Pages/md-drivers-license.aspx#mddlcorrecting.

[506] Maryland Commission on Civil Rights, Public Accommodations Discrimination, https://mccr.maryland.gov/Pages/Public-Accommodations-Discrimination.aspx.

[507] The "MPSSAA Guidance for Participation of Transgender Youth in Interscholastic Athletics," https://www.mpssaa.org/assets/1/6/MPSSAA_Transgender_Guidance_revised_8.16.pdf.

[508] Allegany County, M.D. Public Schools, Department, Athletics, and Title IX compliance, www.acpsmd.org.

[509] Maryland Health Connections www.marylandhealthconnection.gov/wp-content/uploads/2019/04/MHC_Factsheet_LGBT.pdf.

[510] Massachusetts General Laws, Chapter 151B Unlawful discrimination because of race, color, religious creed, national origin, or sex, Section 4(1), https://www.mass.gov/info-details/mass-general-laws-c151b-ss-4.

[511] https://www.mass.gov/how-to/amend-a-birth-certificate-following-medical-intervention-for-the-purpose-of-sex-reassignment.

[512] https://www.mass.gov/how-to/change-information-on-your-drivers-license-or-id-card.

[513] Massachusetts Attorney General's Civil Rights Division, https://www.mass.gov/service-details/public-accommodation-civil-rights-protections.

[514] http://www.miaa.net/gen/miaa_generated_bin/documents/basic_module/GenderIdentityIcon.pdf.

[515] https://www.michigan.gov/documents/act_453_elliott_larsen_8772_7.pdf.

[516] The information sheet listing the requirements is available from the MDHHS, https://tinyurl.com/vxz77pst.

[517] https://tinyurl.com/3bfxrh6h.

[518] https://michiganlegalhelp.org/

[519] 1963 Const., Art. II, and Art. V, Section 29; 1976 PA 220 and PA 453; and Rules Governing Organization and Procedures of the MCRC, Michigan Department of Civil Rights, https://www.michigan.gov/mdcr/0,4613,7-138-4954_4997-16288--,00.html.

[520] The Michigan Youth Risk Behavior Survey is described more fully, Michigan Department of Education, https://www.michigan.gov/mde/0,4615,7-140-74638_74639_29233_41316---,00.html.

[521] The full statement, Michigan State Board of Education, https://www.michigan.gov/documents/mde/SBEStatementonLGBTQYouth_534576_7.pdf.

[522] Senate Bill 218, introduced in the Michigan State Senate on March 10, 2021, by Republican Senators Theis, BARRETT, RUNESTAD, VICTORY, BUMSTEAD, BIZON, DALEY, OUTMAN, NESBITT, LASATA, MACDONALD, ZORN and VANDERWALL, http://www.legislature.mi.gov/documents/2021-2022/billintroduced/Senate/pdf/2021-SIB-0218.pdf.

[523] Michigan House Bill 5958, https://tinyurl.com/235stret.

[524] *City of Boerne v. Flores, Archbishop of San Antonio, et al.*, 521 U.S. 507 (1997), pp. 511.

[525] *City of Boerne*, supra, pp. 519.

[526] Minnesota Human Rights Act, MN Stat. Ch. 393A.01, et. seq., https://www.revisor.mn.gov/statutes/cite/363A.01. See also, the Minnesota Department of Human Rights, https://mn.gov/mdhr/.

[527] https://www.health.state.mn.us/people/vitalrecords/docs/bamendia.pdf.

[528] Email from the Minnesota Department of Public Safety, Division of Driver Services, dated July 21, 2021.

[529] https://onlineservices.dps.mn.gov/EServices/_/.

[530] Minnesota Statutes, Chapter 363A.11, https://www.revisor.mn.gov/statutes/cite/363A.11.

[531] https://tinyurl.com/7jmkhvwm. See also, https://mn.gov/mdhr/news-community/newsroom/?id=1061-377055#/detail/appId/1/id/448604.

[532] Minnesota Revised Statutes, Chapter 363A Human Rights, Section 363A.26 Exemption Based on Religious Association, https://www.revisor.mn.gov/statutes/cite/363A.26.

[533] Mississippi Statutes, not yet codified. The Mississippi Fairness Act was signed by Governor Tate Reeves and became effective on July 1, 2021, see http://www.legislature.ms.gov/legislation/measure-search/.

[534] Mississippi "Protecting Freedom of Conscience From Government Discrimination Act, Sections 1 and 2, http://billstatus.ls.state.ms.us/documents/2016/html/HB/1500-1599/HB1523SG.htm.

[535] Missouri Statutes, Title XII Public Health and Welfare, Chapter 213 Human Rights, Section 213.010(6), https://revisor.mo.gov/main/OneSection.aspx?section=213.010&bid=34591&hl=.

[536] Email from the Missouri Human Rights Commission, dated July 20, 2021,

[537] Missouri Court of Appeals, in *Pittman v. Cooper Paper Recycling Corp*, 478 S.W.3d 479 (Mo. Ct. App. 2015); 128 Fair. Empl. Prac. Cas. 379, https://casetext.com/case/pittman-v-cook-paper-recycling-corp-2.

[538] Missouri Supreme Court, in *Lampley v. Missouri Human Rights Commission*, 570 S.W.3d 16 (Mo. 2019), https://casetext.com/case/lampley-v-mo-commn-on-human-rights-1.

[539] Missouri Code of State Regulations, Title 19, Division 10, Chapter 10, Section 110(9), https://www.sos.mo.gov/cmsimages/adrules/csr/current/19csr/19c10-10.pdf.

[540] https://dor.mo.gov/forms/5532.pdf.

[541] Email received from the Missouri Department of Revenue, Bureau of Driver's Licenses, dated July 16, 2021.

[542] Missouri Statutes, Title XII Public Health and Welfare, Chapter 213 Human Rights, Section 213.065(1), https://revisor.mo.gov/main/OneSection.aspx?section=213.010&bid=34591&hl=.

[543] Missouri Statutes, Title XII Public Health and Welfare, Chapter 213 Human Rights, Section 213.065(2), https://revisor.mo.gov/main/OneSection.aspx?section=213.010&bid=34591&hl=.

[544] Missouri State High School Activities Association, 2019-2020 Official Handbook, https://www.mshsaa.org/resources/pdf/Official%20Handbook.pdf.

[545] https://house.mo.gov/billtracking/bills211/hlrbillspdf/0931H.01I.pdf.

[546] Missouri Statutes, Title I, Chapter 1, Section 1.302, https://revisor.mo.gov/main/OneSection.aspx?section=1.302.

[547] Montana Code Annotated 2019, Title 49, Chapter 1 Basic Rights, Part 1 Basic Personal Rights, Section 49-1-102(1) and (2), https://leg.mt.gov/bills/mca/title_0490/chapter_0010/part_0010/section_0020/0490-0010-0010-0020.html.

[548] https://dojmt.gov/driving/driver-exam-stations/.

[549] https://dojmt.gov/driving/required-docs/.

[550] See Montana Secretary of State, https://rules.mt.gov/gateway/RuleNo.asp?RN=23.3.127.

[551] Montana Department of Justice Diver Licenses, https://dojmt.gov/driving/driver-licensing/#DLID21.

[552] Montana Code Annotated 2019, Title 49, Chapter 2, Part 3, Section 49-2-304(1) https://leg.mt.gov/bills/mca/title_0490/chapter_0020/part_0030/section_0040/0490-0020-0030-0040.html.

[553] https://leg.mt.gov/bills/2021/billpdf/HB0112.pdf.

[554] Email from the Nebraska Equal Opportunity Commission dated July 15, 2021.

[555] Email from the Nebraska Department of Health and Human Services, Vital Records Section, dated July 16, 2021.

[556] Nebraska Revised Statutes, Chapter 71 Public Health and Welfare, Section 604.01 Birth certificate; sex reassignment; new certificate; procedure, https://nebraskalegislature.gov/laws/browse-chapters.php?chapter=71.

[557] Nebraska School Activities Association Non-Discrimination Policy, https://nsaa-static.s3.amazonaws.com/about/nondiscrim.pdf.

[558] Nevada Statutes, Title 53 Labor and Industrial Relations, Chapter 613 Employment Practices, Section 330, https://www.leg.state.nv.us/NRS/NRS-613.html#NRS613Sec330.

[559] https://www.leg.state.nv.us/NRS/NRS-041.html#NRS041Sec270.

[560] Nevada Revised Statutes, Title 41, Sections 270-290, http://selfhelp.nvcourts.gov/self-help/name-changes/overview-of-name-changes.

[561] Nevada Administrative Code, Chapter 440 Vital Statistics, Section 030, https://www.leg.state.nv.us/NAC/NAC-440.html.

[562] Nevada Administrative Code, Chapter 440 Vital Statistics, Section 030, https://www.leg.state.nv.us/NAC/NAC-440.html.

[563] Nevada Revised Statutes, Chapter 651, Section 070, https://www.leg.state.nv.us/nrs/nrs-651.html#NRS651Sec070.

[564] Nevada Interscholastic Activities Association Policy Statement on Gender Identity and transgender participation in school sports https://www.niaa.com/publications/Transgender_Participation__Policy_Adopted_4-6-2016.pdf

[565] New Hampshire Statutes, Title XXXI, Chapter 354A, Sections 6 and 7 on employment discrimination, and the other statutes prohibiting discrimination on the basis of sex, sexual orientation, and gender identity in Section 8-15 for housing, and Sections 16 and 17 on public accommodations, http://gencourt.state.nh.us/rsa/html/nhtoc/NHTOC-XXXI-354-A.htm.

[566] Email from the New Hampshire Department of State, Vital Records Administration, dated July 19, 2021.

[567] Website of the New Hampshire Department of Safety, Division of Motor Vehicles, under Driver Licensing>Record Change Request>Name Change, https://tinyurl.com/ueuf2.

[568] https://www.nh.gov/safety/divisions/dmv/forms/documents/dsmv626.pdf.

[569] New Hampshire Revised Statutes, Title XXXI, Chapter 354-A, Section 354-1:17, http://gencourt.state.nh.us/rsa/html/XXXI/354-A/354-A-17.htm.

[570] New Hampshire Revised Statutes, Title XXXI, Chapter 354-A:27, see also http://gencourt.state.nh.us/rsa/html/XXXI/354-A/354-A-27.htm.

[571] New Jersey Statutes Annotated, Section 10:5-3, https://www.nj.gov/oag/dcr/downloads/NJ-Law-Against-Discrimination.pdf.

[572] https://www.nj.gov/health/forms/reg-l2_1.pdf.

[573] https://www.njcourts.gov/forms/10551_namechg_adult.pdf.

[574] https://www.state.nj.us/mvc/pdf/license/genderchange.pdf.

[575] https://www.nj.gov/oag/dcr/downloads/fact_LAD.pdf.

[576] https://www.njoag.gov/about/divisions-and-offices/division-on-civil-rights-home/public-accommodation-discrimination/.

[577] https://www.njsiaa.org/sites/default/files/documents/2020-10/transgender-faqs-approved-11-15-17.pdf.

[578] Fairness In Women's Sports Act, S3540, was introduced March 11, 2021, https://www.njleg.state.nj.us/2020/Bills/S4000/3540_I1.PDF.

[579] See "Bill to ban transgender HS athletes from girls sports would upend landmark N.J. policy," by Brian Deakyne and Riley Yates, https://www.nj.com/highschoolsports/2021/03/bill-to-ban-transgender-hs-athletes-from-girls-sports-would-upend-landmark-nj-policy.html.

[580] New Mexico Statutes, Chapter 28 Human Rights, Article 1 Human Rights, Section 28-1-7, as amended July 1, 2003, https://www.nmlegis.gov/sessions/03%20Regular/FinalVersions/SB0028.html, see also, the New Mexico Department of Workforce Solutions, Bureau of Human Rights, which enforces the law, https://www.dws.state.nm.us/Human-Rights-Information.

[581] New Mexico Department of Health, Division of Epidemiology and Response, Vital Records and Health Statistics, Vital Records, https://www.nmhealth.org/about/erd/bvrhs/vrp/gdc/.

[582] https://www.nmhealth.org/publication/view/form/5429/.

[583] New Mexico Department of Health, Division of Epidemiology and Response, Vital Records and Health Statistics, Vital Records, https://www.nmhealth.org/about/erd/bvrhs/vrp/gdc/.

[584] New Mexico Statutes, Chapter 28, Article 1, Section 28-1-7(F), https://tinyurl.com/4e5d9ymj.

[585] New Mexico Statutes, Chapter 28, Article 1, Section 28-1-7(G), https://tinyurl.com/4e5d9ymj.

[586] https://www.nmact.org/file/Packet_060513.pdf.

[587] Email received from Adrien Lawyer, Executive Director and Co-Founder, Transgender Resource Center of New Mexico, dated July 20, 2021.

[588] New Mexico Religious Freedom Restoration Act, NM Stat. 28-22-3, https://www.nmlegis.gov/sessions/99%20Regular/FinalVersions/SB0644.pdf.

[589] New York Executive Law, Article 15, Section 296, et seq., https://dhr.ny.gov/sites/default/files/doc/HRL.pdf.

[590] https://www.health.ny.gov/forms/doh-5721.pdf.

[591] https://www.health.ny.gov/vital_records/docs/public_instructions_for_birth_corrections.pdf.

[592] https://dmv.ny.gov/forms/mv44nc.pdf.

[593] https://dmv.ny.gov/forms/mv44.pdf.

[594] https://dmv.ny.gov/address-change/how-change-information-dmv-documents#footnote4_dy584aa.

[595] New York Executive Law, Article 15, Section 296(2)a, https://dhr.ny.gov/sites/default/files/doc/HRL.pdf.

[596] http://nysphsaa.org/Portals/0/PDF/Handbook/2020-21/NYSPHSAA%20Handbook%20002.pdf.

[597] https://www.schools.nyc.gov/school-life/school-environment/guidelines-on-gender.

[598] North Carolina Statutes, Article 49, Section 143-422, et seq., the "Equal Employment Practices Act, https://www.ncleg.net/enactedlegislation/statutes/html/byarticle/chapter_143/article_49a.html.

[599] North Carolina Statutes, Article 4, Section 130A-118(b)(4) https://www.ncleg.gov/EnactedLegislation/Statutes/HTML/ByArticle/Chapter_130A/Article_4.html.

[600] See a map of offices https://www.ncdot.gov/dmv/offices-services/locate-dmv-office/Pages/dmv-offices.aspx.

[601] https://www.ncdot.gov/dmv/downloads/Documents/DL-101.pdf.

[602] North Carolina High School Athletics Association https://www.nchsaa.org/gender-identity-frequently-asked-questions-faqs.

[603] North Dakota Department of Labor and Human Rights, https://www.nd.gov/labor/nddolhr-now-accepting-and-investigating-charges-discrimination.

[604] North Dakota C.C. 14-02.4-02(6), https://www.legis.nd.gov/cencode/t14c02-4.pdf?20150821135716.

[605] North Dakota C.C. 14-02.4-02(18), https://www.legis.nd.gov/cencode/t14c02-4.pdf?20150821135716.

[606] Email from the North Dakota Department of Health, Birth Registration Unit, dated July 22, 2021.

[607] https://www.dot.nd.gov/divisions/driverslicense/docs/Drivers%20Lic%20Sites.pdf.

[608] https://www.dot.nd.gov/forms/sfn61146.pdf.

[609] Email received on July 28, 2021, from the North Dakota Driver's License Division.

[610] https://www.nd.gov/labor/nd-protected-categories.

[611] North Dakota Department of Labor and Human Rights, https://www.nd.gov/labor/human-rights/public-accommodation.

[612] Email from the North Dakota High School Athletic Association (NDHSAA) explaining its policy for transgender students to participate in interscholastic Sports programs

[613] Re-engrossed House Bill 1410, SECTION 1. AMENDMENT. Section 12-44.1-14 of the North Dakota Century Code, Subsection 2(a), https://www.legis.nd.gov/assembly/67-2021/documents/21-0346-10000.pdf.

[614] Ohio Revised Code, Title 41 Labor and Industry, Chapter 4112 Civil Rights Commission, Section 4112.01 Definitions, https://codes.ohio.gov/ohio-revised-code/section-4112.01.

[615] Ohio Revised Code, Title 37 Health and Safety – Morals, Chapter 3705 Vital Statistics, Section 3705.13, https://codes.ohio.gov/ohio-revised-code/section-3705.13.

[616] Email received from Rena Boler, Administrative Officer of the Ohio Department of Health, Bureau of Vital Statistics on July 27, 2021.

[617] *Stacie Ray, et. al., v. Stephanie McCloud, et.al.*, U.S. District Court for the Southern District of Ohio, Eastern Division, Case No. 2:18-cv-272/MHW/JV, Opinion and Order dated 12/16/2020, pp. 27.

[618] This information was obtained during a live chat via the internet with an Ohio BMV agent. The agent stated she did not have the capability to email the information to the author. The agent typed the information into the chat, and the author was able to retrieve it through copy and paste. The information was obtained only after making several attempts to contact the Ohio BMV offices and having used the contact form on the Ohio Governor's website. The Governor's website responded to my request for information on July 29, 2021, by sending me a letter addressed to me stating:

> On behalf of the Office of the Governor Mike DeWine, I am writing to respond to your public records request. Specifically, your request is as follows:
>
> The request for information is what policies and procedures does your driver's license agency have that allows or disallows transgender people from changing the designation of sex on their driver's license?
>
> Please note that you have made a request for information, rather than a request for specific, existing records. State ex rel. *Morgan v. New Lexington*, 112 Ohio St. 3d 33, ¶ 30 (2006) ("[r]equests for information and requests that require the records custodian to create a new record by searching for selected information are improper"); See State ex rel. *White v. Goldsberry*, 85 Ohio St.3d 153, 154, 1999-Ohio-447, 707 N.E.2d 496; Ohio Sunshine Law Manual 2020, pg. 12. Your request would require us to create a record to provide to you, which we are not obligated to do. We are, however, ready and willing to provide specific, existing records.
>
> Further, judging from the language of your request, records responsive to your request (should they exist) would likely be kept by the Ohio Bureau of Motor Vehicles. You may wish to contact that agency. If you have any questions or concerns about this request, please feel free to contact me," The Letter was signed by Sean T. McCullough, Assistant Chief Counsel.

[619] Ohio Revised Code, Title 41, Chapter 4112, Section 4112.01(9) "place of Public Accommodation," https://codes.ohio.gov/ohio-revised-code/section-4112.01.

[620] Ohio Revised Code, Title 41, Chapter 4112, Section 4112.02(G), https://codes.ohio.gov/ohio-revised-code/section-4112.02.

[621] Ohio High School Athletics Association (OHSAA) Handbook for Schools Grades 7 to 12, Section 6 Team Membership, 1-6-1 through 1-6-4, updated July 7, 2020, https://ohsaaweb.blob.core.windows.net/files/SchoolResources/Handbook.pdf.

[622] See Chapter 21 Discrimination toward the bottom of the page, https://www.oscn.net/applications/oscn/index.asp?level=1&ftdb=STOKST25&year=.

[623] Oklahoma Statutes Citationized, Title 25 Definitions and General Provisions, Chapter 21 Discrimination, Article 3 Discrimination in Employment, Section 1301 Definitions, Section 1301(6, https://www.oscn.net/applications/oscn/DeliverDocument.asp?CiteID=73442.

[624] Oklahoma Statutes Citationized, Title 25 Definitions and General Provisions, Chapter 21 Discrimination, Article 4A Discrimination in Housing, Section 1452, https://www.oscn.net/applications/oscn/DeliverDocument.asp?CiteID=73456.

[625] https://vitalchek.com/amendments/home/ok.

[626] https://oklahoma.gov/content/dam/ok/en/health/health2/documents/birth-certificate-application-08-2017-eng.pdf.

[627] https://oklahoma.gov/health/birth-and-death-certificates/acceptable-identification.html.

[628] https://oklahoma.gov/health/birth-and-death-certificates/amendments.html.

[629] Oklahoma Statutes, Title 25 Definitions and General Provisions, Section 25-1402, https://law.justia.com/codes/oklahoma/2014/title-25/section-25-1402. The statutes are also available from the Oklahoma Legislature's website, but are in rtf format, and difficult to navigate or visualize.

[630] Oklahoma Secondary Schools Activities Association, Board of Director's Policies, Section LVII, pp. 35, http://www.ossaa.com/Manual_BoardPolicies.aspx. Clicking on the down arrow in the upper left corner of the document allows the reader to download a copy in pdf format.

[631] Oregon Revised Statutes, Chapter 659A Unlawful Discrimination in Employment, Public Accommodations and Real Property Transactions; Administrative and Civil Enforcement, Section 659A.006, https://www.oregonlegislature.gov/bills_laws/ors/ors659A.html.

[632] https://www.oregon.gov/boli/civil-rights/Pages/gender-identity-at-work.aspx.

[633] https://www.oregon.gov/oha/PH/BIRTHDEATHCERTIFICATES/Pages/rules.aspx.

[634] https://www.oregon.gov/oha/PH/BIRTHDEATHCERTIFICATES/CHANGEVITALRECORDS/Pages/amendbirthinfo.aspx.

[635] https://www.oregonlegislature.gov/bills_laws/ors/ors033.html.

[636] https://www.oregon.gov/oha/PH/BirthDeathCertificates/Pages/findus.aspx.

[637] https://www.oregon.gov/OHA/PH/PHD/Pages/index.aspx.

[638] https://www.oregon.gov/oha/PH/BIRTHDEATHCERTIFICATES/CHANGEVITALRECORDS/Documents/amendreq.pdf.

[639] https://www.oregon.gov/oha/PH/BirthDeathCertificates/GetVitalRecords/Documents/birthor.pdf.

[640] https://www.oregon.gov/oha/PH/BirthDeathCertificates/GetVitalRecords/Documents/45-13A-Long.pdf.

[641] https://www.oregon.gov/oha/PH/BIRTHDEATHCERTIFICATES/CHANGEVITALRECORDS/Pages/amendmentfees.aspx.

[642] https://www.oregon.gov/oha/PH/BirthDeathCertificates/GetVitalRecords/Pages/fees.aspx.

[643] https://www.oregon.gov/oha/PH/BIRTHDEATHCERTIFICATES/CHANGEVITALRECORDS/Pages/amendmentfees.aspx#replacements.

[644] Oregon Health Authority, Center for Health Statistics, https://www.oregon.gov/oha/PH/BIRTHDEATHCERTIFICATES/CHANGEVITALRECORDS/Pages/CourtOrderChangeSex.aspx.

[645] https://www.oregon.gov/odot/DMV/pages/appointments.aspx, https://www.oregon.gov/odot/DMV/Pages/Offices/index.aspx.

[646] https://www.oregon.gov/odot/DMV/Pages/Fees/index.aspx.

[647] https://www.oregon.gov/odot/DMV/Pages/driverid/chg_gender_designation.aspx.

[648] Oregon Bureau of Labor and Industries, Civil Rights, gender identity policy, https://www.oregon.gov/boli/civil-rights/Pages/gender-identity-at-work.aspx.

[649] Oregon Schools Activities Association policy on transgender athletes competing in school sports programs, https://www.osaa.org/docs/handbooks/GenderIdentityParticipationBP.pdf.

[650] "PENNSYLVANIA HUMAN RELATIONS ACT," Act of 1955, Section 2 Findings and Declaration of Policy, P.L. 744, No. 222, AS AMENDED JUNE 25,1997 BY ACT 34 OF 1997, 43 P.S. §§ 951-963, https://tinyurl.com/ywvncpj9.

[651] https://www.health.pa.gov/topics/Documents/Certificates%20and%20Records/Request%20to%20Modify%20an%20Adult%27s%20Birth%20Record.pdf.

[652] https://www.dot.state.pa.us/Public/DVSPubsForms/BDL/BDL%20Form/DL-180.pdf.

[653] Title 54, Chapter 7, Section 701(a.1) of the Pennsylvania Consolidated Statutes, https://www.legis.state.pa.us/cfdocs/legis/LI/consCheck.cfm?txtType=HTM&ttl=54&div=0&chpt=7.

654 See Pennsylvania Human Relations Commission, https://www.phrc.pa.gov/File-A-Complaint/Types-of-Complaints/Pages/DenialofServicesandFacilities.aspx.

655 From the PIAA Policies Procedures document dated 1/7/2021, https://www.piaa.org/assets/web/documents/Handbook%20-%20Section%20II%20-%20Policies%20and%20Procedures.pdf.

656 Pennsylvania Religious Freedom Protection Act, https://www.legis.state.pa.us/WU01/LI/LI/US/PDF/2002/0/0214..PDF.

657 Rhode Island Commission for Human Rights, http://www.richr.ri.gov/about/index.php.

658 https://tinyurl.com/5c6dz384.

659 http://www.dmv.ri.gov/licenses/address/.

660 https://dmv.ri.gov/sites/g/files/xkgbur556/files/documents/forms/license/License-App-v2-RI.pdf.

661 https://dmv.ri.gov/sites/g/files/xkgbur556/files/documents/forms/license/gender_designation.pdf.

662 https://www.ssa.gov/.

663 https://dmv.ri.gov/sites/g/files/xkgbur556/files/documents/forms/checklist/license_checklist.pdf.

664 Rhode Island statutes, Title 11, Chapter 11-24, Section 11-24-1, http://webserver.rilin.state.ri.us/Statutes/TITLE11/11-24/INDEX.HTM.

665 RIIL Rules and Regulations, Article 3, Section 3B), https://www.riil.org/page/3033.

666 https://www.eeoc.gov/laws/guidance/protections-against-employment-discrimination-based-sexual-orientation-or-gender?utm_content=&utm_medium=email&utm_name=&utm_source=govdelivery&utm_term=.

667 South Carolina Human Affairs Commission, https://schac.sc.gov/employment-discrimination/prohibited-practices-discrimination-types.

668 http://www.scdhec.gov/library/D-2595.pdf.

669 https://www.scdmvonline.com/Locations.

670 file:///C:/Users/mwmoo/AppData/Local/Temp/4057.pdf.

671 file:///C:/Users/mwmoo/AppData/Local/Temp/447-NC.pdf.

672 https://www.scdmvonline.com/Driver-Services/Drivers-License/REAL-ID.

673 https://www.eeoc.gov/statistics/south-dakota.

674 South Dakota Administrative Rules, 44:09:05:02, https://sdlegislature.gov/Rules/Administrative/18027.

675 https://dps.sd.gov/driver-licensing/renew-and-duplicate/renew-online/.

676 https://dps.sd.gov/driver-licensing/renew-and-duplicate/appointment-information.

677 https://dps.sd.gov/contact/locations?agency=5.

678 South Dakota Department of Public Safety, https://dps.sd.gov/driver-licensing.

679 South Dakota Division of Human Rights, https://dlr.sd.gov/human_rights/public_accommodations.aspx.

680 South Dakota Senate Bill 124, signed by Governor Kristi Noem on March 10, 2021, https://sdlegislature.gov/Session/Bill/22127/219024.

681 https://www.tn.gov/humanrights/file-a-discrimination-complaint/employment.html.

682 Tennessee Code, Title 4 State Government, Chapter 21 Human Rights, Section 102 Chapter Definitions, https://www.tn.gov/content/dam/tn/humanrights/images/THRC_Statutes_revised_thru_20161.pdf.

683 Tennessee Code Annotated, Title 68 Health, Safety and Environmental Protection, Chapter 3 Vital Records, Part 2 Records – General Requirements, Section 203 Amendment of Records, Paragraph (d), https://tinyurl.com/z4etjhky.

684 Paragraph (c) of 68-3-203 above.

685 www.eeoc.gov.

686 Texas Labor Code, Title 2 Protection of Laborers, Subtitle A Employment Discrimination, Chapter 21 Employment Discrimination, Subchapter A General Provisions, Section 21.051 Discrimination by Employer, https://statutes.capitol.texas.gov/Docs/LA/htm/LA.21.htm.

[687] Texas Fair Housing Act at Texas Property Code, Title 15 Fair Housing Practices, Chapter 301 Texas Fair Housing Act, Subchapter B Discrimination Prohibited, Section 301.021 Sale or Rental, https://statutes.capitol.texas.gov/Docs/PR/htm/PR.301.htm.

The Texas Department of Housing and Community Affairs, at https://www.tdhca.state.tx.us/fair-housing/ refers to Title VIII of the Civil Rights Act of 1968, as well as the Texas Fair Housing Act. Title VIII of the Civil Rights Act of 1968 states:

Sec. 804. [42 U.S.C. 3604] Discrimination in sale or rental of housing and other prohibited practices as made applicable by section 803 of this title and except as exempted by sections 803(b) and 807 of this title, it shall be unlawful-

a) To refuse to sell or rent after the making of a bona fide offer, or to refuse to negotiate for the sale or rental of, or otherwise make unavailable or deny, a dwelling to any person because of race, color, religion, sex, familial status, or national origin.

(b) To discriminate against any person in the terms, conditions, or privileges of sale or rental of a dwelling, or in the provision of services or facilities in connection therewith, because of race, color, religion, sex, familial status, or national origin.

(c) To make, print, or publish, or cause to be made, printed, or published any notice, statement, or advertisement, with respect to the sale or rental of a dwelling that indicates any preference, limitation, or discrimination based on race, color, religion, sex, handicap, familial status, or national origin, or an intention to make any such preference, limitation, or discrimination.

(d) To represent to any person because of race, color, religion, sex, handicap, familial status, or national origin that any dwelling is not available for inspection, sale, or rental when such dwelling is in fact so available.

(e) For profit, to induce or attempt to induce any person to sell or rent any dwelling by representations regarding the entry or prospective entry into the neighborhood of a person or persons of a particular race, color, religion, sex, handicap, familial status, or national origin. https://www.justice.gov/crt/fair-housing-act-2.

[688] Discrimination prohibited under the Rehabilitation Act of 1973, https://www.ada.gov/cguide.htm#anchor65610.

[689] https://dshs.texas.gov/vs/doc/Texas-Birth-Certificate-Change.pdf.

[690] Texas Interscholastic League, https://www.uiltexas.org/policy/constitution/general/nondiscrimination.

[691] https://capitol.texas.gov/tlodocs/87R/billtext/html/HB01239F.HTM.

[692] https://statutes.capitol.texas.gov/Docs/CP/htm/CP.110.htm#110.003.

[693] Texas Religious Freedom, Title 5 Governmental Liability, Chapter 110 Religious Freedom, Section 110.001, https://statutes.capitol.texas.gov/Docs/CP/htm/CP.110.htm.

[694] Utah Code, Title 34 Utah Labor Code, Chapter 5 Utah Antidiscrimination Act, Section 106 Discriminatory or Prohibited Employment Practices – Permitted Practices – Effective 5/10/2016, https://le.utah.gov/xcode/Title34A/Chapter5/34A-5-S106.html?v=C34A-5-S106_2016051020160510.

[695] https://vitalrecords.health.utah.gov/certificates/amend-a-vital-record.

[696] Utah Office of Vital Records and Statistics, https://vitalrecords.health.utah.gov/certificates/amend-a-vital-record where a person can get their records amended.

[697] https://vitalrecords.health.utah.gov/records.

[698] https://eforms.com/images/2017/12/Utah-Adult-Name-Change-Petition.pdf.

[699] Utah Code, Title 13, Chapter 7 Civil Rights, Section 1 Policy and Purposes of Act, https://le.utah.gov/xcode/Title13/Chapter7/C13-7_1800010118000101.pdf.

[700] The Utah High School Activities Association Handbook, https://uhsaa.org/Publications/Handbook/Handbook.pdf.

[701] Utah Code Annotated, Title 63L Lands, Chapter 5 Utah Religious Land Use Act, Section 102 Definitions, https://le.utah.gov/xcode/Title63L/Chapter5/63L-5-S102.html?v=C63L-5-S102_1800010118000101.

[702] https://hrc.vermont.gov/legal/jurisdiction.

[703] Vermont Human Rights Commission, https://hrc.vermont.gov/resources/faq.

[704] https://legislature.vermont.gov/statutes/section/18/104/05112.

[705] https://www.healthvermont.gov/sites/default/files/documents/pdf/HS_VR_BC_Correct_Amend.pdf.

[706] https://www.vermontjudiciary.org/sites/default/files/documents/Pc%20122.pdf.

[707] https://dmv.vermont.gov/sites/dmv/files/documents/VL-040-Replacement_License.pdf.

[708] https://dmv.vermont.gov/faq/what-is-social-security-number-verification.

[709] https://dmv.vermont.gov/licenses/identity-documents/social-security-information.

[710] Vermont Statutes Annotated, Title 9 Commerce and Trade, Chapter 139 Discrimination; Public Accommodations; Rental and Sale of Real Estate, Section 4502 Public Accommodations, https://legislature.vermont.gov/statutes/section/09/139/04502.

[711] Vermont Principals' Association policy on Gender Identity, https://vpaonline.org/athletics/high-school-policies/.

[712] https://law.lis.virginia.gov/vacode/2.2-3900/.

[713] Virginia Code, Title 32.1, Section 261 New certificate of birth established on proof of adoption, legitimation or determination of paternity, or change of sex, https://law.lis.virginia.gov/vacode/title32.1/chapter7/section32.1-261/.

[714] https://law.lis.virginia.gov/vacode/title2.2/chapter39/section2.2-3904/.

[715] The Handbook of the Virginia High School League Transgender Policy, Section 28A-8-1, pp. 81-83, https://drive.google.com/file/d/1bAp-szol6yLz_ZFzFVTbyEgiCBH0ZXGA/view.

[716] Virginia Code Title 57, Chapter 5, Section 02 (Effective until January 1, 2022), https://law.lis.virginia.gov/vacode/title57/chapter1/section57-2.02/.

[717] https://app.leg.wa.gov/RCW/default.aspx?cite=49.60.030.

[718] https://www.doh.wa.gov/Portals/1/Documents/Pubs/422-143-SexDesignationChangeAdult.pdf.

[719] Washington state Department of Health, Vital Records, https://www.doh.wa.gov/LicensesPermitsandCertificates/VitalRecords/SexDesignationChangeonaBirthCertificate.

[720] Washington Administrative Code, Title 308, Chapter 104, Section 0150 Changing sex designation on a driver's license, instruction permit, or identification card, https://apps.leg.wa.gov/wac/default.aspx?cite=308-104.

[721] Revised Code of Washington, Title 49 Labor Regulations, Chapter 60 -Discrimination - Human Rights Commission, Section 215 Unfair practices of places of public resort, accommodation, assemblage, amusement—Trained dog guides and service animals, https://app.leg.wa.gov/RCW/default.aspx?cite=49.60.215.

[722] https://app.leg.wa.gov/RCW/default.aspx?cite=49.60.

[723] https://app.leg.wa.gov/RCW/default.aspx?cite=28A.642.010.

[724] https://app.leg.wa.gov/RCW/default.aspx?cite=28A.600.477.

[725] https://app.leg.wa.gov/RCW/default.aspx?cite=28A.642.020.

[726] https://app.leg.wa.gov/RCW/default.aspx?cite=28A.642.080.

[727] http://wiaa.com/results/handbook/2020-21/Appendices.pdf.

[728] https://leg.wa.gov/CodeReviser/Pages/WAConstitution.aspx.

[729] West Virginia Code, CHAPTER 5. GENERAL POWERS AND AUTHORITY OF THE GOVERNOR, SECRETARY OF STATE AND ATTORNEY GENERAL; BOARD OF PUBLIC WORKS; MISCELLANEOUS AGENCIES, COMMISSIONS, OFFICES, PROGRAMS, ETC., Article 11 Human Rights Commission, Section 9(2) Unlawful Discriminatory Practices, https://www.wvlegislature.gov/wvcode/code.cfm?chap=5&art=11#01.

[730] http://www.wvlegislature.gov/wvcode/code.cfm?chap=48&art=25, read the law on name changes. You may be able to get assistance from the local legal aid organization where you live in West Virginia.

[731] https://transportation.wv.gov/DMV/DMVFormSearch/DMV-99-RO-GenderDesignationForm.pdf.

[732] West Virginia Code, Chapter 18 Education, Article 2 State Board of Education, Section 25(d) Clarifying Participation for Sports Events to be Based on Biological Sex of the Athlete at Birth, https://www.wvlegislature.gov/wvcode/ChapterEntire.cfm?chap=18&art=2&section=25D#2.

[733] Wisconsin Department of Workforce Development, https://dwd.wisconsin.gov/er/civilrights/discrimination/.

[734] https://www.wicourts.gov/contact/docs/clerks.pdf.

[735] https://www.dhs.wisconsin.gov/forms/f0/f05291.pdf.

[736] https://www.dhs.wisconsin.gov/vitalrecords/amendments.htm.

[737] https://docs.legis.wisconsin.gov/statutes/statutes/106/iii/52.

[738] WIAA policy on transgender participation in school sports programs, https://www.wiaawi.org/Portals/0/PDF/Eligibility/WIAAtransgenderpolicy.pdf.

[739] Wisconsin Legislative Council, Information Memorandum, Freedom of Religious Exercise: State and Federal Law, pp. 4, https://docs.legis.wisconsin.gov/misc/lc/information_memos/2015/im_2015_06.

[740] Wyoming Statutes Annotated, Title 27 Labor and Employment, Chapter 9 Fair Employment Practices, Section 105(a), https://tinyurl.com/hfyytm3s.

[741] https://health.wyo.gov/wp-content/uploads/2021/07/WDH_VSS-Correction-Application-Form-2021Corrected.pdf.

[742] Wyoming Department of Health, Vital Statistics Services, https://health.wyo.gov/admin/vitalstatistics/corrections-and-court-order-changes/.

[743] Wyoming Administrative Rules, Department of Health, Vital Records Services, Chapter 10, Section 4(e)(iii), https://rules.wyo.gov/Search.aspx?mode=1.

[744] Wyoming Statutes Annotated, Title 6 Crimes and Offenses, Chapter 9 Miscellaneous Offenses, Article 1 Discrimination, Section 101 Equal Enjoyment of Public Accommodations and Facilities; Penalties, https://tinyurl.com/7aembct6.

[745] Wyoming Statutes Annotated, Title 40 Trade and Commerce, Chapter 26 Wyoming Fair Housing Act, Section 103 Sale or Rental, https://tinyurl.com/374hujsk.

[746] http://www.whsaa.org/handbook/Handbook.pdf at pp. 40.

[747] *DANIELA ARROYO GONZALEZ, et al. v. RICARDO ROSSELLO NEVARES, et al.*, U.S. District Court for the District of Puerto Rico, Case No. 3:17-cv-01457-CCC, at pp. 4., https://www.lambdalegal.org/sites/default/files/legal-docs/downloads/arroyo_opinion_and_order.pdf.

[748] *Gonzalez, supra*, pp. 15.

Made in the USA
Middletown, DE
16 January 2022

58522745R00192